Reshaping Confucianism

Reshaping Confucianism

A Progressive Inquiry

CHENYANG LI

OXFORD
UNIVERSITY PRESS

Oxford University Press is a department of the University of Oxford. It furthers
the University's objective of excellence in research, scholarship, and education
by publishing worldwide. Oxford is a registered trade mark of Oxford University
Press in the UK and certain other countries.

Published in the United States of America by Oxford University Press
198 Madison Avenue, New York, NY 10016, United States of America.

© Oxford University Press 2024

All rights reserved. No part of this publication may be reproduced, stored in
a retrieval system, or transmitted, in any form or by any means, without the
prior permission in writing of Oxford University Press, or as expressly permitted
by law, by license, or under terms agreed with the appropriate reproduction
rights organization. Inquiries concerning reproduction outside the scope of the
above should be sent to the Rights Department, Oxford University Press, at the
address above.

You must not circulate this work in any other form
and you must impose this same condition on any acquirer.

Library of Congress Control Number: 2023942435

ISBN 978-0-19-765763-8 (pbk.)
ISBN 978-0-19-765762-1 (hbk.)

DOI: 10.1093/oso/9780197657621.001.0001

Paperback printed by Marquis Book Printing, Canada
Hardback printed by Bridgeport National Bindery, Inc., United States of America

To
Hong, Fay, and Hansen

Contents

Acknowledgments   ix

Introduction: Progressive Confucianism   1

SECTION I. FOUNDATIONAL CONCEPTS

1. Dynamic Harmony   27

2. Care-Centered Virtue   53

3. Ritual as Cultural Grammar   74

SECTION II. SELF AND OTHERS

4. Filial Care   97

5. Differentiated Gender Equilibrium   117

6. Friendship   137

7. Virtuous Life and Longevity   157

INTERLUDE

8. Can Sages Be Wrong?   175

SECTION III. SOCIO-POLITICAL RECONSTRUCTIONS

9. Freedom through Choosing   199

10. Two Forms of Equality   219

11. Kingliness without Kings   240

12. Education for Humanity   257

Notes   281
References   309
Index   329

Acknowledgments

The process of writing this book began more than ten years ago. I am indebted to more people and institutions than I can acknowledge here. Nanyang Technological University in Singapore provided an ideal environment to conduct academic research. A sabbatical leave allowed me to take a Berggruen/CASBS fellowship at the Center for Advanced Study in the Behavioral Sciences of Stanford University in 2015–2016, where I wrote a substantial part of the book manuscript. Over the years, my research projects benefited from the support of several research grants, especially a generous inaugural Social Science Research Thematic Grant (#MOE2016-SSRTG-007) from Singapore's Social Science Research Council, and two Singapore's Ministry of Education research grants (RG163/14, RG100/21).

Numerous discussions with David Wong at CASBS made me think more clearly about my project; his encouragement helped me firm up a plan to write a care interpretation of *ren* in Chapter 2. Karyn Lai and Winnie Sung provided invaluable input on the organization of the book and its title. Stephen Angle reviewed first the book proposal and then the entire manuscript, providing constructive comments that have been particularly insightful. He also shared with me his book manuscript before its publication, *Growing Moral: A Confucian Guide to Life*, which provided much inspiration. Another reviewer for Oxford University Press, who remains anonymous, provided constructive comments and suggestions. Huang Yijia and Kathryn Lynn Muyskens read the entire manuscript respectively and provided valuable comments and edits. Lucy Randall, my acquisition editor at Oxford University Press, has been wonderfully efficient and supportive, making the publication process such a great pleasure and smooth sail.

I would like to thank the following individuals for their support and friendship: Roger Ames, Daniel Bell, Alan Chan, Michael Puett, Jana Rošker, Jin Li, Anna Sun, Hong Xiao, Joseph Chan, Yong Huang, Bo Mou, Liang Tao, Guo Yi, Dimitris Apostolopoulos, Asma Afsaruddin, Dascha Düring, Robert Neville, Philip Pettit, Philip J. Ivanhoe, Randy John LaPolla, Xinzhong Yao, Frank Perkins, Brook Ziporyn, Sor-hoon Tan, Loy Hui Chieh, Matthew Walker, Ruiping Fan, Ellen Zhang, Peimin Ni, Baogang He, Sungmoon Kim,

Qingjie Wang, Xinyan Jiang, Sai Hang Kwok, Robin Wang, Li Jifen, Qingjuan Sun, He Fan, Liu Linna, Zhang Lili, Mu Xiaofeng, Yang Fang, Tan Wee Ngar Joyce, Christine Tan, Jacob Bender, Hu Jianping, Luo Biming, Zhang Jian, Alice Simionato, Huang Xiaoqian, Zhou Yalin, Mao Xueting, Jonathan Chua, Chen Hai, and Li Luyao. To all of them I owe my sincere gratitude. I would also like to acknowledge my intellectual debt to the late Joel J. Kupperman, Walter Benesch, Raeburne Heimbeck, and Vincent Shen, who provided me with much professional inspiration and personal guidance.

Many of the ideas in this book have been expressed in various publications and presentations even though these ideas have been reformulated and further advanced in their present forms. Chapters 6, 7, 9, 10 are based on previous publications, albeit with significant revisions. These publications are "A Confucian Solution to the Fungibility Problem of Friendship," *Dao: A Journal of Comparative Philosophy*, 2019 (18.4): 493–508; "Confucian Moral Cultivation, Longevity, and Public Policy," *Dao: A Journal of Comparative Philosophy*, 2010 (9.1): 25–36; "The Confucian Conception of Freedom," *Philosophy East and West*, 2014 (64.4): 902–919; "Equality and Inequality in Confucianism," *Dao: A Journal of Comparative Philosophy*, 2012 (11.3): 295–313. I thank these publishers for granting permissions and the audiences at my presentations, whose names I am unable to identify.

Translators of ancient texts usually have their own understandings and interpret texts in certain perspectives. To avoid systematic biases, I have compared and used different translations of Chinese texts, with my modifications when needed. At times I use my own translations as appropriate, with original texts in endnotes. When I cite works published in Chinese, I use either the Traditional or Simplified characters respectively to be faithful to their original texts.

I dedicate this book to my beloved wife Professor Hong Xiao and our two children Fay and Hansen. Their unconditional love and care have made my life especially rewarding and meaningful.

Introduction

Progressive Confucianism

This book aims to accomplish two goals, both that of a research monograph and that of a general introduction to progressive Confucianism. Books on Confucianism usually fall into two categories. One consists of monographs and anthologies on a specific topic, which often exhibit scholarly sophistication and contemporary relevance, yet they do not present an extensive account of Confucian philosophy. The other includes textbooks of a general introduction to Confucianism, which tend to provide informative overviews of its teachings in history but lack in-depth philosophical inquiry and reflection on their contemporary significance. *Reshaping Confucianism* brings together an original research monograph and an introductory textbook into one volume, showcasing both the depth and breadth of recent insight into the Confucian legacy as well as how it continues to influence the present-day world.

Confucianism is a living and evolving tradition. Its teachings have been continuously defined and redefined in response to the changing political and social context of China's history. Extending this effort in reconstructing Confucianism, I critically analyze and progressively develop a series of core ideas that originated from Confucian classic texts and do so in the context of contemporary scholarly discourse. In addition, I combine an in-depth analysis of historical teachings with a systematic deliberation on their contemporary significance, paying attention to the current state of the field of research. Furthermore, a comparative perspective is adopted so that Confucian philosophy is placed in the context of world philosophy. Each chapter presents something new: a novel interpretation from a fresh angle, an insight that has been neglected in scholarship, or a reformed idea that connects tradition with modern sensibilities. Readers will see not only how various seminal ideas were conceived and developed by ancient thinkers, but also how these ideas can be reconstructed and aligned in a sensible Confucian philosophy in response to contemporary challenges. As such, each chapter can be read as

Reshaping Confucianism. Chenyang Li, Oxford University Press. © Oxford University Press 2024.
DOI: 10.1093/oso/9780197657621.003.0001

2 RESHAPING CONFUCIANISM: A PROGRESSIVE INQUIRY

an independent research article, with issues raised to be further explored and debated. Collectively, the chapters present most—albeit not exhaustively—key ideas of Confucian philosophy and hence can serve as an introduction to Confucian philosophy. Study questions are provided toward the end of each chapter to assist students in the classroom to comprehend key points and to develop their own views.

Main topics covered in this book are dynamic harmony (*he* 和), care-centered virtue (*ren* 仁), ritual propriety (*li* 禮), filial care (*xiao* 孝), differentiated gender equilibrium (*bie* 別), friendship (*you* 友), longevity (*shou* 壽), sagehood (*sheng* 聖), equality (*qi* 齊), freedom (*ziyou* 自由), politics (*zheng* 政), and education (*jiao* 教). Some of these are found on the usual list of introductory Confucian philosophy books. Others are newcomers to be (re)formulated for progressive Confucianism, as will be explained shortly. This book raises fundamental questions about Confucian philosophy. How central is *he* as a Confucian value? Is *ren* care-centered? Is it appropriate to interpret *li* as cultural grammar? Is Xunzi's philosophy of filial care more progressive than Kongzi's and hence more suitable for contemporary society? What is the best form of Confucian gender equality today? Can sages—including Kongzi—be wrong? Should and how can freedom become a part of progressive Confucianism? Is the model of "politics without (depending on) political leaders" a viable way of realizing the Confucian political ideal of the good society? These questions are addressed with a set of specific solutions. The views are provocative and even controversial; they are expected to spark further debates on these important issues.

This introduction contextualizes these inquiries by explaining my research goals, orientation, approaches, methodologies, and the outline of the chapters.

1. Progressive Confucianism

"Confucianism" is the Latinized name originally coined by Western missionaries for *rujia* 儒家, namely the School of *Ru* ("Scholar"). It refers to the intellectual and cultural tradition that includes not only "Confucius" (Kongzi 孔子, 551–479 BCE) but also other classical thinkers and texts associated with the tradition.[1] As a philosophy, Confucianism first flourished during the "Spring–Autumn and Warring States" period (ca. 770－221 BCE), when such major thinkers as Kongzi ("Master Kong"), Mengzi (Mencius

孟子, 372–289 BCE) and Xunzi (荀子, third century BCE) gained social prominence. Most of Confucian classic texts during this period or slightly thereafter are without definitive authors, including the *Book of Changes* (*Yijing* 易經), the *Book of Rites* (*Liji* 禮記), the *Book of History* (*Shangshu* 尚書), the *Rites of Zhou* (*Zhouli* 周禮), and the *Book of Poetry* (*Shijing* 詩經). Understood this way, classical Confucianism is "greater pre-Qin Confucianism" (大先秦儒學), as opposed to a narrowly conceived pre-Qin Confucianism that is confined to Kongzi and Mengzi. Subsequent revivals of Confucian philosophy include Neo-Confucianism in the Song and Ming dynasties (ca. 960–1644), when various thinkers re-worked classic ideas under the influence of Buddhism and Daoism, and again its modern renaissance under the label of "New Confucianism" (*xin rujia* 新儒家), which began after the first quarter of the twentieth century and has continued to the present day. In each subsequent period, Confucian thinkers attempted to reconstruct Confucian philosophy by reclaiming ancient ideas and reformulating them with new insights to address perennial human concerns in the context of their respective times. Continuing such a tradition, this book is a study of key ideas of Confucian philosophy with an aim to interpret and formulate them progressively in contemporary perspectives.[2]

This study takes Confucianism as an evolving body of rich cultural resources that provides not only valuable knowledge about a long and distant past but also fundamental insights into the human condition. Admittedly, some of its ideas as conceived by ancient thinkers may no longer be relevant for our times, whereas others remain pertinent, even critically important, to contemporary society. There is no denying, for instance, that ancient Confucian thinkers held sexist views typical of their times. These views are no longer tenable in the modern context. Similarly, ancient Confucian thinkers did not advocate such ideas as democracy, human rights, and political equality, even though some of their humanist views can be extended in these directions today. To make its existence meaningful, Confucian philosophy today must be progressive. Progressive efforts in Confucianism must integrate two components. On the one hand, as far as it is Confucian, progressive Confucianism must maintain its Confucian characteristics. This requires it to preserve an organic connection with its ancient sources and to take into consideration what ancient Confucian thinkers have said about various issues. On the other hand, progressive Confucianism today must advance itself with sensibilities developed through modern-day life experiences, keeping itself answerable to various contemporary challenges.

4 RESHAPING CONFUCIANISM: A PROGRESSIVE INQUIRY

The latter requires a critical attitude toward classic texts, to discriminate between what is alive and what is dead in ancient teachings. Together, these two components create an ongoing tension within the continuation of the Confucian tradition. Handling such tension calls for careful analysis, critical reasoning, rigorous argument, and delicate balancing. Moreover, to advance itself in the multicultural context of the globalized world, progressive Confucianism needs to use resources and heed challenges not only from within its own tradition but also from external sources. The last point makes today's development of Confucianism inevitably cross-cultural and comparative in character.

To my knowledge, the term "progressive Confucianism" was first coined by Stephen Angle in his book *Contemporary Confucian Political Philosophy: Toward Progressive Confucianism* (2012). More recently, Angle further advocated this idea in *Growing Moral: A Confucian Guide to Life* (2022). Angle understands progressive Confucianism as "a Confucianism that, in its efforts to help us and our societies get better, self-critically recognizes that it, too, must respond to changing circumstances" (Angle 2022, 69). He further elaborates that:

> The idea that ethical insight leads to progressive political change, which in turn leads to greater realization of our potential for virtue, lies at the heart of progressive Confucianism. (Angle 2022, 197)

Angle maintains, forcefully, that progressive Confucianism is solidly Confucian in that social institutions advocated by progressive Confucians are valued because of their capacity to assist in the realization of the fundamental human virtues that Confucians have always promoted since ancient times. This book shares Angle's goal of constructing a progressive Confucian philosophy for contemporary times. I am in agreement with Angle on his view of the undisputable rootedness of progressive Confucianism. I also hold that social structures must be changed when they become barriers to the realization of virtue. Hence, progressive Confucianism must support social reform and political reform where reform is needed. Even though political philosophy is undoubtedly an important part, my understanding of progressive Confucianism goes broader to cover various subareas of Confucian philosophy. For instance, we can have a progressive understanding of *he* 和 (dynamic harmony), *li* 禮 (ritual propriety), *xiao* 孝 (filial care), *sheng* 聖 (*sagehood*), and *jiao* 教 (education) as shown in this book.[3]

INTRODUCTION 5

Furthermore, "progressive Confucianism" (with a lower-case p) to me is a descriptive term rather than a proper name; it denotes an orientation in doing Confucian philosophy rather than a specific formulation of Confucian philosophy. Today, there are many formulations of Confucianism. For instance, there are "Citizenship Confucianism" (*Gongmin Ruxue* 公民儒學, Lin 2021) "Life Confucianism" (*Shenghuo Ruxue* 生活儒学, Huang 2017), "*Gongfu* Confucianism" (*Gongfu Ruxue* 功夫儒学, Ni 2022), and "Freedom Confucianism" (*Ziyou Ruxue* 自由儒学, Guo 2017). Each of these provides a particular articulation of Confucianism, with its own prioritized concept, be it citizenship, everyday life, *gongfu*, or freedom. Progressive Confucianism, in contrast, is not confined to advocating any particular formulation of Confucianism. It encompasses all these varieties in so far as they are all part of the progressive movement in contemporary Confucianism, including the form of progressive Confucianism pioneered by Stephen Angle as well as various attempts in this book. Promoters of progressive Confucianism can disagree not only with their more conservative colleagues within the tradition, but also among themselves, as to the most sensible and effective way to preserve and move Confucianism forward. Progress is to be made precisely through sorting out such disagreements by rational argument and engaged debate. Moreover, in the sense as I understand it, there can be progressive Confucianism during any period in history. We can find progressive development in ancient thinkers. As shown in Chapter 4 of this book, on the idea of *xiao* 孝 (filial care) for instance, Mengzi was more progressive than Kongzi; Xunzi was more progressive than Mengzi. In the modern development of Confucianism, Huang Zongxi 黃宗羲 (1610–1695) was undoubtedly progressive in comparison with most of his contemporaries (Britannica 2021). Hopefully, one thousand years from now, there are also new versions of progressive Confucianism in response to the society of that time.

It should be made clear at this point that I am by no means neutral with regard to Confucian philosophy. I accept and endorse its humanistic, relationship-based orientation, its conviction of human moral cultivability, and its ideal of a harmonious world. I believe that Confucian philosophy has something very important to offer the modern world. However, I try to explicate Confucian philosophy not only to an audience who is already immersed in the tradition, but also to make it sensible and accessible to readers who are not already predisposed toward Confucianism. In the meantime, I hold that Confucian philosophy today should live up to contemporary challenges and come up with sensible responses to philosophical problems in the world.

2. Historical and Philosophical Approaches

Confucianism can mean different things to different people. It can be studied through the lens of the history of thought. Through such an approach, one can reconstruct Confucian philosophy within its historical context, evaluate it against its social background, and defend or criticize it in the terms of its own time. Confucianism can also be seen as a living tradition rather than a fixed cultural artifact in history. As such, Confucian philosophy addresses perennial human concerns with evolving social contexts and is to be studied not as an ancient relic but as a living cultural phenomenon that constantly reinvents itself in response to new challenges.

On studying philosophers of the past, Richard Rorty has distinguished two kinds of reconstructions. The first is historical reconstruction. This kind of study treats the history of philosophy as we treat the history of science. In doing so, we "recreate the intellectual scene in which the dead lived their lives—in particular, the real and imagined conversations they might have had with their contemporaries (or near-contemporaries)" (Rorty 1984, 50). Another type of reconstruction is rational reconstruction. In rational reconstruction, we bring past thinkers into conversations with ourselves. We want to know not only what a past thinker said or would have said given the limitations of his or her time. We also want to know what "an ideally reasonable and educable" past thinker could be brought to accept as reasonable. That is, given what we know now about things in the world and what we know of the overall orientation of the past thinker, what we believe the thinker could say on a matter of inquiry. In the latter kind of reconstruction, for instance, "an ideal Aristotle can be brought to describe himself as having mistaken the preparatory taxonomic stages of biological research for the essence of all scientific inquiry" (ibid., 51). In rational reconstructions, we are not dealing with past thinkers as they once lived; we are instead dealing with "the re-educated dead" (ibid., 52). A re-educated dead thinker is a past thinker who we imagine has acquired some pertinent knowledge that we now possess, and hence could adjust his or her views on specific issues. To put it differently, a "re-educated past thinker" is an imagined contemporary person who subscribes to much of the theoretical framework of a past thinker and is informed of modern knowledge and equipped with modern sensibilities. A re-educated Aristotle, for instance, is a contemporary Aristotelian philosopher who has been educated through modern scientific knowledge and is well-informed about modern developments in society. Rorty holds that, ideally, historical reconstructions are ones on which all historians could agree.[4] Rational reconstructions, conversely, "are unlikely to converge, and there is no reason why they should" (ibid., 54). Reasonable people can disagree on whether it is reasonable to expect "an ideally reasonable and educable" past thinker to change his or her views. On some issues, even "an ideally reasonable and educable" past thinker may nevertheless choose an undetermined path.

Rorty's differentiation between historical reconstruction and rational reconstruction provides good tools for us to reflect on different ways of studying Confucian philosophy. Scholars of Confucian philosophy today tend to gravitate around two related yet quite different approaches in parallel with the two types of reconstruction outlined by Rorty. Those who engage primarily in historical reconstructions usually are equipped with a strong disciplinary background in history, classics, intellectual thought, or Chinese studies. Others who tend to do what Rorty has called "rational reconstruction" are mostly with a strong background in the discipline of philosophy. To reveal this important disciplinary difference, I here label these approaches to studying Confucian philosophy as the "historical approach" and the "philosophical approach" respectively, in parallel more or less with the two academic disciplines of history and philosophy. Researchers with the historical approach aim to find out what past thinkers actually said or meant as recorded in classic texts. Kwong-loi Shun has called this approach "textual analysis." Shun writes, "In textual analysis, we seek to approximate the perspectives of past thinkers whose ideas are recorded in past texts," and we attend to the historical, cultural, and individual context in which a past thinker developed the ideas (Shun 2018, 67). In contrast, the philosophical approach aims to philosophize alongside ancient thinkers by bringing them into conversations with us. We explore what these thinkers would have said if they had known what we now know—given their general philosophical orientation. To borrow Rorty's terminology, in the historical approach we deal with "unre-educated" ancient thinkers, whereas in the philosophical approach our conversational partners are "re-educated" ancient thinkers. For instance, an unre-educated Kongzi would say that men and women are unequal, whereas a re-educated Kongzi might say that the two sexes are equal, along the line of Mengzi's thought that all humans are born with similar characteristics (*Mengzi* 2A6). However, a re-educated Kongzi would hold that this sexual equality comes from our shared nature (*xing* 性), which is an important idea within the Confucian philosophical framework, rather than from a God-given right, which is more likely to have come from a monotheistic thinker. As Rorty indicated, engaging in studies of the philosophical approach, people do not have to agree on their conclusions, even though there are varying degrees of plausibility in them.

In this regard, the philosophical approach diverges significantly from the historical approach, even though a researcher may engage in both approaches in the same study.[5] If we use the analogy of reconstructing a house for the reconstruction of Confucian philosophy, we can put their main difference this way. The historical approach requires researchers to reconstruct it as closely as possible to the original shape and the state of the house in the past, including design flaws and distorted parts if any. With this approach, when studying classical Confucian philosophy, researchers need to, as far as possible, present the whole picture of ancient Confucian thinkers as they once were through historical reconstruction. The ultimate goal of such studies is to maximize historical accuracy and textual exactitude. This is the task mainly for historians of intellectual history and researchers of the history of philosophy.[6] One can anticipate various difficulties with achieving the goal of historical accuracy. First, what we are dealing with is not an exact science and ancient thinkers may not have presented their philosophies systematically in clearly articulated essays with rigorous definitions as typically done by contemporary scholars. Textual vagueness leaves room for interpretations. Second, the views of ancient thinkers are often sporadically dispersed in various texts and these views may not be consistent. Sometimes inconsistencies occur even within the same text. Consequently, attempts to construct a coherent reading of their views involve selective readings, and historical reconstruction becomes partial reconstruction, falling short of the goal of the historical approach. The third difficulty is related to inevitable subjectivity in interpretation. Theories of hermeneutics demonstrate that reading a text always involves a degree of subjectivity. This is especially so when we encounter substantial uncertainty in interpreting ancient texts. When an ancient thinker left gaps in their articulation of thought and more than one candidate idea can serve similarly well in filling that gap, no objective way is available—at least for the time being—to determine which is the right candidate idea. These difficulties by no means render the task of the historical approach impossible, however. Various attempts can be made to overcome these difficulties, at least partially. Abundant historical scholarship proves the fruitfulness of the historical reconstruction. It is just that we must bear in mind its limitations. These limitations make the historical

INTRODUCTION 9

approach less distinct from the philosophical approach in researchers' own subjective intervention. Nevertheless, the goals of these two approaches are different: whereas the historical approach aims primarily at historical accuracy, the philosophical approach strives for contemporary sensibility and plausibility.

The philosophical approach to reconstructing the house, in contrast, requires us to remedy its design flaws, replace decayed material, and methodically modify parts that are no longer suitable for modern living, to the best of our ability today. This is done on a recognition that the old house is valuable in important ways and is mostly worthy of inheriting. Hence, rather than creating an entirely different and new house, we re-create the project that the ancient housebuilders had attempted while also taking into consideration what they would have opted for if they were living today. If the actual ancient house was designed with defects, the reconstructed modern house need not replicate those flaws. Making changes to the design naturally involves imagination as to what preferences the ancient builders would have had if they were re-educated today as Rorty put it. A philosophical reconstruction, therefore, is always selective and developmental. It differs from building an entirely new house as a philosophical reconstruction involves restrained innovation appropriate for the overall framework of the project. Disagreements naturally emerge as to how much of the old house should be preserved and what modifications should be implemented, even though they are often related also to disagreements regarding the original state of the old house. For all these reasons, philosophical reconstruction by its very nature involves different opinions and is subject to reasonable dispute. Yet, it is through differences and controversies that new philosophical ideas emerge and advance.

In studying Confucian philosophy, both approaches are needed, with each serving different purposes. We want to know what views ancient thinkers actually held; we also want to reconstruct Confucian philosophy for our times. Researchers of the philosophical approach can benefit from studies of the historical approach. We need to know what was said before we reason about what could have been said and what should be said today. While these two kinds of research can be beneficial to each other, we should avoid using one approach to assess and criticize the other approach. Criticizing a philosophically reconstructed house for failing to replicate a poorly designed portion of the historical house is not a meaningful criticism in philosophy.[7] In the meantime, philosophers should not pretend that they are representing accurate history. They should not deny that the house once had poorly designed parts as historians remind us; historians should not reject possible reconstructions by philosophers of the house without these parts. Through good coordination, these two approaches complement each other with each providing a necessary component for studying Confucian philosophy in the twenty-first century.

This book incorporates both historical and philosophical approaches. Parts of this book engage Confucian ideas with a historical approach. For instance, through a historical reconstruction, I discover that *you* 友, the Chinese concept for friend, originated from its earlier meaning of kinship. This finding helps to solve a puzzle in understanding Confucian friendship, one of the five cardinal human relationships in Confucianism. Ancient thinkers provided abundant reasons for becoming *you* with certain kinds of people, but they did not give a justification for why *you* should be treated like family even though they did hold such a view. The discovery of the etymology of *you* provides an explanation, i.e., *you* already means family (see detailed discussion in Chapter 6). There are also parts of the book that are mainly philosophical in character. For instance, interpreting the Confucian philosophy of friendship as based on a family model and on particularized virtues, I argue for a Confucian response to the fungibility problem of friendship. This does not mean that ancient Confucian thinkers already formulated such an argument against the fungibility of friends. It is important, therefore, for readers to differentiate philosophical argument from the historical reconstruction in the book.

The main orientation of this book, however, belongs to the philosophical approach. This is a volume on Confucian philosophy in its contemporary context rather than a book of the history of Confucian philosophy. Taking readers on a journey to investigate Confucian philosophy in its evolving context, this book scrutinizes various elements of Confucian philosophy and considers their relevance, or the lack thereof, for the modern world. On selected topics, I examine critically what was construed in ancient times, what has gone through the test of time, and what can be amended or further developed in response to contemporary concerns. That is, I examine not only what ancient thinkers actually said on various issues and make appropriate assessments accordingly, but also what they would have said on these issues in new social contexts in light of their overall views concerning humanity and the world. For example, when Kongzi advocated "education regardless of social classes" (*you jiao wu lei* 有教無类), he evidently did not consider female students. However, because Confucian thinkers today accept gender

INTRODUCTION 11

equality, they should, therefore, include female students under this principle of education. Thus, the fact that ancient Confucian thinkers were sexist does not need to preclude Confucian philosophy from taking a stance on gender equality in education in the twenty-first century. This kind of argument makes contemporary progressive Confucianism possible.

3. Principle of Progressive Humanity

In philosophy, people generally accept the need to apply the principle of charity in interpreting the beliefs and utterances of others. The principle of charity requires us, whenever plausible, to interpret an idea or text in ways that maximize its truth value or rationality, making it as intelligent as possible. Daniel Dennett has argued that the principle of charity should be supplemented by a "projective principle," otherwise called the principle of humanity. The principle of humanity requires us to make sense of an idea or text by attributing to the idea holder "the propositional attitudes one supposed one would have oneself in those circumstances" (Dennett 1989, 343). Even though we do not agree with someone's view, we can imagine that, had we been in a similar community surrounded by a similar environment, we ourselves would have held such a view.

Both principles can be applied to interpreting classical Confucian philosophy. Articulated in classical Chinese, propositions in classic Confucian philosophy are often subject to varied interpretations. The principle of charity helps us to make the best sense of these views as what rational and intelligent beings would hold. The principle of humanity, similarly, calls on us to place ourselves in the circumstances of ancient thinkers and to understand them as sensible people shaped by the society of their times.

These principles can be complemented by the two tenets of scholarship proposed by the Chinese philosopher Zhang Xuecheng 章學誠 (1738–1801). Zhang argued that, in studying classic texts, we much practice two virtues of scholarship (*wende* 文德) in the form of two tenets.[8] One such tenet is empathetic understanding (*shu* 恕), which is a primary Confucian value (*Analects* 4.15, 15.24). *Shu* is not about tolerance of ancient ideas; rather it is about placing oneself in the specific situation of ancient thinkers to make sense of their views. Zhang maintained that without understanding the social environment in which ancient thinkers lived, we have no adequate basis to assess their works; without understanding the lives of ancient thinkers, we

12 RESHAPING CONFUCIANISM: A PROGRESSIVE INQUIRY

cannot sensibly comment on their works. Zhang's tenet of empathetic understanding for interpreting ancient thinkers can aid the application of the principle of humanity in the context of studying ancient Chinese philosophy. The other tenet espoused by Zhang is respectfulness (*jing* 敬). Here *jing* is not about cultivating the general virtue of respect; it is rather understood specifically as restraining one's thought from roaming wild (*buzong* 不縱) in thinking and writing about ancient thinkers. It is about presenting appropriate interpretations in reading ancient texts (*zhongjie* 中節). In the context of our discussion here, Zhang's tenet of respectfulness implies one should not under-interpret or over-interpret ancient thinkers by straying from what they actually held. As we apply the principle of charity in interpreting ancient thinkers, we should also uphold Zhang's virtue of respectfulness; in particular, we should not be excessively "charitable" by attributing modern ideas to ancient thinkers, as opposed to making our own development of ancient ideas.

These principles and tenets, however, are more appropriate for studying Confucian philosophy with the historical approach. Taking the philosophical approach as not only an interpretation of ancient thinkers but also a development of their ideas in view of modern moral sensibilities, I would like to propose another principle, "the principle of progressive humanity," which can be seen as an enhanced version of the principle of humanity for developing ancient ideas. With the principle of progressive humanity, we understand humanity in a progressive process of human society. On this enhanced principle, we should not only make sense of ancient thinkers by placing them under their own historical circumstances as prescribed by the principle of humanity, but also expand their ideas on the basis of their overall philosophical dispositions in accordance with our modern sensibilities. That is, from an ancient thinker's general attitude and philosophical framework, we propose new views that someone sharing such attitude and framework may come to hold under modern circumstances. In doing so, we formulate modern views out of an ancient thinker's own general conceptual framework. To borrow Rorty's language, we bring "an ideally reasonable and educable" past thinker into conversation with us. For example, Mengzi is well-known for his views that the people are more important than the ruler (*Mengzi* 7B14) and that overthrowing a bad ruler can be justified (*Mengzi* 1B8). Mengzi also cites the *Book of History* that "Heaven sees through the way the people see and Heaven hears through the way the people hear" (*Mengzi* 5A5). Mengzi nevertheless did not envision a democratic social institution due to his own historical limitations. We can imagine, however, had he lived in the twenty-first century, Mengzi would or might have embraced democracy out of his overall philosophical dispositions. If the people are the most important in society and they are the legitimate judges of whether a bad ruler should be replaced, then democracy seems to align well with Mengzi's thought, and one could argue that a "re-educated" Mengzi would be in favor of it. Therefore, we can develop a political philosophy along the line of Mengzi's ideas and call it a modern Mencian philosophy. Of course, this is not to say that Mengzi, the ancient thinker of the fourth century BCE, was actually for democracy. We can call it "Mencian" because the overall orientation of Mengzi's philosophy is predisposed this way. In comparison, given the overall propensity of Xunzi's philosophy, we are less justified to claim that Xunzi would be just as predisposed as Mengzi toward democracy, even less so with Xunzi's students, the legalists Han Fei 韓非 and Li Si 李斯.

The principle of progressive humanity is useful as we endeavor to develop Confucian philosophy for the modern world. To be sure, people's modern sensibilities are not the same, be it moral or political. Today's Confucians may disagree as to what extent Confucianism can be democratic or gender-egalitarian, for instance. Nevertheless, on such important issues, most contemporary authors share considerable common grounds; our audiences of the twenty-first century are significantly different from those of the ancient thinkers over two thousand years ago. Even the most conservative Confucian thinkers today accept the need for at least some level of democracy for contemporary society. Researchers of Confucian philosophy are overwhelmingly supportive of gender equality. These shared sensibilities today, even though far from uniform, provide enough common grounds for the principle of progressive humanity to operate. In studying Confucian philosophy as a living and evolving tradition, such a principle enables us to advance seminal ideas produced by ancient thinkers and helps us to reformulate these ideas in response to modern challenges. Augmenting the philosophical approach explicitly with the principle of progressive humanity enables us to rationally reconstruct Confucian philosophy in contemporary contexts with a progressive impetus, as I attempt to demonstrate through the chapters in this book.

4. Comparative Perspectives

The principle of progressive humanity provides a guide for studying Confucian philosophy on its upward vertical dimension, along its temporally

14 RESHAPING CONFUCIANISM: A PROGRESSIVE INQUIRY

progressive trajectory. In the meantime, we need to take into consideration another important dimension in studying Confucian philosophy in the twenty-first century, its multicultural global context. This is a horizontal dimension.

The modern world is now a global world. In this regard, the context of developing Confucian philosophy today has varied fundamentally from its ancient past. When Kongzi and his followers philosophized in the "Spring–Autumn and Warring States" period, their world was a very limited one, in space as well as in conceptual scope. Their own culture was the only civilization known to them. The main task of these thinkers was to persuade contemporaries within their own culture, as the outside world, in their minds, was occupied by "barbarians" who needed to be brought into the only civilization known to them. In this regard, their model of "intercultural" communication was strictly one-directional. It was almost entirely about civilizing "un-cultured" peoples into their own culture. Even though such a view does not constitute racism, it was not appropriate toward other cultures. Today, our understanding of the world has since changed enormously. We now live in a multicultural world. In such a globalized world, Confucianism and Chinese culture at large are not the only game in town. Confucian philosophy needs to communicate and engage with other cultural traditions. It needs to use language that is sensible not only to an audience within its own cultural tradition but also to that of other cultures. In this regard, doing Confucian philosophy in a global context today involves a twofold task. On the one hand, we need to make sense of Confucian philosophy to people of non-Confucian cultures as well as of the Confucian culture. On the other, we must learn from other cultures to enrich and to advance Confucian philosophy itself. Toward such a twofold goal, Confucian philosophy needs to be explicated and developed via comparative philosophy.

"Comparative philosophy" usually implies intercultural philosophy.[9] It has a narrow meaning and a broad meaning. In its narrow meaning, comparative philosophy means to understand a philosophy by comparing and contrasting it with another philosophy. Comparative philosophy in this sense is useful when studying a philosophy in its given form, especially as a matter of the history (including contemporary history) of philosophy. For instance, by comparing Aristotle with Kongzi we learn their shared insights as well as important differences and we better understand both great philosophers. In its broad meaning, comparative philosophy actively seeks to solve problems and develop new ideas by taking into consideration different philosophical

INTRODUCTION 15

perspectives, challenges, alternative formulations, and solutions from other cultural traditions. In the latter sense, comparative philosophy is to *philosophize comparatively*. Thus, it is not merely a methodology of learning from the history of philosophy, but also a creative activity—a way of generating new insights through bringing together divergent traditions. The above-mentioned example of introducing democracy into Confucianism is one such case. Mengzi's philosophy, even with morally permissible revolutions, cannot solve the problem of responsible government. Introducing democracy provides a good way forward. By learning from modern Western political philosophy, such as that of John Locke and Immanuel Kant, contemporary Confucian philosophers of the twentieth century, such as Mou Zongsan, Tang Junyi, and Xu Fuguan have attempted to incorporate democracy into Confucian philosophy. Xu Fuguan, for example, has argued that Confucianism can and should embrace democracy to implement the rule of law, protection of freedom, and the importance of elections. In the meantime, Xu also maintains that the Confucian ideal of "rule by virtue" must be retained and integrated with democratic elements (Elstein 2015, 67–89). Xu's progressive version of Confucianism is one of the numerous fruits from the tree of comparative philosophy in the broad sense. Taking comparative philosophy in its broad sense, as philosophizing comparatively, it has an indispensable and non-replaceable role in contemporary philosophy, and it will continue to help us advance contemporary philosophy as long as there are different cultures in the world.

Comparative philosophy builds bridges across cultures (see Li 1999, 5–6). Such bridges invite and facilitate two-way traffic, not only enabling Confucian philosophers to learn from the world as exemplified above but also offering the resources of Confucian philosophy to other cultural traditions. Take the Chinese idea of *he* 和 as an example. *He* is usually translated as harmony. The English word "harmony" as commonly used, however, does not convey the Confucian idea of *he*. *He* is much more than congruence or peacefulness, as usually connoted by "harmony" and its likes in Western languages.[10] Without any doubt, *he* has been used in various senses over a long period of time in China, including the sense of peacefulness. But as a philosophical idea, *he* is far richer than that. To put it in very brief terms, *he* stands for a dynamic process through which various parties join hands by way of interaction, coordination, collaboration, mutual enhancement, and mutual transformation in order to reach "optimizing symbiosis," to borrow the expression from Roger Ames (2020). And there is a "critical" element in its operation,

16   RESHAPING CONFUCIANISM: A PROGRESSIVE INQUIRY

which requires societal criticism and acknowledges differences of opinion (Ho and Barton 2020). We can translate it as "harmony" and its Western linguistic variations only in a rehabilitated sense of the word. The difficulty with the translation itself suggests that there is no close counterpart of this concept in Western philosophy. Confucian philosophy has something very valuable to offer the world in this regard; Confucian philosophers' role is to develop and explicate a philosophy of *he* that is based on the idea upon which ancient Chinese thinkers have fruitfully worked. To be effective, a contemporary philosophy of harmony should be developed in the context of world philosophy rather than merely as an idea for and within Confucian philosophy.[11] It should show how such a concept can be helpful in addressing the contemporary world's problems at large.

In this book, I attempt to critically examine and progressively advance Confucian ideas with intercultural sensibilities. In doing so, I adopt both a philosophical approach and a comparative perspective, integrating the vertically progressive movement with a strategy of horizontal openness. These two dimensions mutually enhance each other. Formulating and presenting Confucian philosophy progressively makes it meaningful to the contemporary world. Taking note of and utilizing cultural resources from the rest of the world helps us bring Confucian philosophy forward on the world stage.

5. Summary of Chapters

This book consists of three sections. Chapters 1 to 3 constitutes the first section, investigating *he*, *ren*, and *li*, three topics that are foundational in Confucian philosophy. The second section, including Chapters 4 to 7, is on "Self and Others," covering some main Confucian ideas of persons and their relational existence in society. The interlude space, taken by Chapter 8, discusses a single yet very important issue: whether Confucian sages, including Kongzi, can be wrong. The last section, Chapters 9 to 12, probes "Socio-Political Reconstructions," with aims to reformulate four ideas that are traceable to ancient Confucian thinkers but need to be reformed progressively to make Confucianism viable in contemporary society.

In Section I, I begin with *he* 和, or harmony, as the first concept of this study. This arrangement calls for an explanation as most Confucian books begin with *ren* 仁, which has often been interpreted as humaneness. I argue that *he* is a foundational concept in Confucian philosophy. Cosmologically and metaphysically, this concept sets the general orientation of the Confucian worldview. Socially and politically, it directs social institutions and human relations. Ethically, *he* has been assigned a leading role in coordinating other key virtues in Confucian moral philosophy. We need to make sense of this concept before we can understand how other concepts work their ways along with one another in Confucian philosophy and see how the ideal society and the virtuous personhood are to be achieved. In comparison, *ren* is primarily a human virtue in the domain of ethics, and by extension in social and political philosophy. As far as studying Confucianism as a philosophy rather than merely an ethic, the relevance of *ren* is limited. Some scholars of Chinese philosophy have attempted to expand the notion into the ontological and cosmological domains by arguing that *ren* is a substance (*benti* 本體, e.g., Chen 2014). I believe ontologizing the concept of *ren* inevitably obscures its proper meaning as a personal virtue and hence undermines its central importance in Confucian moral and social philosophy.[12] In contrast, *he* is a broad-ranging concept that encompasses every level of existence. This chapter shows that, unlike predominant conceptions of harmony in the West, the Confucian *he* is neither pure accord nor conformity to a pre-set order in the world. It is "deep harmony" in the sense that *he* defines the entire Confucian cosmology and penetrates all levels of existence without eternally fixed ultimate principles. It is "dynamic harmony" in the sense that, rather than a static state of concord, *he* is a continuing process that brings various participating components together through mutual adjustment and accommodation. Characterized as "harmony with differences," this notion stands for an integrative process that involves creative tension and transformation. Confucian harmony is dynamic harmonization on the personal, familial, communal, societal level, which finally culminates as harmony in the entire world. Interpreted thus constructively, harmony is a recurring theme throughout this book. The focus of this chapter, however, is on elucidating harmony as the fundamental and deep-rooted concept in Confucian philosophy.

The next chapter presents the idea of *ren* 仁. A central concept to Confucian ethics, *ren* has two closely related meanings. Its root meaning is associated with the psychological states of empathy and compassion. This sense of *ren* is best elucidated in Mengzi's philosophy where *ren* is placed along with three other cardinal human virtues (rightness, propriety, wisdom) to form the four fundamental virtues of humanity. *Ren* also contains meaning on a higher order, standing for a comprehensive and holistic quality of the moral personhood. Students of Confucian philosophy often shift between these two senses without making conceptual connections. This chapter makes the case that the Confucian concept of *ren* is rooted and anchored in care, promotes a caring moral disposition, and culminates in a care-centered comprehensive virtue.

Chapter 3 addresses *li* 禮 or ritual propriety. The Confucian conceptualization of *li* is alien to most Western readers. To make sense of this important concept, this chapter explicates *li* in terms of cultural grammar. *Li* constitutes the operating infrastructure within a culture and provides protocols for people acting appropriately in social interactions just as grammar provides rules for the proper use of language in communication. Understood this way, *li* has both a descriptive and a normative function in society. Each culture has its own cultural grammar; understanding a culture requires people to know its *li*; whether one can behave in accordance with its *li* is indicative of the person's maturity and virtuosity in a culture. In the meantime, *li* evolves as grammar does over time. This interpretation of *li* provides a fruitful perspective for understanding *li* across cultures in contemporary times as well as a coherent reading of various sayings about *li* in classic texts.

Sections II opens with Chapter 4 on *xiao* 孝. It investigates one of the most important values in the Confucian tradition and argues for its interpretation as filial care. By tracing the evolution of this Confucian idea from Kongzi, to Mengzi, and then to Xunzi, this chapter argues that the common interpretation of *xiao* as "filial piety" does not accurately reflect the liberalizing evolution of this important Confucian notion. Through these three classical thinkers, a gradual shift in the requirements of *xiao* took place on the basis of their varied conceptualizations of respect (*jing* 敬) for parents. Based on various discussions by these thinkers, Confucian *xiao*, on the whole, is best understood as filial care that encompasses the physical, psychological, and moral dimensions of the lives of parents. Understood this way, it remains meaningful for contemporary societies.

The issue of gender equality has posed major challenges to Confucianism. One such challenge is whether Confucianism can preserve its ideal of gender differentiation (*bie* 別) without sexual discrimination and inequality. This chapter attempts to strike a balance between preserving and reforming tradition. By identifying discriminative and reasonable differentiations between the two genders, Chapter 5 ventures for Confucianism to achieve gender equality in families through flexible equilibrium on a new model of *yin-yang* philosophy. At the center of this new formulation is the argument that people's *yin-yang* differentiating roles can and should be detached from biological sexes. I argue that, on such a new model, Confucian gender equality can be achieved through gender differentiation without discrimination between the two sexes. Predictably, such a proposal will be controversial. Some readers will find it unsatisfactory because my proposal has gone too far from traditional Confucianism, whereas others will think it is not far enough. On an issue as important as gender equality, considerably more engagement is needed. I hope this chapter serves as one more starting point for further explorations.

You 友, the Confucian concept of friendship occupies Chapter 6. Friendship is one of the five cardinal human relationships in Confucianism. It constitutes an important dimension of the Confucian conception of a meaningful life. Friendship is particularly significant in modern societies where more and more people live urban lives, as opposed to ancient agrarian societies when people were mostly confined to kinship-based communities. By examining exemplary Confucian friends depicted in classical literature, this chapter makes the case that Confucian friendship is based on a family model and that Confucian friends are taken as extended family. As such, friends have mutual responsibilities to some extent analogous to family members. This interpretation is supported by a study of the evolution of the notion of *you* that connects to familial relationships. Furthermore, Confucian friendship is built on virtue. Personal virtues, however, are particularized in each person and thus contribute to people's individuality rather than making them faceless. This integrated conception of friendship, friends as family with particularized virtues, provides the basis for a Confucian solution to the challenge of the fungibility problem in the philosophy of friendship.

Chapter 7 investigates the connections between virtuous living and longevity (*shou* 壽). Although this idea is usually missing from the lists of Confucian concepts, longevity has been an ideal in close connection with virtuous living in Confucianism. By investigating the linkage between the Confucian ideal of longevity and cultivating virtue, this chapter makes the case that the Confucian virtuous life is founded on the ideal of personal harmony, and in that connection, it promotes a holistic, healthy life, which tends to lead to longevity. Such longevity is healthy and virtuous longevity. These Confucian ideas remain relevant to contemporary society.

The investigations thus far have brought readers to an inevitable question: Can Confucian sages, including Kongzi, be wrong? Now we take an interlude with Chapter 8 to examine an issue of profound significance for studying Confucian philosophy in contemporary times. Traditionally,

20 RESHAPING CONFUCIANISM: A PROGRESSIVE INQUIRY

Confucian teachings have been presented as words of the sages (*sheng* 聖). The sages have been regarded as possessing perfect knowledge and utmost virtue. Yet, some of their teachings appear problematic against modern moral sensibilities. This chapter traces debates in history regarding the perfection of Confucian sages and argues for their fallibility. Confucian sages are humans; no matter how good they have become; they can still make mistakes. The fallibility of Confucian sages marks a major difference between Confucianism and monotheistic traditions regarding respective sacred classic texts. It enables us to critically reexamine ancient Confucian teachings and to present Confucian philosophy as an enterprise that evolves through its internal dynamics to adapt to contemporary times. Recognizing the fallibility of Confucian sages is a crucial step for progressive Confucianism.

The last section, Section III, is composed of four reconstructions of Confucian socio-political philosophy. Chapter 9 attempts to articulate a Confucian philosophy of freedom through its intrinsic connection with the ancient Confucian notion of choice (*ze* 擇). It argues that such a modern concept of Confucian freedom can be reconstructed on the basis of the Confucian ideal of "choosing the good" (*ze shan* 擇善). Drawing on contemporary feminist theories of competency-based autonomy and linking virtue with competency, this chapter advances a Confucian conception of freedom whose realization is liberating, empowering, and fulfilling.

Chapter 10 investigates the Confucian conception of equality in moral, social, and political dimensions. Confucianism has long been known for its hierarchical character. This does not mean, however, that it has no conception of equality. There are two kinds of equality embedded in Confucianism. One is numerical equality, rooted in the Confucian belief in the same moral potential possessed by every person. Such a notion provides a foundation for constructing universal human dignity and political equality in contemporary society. The other is proportional equality. This kind of equality is accorded to individuals on the basis of the levels of their contribution and achievement in society and of refinement as good persons. The combination of these two notions of equality serves as a cornerstone for the Confucian vision of a just society. A major task for contemporary Confucians is to sensibly rearticulate and progressively implement these conceptions of equality for justice in society.

Chapter 11 proposes a major departure from the mainstream views of the contemporary "Confucian democracy" discourse and opts for participatory democracy as an effective means for achieving Confucian political goals. The general ideal of Confucian philosophy has often been captured in the slogan of "inner sageliness and outer kingliness" (*neisheng waiwang* 內聖外王). "Inner sageliness" is about self-cultivation toward the goal of sagehood; "outer kingliness" is about realizing the Confucian ideal of good society through political involvement. The latter has been pursued primarily in the form of service in government. In a provocative attempt, this chapter argues that the traditional understanding of Confucian political participation is not only extremely limited but also fundamentally flawed. This vital flaw is due to the fact that the very nature of power politics jeopardizes the traditional means to achieve Confucian moral and social ideals, as the moral and political failures of countless ancient Confucian officials have evidenced throughout history. Thus, a fundamental shift of strategy is needed. In a democratic era, the ideal of "outer kingliness" can be realized effectively by active participation in democratic processes in society. Thus, the Confucian ideal of "outer kingliness" is to be realized without "kings," or more aptly, through "politics without (depending on) political leaders."

Finally, Chapter 12 explores the role of Confucianism in contemporary civic education. From its earliest conception, the Confucian social project has primarily been educational (*jiao* 教) in character, with the purpose to prepare people for productive and virtuous lives. With regard to Confucian educational philosophy in relation to contemporary society, this chapter argues that Confucian virtue-centered philosophy is secular and this-worldly, and hence is particularly suitable for civic education in a multicultural world. By updating its value configuration, Confucian civic education can equip citizens with civic knowledge, civic skills, and civic disposition, preparing them to be effective participants in democratic social lives. Thus, a progressive Confucianism can play an important role in civic education not only in modern China and East Asia, but also throughout the world.

6. Summary

Reshaping Confucianism contributes to the discourse of progressive Confucianism by identifying key concepts and providing philosophical reconstructions that are important to Confucianism in contemporary times. The chapters provide a general picture of today's Confucianism in progressive

22   RESHAPING CONFUCIANISM: A PROGRESSIVE INQUIRY

transformation. In this author's view, a progressive Confucianism reshaped for the twenty-first century will continue to uphold the general ideal of "inner sageliness and outer kingliness" (*neisheng waiwang* 內聖外王). It is to be realized, however, in the form of "sageliness without sages and kingliness without kings" (*meiyou shengren de shengdao; meiyou xianwang de wangdao* 沒有聖人的聖道；沒有賢王的王道). "Sageliness," or *shengdao* (sagely way), signifies the Confucian ideal of people's moral cultivability; now it has to be pursued without hopes for perfect sages. "Kingliness," or *wangdao* (kingly way) stands for the Confucian political ideal of caring government and flourishing society; now it must be realized through democratic activism without relying on sagely leaders.

The book does not aim to systematically present one particular formulation of a comprehensive Confucianism. Instead, my explorations are open-ended and call for further discourse. As Richard Rorty has suggested, we contemporaries do not have to agree on what reasonable and re-educated ancient thinkers would say in modern contexts (Rorty 1984, 54). That is the nature of philosophy. The same applies to the cases in this book. However, it is this author's hope that the investigations and explorations in this book have provided meaningful material for further discussion.

Study Questions

1. How is Confucian philosophy related to Kongzi?
2. Explain the following terms:
   a) historical reconstruction
   b) rational reconstruction
   c) historical approach
   d) philosophical approach
   e) principle of charity
   f) principle of humanity
   g) principle of progressive humanity
3. What approach(es) does the author take in this book?
4. In what way can Zhang's two tenets for interpreting ancient texts complement the principle of charity and of humanity?
5. Is the author neutral with respect to Confucianism? If not, will it be a problem in explicating progressive Confucianism?

INTRODUCTION   23

6. In your view, is there a need to preserve cultural traditions? Why or why not?
7. If your answer to #6 is yes, how should we balance cultural preservation and cultural innovation?
8. What does the author mean by "sageliness without sages and kingliness without kings?" What is your view on such moves?

SECTION I
FOUNDATIONAL CONCEPTS

1

Dynamic Harmony

Usually translated as "harmony," *he* 和[1] is a foundational idea that sets the overall outlook of Confucian philosophy. It is one of the most extensive concepts, encompassing cosmology, metaphysics, epistemology, ethics, and social-political philosophy.[2] Without a good understanding of *he*, we cannot adequately comprehend Confucian philosophy. For these reasons, we take on *he* as the first concept of study in this book.

He is also the most misunderstood and underappreciated Confucian concept in contemporary times, especially in the West. This regrettable misfortune is due mainly to two reasons. First, since early on *he* has been misinterpreted and ill-implemented politically to suppress differences, until this day in China. Such political uses contaminated the concept and obscured its proper philosophical meaning. Little has been done to reclaim this concept. Second, in modern Western philosophical discourse, "harmony" has often been interpreted in a Platonic sense, which overshadows individual liberties and initiative by the collective,[3] or construed in superficial ways as happy concordance, making it either too idealistic or uninteresting, or both. These biases make studying *he* in the name of "harmony" unattractive. Reinvigorating the study of *he* requires us to explicate and restore its proper meaning in Confucian philosophy and to differentiate it from "harmony" as commonly understood in the West.

This chapter investigates *he* as dynamic and creative harmony and shows its vital importance in Confucian philosophy. It demonstrates how the notion of *he* was initially articulated precisely to counter oppressive conformity and to characterize the rich and energetic nature of the human life and the world at large. I will begin by investigating the formation of the concept before exploring its metaphysical significance.[4] I will further elucidate the metaphysical dimension of harmony by analogizing some of its characteristics with those of the theory of evolution. This chapter concludes with an elaboration of the personal, social, and environmental implications of the Confucian philosophy of harmony.

Reshaping Confucianism. Chenyang Li, Oxford University Press. © Oxford University Press 2024.
DOI: 10.1093/oso/9780197657621.003.0002

28 RESHAPING CONFUCIANISM: A PROGRESSIVE INQUIRY

1. Formation of the Concept of Dynamic Harmony

One of the earliest definitions of *he* as dynamic harmony can be found in the *Discourse on the States* (*Guoyu* 國語), a classical text written during the Spring and Autumn period (770–476 BCE). The text proposes that *he* designates the effect "when sounds respond to and mutually enhance (*xiangbao*) one another"[5] (Lai 2000, 166). The ancient Chinese lexicon *Shuowen* defines *bao* 保 as *yang* 養, namely "to foster." *Xiang bao* thus means to mutually foster one another. In this understanding, *he* takes place when various sounds resonate with one another in a mutually complementing and enhancing way. From here it can be readily extended, by analogy, to mean similar effects in other things and hence to construe a general concept of dynamic harmony.

In Chapter Zhengyu of the *Discourse on the States*, philosopher Shi Bo[6] elaborates the idea this way:

> Harmony (*he*) generates things indeed, whereas sameness does not advance growth. Counterbalancing one thing with another is called harmony. For this reason things come together and flourish. If one uses the same thing to complement the same thing, that is a dead end and will become wasted.[7] (Lai 2000, 746)

Shi Bo posts *he* in direct contrast with sameness (*tong* 同). This indicates that *he* itself already implies heterogeneity. He illustrates that a single sound in music is not much to hear, a single color in painting does not make a pattern, a single flavor in cooking does not satisfy the taste. From these examples, one can conclude that a single thing does not harmonize[8] (Lai 2000, 747). Shi Bo's elaboration confirms two of the features already implied in the initial definition of *he* in terms of sounds. First, *he* is a generative and productive process; second, such a process requires heterogeneity. Without diverse things coming together, there would be no basis for harmony. When diverse elements come together and interact in mutually enhancing ways, new things or effects are generated. This is *he*.

He is not merely an abstract and speculative idea. According to Shi Bo, it was the philosophy of ancient sage-kings in action, which enabled their societies to thrive:

> The early kings mixed Earth with Metal, Wood, Water, and Fire in producing varieties of things. They balanced one's taste with the five flavors,

strengthened the four limbs in order to guard the body, harmonized (*he*) the six measures of sounds to improve the hearing, made the seven parts of the body upright to maintain the heart/mind, balanced the eight body parts to complete the whole person, established the nine social rules to set up pure virtues, and put together the ten offices to regulate the multitudes ... Thus, it was harmony (*he*) at the highest level.[9] (Lai 2000, 746–747)

Earth, Metal, Wood, Water, and Fire are the five processings of *qi* 氣 (physical energy) that serve as the basic elements of Chinese cosmology. Appropriately integrating these factors enabled ancient kings to generate varieties of things productively. These sage-kings established themselves as examples in promoting *he*, making it a normative quality for people to implement. By Shi Bo's account, these sage-kings engaged themselves in a harmonious unity (*he-tong* 和同) by bringing together and maintaining diversity: marrying their wives from other families, seeking wealth in all directions, and choosing ministers who could remonstrate with the ruler (Lai 2000, 747). For Shi Bo, a healthy and prosperous world relies on various things working well together.

In the *Discourse on the States*, we see how the idea of *he* was first conceived as a philosophical concept, however rudimentarily, out of observing musical interplay, and it was then used to account for the successful ways of ancient sage-kings to manage society. The text's alleged author or one of the authors, Zuo Qiuming 左丘明 (circa 502–422BCE) was a contemporary of Kongzi.[10] Zuo is also associated with another important text on harmony, the *Zuo Commentary on Spring and Autumn Annals* (*Zuozhuan* 左傳), one of the Confucian *Thirteen Classics*. The *Zuo Commentary* records a discussion of *he* by another philosopher, Yanzi 晏子 (?–500BCE):

> Harmony (*he*) is like making soup. One needs water, fire, vinegar, sauce, salt, and plum to cook fish and meat. One needs to cook them with firewood, mingle (*he*) them together in order to balance the flavors. One needs to compensate for deficiencies and reduce excessiveness. The virtuous person (*junzi* 君子[11]) eats [such balanced food] in order to maintain peace in his heart-mind.[12] (TTC 1980, 2093)

In comparison with Shi Bo, Yanzi's account is more elaborate and more sophisticated in emphasizing not only heterogeneity but also the process of balancing differences. In Yanzi's view, harmony involves integrating differences

30 RESHAPING CONFUCIANISM: A PROGRESSIVE INQUIRY

and opposites by actively balancing them. This can be seen in the typical cooking process. A cook needs divergent ingredients to make a rich soup. The mentioning of water and fire may suggest a tension between ingredients that may be implied in Shi Bo's expression of "counterbalancing." When managed well, however, such tension is creative tension, as between water and fire used in cooking. The cook needs components that taste and smell very different. One important aspect of good cooking is the ability to balance one strong flavor with another. When diverse ingredients are integrated well, each contributing to the taste of the soup and none of them overwhelming others, it would be a successful culinary product. In such a process, each ingredient realizes its potential by transforming itself as well as contributing to the transformation of others. This reflects a process of dynamic and generative harmony.

In addition to this culinary metaphor for harmony, Yanzi uses a musical metaphor. He says:

> Sounds are like flavors. Divergent elements complete one other: one breath, two styles, three types, four instruments, five sounds, six measures, seven notes, eight winds, and nine songs. Divergent sounds complement one another: the pure and the impure, the big and the small, the short and the long, the fast and the slow, the sorrowful and the joyful, the strong and the tender, the late and the quick, the high and the low, the in and the out, and the inclusive and the non-inclusive. Listening to this kind of music, the virtuous person (*junzi* 君子) maintains peace in his heart-mind.[13] (TTC 1980, 2093–2094)

In this musical metaphor, harmony is achieved by various sounds complementing one another and integrating into a coherent piece of music.

Contemporary thinkers, however, have read these two metaphors in different ways. Alan Chan has argued that the musical metaphor for harmony suggests "conformity with certain norms" (Chan 2011, 40). In the musical metaphor, "harmony is the absence of strife (*bu he* 不和), and this absence can only be brought about if contention gives way to concord" (ibid. 41). Chan concludes:

> Confucian harmony in this understanding is characterized by sage and benevolent leadership "above" and grateful and joyous compliance "below." This is the overall score that Confucian ethics aims to orchestrate. (ibid., 42)

DYNAMIC HARMONY   31

Chan's reading raises important questions for interpreting these metaphors for Confucian harmony. A metaphor can always be read in different ways. One can definitely find an undercurrent of compliance and even conformity in ancient Chinese discourses of harmony. Shi Bo's story of sage-kings, for instance, can be read this way. In fact, the history of harmony discourse includes contested conceptions. Both the culinary and musical metaphor may strike readers as implying that a master figure, either a cook or a musical conductor, is needed to generate harmony. There are reasons, however, for not interpreting the musical metaphor as requiring a manipulating master. First, the original definition in the *Discourse on the States*, that *he* takes place "when sounds respond to and mutually enhance one another" (Lai 2000, 166), is more accurately a metaphor of blending sounds rather than a metaphor of merely man-made music. Such a definition includes the interplay of natural sounds. For instance, the *Book of Changes* states, "a crane sings in the forest; her babies *he* their mother" (*minghezaiyin, qizi he zhi* 鳴鶴在陰，其子和之, TTC 1980, 79).[14] Second, ancient Chinese integrated music—unlike Western orchestral music—requires no conductor and hence there is no central control. Instead, layers of various instruments coordinate and collaborate with one another to generate music. Importantly, in such performances, the listeners are in fact listening to each other and playing responsively. The mode of music production is more like jazz than an orchestra. The performance of ancient Chinese music is the manifestation of *he*, as the performers are mutually supportive and are working together for an outcome that is enriched by the collaborations and that cannot be achieved by one person. Third, Yanzi begins his musical metaphor by claiming explicitly that "sounds are like flavors (in producing a soup)," and he explicates in specific terms how various musical notes work together to generate harmony, rather than speaking of the need for a controlling force. For Yanzi, good music requires a variety of sounds in various modes and these diverse sounds complement and complete one another in a conjoined process of production. Understood this way, harmony can take place without a predominant force and, as will be shown in the next section, harmony can ultimately be a self-generating process.

Moreover, Yanzi articulated the idea of harmony precisely as an alternative to conformity. He explicitly argues that *he* must be distinguished from another notion, *tong* 同. Here *tong* literally means sameness, uniformity, or conformity, even though the word has also been used to mean "coming together" elsewhere. Forced *tong* is conformity. In Yanzi's conversation with

32   RESHAPING CONFUCIANISM: A PROGRESSIVE INQUIRY

the ruler of Qi, the ruler evidently confuses *he* with *tong* when he praises how "harmonious (*he*)" the relationship is between him and his minister Ju 據. Yanzi counters that the relationship between the ruler and Ju is *tong*, not *he*. Yanzi uses the above examples of cooking and making music to show that *he* is not to be confused with *tong*. Both metaphors are used in direct contrast to Ju's case of conformity (*jin Ju bu ran* 今據不然). Yanzi explains:

> When the ruler says "yes," Ju also says "yes"; when the ruler says "no," Ju also says "no," This is like mixing water with water. Who can eat such a soup? This is like using the same kind of instrument to produce music. Who can enjoy such music? This is the reason for why it is not all right to be *tong*. (TTC 1980, 2094)

For Yanzi, the kind of relationship between the ruler and his minister Ju is sameness or conformity, not harmony. A harmonious relationship presupposes that they have different perspectives and often divergent views on various issues. Such differences inevitably bring out some form of tension in the relationship; a completely tensionless relationship is not harmony and will instead be one of *tong*, as the one between the ruler and Ju. Differences and tension should be managed in ways conducive to harmony. This is of course not to·say that harmony does not need some common ground between the parties. A certain kind of commonality is needed for harmony to take place. After all, various sounds in music production are nevertheless all sounds; many ingredients in soup-making are food products. The point is rather that *tong* without adequate differences precludes harmony. Such a state is like making a soup with only one ingredient ("mixing water with water") or producing a symphony with only one kind of instrument. A soup made of only one ingredient is tasteless, a symphony composed of only one instrument is boring, and a government consisting of only one voice is stagnant and dangerous. Against a common confusion represented by the ruler of Qi, Yanzi's emphasis is undoubtedly on difference rather than commonality.

Along the line of Yanzi's elaboration, we can say that, philosophically, *he* is a third way, markedly distinct from forced uniformity and unmanageable scatteredness. Forced uniformity implies oppression; unmanageable scatteredness amounts to chaos. *He* presupposes the existence of different things and implies a certain favorable relationship among them that is achievable through mutual adjustment and mutual complementation. It is a process that brings together diverse elements to work together without imposing uniformity. This sense of harmony is not about conforming to a fixed order in the world. On the contrary, it is about creating order out of heterogeneity that maintains well-coordinated diversity. Thus, *he* from early on carries with it an explicit orientation toward diversity and difference, against uniformity.

Linking Yanzi's description of *he* with Shi Bo's explicit statement that *he* is generative, we can understand *he* not merely as a state of different things hanging together in a congenial way, but as a process through which various participating parties are transformed and mutually enhanced in productive ways. In such a process there are differences and tensions, even though they are managed appropriately to avoid serious breakdowns. Here emerges the basis for a Confucian idea of harmony.

Roger Ames has characterized this harmonious order as "a continuing aesthetic achievement made possible through *ars contextualis*, 'the art of optimal contextualizing within one's roles and relations'" (Ames 2011, 84). Ames's use of "one's roles and relations" may suggest harmony only in the social realm. Philosophically, however, Confucian harmony concerns more than mere human beings. As Ames says, harmony reflects "a collaboration among the participating elements to make the most out of the situation" (ibid.). This conception of harmony is transformative and uplifting. It is a generative process that is inter-relational, interdependent, integrative, and innovative. In such a way, it brings about new outcomes in the world. Understood this way, productivity in the sense of generating new synergy through contextualized optimization of a situation is at the core of the Confucian conception of harmony.

The ideas from Shi Bo and Yanzi were later appropriated by Confucian thinkers and became a central ideal in Confucianism. All major Confucian classics recognize the importance of harmony, even though they emphasize its manifestations in different dimensions of the world and weigh it differently. In Kongzi's *Analects* and the book of *Mengzi* harmony is taken as a moral and sociopolitical concept, and it figures far less prominently than in the *Book of Changes* (*Yijing* 易經) and the *Zhongyong* 中庸. In *Analects* 13.23 Kongzi adopts the moral ideal of *he*, making *he* a criterion for virtuous persons (*junzi* 君子). Echoing Yanzi, Kongzi says that "The *junzi* harmonizes but does not seek sameness (*tong*), whereas the petty person seeks sameness but does not harmonize" (*Analects* 13.23). As discussed earlier, heterogeneity is the most important precondition for Confucian harmony. For Kongzi, a sensible person should be able to respect different opinions and be able to

34 RESHAPING CONFUCIANISM: A PROGRESSIVE INQUIRY

work with different people in a harmonious way. Distinguishing harmony from sameness (conformity) is the most important feature of the conception of harmony as explicated by Yanzi. Kongzi incorporated such a philosophy, as opposed to the construal of harmony as sameness by the ruler of Qi, into his philosophy of *li* 禮 (rites, ritual propriety). *Li* is one of the most important concepts in the *Analects* (see Chapter 3 of this book). The text takes *li*'s function precisely as to harmonize people of various kinds, both within each person and within relationships. Kongzi's disciple Youruo 有若 is recorded as saying that "of the functions of *li*, harmonization is the [most] precious" (*Analects* 1.12).[15] In this view, there is a direct connection between *li* and harmony. According to another Confucian classic, the *Rituals of the Zhou* (*Zhouli* 周禮), one of the six primary functions of the state official Greater Minister is "[to minister] state rituals (*li*), in order to harmonize the country" (TTC 1980, 645). Accordingly, we cannot understand *li* without connecting it with harmony.

Echoing Kongzi's view on harmony with difference, Mengzi maintains that the lack of uniformity is in the nature of things in the world, and if we force them into sameness, we upset their natural order and cause chaos in society (*Mengzi* 3A4). Mengzi comments that among the three important things in human affairs, harmony between people is the most important: "good timing is not as good as being advantageously situated, and being advantageously situated is not as good as having harmonious people" (*Mengzi* 2B1). To achieve important goals in social affairs, one would need all three: good timing, an advantageous position, and having harmonious people. The most precious thing, however, is to have people who work harmoniously with one another.

In the *Xunzi, he* is used in two different senses. One is the positive sense of harmony. Concurring with Kongzi on the importance of ritual propriety (*li*) to harmony, Xunzi says that "[only] when following ritual propriety is one harmoniously (*he*) adjusted"[16] (*Xunzi*, chapter 2). In the negative sense, Xunzi warns people not to use "harmony" as an excuse for abandoning principles: "To harmonize with others for the sake of what is good is being reasonably accommodating" and "to harmonize with others for the sake of what is bad is toadying" (*Xunzi*, chapter 2; cf. Knoblock 1988, 153). He further elaborates, "To recognize as right what is right and as wrong what is wrong is called wisdom. To regard as wrong what is right and as right what is wrong is called stupidity" (ibid.). For Xunzi, real harmony is not without principle. It is not about pleasing other people and avoiding conflict at any cost, as in the case of minister Ju of Qi. Real harmony goes with wisdom. Xunzi's view strikes a similar chord with Kongzi, whose ideal of harmony is "harmony without mindlessly following others" (*Zhongyong* 10; TTC 1980, 1626). To follow others mindlessly is to conform to others; Confucian harmony is not to be confused with it.

While harmony is treated as a moral ideal in the *Analects* and the *Mengzi*, it is treated as a broader philosophical concept in other Confucian classics. The Confucian classic *Book of Rites* (*Liji* 禮記) states, "when *yin* and *yang* harmonize, the myriad things get their due" (TTC 1980, 1446). Xunzi elaborates on the same idea in more detail:

> With the great transformation of *yin* and *yang*, the generous supply of wind and rain, the myriad things each get harmonized so they can live, and get nurtured so they grow. (*Xunzi*, chapter 17; cf. Hutton 2014, 176)

Xunzi's statement concurs with the *Book of Changes*, which in its *Tuan Commentary* develops the notion of "Great Harmony" (*dahe* 大和):

> How great is the *Qian* 乾 (Heaven)! From it the myriad things originate under Heaven. . . . With the changes of the *Qian* way, the myriad things all keep on their own path of life. Thus, they preserve the Great Harmony.[17] (TTC 1980, 14)

"Great Harmony" is the highest ideal in the *Book of Changes*. In such a view, while the world is full of different things, all these things harmonize as they go through incessant changes. Such Great Harmony is taken as the overall trend in the world.

Perhaps the most focused articulation and elaboration of this Confucian ideal of harmony is found in the *Zhongyong* 中庸, one of the Confucian canonical *Four Books*. The *Zhongyong* states:

> Centrality is the great foundation under Heaven, and harmony is the great way under Heaven. In achieving centrality and harmony, Heaven and Earth maintain their appropriate positions and the myriad things flourish. (TTC 1980, 1625)

In the context of our study, this passage can be interpreted as follows. Centrality and harmony are directly linked because harmony is situated in

36   RESHAPING CONFUCIANISM: A PROGRESSIVE INQUIRY

the middle between forced uniformity and conformity on the one hand and scattered divergence on the other. By taking the middle way, Confucians aim to connect diverse elements in the world in a mutually beneficial way and to avoid completely losing unity in absolute scatteredness. In this view, Heaven and Earth can only operate appropriately through dynamic harmony, without which they will lose their proper place and things in the world will not flourish.[18] Thus, in the *Zhongyong*, a text which lays out the foundation for Confucian moral metaphysics, harmony is set as the highest ideal.[19]

Post-Qin Confucian thinkers inherited this philosophy of harmony. Dong Zhongshu 董仲舒 (179–104 BCE), an influential Confucian thinker during the Western Han, insists, "There is no virtue greater than harmony" (TTM, 805).[20] Dong also maintains faith that, "although there are disharmonies, they are bound to be converted into harmonies. This is the Way of Heaven and Earth" (TTM, 805).[21] Harmony as a central concept re-arose prominently in the ideas of the Song Confucian philosopher Zhang Zai 張載 (1020–1077). His major work, *Zheng Meng* 正蒙, summarizes and presents his general philosophy. The work opens with a chapter on "Great Harmony" (*taihe* 太和) and concludes with a chapter on forming one body with the cosmos, a chapter that has been usually presented under the title of "Western Inscription." The opening chapter sets the tone for the entire work. Zhang writes:

> The Great Harmony is called the Way (*Dao*). It embraces the nature which underlies all counter processes of floating and sinking, rising and falling, and motion and rest. It is the origin of the process of fusion and intermingling, of overcoming and being overcome, and of expansion and contraction. At the commencement, these processes are incipient, subtle, obscure, easy, and simple, but at the end they are extensive, great, strong, and firm. . . . Unless the whole universe is in the process of fusion and intermingling like fleeting forces moving in all directions, it may not be called Great Harmony. (Chan 1963, 500–501)

For Zhang, the Way (*Dao*) as the universal nature or reason of the world is to be accounted for by harmony. Zhang takes *qi* 氣 (physical energy) as primary in the cosmos. In his developmental view of the world, the operation of *qi* through the forces of *yin* and *yang* leads to the formation of the world as we know it and these two forces harmonize in guiding its operation. On such an account, out of formless *qi* emerge various forms of things; when there are different forms of things, there comes tension and opposition; tension and opposition may lead to conflict; and finally, conflict needs to be resolved in harmony.[22] Zhang's philosophy culminates in the closing chapter of the work by presenting a view of universal love. Zhang writes:

> Heaven is my father and Earth is my mother, and even such a small creature as I finds an intimate place in their midst. Therefore, that which fills the universe I regard as my body and that which directs the universe I consider as my nature. All people are my brothers and sisters, and all things are my companions. (Chan 1963, 497)

In Zhang's philosophy, harmony penetrates the deepest level of the universe and yet manifests itself on every level, from forming physical entities and generating life forms, to practicing personal ethics, and to the operation of social and political institutions.[23]

The above reconstruction shows that the idea of dynamic harmony has been an important component of Confucian philosophy across historical periods. As such, it has been rooted deeply in Confucian thinking. It deserves serious scholarly treatment.

Before I conclude this section, one pertinent question needs to be addressed. Given that *he* is used to mean a dynamic process of interaction and integration of various elements through coordination, should it be translated as "harmony"? "Harmony" usually means agreement and accord in modern English usages (Oxford 2022). There are three reasons as to why I used "harmony" as the translation for *he*, despite its imperfections. First, there is no exact equivalent word for *he* in English. Using a new phrase may be awkward while at the same time inhibiting the expression of its full meaning. For instance, even a phrase like "productively coordinated diversity in unity" does not reveal the dynamic characteristic of *he*. Second, the translation is already widely accepted and used among scholars of Chinese studies. It is more convenient to continue using it while elucidating its rich meanings rather than picking up an unfamiliar term. Third, tracing back to ancient Greek philosophy, "harmony" (*harmonia*, αρμονία) has been used in ways similar to those in ancient China, even though modern Western philosophical discourse has only seen it in a narrow sense that implies uniformity and conformity.[24] Readers are gently reminded that "harmony" here stands for the Confucian concept of *he* as it is explicated in this book, and from time to time, I will say "dynamic harmony" as a reminder.

38 RESHAPING CONFUCIANISM: A PROGRESSIVE INQUIRY

2. Harmony as a Deep Concept

The above investigation shows the formation of *he* as a metaphysical, social, and moral concept in early Confucian philosophy. In this section, I will further reconstruct *he* as a fundamental philosophical concept along the lines of its development mainly through the *Book of Changes*, the *Zhongyong*, Xunzi's and Zhang Zai's philosophy. I argue that, philosophically, this concept of harmony is a deep concept. It is "deep" in three senses. First, harmony is not a superficial phenomenon. It penetrates the surface to reach the deep level of the entire process of each instance of harmonious existence. Second, Confucian harmony is not merely a moral or social concept, it has deep metaphysical roots, indicating how the world operates at its fundamental level.[25] Third and most importantly, at each stage of the evolution of the world, harmony takes place with existing preconditions and within contexts, both of which are themselves the results of preceding processes of harmonization. Ultimately, there are no absolute pre-determined orders or prototypes in the world that are ontologically prior to harmony. Harmony is traced to the very beginning of the cosmos.

Against the background of a widely shared worldview in ancient China, we will see that the emphasis on harmony in early Chinese philosophy is closely connected to its ontology of *qi* 氣 (physical energy). Taken as the primordial stuff in the universe, *qi* in itself is formless and orderless. It takes shape and form through a process of harmonization. A prominent theme of ancient Chinese cosmogony is that the world began with *hundun* 混沌, or orderless original matter, often labeled as the primordial *qi*. By the time of the Eastern Zhou period (770–256 BCE), *hundun* had become a common theme across various streams of thought (Girardot 1984, 54). The idea of *hundun* and its evolution can be found in a variety of ancient texts. For instance, the *Chu Silk Text A* 楚帛书甲篇, which has been seen as the "Chinese Genesis" (Dong 2002), describes the initial state of the universe in terms of *mengmengmomo, wangzhangbibi* [26] (Rao and Zeng 1985, 11). The two expressions describe an undifferentiated original state of the universe. Namely, at the beginning stage of the universe, things have not taken their forms (Rao and Zeng 1985, 11). The world emerges from such a primeval state.

The Daoyuan 道原 article of the *Mawangdui Silk Texts* describes the original state as the "One" and expresses a similar view: "In the very beginning, all things were undifferentiated and unsubstantiated. The undifferentiated and unsubstantiated is the One; the One perseveres"[27] (Chen 2007, 38). This "One" is the original whole of the chaos. The author of the text explicitly designates the working of the One as *he*, "Its name is One, its home is non-substantiation, its nature is effortless action, and its function is harmony"[28] (ibid.). In this view, the "One" does not have a pre-given form. The subsequently formed world is generated through a process of harmony.

In a similar vein, the Jing: Guan 經:觀 article of the *Mawangdui Silk Texts* quotes the Yellow Emperor as speaking of the beginning *hundun*:

> There was neither darkness nor brightness, neither *yin* nor *yang*. With *yin* and *yang* not being set, I have nothing to name for. Then it started to be divided into two, as *yin* or *yang*, and further divided into the four seasons.[29] (Chen 2007, 210)

Darkness and brightness suggest day and night. The text claims that the world had no such differentiation at the beginning. This original oneness gives rise to *yin* and *yang*, the harmonizing interaction of which jointly leads to the generation of the myriad things (ibid.).[30] The concepts of *yin* and *yang* can be understood here in either a thick or thin sense. Understood thickly, one can take the former of the pair as endowed with characteristic features such as dark, soft, wet, short, slow, feminine, and so forth, whereas light, firmness, dryness, quick, long, masculine, and so forth in the latter. It is difficult, however, to see what these features on each side have in common to make either *yin* or *yang* a distinct concept. When they are taken in a thin sense, these two forces stand for divergent features that interact and complement each other, without definitive particular features as described in the thick reading. Neither *yin* nor *yang* can exist in and of itself; they are in tension and harmony from the beginning. In this way, *yin* and *yang* are symbols of harmony. In the context of these classic texts, we can say that the undifferentiated One evolves as harmony makes its way in the world, and this originally formless One generates everything in the world through a process of harmonization.

Contemporary philosopher Ding Sixin 丁四新 writes:

> In the Daoyuan text, the idea of "harmony" is not about harmonious relations among formed things. Rather it is the necessary and sufficient condition for generating the myriad things. Fundamentally speaking, without harmony there cannot be the generation of concrete things. (Ding 2015)

40 RESHAPING CONFUCIANISM: A PROGRESSIVE INQUIRY

Harmony in this sense is prior to every thing and any thing, prior even to Heaven and Earth. I call this kind of harmony "deep harmony" as it does not presuppose an ultimate pre-set order in the world, whether in the form of an intelligent mind (the divine), Pythagorean numbers, or Platonic forms. Deep harmony is a self-generating harmony that reaches the most fundamental level of the world.

There is no need to inquire whether this account is based on the evidence of scientific research. It is obviously not. Rather, it is a conceptual framework that underpins how the early Chinese understood the ways in which humans are embedded in the world. It takes harmony as the ultimate impetus for the generation of the universe. As such, the concept of harmony in Chinese philosophy carries significant explanatory power for understanding our world.

Modern scientific theories, nevertheless, can help us make sense of the concept of harmony in Chinese philosophy. There are some parallels, though limited, between the Chinese cosmogony of *qi* and the contemporary scientific cosmological theory of the Big Bang.[31] Highlighting these parallels, as crude as they seem, can help us make sense of the orientation of Chinese harmony thinking. Speaking of the primordial status of the Big Bang, Stephen Hawking argued:

> You can't get to a time before the Big Bang because there was no time before the Big Bang. We have finally found something that doesn't have a cause, because there was no time for a cause to exist in. (Hawking 2018, 37–38)

Similar things can be said of the original *qi* in Chinese cosmogony. Furthermore, whereas the Chinese have used the terminology of the forces of *yin* and *yang*, Hawking's scientific counterpart points to positive and negative energy. According to Hawking, when the Big Bang produced a massive amount of positive energy, it also produced an equal amount of negative energy; there is a kind of perfect symmetry in the universe. This is like, in Hawking's words: if you build a hill, you dig a hole. The balance between positive energy and negative energy adds up to zero (Hawking 2018, 32). Such a view seems to align well with the Chinese *yin-yang* energy theory that grounds cosmic harmony, even though the ancient theory was articulated in pre-scientific language.

Also, we do not know scientifically what happened immediately after the Big Bang in the modern cosmogony. We can only imagine some processes to fill the gap between the beginning of the universe and the world as we know it today. What is significant for the purposes of this study is that such a Chinese cosmogonic theory provides a meaningful background for us to contextualize harmony. In the Confucian view, dynamic harmony is the process that bridges the gap between the original undifferentiated oneness and our world today. As Xunzi claims, with the harmonious interplay of *yin* and *yang* there come favorable natural conditions (e.g., winds and rain) for the myriad things to be produced and maintained (*Xunzi*, chapter 17).

Another scientific idea useful to our understanding here is evolution. Evolution has played an important role in shaping our world. Charles Darwin's theory of evolution explains how organisms evolve over time without intelligent design or a blueprint for progress. According to the theory of evolution, individual organisms have biological traits either through inheritance or mutation. Some of these traits are conducive to survival in the changing environment whereas other traits may not be. Individuals with traits favorable to survival are likely to persist and to pass genes to future generations and, in that sense, they are "selected" by nature to continue. As a result, the vast majority, if not all, of existent organisms are those which continue to be well fitted to their environment. An often-cited example of such selections is color changes of the peppered moth in nineteenth-century England. The dark-colored peppered moth was not known before the nineteenth century. But they became popular in heavily polluted areas during the industrial revolution, where their dark color protected them from being easily spotted and preyed on by predators. Evolution can serve as a helpful metaphor for understanding the Confucian idea of dynamic harmony. For the purposes of our discussion, four important features of the evolution process are worth noting.

First, mutation is a natural occurrence in nature. Things are not fixed but changing. Changes, both internal mutations in the organism and in the environment, give impetus to evolution. Evolution does not explain mutation; rather, mutation is a piece of the puzzle that explains evolution.

Second, surviving individual organisms must have the capacities that align with the conditions of the environment, which also changes. The suitability of a trait is not determined by the trait in itself; rather it depends on joining and forming some kind of pattern with the environment. There is usually tension in the fitting process. For the peppered moth, light color is a good trait in a lighter-colored environment whereas dark color is more conducive to survival in a heavily polluted environment. We can imagine that, as the peppered moth turned dark and difficult to spot, over time, birds would have

42   RESHAPING CONFUCIANISM: A PROGRESSIVE INQUIRY

to evolve with better eyesight to survive in that environment (leaving aside other considerations). In this sense, fitness is a mutual and multidirectional process between the organism and the various conditions of its environment.

Third, the outcome of evolution is the continuation of some species and the generation of new ones. In evolution, new traits develop through mutation and, insofar as they have a central role in the organism's survival and success within the environment, the species would do well to continue propagating the specific traits in successive generations. At some junctures, new species emerge. These are the main product of evolution.

Fourth, for any particular species, its evolutionary process can break down and the species can cease to exist. Countless species have gone extinct due to failure to adapt to new environments. Yet, evolution itself persists in the world. Other species carry on the process and nature moves along in this way.

Confucian harmony is not the same as evolution. For one thing, dynamic harmony is not confined to living species. It covers the entire realm of existence, traceable all way to the beginning of the world from the orderless. Harmony occurs in astronomical processes as well as in various physical phenomena around us on earth; we find harmony in the four seasons as well as in beaches, in the symbiosis of species as well as in human relationships. Nevertheless, this notion of harmony as occurring in the natural world resembles evolution in important ways.

First, Confucian cosmogony presupposes change as a natural occurrence. Just as we cannot understand evolution without seeing it as an ongoing process of change, harmony must also be understood as a dynamic process. In comparison with relatively static worldviews held by most Greek philosophers, as represented by major thinkers such as Plato and Aristotle, Chinese worldviews tilt overwhelmingly toward change ("becoming"). The *Book of Changes* underscores this fundamental feature of the world as in a state of constant change. It defines the Way (*Dao*) of the first hexagram *Qian* as "change," which is linked to "Great Harmony" (TTC 1980, 14). As with evolution, harmony does not explain the origin of change even though it induces changes; it takes change as an eternal phenomenon that contributes to our understanding of dynamic harmony in the world. Only change causes change. Indeed, as depicted in the *Book of Changes*, change is a fundamental presupposition for harmony.

Second, harmony involves beings that are inter-relational and interdependent. For anything to become involved in the process of dynamic harmony, it must work in collaboration with other things in the world and join them in the process of creating new patterns. Tension exists in such a process. Evolution is not individual-based. Individuals are members of species. Individual mutations contribute to evolution only when they affect the species. Such an understanding helps us make sense of how the inter-relationality of individuals affects patterns of the existence of species. Scientists have long been intrigued by a phenomenon called "quorum sensing." Quorum sensing is a mechanism that allows individual bacteria to communicate and coordinate group behavior through exclusively local interactions. It enables bacteria to determine population densities to coordinate activities of the entire community. Similar mechanisms also exist among macroscopic organisms such as ants and bees. How is it possible for individual members in a population that can interact through local means to coordinate behavior with other members at a distance without central control? Using a computer modeling method called "cellular automaton" researchers have been able to simulate the process. Computer scientist Wim Hordijk describes the method as follows:

> In its simplest form, a cellular automaton (CA) consists of a linear array of "cells," each of which can be in one of two states, say zero or one. At discrete time steps (or iterations), all cells simultaneously update their state according to a fixed update rule, which depends on their current local neighborhood configuration consisting of a cell itself together with its left neighbor and right neighbor. This update rule simply states for each possible local neighborhood configuration what the new state of the center cell will be. (Hordijk 2018)

This is a continuing process. Each cell continues to change in accordance with its neighboring cells that also continue to change. Such a process continues to evolve so that the entire population achieves some sort of optimal equilibrium in a relatively stable state, until further mutation or variations in the environment call for further adjustment.[32] From the perspective of Confucian harmony, such a process can be used as a good illustration of dynamic harmony in a crude form. Even though the domain of action for each individual item in the world may be confined in one way or another, yet harmonization nevertheless takes place through chains of interactions and eventually permeates a large domain of existence beyond the initial localities without centrally controlling agency. Harmony is a from-the-ground-up process.[33]

44 RESHAPING CONFUCIANISM: A PROGRESSIVE INQUIRY

The third parallel between harmony and evolution is that both processes bring about new things in the world. The outcomes of evolution include new species and adapted species whose traits are more adaptive to the environment. The outcome of harmony lies in the generation of new things and new phenomena in the world. As the ancient thinker Shi Bo said, an important efficacy of harmony is that it is generative of things (Lai 2000, 746). When harmony is achieved, existing things are transformed into new states or new relations, their statuses are elevated to new heights, or new things are produced. The generation of new things is, however, not pre-determined. Like evolution, harmony is generative and creative without pre-destination. Evolution does not take place *in order to* produce longneck giraffes and fast-running deer, for instance; rather it explains the special features of these animals. Similarly, harmony in the natural world does not occur *in order to* produce various good things; rather it explains their emergence. Humans affect harmony with purposes to generate desirable states. Such outcomes, however, must be accounted for by actual processes as well as purposes. New things emerge as a result of the processes of harmonization, in the natural world as well as the human world.

Fourth, harmony can break down for individual beings or collectives. When a species fails to keep up with evolution, it goes extinct; new species emerge, and existing species continue to evolve. Similarly, when a harmonious process breaks down, further harmonizing forces overcome them and move forward. People suspicious of the idea of harmony often point to disharmonies in the world to show that the world is not harmonious. Undoubtedly, both harmony and disharmony exist in the world. From the perspective of a harmony philosophy, harmony includes the process of overcoming disharmony.

One such example of harmony overcoming disharmony can be seen in the reintroduction of wolves in the Yellowstone National Park in the United States. Wolves are often seen as a cause of disharmonies in nature. In the 1920s, the last wolf pack was killed in Yellowstone by park employees as part of the policy of the time to eliminate all predators. In the subsequent seventy years without wolves, Yellowstone's ecosystem fell out of balance. The elk population exploded, taking a heavy toll on willows and aspens. Without those trees, songbirds declined, beavers were unable to build their dams, and riverbanks started to erode. Furthermore, without beaver dams and the shade from trees and other plants, water temperatures were too high for cold-water fish (Randall 2020). In 1995, wolves were reintroduced back to the park. The elk and deer populations started responding immediately. Willows rebounded approximately ten years afterwards, and in twenty years the aspen began flourishing, riverbanks stabilized, and songbirds returned as did beavers, eagles, foxes, and badgers (ibid.). In itself, the killing of prey by wolves is a kind of disharmony. Yet, these deaths pave the way for harmony in nature on a larger scale.

In the Confucian view, disharmony can be seen as a component of, or a transitional stage for, achieving further harmony. Disharmony contributes to harmony in two ways. First, it serves as a necessary component for harmony on another level. When wolves kill preys in the Yellowstone National Park, these killings in themselves are disharmonies. They nevertheless are constitutive of the overall harmony at the park. Second, disharmony can lead to and pave ways for harmony. A revolution itself is disharmony. It nevertheless can be a necessary means for people to overthrow an oppressive government so they can build a harmonious society. From the perspective of a harmony philosophy, disharmonies in either case should be kept at the absolute minimum level, especially when human suffering and death are concerned. The value of a philosophy of harmony is, at least in part, to provide us with a positive outlook and mindset for harmony, so we prioritize it as an important value to pursue and promote in the world.[34]

Contemporary thinkers have offered sophisticated discussions of Confucian harmony. Brook Ziporyn speaks of two types of coherence in Chinese philosophy, the non-ironic and the ironic. Non-ironic coherence is found in such texts as the *Analects* and the *Mengzi*. It means "the hanging together of items into groupings, but also coherence in the sense of intelligibility (visibility and readability) and as value" (Ziporyn 2012, 87). Ironic coherence is found the *Daodejing* and the *Zhuangzi*, where we find such ideas as "the true knowing is the knowing that does not know," namely "knowing without knowing," as well as "doing without doing" and "being without being." In the latter sense, "true coherence is the coherence which is not 'coherent'" (ibid.). Indeed, Daoist ideas are often expressed in paradoxical terms whereas Confucians, as Ziporyn has summarized, tend to understand coherence—and harmony—in non-ironic ways. However, if we take the Confucian concept of dynamic harmony as a continuing process to overcome disharmony and to renew itself toward an undetermined future, we will find a similar "ironic" dimension. For harmony to take place, its precondition is for there to be things that are yet to be harmonized. In this sense, disharmony is indispensable in conceptualizing dynamic harmony. Failures

46 RESHAPING CONFUCIANISM: A PROGRESSIVE INQUIRY

of individual species in nature do not disprove evolution. Evolution succeeds in the midst of countless failed and extinct species; likewise, the existence of disharmony is not a counterproof of harmony. Harmony prevails precisely on the basis of disharmony and in overcoming disharmony. Harmony is made intelligible through the contrast, like the light with the darkness. In this aspect, conceptually, harmony and disharmony are dependent on each other.

In his rich study of harmony, Stephen Angle connects harmony with coherence from another perspective. He argues that "harmony is the realization of coherence" (Angle 2009, 68). "Coherence" here is used by Angle to translate the Chinese concept of *li* 理, usually translated as "principle" (e.g., Chan 1963, 590). In Angle's interpretation, "coherence" suggests that various things fit together in a consistent, unifying way, producing an agreeable pattern. On such an interpretation, Angle argues that we can understand the important Neo-Confucian notion of the *li* of human nature (*xing zhi li* 性之理). On Angle's reading, on the one hand, *li* is the appropriate way in which our various feelings and capacities fit together. On the other, it also stands for a relationship that one forms with other things in the world, fitting harmoniously with the rest of the world (Angle 2009, 34). He writes:

> *Li* 理 is indeed a kind of pattern or network of interdependencies, a pattern that is partly constituted by my own "profoundest reactions." Coherence— the valuable, intelligent way things fit together—is part and parcel of my own reaction to my environment. (Angle 2009, 35)

Angle's discussion of coherence is helpful for our understanding of harmony. There is, however, an important difference between Angle's and my understanding of harmony. The *li* or coherence that Angle expounds is based largely on the idea of the Neo-Confucian philosopher Zhu Xi 朱熹 (1130–1200), for whom, *li* is an eternal, pre-set order of the universe. Zhu Xi claims that *li* is "prior to *qi*."[35] The contemporary philosopher Zhang Liwen explains this as meaning that "*li* is the source and foundation of the innumerable events and things in the world" (Zhang 2015, 24). As such, "*li* transcends the limits of time and space," and that as "the unlimited thus [*li*] becomes the root or basis for limited beings, such as people" (ibid., 25). Along these lines, saying that "harmony is the realization of coherence," as Angle does, may imply that harmony is the process by which a pre-determined order (*li* 理) is brought into the world. Angle seems aware of such a problematic implication of Zhu Xi's idea of *li* and resists Zhu's notion of a reified *li* (Angle 2009, 41). Yet, Angle does not offer an account of the origin of coherence (*li*) in the first place, while making harmony a consequence ("realization") of coherence. In contrast, my concept of deep harmony does not accept an ultimate pre-set order, "coherence" or otherwise; in my view, deep harmony *generates* coherence in the world, even though a generated order, in turn, contributes to further harmony in the world. In most versions of the Big Bang theory, space, time, and physical laws did not exist in the first place; they are products of the Big Bang and consequently become the conditions for further changes in the world. Similarly, in Confucian harmony philosophy, coherent patterns in the world are outcomes of prior harmony, not the other way around. Subsequent harmony processes take place in the context of what has been generated through prior harmony processes.

From the above discussion, we can now summarize the Confucian concept of harmony as follows. First, harmony as a foundational concept is deep as it penetrates the entire realm of existence, both the metaphysical/intangible (*xing er shang* 形而上) and the physical/tangible (*xing er xia* 形而下), without an ultimately pre-determined order. Second, harmony is dynamic, referring more to a process than a state. Harmony is harmonization. Third, harmony in the world is built on heterogeneity as it is multilateral and interrelational, taking place among various elements or parties and bringing them together. It is a counterforce to uniformity and conformity, as well as to mere chaos. Fourth, harmony is creative and generative. Like evolution, harmony is essentially a forward-oriented movement. Through harmony, things are transformed, enhanced, and renewed. Fifth, harmony is advocated as a value. In the Confucian view, problems in the world are disharmonies or results thereof, be it separation, stagnation, or oppression. Harmony as harmonization is a process of overcoming disharmony. The Confucian mission, therefore, is to advance harmony in the world. Confucians hold that the overall trend of the world is harmony rather than disharmony. Such a stance can be grounded in the Confucian view of the cosmogenic transformation from the original orderless and valueless chaos to the present world that possesses overall positive value. This transformation is achieved through harmonization. In other words, our present world endowed with overall positive value is the effect of the processes of harmony. For this reason, harmony itself is of positive value.[36]

On this account, harmony provides an overall conceptual framework in which other values are situated and vindicated. For instance, by analyzing the

Confucian virtue of *jing* 敬, respect or respectfulness, Kwong-loi Shun argues that Confucians advocate *jing* toward other people not so much because they have intrinsic worth but because "doing so conduces to social harmony and peaceful coexistence, and helps to build a community characterized by mutual respectfulness" (Shun 2013, 54). Confucian cardinal virtues such as *ren* 仁 (human-heartedness), *yi* 義 (rightness, appropriateness), *li* 禮 (ritual propriety), *zhi* 智 (wisdom), *sheng* 聖 (sageliness), are key virtues because they, at least in part, contribute to generating social harmony. Without reference to harmony, we cannot adequately explain the significance of these virtues in Confucian philosophy.

3. Harmony as Social and Moral Ideal

The above study shows that the Confucian conception of harmony is neither "innocent harmony," a naïve ideal of harmony without tension, as Martha Nussbaum described in her discussion of harmony (Nussbaum 1986, 78; 1990, 131), nor oppressive harmony that suppresses difference, as Karl Popper found in Plato's *Republic* (Popper 1945, 77, 88, 94).[37] It is rather a third alternative conception for dynamic harmony. In the Confucian conception, harmony takes place either with or without human agency. When the *yin* and *yang* forces in nature generate patterns out of chaos through interaction and mutual adjustment, there is harmony without human agency. When a good cook produces a delicious soup or two persons form a well-coordinated team, there is harmony with human agency. In the human world, people establish and maintain harmonious relationships in the forms of family, community, country, and international institutions. Such a relationship extends also to the environment. For Confucians, harmony defines the kind of life a person should live, the kind of society people should construct, and the kind of world humanity should maintain. At each level, there is heterogeneity, there is tension, and there is transformation toward future and greater harmony.

Harmony can take place at various levels of the human world. It can take place within the individual as intrapersonal harmony. A person can harmonize various parts of his or her body, the heart-mind, and various pursuits in life into a well-functioning, organic whole (see more discussion in Chapter 7). Kongzi advises that people should regulate their internal energy, *qi*, to maintain a balance for the good life (*Analects* 16.7). The *Zhongyong* states that one is in harmony if he lets various emotions, joy, anger, sorrow, and pleasure, arise to an appropriate degree. An optimal proportion of various emotions is essential to a good life. More importantly, Confucian harmony defines virtue itself. The *Wuxing* 五行 text of the excavated *Guodian Chu Bamboo Slips* states:

> The harmony of the Five virtuous practices is called Virtue; the harmony of the Four practices is called Goodness. Goodness is the human Way. Virtue is the Heavenly Way. (Liu 2003, 69)

The four virtuous practices are *ren* 仁 (human-heartedness), *yi* 義 (rightness, appropriateness), *li* 禮 (ritual propriety), and *zhi* 智 (wisdom); the five virtuous practices also include an additional *sheng* 聖 (sageliness), which is held to extend beyond humanity and to connect with Heaven. Various virtues have their respective value and serve different needs in life and society. However, according to the author of the *Wuxing*, what makes these virtues most valuable is not each virtue alone, but a good balance and integration of various virtues in harmony. The harmonious practices of the four virtues are the human Way. The harmonious practices of the five virtues are the Heavenly Way, adding a spiritual dimension to the human world. This important coordinating role of harmony makes it the virtue of the virtues. A good person not only possesses various good virtues respectively but also possesses and practices them in a harmonious way.[38]

As a process of mutual adjustment and transformation as well as a reasonable accommodation, this kind of Confucian dynamic harmony can take place between individuals and between groups of people. Confucians especially emphasize harmony in the family. Mengzi advocates affection between parents and children, differentiated roles between spouses, and precedence between elder and younger siblings (*Mengzi* 3A4). Affection between parents and children requires parents to love and care for their children and children to respect and assist their parents. Husband and wife should play different roles in the family to work effectively and efficiently as a team (see more discussion in Chapter 5 of this book). In the family, elder siblings are given responsibilities either to care for their younger siblings or to assist their parents in raising small children. Elder siblings are to be kind toward the younger and the younger are to defer to their elder brothers or sisters. All these stipulations are meant to foster harmony in the family. Confucians see harmony in the community as an important dimension of social harmony.[39]

Mengzi emphasizes the vital importance for people to have adequate means of production for a healthy society. In the agricultural society of his time, this meant mainly giving people farming land to support their lives. He says, "When people have land, they settle down for the long term; otherwise they are fickle" (*Mengzi* 3A3). In Mengzi ideal social arrangement, people have parcels of land adjacent to one another. They work side by side, assist one another and take care of one another in need. Thus, they grow affectionate and become harmonious with one another (*Mengzi* 3A3). In such a society, harmonious human relationships are built on adequate economic foundations. For Mengzi, social harmony also requires virtuous political leadership. However, the foundation of social harmony arises from the grass roots in society.

The role of Confucian political leadership seems to lie mainly in solidifying such grassroots harmony in society and in providing a bridge to expand such harmony throughout the entire world. Chapter *Zhouguan* of the *Book of History* (*Shangshu* 尚書) describes that sage-kings governed this way:

> At court, there were the general regulator and the chief of four mountains; abroad, there were the pastors of the provinces and the princes of states. Thus, the various departments of government went on harmoniously, and the myriad states all enjoyed repose. (Waltham 1972, 201)

The *Yaodian* Chapter of the *Book of History* sets the goal of political leadership as to promote virtues in society to make all tribes friendly toward one another and all states in harmony (TTC, 119).[40]

Finally, the ideal of Confucian harmony extends beyond the human world to nature and espouses a harmonious relationship between humanity and its environment. Of all classical thinkers, Xunzi was the most advanced in elaborating an appropriate relationship between humanity and nature. For Xunzi, a good human–nature relationship is not only a matter of avoiding the overuse of natural resources but also about actively building a harmonious relationship. Such a relationship is not a one-way street but bidirectional. Specifically, not only must humans avoid abusing nature, but they should also help nature grow and thrive. In his words, such a philosophy leads to a situation where humans do not confine their desires to things already in nature, and things in nature are not exhausted by humans in pursuit of these desires. On the one hand, what is already available in nature should not be the limits of human pursuit; humans can aspire for more than what is already in nature by extending and growing nature and making nature more resourceful than it has been. On the other hand, it is also important that we make sure we do not exhaust natural resources in pursuit of desires. These two things, human pursuits and natural resources are meant to grow concomitantly in support of each other (*Xunzi*, chapter 19.1).[41] This is evidently a form of dynamic harmony. It seeks to achieve a dynamic equilibrium between satisfying human needs and growing natural resources as both move forward and sustain each other.

Furthermore, Xunzi maintains that to achieve such a goal, human society must become harmonious in the first place. He believes people achieve social harmony when ritual propriety fulfills its proper function and people cooperate in social production rather than fighting with one another. Social harmony in turn leads to harmony with nature. Xunzi says:

> If the myriad things obtain their appropriate function, affairs as they undergo change obtain a suitable response, above the natural sequence of the seasons is obtained from Heaven, below the benefits of Earth are gained, and in the middle the harmony of humanity is obtained, then goods and commodities will come as easily as water bubbling up from an inexhaustible spring . . . Hence, if the Confucian way is thoroughly carried out, the result will be riches that spread out and reach everywhere in the world, even in times of leisure there will be accomplishment, and when the bells are struck and the drums beaten, harmony will prevail. (*Xunzi*, chapter 10; Knoblock 1990, 130, modified)

Because humans can make conscious decisions and by being socially organized beings, humans have power over nature, it is imperative that we first harmonize among ourselves and then exert a concerted effort to harmonize with nature.

On such a view, to grow toward the realization of its potential and to become complete with its nature, anything in the world—human as well as nonhuman—must follow the route of harmony. When a plant is harmonized with its surroundings it thrives; when a person is harmonized with her environment, she flourishes. The ideal for an individual is not only to harmonize within one's own person, but also with other individuals. The ideal for a society is not only to harmonize within the society, but also with other societies. The ideal for humanity is not only to harmonize among its members and between groups but also with the rest of the cosmos. If we humans can achieve both harmony in society and harmony with nature, we achieve the highest goal in Confucianism.[42]

Study Questions

1. What are the primary metaphors in explicating harmony in ancient China? Explain these metaphors.
2. According to the philosopher Yanzi, how is harmony different from conformity/sameness (*tong*)?
3. What is the role of tension in harmony?
4. In what sense is harmony "the virtue of the virtues"?
5. What does the author mean by "deep harmony"?
6. What are some parallels between deep harmony and evolution?
7. The author argues that "harmony can take place at various levels." What are these levels?
8. What is Xunzi's view of human beings' harmonious relation with nature?
9. Can you summarize the main features of Confucian harmony?
10. Do you think the Confucian idea of harmony is useful? Can you explain the idea with your own experience?

2

Care-Centered Virtue

Ren 仁 is a key concept in Confucian ethics. The word has been translated into English in various ways, most commonly as "love," "humaneness," "benevolence," "humanity," and "virtue." All these translations reveal some aspects of *ren*. Yet, for different reasons, none is satisfactory in accurately conveying its meanings. Difficulties in translating this notion are due mainly to two reasons. The first is cross-cultural differences in conceptualization. Philosophical concepts often reflect broad conceptualizations of human experiences. They take place in various parts of the world at different times and are often done in different ways, especially at a general level. This phenomenon makes it difficult to find good matching words in cross-cultural translation. It does not mean that cross-cultural translation is impossible. As often is the case, various translations may reveal different dimensions of the same concept. Contextualization is needed to avoid biases, to connect different senses of the same concept, and to find adequate interpretations of the concept in question. The second main reason for the difficulties in translating *ren* is that, as will be shown, the word has two overlapping yet different meanings, both of which play important roles in Confucian ethics. In classic texts, it is often ambiguous on which meaning of the word is being used.

In this chapter, I tackle these difficulties with a focus on elucidating the meanings of *ren*. I accept the unavoidable difficulty in translation and leave the word untranslated, as is the convention with other Chinese terms like *dao*, *yin*, and *yang*, to avoid unnecessary disputes. By examining the concept itself and the nuances in various translations and interpretations, I establish the two principal meanings of *ren* as a specific virtue and as a comprehensive virtue, and I argue that *ren* as a comprehensive virtue is rooted in care as a specific virtue, with care as its central characteristic.[1] I also highlight some important features of Confucian *ren* ethics in comparison with Western feminist care ethics to contextualize this important Confucian concept from a cross-cultural perspective.

Reshaping Confucianism. Chenyang Li, Oxford University Press. © Oxford University Press 2024.
DOI: 10.1093/oso/9780197657621.003.0003

1. Interpretations of *Ren*

Ren occupies a prominent place in Kongzi's *Analects*. The word *ren* appears 105 times and in sixty of its 503 conversations in the text (Chan 1963, 16; Lai 2014, 83). There is a consensus among scholars that Kongzi made a major contribution to developing Confucian ethics by transforming the meaning of *ren* from a specific personal trait into a comprehensive virtue of persons with high moral attainment. Understanding the connection between these two meanings is crucial to comprehending *ren*.

The meaning or meanings of *ren* in early antiquity was not clearly defined. But its uses in classic texts present some cues. In the *Book of Poetry* (*Shijing* 詩經), *ren* is used along with *hao* 好 (good, pleasant), *wu* 武 (combative, masculine), *quan* 鬈 (strong), and *cai* 偲 (talented), with each respectively in conjunction with *mei* 美 (beautiful), indicating *ren* is a praiseworthy personal trait.[2] The fact that *ren* is used as one trait along with many other traits, and that each of these is paired with *mei* (beautiful), suggests that *ren* is a specific trait even when the exact meaning is not obvious in these uses, whereas "beautiful" is a good quality of a higher order than *ren*. In her study of early Chinese texts, such as the *Book of Poetry* and the *Book of History* (*Shangshu* 尚書), Fang Ying-hsien has concluded that the original meanings of *ren* include the tender aspect of human feelings (*rouhe xingqing* 柔和性情), friendly actions toward others and mutual assistance (*youshan, huzhu* 友善與互助), being amicable (*qin he* 親和), and mutual love (*hu ai* 互愛). Accordingly, *ren* in its early usages carried an other-regarding orientation and stands for a tender loving concern for others (Fang 1976).[3]

In the *Analects*, *ren* is used both in a narrow sense as a specific virtue and in a broader sense as a comprehensive virtue (Chan 1963, 16). A specific virtue is a trait of a person, such as bravery or generosity. *Ren* in this narrow sense can be placed side by side with other simple qualities such as *quan* 鬈 (strong) and *cai* 偲 (talented). When *ren* is taken in a broad sense as the overall quality of a good person, it is a comprehensive virtue that encompasses other specific virtues. A person of *ren* in the latter sense is one with a fully developed moral character. Through Kongzi's creative construction, *ren* was transformed from a specific virtue to a comprehensive virtue that is central to Confucian ethics, even though the sense of tender loving concern for others in its narrow meaning survives such a transformation. Now the question is how to interpret *ren* in this broad sense.

In considering this question, we should differentiate translation from interpretation even though the two are closely linked. In translation, we need a handy and catchy word or phrase in rendering a foreign expression. In interpretation, we can elaborate on the nuances of a concept and delineate its precise meanings. Of course, translation also comes with some form of interpretation, though in a limited way. By choosing a word or phrase in translating a foreign concept, we want the word or phrase to best reflect the meaning of the original concept. Ideally, we wish to find a word or a handy phrase that both translates and interprets the original one. When this is not possible, especially when a simple translation can be seriously misleading, we should leave the word untranslated while focusing on its interpretation. The Confucian *ren* is one such case in point. In the following, I will examine several influential English translations of *ren* and show their inadequacies, even though they all reveal some important aspects of the concept.

One of the most common interpretations and translations of *ren* is humaneness. Humaneness is closely associated with the psychological states of kindness and compassion. The sense of *ren* as humaneness is probably most salient in the book of *Mengzi*. Irene Bloom has translated a famous passage by Mengzi as follows:

> The heart's feeling of pity and compassion is the sprout of humaneness [*ren* 仁]; the heart's feeling of shame and aversion is the sprout of rightness [*yi* 義]; the heart's feeling of modesty and compliance is the sprout of propriety [*li* 禮]; and the heart's sense of right and wrong is the sprout of wisdom [*zhi* 智]. (*Mengzi* 2A6; Bloom 2009, 35, modified)

Mengzi traced the origin of human moral sensibilities in the heart (*xin* 心). He even said that "*ren* 仁 is the human heart" (*Mengzi* 6A11). The heart that cannot bear others' suffering is a heart of compassion, which is the sense of *ren* that reflects the gentle and tender aspect of the human heart. This understanding of *ren* has a close connection to its pre-Kongzi meaning of a tender loving concern for others as indicated in the above-cited study by Fang (1976). Closely related to the translation of *ren* as "humaneness" is "benevolence." D. C. Lau, for example, uses "benevolence" for *ren* in his translation of the *Analects* (1979) and the *Mengzi* (1984). "Benevolence" connotes charitableness and generosity. It is also associated closely with the meaning of a tender loving concern for others. In classical Confucian literature, *ren* carries the meaning of benevolence particularly when it concerns rulers and government. The sense of benevolence can be derived or extended from that of humaneness. Presumably, a humane ruler cannot bear seeing his subjects suffer and such a ruler will practice benevolent government.

However, humaneness or benevolence conveys only the narrow meaning of *ren*. In its broad sense, *ren* is comprehensive. It is not merely a caring disposition toward others, but also a general virtue of a higher order that is to be achieved by developing a broad range of other virtues. Kongzi says that one becomes *ren* by being respectful in private life, being serious in handling affairs, being loyal in dealing with others, and being persistent in challenging situations (*Analects* 13.19). He also says that one becomes *ren* by practicing the five virtues of respectfulness (*gong* 恭), tolerance (*kuan* 寬), trustworthiness (*xin* 信), diligence (*min* 敏), and kindness (*hui* 惠) (*Analects* 17.6). The ancient Chinese lexicon *Shuowen* explicates *hui* straightforwardly in terms of *ren* 仁 (Xu and Duan 1992, 159). The only way to make sense of this linkage is to take the use of *ren* by Xu and Duan in the narrow sense as a specific quality or disposition. This shows that *ren*, as a comprehensive virtue, encompasses *hui* (i.e., *ren* in the narrow sense) as a specific virtue. "Humaneness" and "benevolence" may work in translating the meaning of *ren* in the narrow senses. Neither, however, captures the meaning of *ren* as a comprehensive virtue.

While using "benevolence" to translate *ren* as a specific virtue, Wing-tsit Chan has translated *ren* in its broad sense as "humanity" (Chan 1963, 25–26). Such a translation reveals the sense of *ren* as a comprehensive virtue. Unlike in Mengzi, who takes the seed of *ren* as humaneness to be an inborn quality, such a comprehensive virtue for Kongzi must be acquired through broad learning and persistent cultivation. It is achievable through personal effort and positive socialization. Kongzi said that one becomes *ren* by observing ritual propriety (*Analects* 12.1), and that a person of *ren* helps establish others when he wishes to establish himself and helps others succeed when he wishes himself to succeed (*Analects* 6.30). Kongzi also said that a person of *ren* does not do unto others that which he does not wish to be done onto himself (*Analects* 12.2). These statements indicate that *ren* extends beyond humaneness and benevolence, pointing to an ideal moral personhood in Confucian ethics.

In this sense, there is a close connection between *ren* and the moral ideal of humanity. In Confucian ethics, humanity is not a biological category but a moral one. One becomes "human" through moral cultivation. If we ask what kind of person one would become if she had fully realized her humanity, the Confucian answer is a person of *ren*. In other words, humanity is defined by *ren* in the sense of a comprehensive virtue. One can find support for Chan's translation in Confucian classics. For instance, Section 20 of the *Zhongyong* states that "*ren zhe, ren ye*,"[4] which Chan translates as "humanity (*ren*) is (the distinguishing characteristic of) man" (Chan 1963, 104). However, "humanity" as a broad concept does not work well in translating *ren* in its narrow sense as a specific virtue. When a similar expression appears in *Mengzi* 7B16, Chan translated it in the same way as, "humanity is (the distinguishing characteristic of) man" (Chan 1963, 81). This is problematic. Mengzi takes *ren* as one of the four specific virtues to be *a* characteristic rather than *the* characteristic of humankind. Mengzi says:

> One without the feeling of commiseration is not human; one without the feeling of shame and dislike is not human; one without the feeling of deference and compliance is not human; and one without the feeling of right and wrong is not human. (*Mengzi* 2A6)

For Mengzi, the feeling of commiseration is the seed of *ren* (Bloom 2009, 35). Evidently, it is only one of four fundamental characteristics of humanity. For this reason, "humanity" is too general in translating *ren* in its narrow sense.

Furthermore, "humanity" is vague in translating *ren* as a comprehensive virtue. As indicated earlier, humanity is defined by *ren* in Confucianism. It can also be defined differently in other philosophical traditions. For Aristotle, for instance, humanity is understood in terms of *eudaimonia*. Translating *ren* into a broader concept of humanity, which itself must be defined by *ren* in the tradition, does not convey its meaning to readers unfamiliar with the Confucian tradition.

In an effort to avoid forcing Chinese concepts onto Western concepts, Roger Ames has rendered *ren* as "consummate person or conduct." He writes:

> "Consummate" has the virtue of using the collective and intensive prefix "con-," denoting the sense of "together, jointly" that does justice to the irreducible relationality and thus particularity of *ren*. In addition, *summa* is that form of "completion" that suggests disclosure more than closure, a transactional maturation and fruition more than the actualization of some given potential. *Summa* is the higher efficacy in some particular achievement and not merely a replication of something previously accomplished, and as such, is high praise by the community for someone's particular attainment (*summa cum laude*). (Ames 2011, 179)

58 RESHAPING CONFUCIANISM: A PROGRESSIVE INQUIRY

"Consummate" means the highest (good). Unlike Chan, Ames emphasizes the particularity of *ren* and the context in which *ren* is realized. Ames also claims that "*ren* is not primarily a retrospective 'what' but a prospective 'how'" (Ames 2011, 182). For Ames, *ren* should not be understood as "*a* good" in general terms, but should be understood as being good at, good in, good to, good for, good with. As such, *ren* is the general characteristic of the good person, even though it should always be understood in the context of relational actions in one's social environment. However, something seems missing in Ames's exposition. For one thing, "consummate person or conduct" sounds vacuous, aside from his noting the relational hint of the prefix "con-." Saying that *ren* is the "completion" of something tells us nothing about what is to be completed in order to be *ren*. For another, explicating *ren* in terms of being good at, good in, good to, good for, good with, etc., does not reveal why some act is considered "good" in the first place. We still need to give *ren* a specific formulation to make sense of its conceptual content. As sophisticated as it is, Ames's approach is inadequate because his translation does not provide a substantive sense of *ren*.

Realizing the difficulties in translating and conceptually explicating *ren*, some scholars in recent years have attempted to provide alternatives to theoretical interpretations. They have proposed to understand Kongzi, the *Analects* in particular, as providing practical instructions for a good life instead of theoretical articulation. In his lucid book, *Confucius, The Man and the Way of Gongfu* (2016), Peimin Ni presents an "artistic" interpretation of Kongzi. According to Ni's reading, the *Analects* is about how to live a good life; Kongzi is concerned with the "art" of good living. At the core of Ni's move is the concept of *gongfu* 功夫, which stands for "the arts of life that require cultivated abilities and effective skills" (Ni 2016, xii). *Gongfu* serves as a lens through which we can see things in a certain way and understand things from a particular angle. Ni's *gongfu* approach can be better understood by contrasting it with a theoretical system of teaching. While a theory usually begins by laying out premises and building to a conclusion, a *gongfu* system "starts from the existing condition of the practitioner and, through step-by-step guidance and practice, gradually reaches higher levels of artistic perfection" (Ni 2016, xii). In such a system, different constituents are linked together through their practical rather than theoretical implications. Ni writes:

> Through the lens of *gongfu* perspective one shall further realize that as a way of *gongfu*, Kongzi's teachings are ultimately aimed not at setting up

CARE-CENTERED VIRTUE 59

moral rules to constrain people, but rather at providing guidance to enable people to live good, artistic lives. In other words, Confucianism is more aesthetic than it is moralist. (Ni 2016, xiii)

In Ni's reading, *ren* is about becoming an authentic person through practicing *gongfu*. Hence, conceptually describing *ren* misses its point. In his view, even if *ren* can be described conceptually, it will not be constructive as one cannot become an authentic person by following theoretical instructions, just as one cannot acquire the good taste of delicious food by studying the menu. As far as an artistic life is concerned, an action manual is useless. There are no rules for achieving such a goal. Therefore, Ni maintains, we should understand *ren* as an art and strive to achieve it artistically.

I can appreciate Ni's effort in bringing our attention to an underappreciated dimension of understanding Kongzi. I note, however, that Ni's approach differs from the view that we should use the artistic to supplement the philosophical in interpreting Kongzi. Instead, it places the artistic at the center of Confucian hermeneutics. On Ni's approach, we simply cannot conceptually articulate a Confucian moral philosophy. Such a move is so radical that it risks philosophical nihilism in doing Confucian philosophy. In Ni's direction, Confucianism would fall into the category of wisdom and would have to give up on its claim to be philosophy because philosophy must provide reasons and arguments, and it is not merely practical but also theoretical.

Karyn Lai shares some of Ni's concerns with the difficulties in presenting Kongzi as a theoretical philosopher. She offers a less radical solution. Lai argues that Kongzi's words should be read non-prescriptively, which has the effect of liberating modern readers from the normative grip. With such an approach, the *Analects* offers not only theoretical insights that challenge how we think about the moral life, but also resources to develop moral practice. Reading the *Analects* this way helps readers develop a moral repertoire for the Confucian good life. She explicates *ren* via depicting an exemplary life out of the conversations recorded in the *Analects* (Lai 2014). Like Ni, Lai emphasizes the practical dimension of *ren*. She writes, "The hallmark of an exemplary person is not simply her ethical beliefs, virtues or moral dispositions but her capacity to realize them" (Lai 2014, 91). By focusing on the realization of *ren*, Lai argues that *ren* sits at the intersection of a person and his action and that it concerns both agency and action. In Lai, we see a delicate attempt to balance theory and practice in deciphering Kongzi's teachings. Furthermore, Lai deliberately uses the expression of "*an* exemplary life" rather than "*the* exemplary life," to allow for different instantiations of exemplary lives, highlighting her point that the *Analects* does not recommend a one-size-fits-all model of good lives. She writes:

> The term "exemplary" is also used to indicate that the life of the person who manifests *ren* is inspirational without it necessarily being *paradigmatic*. This is to avoid the suggestion that there is a *typical* example of a good life. (Lai 2014, 84)

Lai is right that Kongzi did not prescribe a singular way of life that everyone should emulate. There are a variety of ways to become a person of *ren*. For each person, the path toward a life of *ren* is irreducibly contextual and situational.

Lai's account, however, does not exempt us from the need to philosophize and theorize on the concept of *ren*. We surely can and should have different instantiations of exemplary lives, but we also need to answer the question of what makes them exemplary, and moreover, why some lives are exemplary of *ren* rather than of something else. While an individual life may be irreducibly particular in character, whether it can be taken as an exemplary life for *ren* still depends on what *ren* is taken to be in the first place. A set of individual instances can exemplify a variety of things. In historical cases that we extrapolate from the *Analects*, these can be instances of the lives of ancient people, ancient Chinese people, morally conscientious people, intelligent people, and so forth. But what makes all these exemplary lives of *ren*? This question cannot be answered by looking at individual examples alone. We still need to come up with an account of the Confucian concept of *ren*. There is just no way to get around it regardless of the difficulties in articulating such an account.

So far, we have examined various translations and interpretations of Confucian *ren*. These approaches can be placed in three categories. The first translates *ren* as humaneness and benevolence. Other translations such as "kindness" and "human-heartedness" also belong to this category. This treatment of *ren* is too narrow, unable to convey the meaning of *ren* as a comprehensive virtue. The second translates *ren* as humanity. This category can also include such renderings as "virtue" and "human excellence." This treatment is too general. It does not convey *ren* as a specific virtue, nor does it reveal the characteristic of *ren* as a comprehensive virtue. I also place Ames' view in this category for its lack of substantive content. The third approach eschews

CARE-CENTERED VIRTUE 61

theoretical reconstructions; instead, it describes *ren* through looking into concrete actions and behaviors. This approach loses the concept of *ren* on the philosophical and conceptual level. We need to find a better way.

2. *Ren* as a Care-Oriented Comprehensive Virtue

Instead of attempting to translate *ren* into a single word, I present an interpretative reading to help readers understand its meanings. Specifically, I propose to connect the two senses of *ren* with care.[5] An important consideration for interpreting *ren* in association with care is the significance of care in contemporary Anglophone philosophy. The rise of feminist ethics in the last quarter of the twentieth century, represented by such thinkers as Carol Gilligan (1982) and Nel Noddings (1984), has elevated care as a legitimate key concept in moral philosophy. The rectified status of care in western philosophy makes it possible to understand Confucian *ren* as care without degrading the philosophical significance of Confucian ethics. On the contrary, such an association shows that, unlike in mainstream Western philosophy, care has always been a key requirement in Confucian moral philosophy.

I argue that *ren* in the sense of a specific virtue of humaneness-benevolence should be understood in the context of care, with its core meaning rooted in a tender loving concern for others, and that *ren* in the sense of an overall virtue is a care-oriented comprehensive virtue. Along this line of understanding, when *ren* is taken as a comprehensive virtue that encompasses other specific virtues, its primary meaning is still grounded on its specific meaning of a tender concern for others. In the following, I will first discuss a definition of virtue and then turn to show why *ren* as a virtue is closely associated with care.

Rosalind Hursthouse and Glen Pettigrove define "virtue" as follows:

> A virtue is an excellent trait of character. It is a disposition, well entrenched in its possessor—something that, as we say, goes all the way down, unlike a habit such as being a tea-drinker—to notice, expect, value, feel, desire, choose, act, and react in certain characteristic ways. (Hursthouse and Pettigrove 2019)

This definition is for specific virtues.[6] A specific virtue is a disposition to incline its possessor to feel, value, choose, act, and react in a certain range of appropriate ways. A person with a specific virtue possesses a certain complex mindset that determines what considerations are good reasons for action. On my account, Confucian *ren* is a virtue in that it is a trait of character with a certain mindset. Persons of *ren* notice, expect, value, feel, desire, choose, act, and react in characteristic ways. This is the case with *ren* as the specific virtue of care, as I will explicate below. *Ren* in the broad sense is comprehensive in that it encompasses a variety of specific virtues; a person of *ren* in the broad sense is a person of well-rounded virtue, who is also able to manage delicate relations between various specific virtues, and able to harmonize them in daily life (as discussed in Chapter 1 of this book).

David Wong has argued that *ren* can be understood as a comprehensive virtue viewed under the aspect of affective concern and respect toward others, noting the significance of a thread running through many of Kongzi's remarks about *ren* that have to do with love, care, deference, and tolerance of others. Wong writes, "The unity of *ren* as a comprehensive virtue that includes all the particular virtues lies in the fact that the component virtues manifest affective concern and respect" (Wong 2014, 178).[7] Along a similar line, I argue that a central aspect of *ren* as a comprehensive virtue is care. Care begins as a mental attitude that can be, and usually is, turned into action. It comprises emotions, emotional predispositions, and desires (Jaworska 2007). On such an account, care as a virtue predisposes its possessor toward the cared-for (person or object) with a tender concern about them. In caring, one feels the relevance or importance of the cared-for and is concerned about their welfare. One attunes to the fortunes or misfortunes of the cared-for, tends to act for their benefit, and wishes for their good. In this connection, a person of *ren* deeply cares about other people, social affairs, and things in the world. Care is the driving force that enables and motivates such a person to acquire and exert other specific virtues. Thus, Confucian *ren* in its broad sense as a comprehensive virtue is rooted in care and anchored on care. By "rooted" I mean that *ren* as a comprehensive virtue historically grew out of *ren* as a specific virtue of care; by "anchored" I mean that various dimensions of *ren* as a comprehensive virtue are still grounded on *ren* as a specific virtue of care.

My argument is based on my interpretation of the idea of *ai* 愛 that has been associated closely with *ren* in the evolution of the concept. The Chinese philosopher Tang Junyi 唐君毅 maintains that "since the time of Kongzi, explicating *ren* in terms of *ai* gets the closest to its meaning and is also the most popular view."[8] Tang writes:

Of the meanings of *ren* in juxtaposition with other virtues, the most deeply rooted and broadly used is *ai*. For instance, Chapter *Zhuoyu* of the *Guoyu* 國語 (*Discourse on the States*) says "*ren* is the *ai* of the cultured ones," "being *ren* by *ai*'ing people," and "caring for the people by being *ren*." Chapter *Chuyu* says, "leading to *ren* by promoting *ai*."[9]

Kongzi famously said that *ren* is "to *ai* people" (*Analects* 12.22). This saying has often been translated as "to love people." "Love" in English covers a wide range of feelings and sentiments. Its primary import is an intense feeling and strong affection. In comparison, "care" in its common sense is not associated as heavily with affection. While *ai* 愛 in Chinese can also convey the meaning of an intense feeling and strong affection,[10] it is often used to express a broader range of attitudes and sentiments, including those that should be more appropriately called "care" rather than "love." In *Analects* 3.17, for instance, Kongzi's student Zigong wished to spare the sheep in a sacrificial ritual. In disapproval, Kongzi said, "you *ai* the sheep, but I *ai* the ritual." In Kongzi's view, the integrity of the particular ritual required sacrificing a sheep. Obviously, here it is not a matter that Zigong loved the sheep. He probably never even saw the sheep in question. It is more appropriate to interpret Kongzi's comment as "you care about the sheep, but I care about the ritual." In *Mengzi* 1A7, Mengzi discusses King Liang Hui's act of replacing a sacrificial ox with a sheep. The king said that he did it not because he was stingy with the expenses, but because he could not bear seeing the ox's frightened appearance. The king said, "even though the state of Qi is small, but how could I *ai* an ox?" By this, he evidently meant that although his state was small, without abundant resources, he still could afford the expense of a sacrificial ox. Here it is obviously not a matter of the king loving the animal. His statement should be interpreted as "even though the state of Qi is small, how could I care so much about the expense of an ox (with no regard for the integrity of the ritual)?"

From the above, we see that, although *ai* can mean love in certain cases, its meaning is broader than love and it encompasses an attitude less intense than love as in its common English usage. It is more appropriate to translate it as "care." When a person cares about someone or something, she may or may not love him or it. When she loves someone or something, she definitely cares about him or it, even though how well she cares often depends on her knowledge, skills, and experience. To borrow from Philip Pettit (2015), we can say that love is a robust form of care.[11] It is not the case, however, that

64 RESHAPING CONFUCIANISM: A PROGRESSIVE INQUIRY

whenever one cares about someone or something, she necessarily loves him or it. Mengzi once said that morally refined persons (*junzi* 君子) should "*ai wu* 愛物" (*Mengzi* 7A45). *Wu* stands for things at large. To *ai wu* does not require us to love them. Rather it means to care about them.[12] "Care" as a broader concept works more appropriately in translating *ai* than "love" in the broad context in which *ai* is used.

The meaning of *ren* as care is evident in Mengzi. Mengzi's use of *ren* reflects a meaning somewhat between a specific trait as it appears in the *Book of Poetry* and a comprehensive virtue as it appears in the *Analects*. As discussed earlier, a poem in the *Book of Poetry*, which predates Kongzi, took *ren* to be one of the specific traits along with others, on a lower order than *mei* 美 (beautiful). Mengzi largely retained the primary meaning of *ren* as care (*ai*), but he elevates it to be one of the four cardinal virtues along with *yi* 義 (rightness), *li* 禮 (ritual propriety), and *zhi* 智 (wisdom). The status of *ren* as one of the four cardinal virtues is still a specific virtue rather than a comprehensive one. In a conversation with the duke of Qi, Mengzi argued that the duke should extend his tender heart toward a sacrificial ox to caring about his people, and that he should spare his people from hardship and suffering by reducing taxation and promoting their welfare. If the duke could follow his tender heart, he would be able to rule with a *ren* government (*ren zheng* 仁政). Mengzi said:

> If you wish to put this [*ren*] into practice, why not go back to fundamentals? If the mulberry is planted in every homestead of five *mu* of land, then those who are fifty can wear silk; if chickens, pigs and dogs do not miss their breeding season, then those who are seventy can (afford to) eat meat; if each lot of a hundred *mu* is not deprived of labor during the busy season, then families with several mouths to feed will not go hungry. Exercise due care over the education provided by village schools, and discipline the people by teaching them duties proper to sons and younger brothers, and those whose heads have turned grey will not be carrying loads on the roads. When the aged wear silk and eat meat and the masses are neither cold nor hungry, it is impossible for their prince not to be a true king. (*Mengzi* 1A7; Lau 1984, 59)

Mengzi's point is that, as the king cared about the ox and spared it, he should also care about his people and practice caring government so that people would live well. We should note that here Mengzi is not talking about abstract or general concepts. He is specific about what a good ruler should do in concrete actions. In Mengzi's view, out of a tender heart, a person can become *ren* in interacting with others. When such a person is or becomes a ruler, he can exercise *ren* in government and the country will prosper. In Mengzi studies, *ren* is often translated as "humaneness" or "benevolence." Both these meanings can be covered under the broader concept of care. In these cases, we can see that while interpreting *ren* as love may work in some contexts, it does not work well in some other contexts (e.g., the case of sparing the ox in *Mengzi* 1A7). Using "care" in its general sense can bridge such a gap and make sense in all these contexts.

Now, let us examine the concept of *ren* as constructed in the *Analects* and show how care is the anchoring factor in the concept of *ren* as a comprehensive virtue. Through Kongzi's innovative work of expanding *ren* from a specific virtue into a comprehensive one, it still carries its original meaning of care. Both meanings are present in the *Analects*. Of the specific virtues encompassed in *ren*, caring about people is primary. Adopting care as an anchoring meaning of *ren* as the comprehensive virtue can help us understand *ren* in a balanced way. When his disciple Zilu asked, "Is there a single saying which can serve as the guiding principle for conduct throughout life?" Kongzi responded, "It is sympathetic understanding (*shu*).[13] Do not do to others what you do not want them to do to you" (*Analects* 15.24). Kongzi's disciple Youzi places brotherliness at the roots of *ren* (*Analects* 1.2). Brotherliness is characterized by reciprocal care. When a child grows up in a brotherly (or sisterly) environment and develops brotherliness for others, he or she has a good foundation to cultivate such a virtue to become *ren* as a virtuous person in the comprehensive sense. In *Analects* 4.3, Kongzi said that "only persons of *ren* are able of liking people and despising people." A person of *ren* cannot see good people without liking them, nor can they see bad people without loathing them because she cares deeply. Xunzi says, "the person of *ren* indeed cares for others, but it is because he cares for others that he hates for people to harm them" (*Xunzi*, chapter 15; Hutton 2014, 155). People who do not care will be neither attracted to good people nor annoyed by bad people. They do not bother to feel affinity and admiration toward good people nor disdain and contempt toward bad people. There is a Chinese expression in terms of *mamuburen* 麻木不仁. *Mamu* literally means numb; *buren* mean "not *ren*." Initially a medical expression, this expression means that a person has become numb and has lost responsive sensitivities. It has later been commonly used to describe those who have

66   RESHAPING CONFUCIANISM: A PROGRESSIVE INQUIRY

lost empathetic abilities in response to the need or sufferings of others. That is, they are unable to care and do not care. This phrase suggests a strong connection between *ren* and care.

In a famous passage, Kongzi said:

> A person of *ren* establishes others if he wishes to establish himself, and realizes others if he wishes to realize himself. Being able to use as analogy what is near at hand can be called the method of becoming *ren*. (*Analects* 6.30)

Using what is near at hand, whether within oneself or close to oneself, to think about others and their situations implies empathizing with others. Empathy is a form of care. A fully developed virtuous person relates to others through care. Care, therefore, is the anchoring idea in understanding Kongzi's concept of *ren* as a comprehensive virtue.

It may seem puzzling at first when we read Kongzi saying that "a person of *ren* is bound to be courageous even though a courageous person may not be *ren*" (*Analects* 14.4). Here *ren* is to be understood as a comprehensive virtue rather than a specific one. We can understand this saying on the basis of definition, that *ren* is defined as a comprehensive virtue, and therefore it encompasses courage, whereas courage is a specific virtue and does not encompass *ren* as the comprehensive virtue. We can make better sense of Kongzi if we take *ren* to be a comprehensive virtue that is anchored on care. For if one sufficiently cares about someone or something, she will summon enough courage to act on his or its behalf. A caring mother, for instance, will risk her own life to protect her child. A caring person is attentive in learning and in cultivating oneself with various specific virtues so she can lead a caring life.

To recapitulate, Confucian *ren* as a comprehensive virtue is anchored on care in two ways. First, *ren* as a specific virtue carries a strong sense of care. This aspect of *ren* is inherited by Kongzi in his transformation of the concept from a specific virtue to a comprehensive virtue. Second, after Kongzi's transformation, care remains at the core of the broad concept, providing a foundational sense for the concept, to the extent that we can say *ren* as a comprehensive virtue is anchored on care. Such an understanding does not imply that *ren* as a comprehensive virtue is equivalent to care, nor that other dimensions (specific virtues) of *ren* are unimportant. Instead, it allows us to understand the characteristic of *ren* in a fruitful way.

3. Confucian Care in a Comparative Perspective

Linking *ren* with care is not without challenges. Some feminist thinkers reject Confucianism due to its sexist biases in history, and hence refuse to be associated with it (e.g., Yuan 2002), whereas some contemporary Confucian thinkers also eschew involvement with care ethics so they would not appear to think "like women" (Ebrey 2000, xii). Neither tendency, however, is constructive for cross-cultural understanding and philosophical exploration. In this section, I will highlight important common features of *ren* with care as it is illustrated in care ethics, as well as their differences, to help us understand better some characteristics of Confucian *ren*.

In contemporary feminist literature, care has been defined in various ways (see Held 2004). It can be an activity, a practice, and a mental state. As a disposition to be attentive and responsive to the feelings and needs of others, care originates in a person as a mental state and is fully realized through activity and practice. In its full sense, care cannot be separate from the act of caring even though it may sometimes not require action. Nel Noddings has given us such an example. Consider two lovers who cannot marry because they are already committed to satisfactory and honorable marriages. One lover learns that his beloved is ill. All his thoughts push him toward her bedside. Yet, he also understands the trouble he may bring her if he follows his wishes. So, he decides not to see her, no matter how worried he is (Noddings 1984, 10). Even though there is no action, he nevertheless cares. Conversely, the mere performance of actions that are usually considered as care without proper mental attitudes may not count as care in the sense we discuss here. We will not characterize a nursing home worker's service as caring, for instance, if he does not possess appropriate attitudes and is inattentive to his patients when performing services. Hence, whether we understand care or caring as activity or practice, it inevitably encompasses mental, attitudinal states. The mental attitude or disposition of caring is described as "engrossment" by Noddings (1984), and "empathy" by Michael Slote (2007). These characterizations vary in degree, yet they both capture the significance of the mental and attitudinal dimensions of care.

Mengzi holds that our moral sensibilities originate from an inborn heart. He invites us to imagine a scenario when a small child is on the verge of falling into a well (*Mengzi* 2A6). He says we would certainly be moved by compassion. We do so not because we want to get in the good graces of the child's parents, nor because we want to win praise from others. The thought

68 RESHAPING CONFUCIANISM: A PROGRESSIVE INQUIRY

that we would rush to save the child's life is out of our "natural" disposition, traceable all way to our inborn heart, rather than out of rational deliberation. One may or may not agree with Mengzi about the inborn nature of this disposition, but such a disposition is undoubtedly one of care. In Kongzi, *ren* as either a specific or a comprehensive virtue is not devoid of mental or psychological components. As discussed in the previous section, various pertinent statements reveal the dimension of *ren* as a caring attitude or disposition. As such, *ren* carries with it a motivational force that propels people toward acting in caring ways.

Another important feature of the Confucian concept of *ren* that resonates a great deal with care ethics is its strong emphasis on the family. Family life is arguably the foremost environment for care. The *Analects* takes fostering virtues in the family as fundamental to becoming *ren* (1.2). Obviously, caring dispositions should be cultivated when a person is young. Such cultivation should begin first in the family. Family virtues such as filiality and brotherliness—today we should say sibling love broadly—are the first step toward fostering a caring personality. Feminist literature has elevated profoundly the significance of family life in contemporary moral theory. In her book *Starting at Home, Caring and Social Policy*, Nel Noddings argues:

> Caring, as a moral orientation, is neither domain nor gender specific, but taking this position does not compel us to deny that the *origins* of care may be domain specific—that they lie in the small group setting that we have come to call "home" and, probably, in parental love. If this is true—if, that is, our sense of caring and being cared for starts at home—then it is reasonable to examine this beginning seriously, to study it philosophically. (Noddings 2002, 1)

Noddings' statement suggests that an adequate description of the moral person should neither be a one-dimensional rational choice-maker nor an abstractly described member of specific groups. One grows into a moral person. Such growth starts at home. Furthermore, in consonance with the care theory that she has developed, Noddings explores how the attitudes and responses characteristic of the best homes can be extended into public policy making (Noddings 2002, 6). One may argue that Noddings' conception of virtues grown out of the best homes is more balanced than the Confucian conception that heavily concentrates on filial virtues, and that ancient Confucians evidently wanted to extend the family environment to

CARE-CENTERED VIRTUE   69

society for virtuous growth much more than Noddings. Nevertheless, they both emphasize the vital role of the family for moral development and the connection between family and society, without a sharp divide between the "private" and the "public" spheres. Thus, both Confucianism and care ethics highly value family life and see an intimate connection between family life and care.[14]

Some feminist thinkers emphasize the distinctiveness of care in care ethics. Virginia Held writes, for instance:

> I disagree with the view that care is the same as benevolence because I think it is more the characterization of a social relation than the description of an individual disposition, and social relations are not reducible to individual states. It is caring relations that ought to be cultivated between persons in their personal lives and between the members of caring societies. (Held 2004, 69)

To be sure, here the "benevolence" that Held discusses may not be the same as *ren*. But her comment is relevant to our discussion as *ren* does contain a sense of benevolence, especially when it comes to the moral quality of good rulers. As articulated by Mengzi, rulers' caring mentality can lead to "benevolent government" (*ren zheng* 仁政; *Mengzi* 1A7). For Held, however, benevolence is not care because care signifies a social relation and is produced, developed, and sustained in relations, whereas benevolence is a personal disposition, which does not require a social relation. Held maintains that even for more distant people, caring relations of a weaker kind must exist to allow them to trust one another enough to live in peace and to respect each others' rights. She claims, "For progress to be made, persons need to care together as a group for the well-being of their members and of their environment" (Held 2004, 69).

Nel Noddings has also emphasized the relational nature of care in her version of care ethics and draws thereby a distinction from the virtue of Confucian *ren*. She writes:

> The caring relation remains central to the fully developed ethic, and even the definition of caring as a virtue depends on the regular establishment and maintenance of caring relations. In contrast, the prominent Confucian philosopher Mencius starts with a concept very like caring (*ren*, or *jen*) but uses it to arrive at a more fully moral *virtue*. (Noddings 2010, 138)

70 RESHAPING CONFUCIANISM: A PROGRESSIVE INQUIRY

Without a doubt, the kind of care encompassed in the Confucian concept of *ren* is also rooted in human relationality. The common version of the Chinese character for *ren* 仁 consists of components of a person and two horizontal strokes, often interpreted as signifying a person in relationships. It has been rendered as "co-humanity" in Anglophone Confucian scholarship, to highlight the relationality of the concept (e.g., Tu Weiming 1981, 47). Confucian care as a virtue must be cultivated through social relations; it often takes place in relations. However, Confucian care does not require existing social relations for it to be exercised. One can care about others both nearby and faraway, with or without personal relations.

I believe it is problematic to confine care solely to relations. Let us take again Noddings' lover example (Noddings 1984, 10). Imagine that the man's love for the woman is unrequited. There is no relationship between them. When she falls ill, he nevertheless cares deeply about her. Thus, insisting on the necessity of relations for care unduly excludes authentic care from the category of care. In this regard, Confucians concur with the contemporary philosopher Michael Slote on caring about all humanity. Slote maintains that "an ethic of caring can take the well-being of all humanity into consideration" (Slote 2001, ix), and hence, our benevolent feelings for distant others can be conceptualized as caring. In everyday life, a good Samaritan cares about someone with whom she has no relation; good philanthropists care about total strangers affected by their charitable projects.

Furthermore, confining care as a relation-based practice risks making care ethics irrelevant to ethical problems that do not involve relations, such as our moral obligations toward people of future generations or the environment (animals, rivers, and trees, etc.). Mengzi said, "persons of *ren* care (*ai*) for all, but they consider the effort to cultivate an affection for the worthy to be the most urgent"[15] (*Mengzi* 7A46; Chan 1963, 81 modified). He explicitly included animals and physical objects in the domain of caring, as in *ai wu* 愛物 (*Mengzi* 7A45). Contemporary environmental ethicists have also extended moral patients to include animals and other living species, as objects of care. Such caring does not require relations.

Moreover, Confucian care can establish new relations. One's caring for a stranger in need may lead to establishing a relation with the stranger, even though it is perfectly conceivable that it may not. We can even say that a person's care for the environment may lead to establishing a relation with the environment, be it a particular mountain or river, even though not necessarily so.[16] When these events happen, care is prior to relations, not the other way around. Unlike Held and Noddings, for Confucians, having relations is neither a precondition nor a necessary consequence of care, even though people's initial disposition of care usually grows with or out of existing relations.[17]

On another note, Noddings draws an important distinction between natural caring and ethical caring (Noddings 1984, 81–83). In her descriptions, natural caring is what one "wants" whereas ethical caring is what one "must." Ethical caring takes place when one acts out of a moral belief of care. Noddings has argued that natural caring is preferred to ethical caring (Noddings 2010, 138). For Confucians, the opposition in moral considerations is between *ren* and un-*ren*, between caring and uncaring, rather than between two kinds of caring, "natural" and "ethical." In Mengzi's famous example, one has an inborn heart not to bear seeing a child fall into a well (*Mengzi* 2A6). Such a natural disposition nevertheless should be further cultivated and strengthened so one becomes a reflective moral agent, with a strong sense of "must." Then, the goal of Confucian moral cultivation is to make people "want" to do what they ethically "must" do. In such caring, the "I want" and the "I must" coincide. Lawrence Kohlberg's theory of moral development claims that behaviors associated with caring belong to a lower stage of moral development. For him, once a person has reached moral maturity and is able to follow self-chosen universal principles of justice, caring as an ethical practice has been transcended and discarded. In contrast, although in history Confucian *ren* as a comprehensive virtue grew out of *ren* as a specific virtue of care, *ren* as a comprehensive virtue retains the sense of *ren* as a specific virtue, giving care a prominent role in Confucian moral practice throughout a person's life.

In Carol Gilligan's moral development theory, a person grows through six stages at three levels, from the preconventional concrete individualistic perspective to the conventional social perspectives, where one sees things from perspectives of others. Then, a person grows to the postconventional level where one eventually reaches a stage in which people make moral judgments through impartial reasoning on the basis of universally accepted principles of justice. Gilligan's last stage differs from that of Kohlberg's in that, for Gilligan, ethics at its maturity does not transcend care but advances care with integrity. At this stage, through redefining care, persons of care continue to practice care in their moral lives, but in a different light. Gilligan writes:

> When the distinction between helping and pleasing frees the activity of taking care from the wish for approval by others, the ethic of responsibility

can become a self-chosen anchor of personal integrity and strength. (Gilligan 1993, 171)

At the stage of moral maturity, caring is no longer a matter of pleasing others but an act of helping others as a self-chosen action. One cares with integrity and strength. Such a view meshes well with Confucian *ren* ethics. Kongzi's disciple Zengzi said a morally refined person cares about others on the ground of virtue, whereas a morally unrefined person cares about others to appease them.[18] Kongzi also reminded his disciple Zilu that being fond of *ren* without being fond of learning leads to foolishness (*Analects* 17.8). *Ren* in this context refers to the specific virtue of care, as it is discussed along with other specific virtues such as trustworthiness (*xin* 信) and courage (*yong* 勇) in the same conversation. Through persistent learning, however, one overcomes such problems by balancing various virtues by harmonizing them (see Chapter 1 of this book). In other words, *ren* as care in its primitive form is inadequate and needs to be brought into *ren* as a comprehensive virtue, to be complemented with other virtues, to become part of a holistic moral character.

Confucian care differs from Gilligan's theory in two major aspects. First, even though anchored on care and with care as its main characteristic, Confucian *ren* ethics focuses on moral cultivation toward building a strong character. The expression of "*ren zhe* 仁者," i.e., "person of *ren*," appears repeatedly in the *Analects*, indicating that the discourse on *ren* is focused on personal character rather than on the trait itself. In contrast, Gilligan focuses on moral principles. Even though she disagrees with Kohlberg in important ways, in the end, she embraces the universal moral principles as the ultimate indication of moral maturity. Second, Gilligan attempts to derive a non-gendered ethics from her gendered studies of young women (e.g., Gilligan 1993, xiii). She detects a "different voice" from women but advances it as a non-gendered ethics. Historically Confucians have taken a different route. Conceptually, *ren* ethics is not gendered. The Chinese words employed in it for "person" such as *ren* 人 and *zhe* 者 are gender-neutral. However, Confucian ethics was first developed in the patriarchal society of ancient China and its forerunners definitely added gendered biases to its application. Whatever the historical context it once had, today we can say without any hesitation that Confucian *ren* ethics is to be practiced by both genders. In such a way, Confucian *ren* ethics and Gilligan's care ethics converge.

In summary, this chapter presents an interpretation of Confucian *ren* in the sense of care as a specific virtue and as a care-oriented comprehensive virtue. I have first argued that *ren* is care as its primary sense. Such an interpretation reveals the substantive meanings of *ren*. Second, Kongzi's transformation of *ren* from a specific virtue to a comprehensive virtue has retained the sense of care and made it an anchoring element of the comprehensive virtue. Third, important similarities and differences exist between Confucian care-oriented ethics of *ren* and feminist care ethics. Recognizing these similarities and differences is important for understanding Confucian *ren* ethics in the twenty-first century.

Study Questions

1. What is the pre-Kongzi meaning of *ren* ?
2. What are the two main meanings of *ren* in Kongzi's *Analects* ?
3. What are some common translations of *ren* ? Why are they inadequate?
4. Why should *ai* be understood as care rather than love?
5. What does *mamuburen* mean? How is it related to our discussion of Confucian *ren* as care?
6. In Confucian ethics, does the practice of *ren* require personal relations? How does it contrast with some Western care ethicists?
7. What are some other similarities and differences between Confucian *ren* ethics and feminist care ethics?
8. What is your view of the strengths and weaknesses of Confucian *ren* ethics?

3

Ritual as Cultural Grammar

Li 禮 is a fundamental concept in Confucian philosophy. Of the *Thirteen Classics* in the tradition, three are dedicated specifically to *li*, namely the *Rituals of Zhou* (*Zhouli* 周禮), the *Book of Rituals* (*Yili* 儀禮), and the *Book of Rites* (*Liji* 禮記). The general meaning of *li* is ritual or the rules of conduct. The use of the word in this sense is abundant in the above-mentioned texts as well as in the *Analects*, the *Mengzi*, and the *Xunzi*. There is, however, another crucially important meaning of *li* as a personal virtue that guides people's proper behavior, especially in interactions with one another. It is in the latter sense that Mengzi emphasizes that, along with other key virtues, *li* grows out of an inborn sense of propriety (*Mengzi* 6A6). The excavated text *Wuxing* 五行 also presents *li* as an inner quality, along with other virtues. These two meanings are integrated dimensions of *li* in Confucian philosophy. On the one hand, *li* stands for social norms that guide people's behavior. On the other hand, it refers to people's inner sense of propriety in conducting themselves. I use "ritual propriety" to translate *li*, covering both the external and inner senses of the concept. This chapter explicates *li* in two ways. First, it examines and analyzes textual evidence to clarify the key meanings of *li* in Confucian philosophy; second, it promotes intercultural understanding by expounding the role of *li* in society as cultural grammar. Toward the end, I will also discuss the significance of *li* in modern times.

1. The Various Dimensions of *Li*

The origin of *li* and its associated phenomena and activities predate Confucianism. Given its long history and the extensive corpus of commentaries, it is no surprise that *li* can be analyzed and explicated from various perspectives. The character 禮 is made up of two components, 示 (*shi*), and 豊, which is also pronounced as "*li*." The original meaning of *shi* is to decipher celestial phenomena for ominous or auspicious signs. 豊, in

Reshaping Confucianism. Chenyang Li, Oxford University Press. © Oxford University Press 2024.
DOI: 10.1093/oso/9780197657621.003.0004

the Oracle form of 豐, stands for instruments used during activities of *shi*. Etymologically, therefore, the character 禮 signifies the use of certain instruments to communicate with supernatural forces. The ancient lexicon *Shuowen* defines *li* 禮 in terms of *lü* 履, "to fulfill" and "to carry out," and identifies its purpose as "to serve the gods in order to receive good fortune" (Xu and Duan 1992, 2). The *Book of Rites* attributes the origin of *li* to primitive people's use of food in worshipping the gods (*TTC* 1415; cf. Legge 1885 III, 368). Accordingly, the original meaning of *li* has direct connections to religious rituals in ancient times.

Xunzi, however, attributes *li* to a non-religious origin. Xunzi writes:

> From what did ritual arise? I say: Humans are born having desires. When they have desires but do not get the objects of their desire, then they cannot but seek some means of satisfaction. If there is no measure or limit to their seeking, then they cannot help but struggle with each other. If they struggle with each other then there will be chaos, and if there is chaos then they will be impoverished. The former kings hated such chaos, and so they established rituals and *yi* in order to divide things among people, to nurture their desires, and to satisfy their seeking. They made sure that the pursuit will not be confined to existing material things and material goods will never be depleted by desires, so that the two support each other and grow together.[1] This is how ritual arose. (*Xunzi*, chapter 19; Hutton 2014, 201, modified)

For Xunzi, *li* was established to address crucial needs for order in society. Following appropriate rules of *li*, people can use resources in an orderly manner and generate wealth without chaotic contention.

It is possible that *li* emerged from both early religious rituals and non-religious rituals as two independent sources, which later converged into one general social mechanism. This possibility may explain the fact that *li* is meant to achieve mainly two purposes, both as rituals and rules. As rituals, *li* has a demonstrative function; it provides models for people to follow as they engage in orderly social activities. As rules, *li* has a regulative function; it obliges people to do certain things in certain ways in social and personal lives. Linking these two roles together, there appears a norm-normal-normative continuum. A norm signifies a normal practice; a normal practice can become normative in directing social behavior.

76 RESHAPING CONFUCIANISM: A PROGRESSIVE INQUIRY

With the two aspects combined, ritual propriety affects every aspect of human life. The *Book of Rites* asserts, "*Li* regulates the myriad things" (Chapter *Liqi*; TTC, 1430–1431; cf. Legge 1885 III, 395). It states:

> Without *li*, there can be no morals or rightness. Without *li*, there can be no education or correct custom. Without *li*, there can be no solution to disputes and litigation. Without *li*, proper relationships between ruler and ministers, superiors and inferiors, father and sons, older and younger brothers, cannot be established. Without *li*, teacher and students can have no bond. Without *li*, there can be no solemnity in court ceremonies, military drillings, and official enforcement of the law. Without *li*, there can be no sincerity and solemnity in ancestor-worshiping and making sacrifice to the gods. That is why cultivated persons are respectful, courteous, and deferential in manifesting *li*. (Chapter *Quli* A; TTC, 1231; cf. Legge 1885 III, 63–64)

Thus, *li* is a key concept in Confucian moral discourse. A person of *li* not only acts appropriately but also behaves ethically.

Kongzi makes a close connection between *li* and *ren* in the *Analects*. However, their exact relationship has been a matter of dispute. Some scholars have held that *li* is instrumental to *ren* whereas others have maintained their equivalence, namely, that performing *li* is being *ren* (see Shun 1993; Li 2007). These disagreements are partially due to the various uses of the term *li* in classic texts, each of which emphasizes different dimensions or layers of meanings of *li*. To move the discussion forward, it is important for us to look into these meanings.

Confucian *li* is a multifaceted concept, encompassing *li-yi* 禮意, *li-ju* 禮具, and *li-wen* 禮文 (Huang 1998, 26). First, *li-yi* is the intended meaning of *li*. For example, the purpose of a university commencement is to celebrate the achievements of graduates and to express good wishes for their future success. We can label it "*li*-meaning" for convenience. Second, there is *li-ju*, the instruments used in the ritual. At a commencement, typically graduation gowns are used. Usually, organizers also prepare graduation diplomas (or their symbolic cases) to hand out to graduates, etc. Thirdly, there is also *li-wen*, the procedures and specifications of the ritual. A commencement usually has a presider, who opens the event and is followed by other speakers, often including a graduate representative, then graduates walk on stage to be recognized, and there would be a certain expected duration for each segment, etc. All three components are important to the successful performance of a good ritual, even though they jointly aim to achieve the *li*-meaning of the event. *Li*-meanings are based largely on social conventions rather than the material qualities of formal elements, *li-ju* or *li-wen*. In some countries, pedestrians walk on the right side of the road whereas in other countries on the left. This can be an arbitrary matter when the rule is initially established. Once the rule has been established and accepted by the public, it picks up its *li*-meaning. It would not be very polite to walk on the opposite side, particularly during rush hours. In the *Analects*, Lin Fang asks Kongzi about "the *ben* (fundamental) of *li*." Kongzi praises him for raising "a great question" and says that *li* 's form should be frugal rather than lavish, and for funeral rituals, one should mourn sincerely rather than being indifferent (*Analects* 3.4). For Kongzi, the most important dimension of *li* is the inward one, the intention and purpose, not its external appearance or expression.

We can say that *li* has a formal component and a substantive component of the intended content. On the one hand, the formal is the mechanical, ritual aspect of *li* (*li-ju*, *li-wen*), such as the equipment used in a ritual and the physical motions performed during a ritual. On the other hand, the content refers to the ethical and social meanings (*li*-meaning) that the performer of *li* intends to convey through the process. In such an understanding, the whole concept of *li* has a "hardware" and a "software" component. The "hardware" is the physical mechanism that expresses *li*. The "software" is the meaning of the ritual. To perform *li* well, one needs to integrate both elements in action. In the *Analects*, *li* mostly stands for the whole integrated *li* in a thick sense, including both the form and the content, but sometimes it is used to emphasize the form and at other times the intended content. In phrases like *wei li bu jing* 為禮不敬, "practicing *li* without respectfulness" (*Analects* 3.26), *li* refers mainly to the form, that is, to the mere formality of rituals and rules of social conduct. Evidently, one could perform *li*, religious or social, without being reverent or respectful. Kongzi reminds us that *li* should not be taken merely in its form. He says, "When [we] say *li*, does it merely mean the jade and silk?" (*Analects* 17.11). The jade and silk are mere *li-ju*, items used in some rituals. *Li* in the integrated sense has to do with how the ritual is performed, by what kind of people, and with what kind of attitude and intention.

The Confucian concept of *li*, thus developed, became a general name for social norms in constructing the good society. It became a central concept

78 RESHAPING CONFUCIANISM: A PROGRESSIVE INQUIRY

in Confucian philosophy to provide objective operating patterns in society. Chapter *Jiyi* of the *Book of Rites* is specific about the function of ritual propriety:

> To trace one's origin, to demonstrate dedication to the gods, to facilitate the harmonious use (of resources), to uphold rightness, and to induce courtesy. Tracing the origin makes people value their roots; dedication to the gods fosters respect for superiors. Harmonious use of resources provides a foundation for people to become disciplined. Rightness keeps people of all social levels from strife. Courtesy prevents contention. These five combined form the ritual propriety (*li*) for regulating all in the world. (TTC, 1595; cf. Legge 1885 IV, 219–220)

Various functions of *li* cover people's religious, social, and ethical lives. These can be enumerated in the following categories.

First, *li* regulates religious activities. The *Book of Rites* states, "forms of *li* under Heaven are for honoring the gods and the spirits" (Chapter *Jiyi*; TTC, 1595; cf. Legge 1885 IV, 219). Kongzi participated in religious rituals and took them seriously (*Analects*, 3.12; TTC, 2467). For him and his followers, practicing the appropriate ritual is the only proper means to worship the gods.[2]

Second, *li* regulates ethical relations. *Li* is the vehicle through which morals are obtained. People become moral by cultivating themselves through the practice of ritual propriety and by following the rules of ritual propriety. The *Book of Rites* states, "*li* is like the human body. The virtuous do not regard a person without it as a full person" (Chapter *Liqi*; TTC, 1435; cf. Legge 1885 III, 404). A person becomes refined morally through practicing ritual propriety. Kongzi famously said that cultivating one's self with *li* leads to *ren* (*Analects* 12.1). For Confucians, ritual propriety is the cornerstone of moral goodness.

Third, *li* regulates governmental affairs. In the *Book of Rites*, Kongzi is quoted saying, "The first business of governance in antiquity was to care (*ai*) for the people; for the purpose of cultivating care, the most important is to practice *li* "[3] (Chapter *Aigongwen*; TTC, 1611; cf. Legge 1885 IV, 266). This is so because ritual propriety provides ground rules for any good government to operate and accomplish its tasks. Kongzi contrasts two primary means to regulate society: *li* and *xing* 刑 (punishment, penal code). He advocates the use of *li* rather than punishment (*Analects* 2.3).

RITUAL AS CULTURAL GRAMMAR   79

Fourth, *li* involves the economic life of society. In this regard, the function of ritual propriety in ancient times was twofold. On the one hand, it regulated governmental policies on the economic life in society. For example, the *Book of Rites* records that the earlier rules of ritual propriety included "no trading of graveyards" (Chapter *Wangzhi*; TTC, 1338; cf. Legge 1885 III, 227–228). The *Zuo Commentary* states, "It is a violation of *li* to start imposing taxes by the acreage of farming land" (Chapter *Xuangong 15*; TTC, 1888; cf. Legge 1861, 329).[4] On the other hand, ritual propriety also sets guidelines for economic activities themselves. The *Book of Rites* records a variety of rituals related to economic activities such as hunting, fishing, raising silkworms, and raising domestic animals in the chapters *Yueling*, *Sheyi*, and others.

Fifth, *li* sets the parameters for judicial punishment, among other forms of laws to be developed later. The *Book of Rites* stipulates that old people in their eighties and nineties "should not be subjected to corporal punishment even if they have committed crimes" (Chapter *Quli*; TTC, 1232; cf. Legge 1885 III, 66). The *Zuo Commentary* states, "There should be no severe corporal punishment of women," and "if such punishment is to be applied, it should not be in public" (Chapter *Xianggong 19*; TTC, 1968; cf. Legge 1861, 483). Corporal punishment was a standard form of criminal penalty in ancient China. Sparing women such punishment, or at least the humiliation of it in public, was a major accommodation in the name of ritual propriety.

Sixth, *li* also regulates many other aspects of everyday life, including weddings, funerals, banquets, sports hunting, wardrobe, receiving guests, and so forth. Whereas ritual propriety during the Xia period (twenty-first to sixteenth century BCE) was primarily a religious affair, during the Zhou (eleventh century to 249 BCE) it shifted primarily to govern human affairs. The *Book of Rites* states that, in a person's life:

> *Li* commences with capping (the ceremony of adulthood), sets its foundation in wedding, exhibits its importance in funeral, demonstrates respect in visiting the worthy, and achieves harmony in drinking and hunting rituals of the community. These are the principal points of *li*. (Chapter *Hunyi*; TTC, 1681; cf. Legge 1885 IV, 430)

The text provides abundant and detailed records of these rituals. Its chapters *Zaji*, *Wensang*, and *Bensang*, for example, contain specific instructions on behavior at various types of funerals. Many of these rituals would be too complicated to be feasible in modern times; they may have never been embraced in practice by common people even in ancient society. Nonetheless, they were an important part of the Confucian ideal social life in ancient times.

Accordingly, ritual propriety regulates every aspect of society. In Confucian philosophy, all these forms of *li* come under one general category because they regulate people's behavior for their own good and for the good of society, and they all direct people as to what ought to be done in an uplifting spirit as opposed to penal laws (*xing*) that threaten people with punishment.[5] In this sense, *li* is positively constructive and edifying whereas punishment is negatively preventive. A good society, in the Confucian view, should be directed primarily by *li* rather than relying on punishment for its operation. The *Zuo Commentary* defines the purpose of ritual propriety as "to manage the country, to stabilize society, to regulate people, and to provide for the good of posterity" (Chapter *Yingong 11*; TTC, 1736; cf. Legge 1861, 33). For Confucians, ritual propriety serves as the foundation of an orderly society and is the vehicle for social harmony and prosperity. When *li* is understood holistically, people who have as a strong sense of *li* and act accordingly exemplify an ideal personhood in society. Such people are also persons of *ren* (*Analects* 12.1).[6]

Without a reliable legislative mechanism in ancient society, the alternative to *li* was the ruler's arbitrary decrees. For this reason, *li* had been a countering force, as limited as it was, to the whims of rulers in pre-modern China. In contemporary times, an orderly society is founded primarily on the rule of law. Part of the role of *li* has thus been replaced by law. Yet, the law does not cover all aspects of *li*. The smooth operation of much of the society still relies largely on *li*.[7]

Various forms of *li* in Confucian society can find their counterpart in other societies, even though they are usually not conceptualized under one umbrella concept, but in different categories as norms, laws, protocol, etiquette, and ceremony. Then, how should we make sense of this comprehensive concept in Confucian philosophy? The next section turns to this issue.

2. *Li* as Cultural Grammar

Confucian *li* was initially designed and developed by Confucian thinkers and practitioners in ancient Chinese society. Yet, the concept is meant not merely for Confucian society alone. In the Confucian view, *li* is necessary for guiding and regulating interactions in society and therefore is indispensable to all civilized societies. Today, how should we understand *li* conceptually from cross-cultural perspectives? I propose that one helpful way to understand the role of *li* in society is to see it as cultural grammar. In the Confucian conception, *li* performs the role in culture analogous to the role of grammar in language.

"Grammar" denotes linguistic rules or systematic patterns used to generate meaningful sentences and phrases for effective communication. There are different theories of grammar. Whereas formal grammar theorized by scholars such as Noam Chomsky is without semantic contents, other grammatical theories do take semantic contents into consideration. Functional theorists, for example, do not take grammar as purely formal. They emphasize the social nature of language and pay particular attention to the context of linguistic behavior. Michael Halliday coined the term "lexicogrammar" to describe the continuity between grammar and lexis (vocabulary). His systemic-functional grammar connects linguistic "form" with "meaning," emphasizing both grammatical forms and the meanings they make. His theory shows how grammar has evolved in particular ways to construe meanings (Halliday and Matthiessen 2004). For functional linguists, grammar is a cultural convention. Grammar refers to patterns in a language with which users make meaning and communicate with one another. In comparison with formal grammar, functional grammar is a kind of "thick" grammar, i.e., formal grammar with semantic contents.[8] Or, to borrow from Wittgenstein, instead of being abstract rules, grammar is situated within activities with which language-games are interwoven, and it is part of "a form of life" that we live (Wittgenstein 2009, 15e; PI§23).

From such a perspective, perhaps we can say that, when merely taken formally, in the sense of *li-wen* (formal descriptions of *li*) as discussed earlier, *li* is analogous to formal grammar; however, when we take Confucian *li* as a broad umbrella concept in its "thick" sense, one that comprises both its "hardware" and "software" (*li-yi*), *li* is more analogous to functional grammar, which takes all constituents, whether affixes, words, phrases, or sentences, to have semantic, syntactic, and pragmatic functions. I propose that such grammar provides a good metaphor for us to understand *li*. Even though *li* is not literally grammar and many disanalogies can be found between them, my strategy here is to use the metaphor of grammar to elucidate some of the most important characteristics of *li*, even though such approach may not exhaust all dimensions of the meanings of *li*.[9]

82   RESHAPING CONFUCIANISM: A PROGRESSIVE INQUIRY

Grammar is embedded in language. It provides general rules or patterns for the use of words in constructing sentences. A child begins learning language by hearing and repeating it, usually by imitating adults' patterns of everyday linguistic behavior. Having grown older, he or she will learn and develop a sense of grammar. Competent language users may speak a language without being conscious of grammar. But if a person is incompetent, we usually explain his flaws in terms of incorrect grammar. Additionally, although the core of grammar remains stable, grammar does change over time. New linguistic expressions emerge and gain currency. That is the evolution of grammar and language. Today we also know that different languages have different grammars. Until the nineteenth century, in the West, Latin grammar was considered universally applicable to all languages. It was believed that any language deserving the name would have to conform to Latin grammar. Only after contact with languages of indigenous peoples, such as Native Americans, did Western linguists realize that different languages have different grammars, rather than no grammar.[10] Understanding a language implies understanding its grammar, at least implicitly. When a person does not know the grammar of another language, he or she does not understand that language. Obviously, a person can be at home with the grammar of one's own language without understanding those of other languages. To a large extent, one's knowledge of grammar defines one's knowledge of a language.

Cultural grammar functions in analogous ways. A culture, as a form of life, is like a language in practice; as the basic rules and norms of human behavior in a society, *li* is embedded in people's everyday behavior just as grammar is embedded in everyday expressions. People usually do not learn *li* in abstract forms, nor do they usually learn grammar in abstract forms. One becomes proficient in practicing *li* by following patterns of human activities in daily life as one becomes grammatically proficient by using linguistic patterns. A person who has become skillful in performing *li* does not have to think about it all the time—one can act instinctively in accordance with *li*—however, when someone does not behave appropriately, we will quickly notice that he or she violates some rules of *li*. A child begins learning social behavior by imitating adults who have already grasped *li*. Nevertheless, society has to figure out specific ways to teach children the rules of *li*. One way or another, children have to attend the "grammar school" of *li* by learning their lessons. Early Confucians apparently thought that only the specific form of *li* of their own society and time (inherited *li* from the Zhou dynasty) was legitimate, and other societies were without *li* and therefore were barbarians. Of course, these Confucians were wrong about *li* just as linguists in the nineteenth century West were wrong about grammar.[11] Different cultures have different forms of *li*. What they all share in common is that the set of *li* in each culture provides for the stable operation of society, more or less in ways that each culture deems appropriate in accordance with its shared or dominant understanding of human needs and their fulfilment. Human needs across cultures are largely similar in generic terms, even though the interpretations of such needs can vary from culture to culture. This common ground in human needs and the particularities in interpretations provide a plausible account for both commonalities and particularities of *li* across cultures. Understanding the *li* of other peoples is necessary for one to understand their cultures; learning the *li* of a culture is a necessary condition for behaving appropriately in that culture.

Roger Ames and David Hall have called *li* "social grammar." They write, "*li* are a social grammar that provides each member with a defined place and status within the family, community, and polity" (Ames and Hall 2001, 70). I use "cultural grammar" to emphasize that *li* is an accomplished form of life, as Kongzi evidently considered *li* to be an indication of civilization. Early Confucians presumably did not think "barbarian societies" had adequate *li* even though these societies had their own social rules. I also want to suggest that *li* is a cultural phenomenon and is culture-specific—each culture with its own set of *li*—even though early Confucian thinkers may not have thought that way. The same society may have two cultures; there may be two sets of *li*, namely two ways of life with different grammars, at least in some important aspects of their social lives. Another difference between my formulation and that of Ames and Hall is that while they emphasize the social-ontological dimension of *li*, namely the function of *li* in assigning people appropriate places in society, I emphasize the performative dimension of *li*, namely the function of *li* in guiding people's actions. The two dimensions are, of course, related. According to my interpretation, a culture is analogous to a language practice, observing the *li* of one's culture is a demonstration of fluency and mastery, just like speaking one's native language with polished grammar. Grammar sets ground rules for using a language and helps speakers master a language; *li* lays out the protocol and rules for appropriate behavior in a culture.

We can compare key characteristics of *li* to grammar to highlight some important similarities. First, grammar is by its nature a public property. As

84 RESHAPING CONFUCIANISM: A PROGRESSIVE INQUIRY

Wittgenstein indicated, there is no such thing as private grammar; a private language with its linguistic rules *in principle* inaccessible to the public is impossible. *Li* is also essentially a public phenomenon and it presupposes a community in which people interact with one another. As Tu Weiming has pointed out, "the problem of *li* does not even occur when one has absolutely nothing to relate to" (Tu 1979, 21). Participating in ritual activities is necessarily a public affair in the sense that it involves more than one person, as it is the act of relating to others in society. A private *li* that is *in principle* inaccessible to other people is not a real *li*. Understanding *li* in terms of cultural grammar helps us see the public nature of *li*.

Second, grammar, at least in natural languages, is rooted in tradition. It is passed on from generation to generation. *Li* is rooted in tradition, too. It has its own evolutionary process and is not something that a later society makes up from scratch. Kongzi said that "Yin followed the *li* of Xia, . . . Zhou followed the *li* of Yin" (*Analects* 2.23). There was a continuity of *li* through the Xia dynasty, the Yin (Shang) dynasty, and the Zhou dynasty. Without *li*, a cultural tradition can neither exist nor survive, because the continuation of a tradition is at least in part constituted by the continuation of its *li*. The continuity of *li* through generations and dynasties sustains the continuity of a culture.

Third, grammar has a descriptive function. By examining how its grammar works, we can learn about a language, and through comparison with other languages, we see where and how these languages differ. For example, a native Chinese speaker gets a sense of how English differs by learning how the word "the" is used in forming sentences. A native English speaker learns the same about the Chinese language in getting to know that in Chinese sentences verbs do not have the past tense; instead in Chinese the past is indicated by using a phrase like "in the past," "last year," or "earlier today." Similarly, *li* describes how people in a society are expected to behave. In understanding a society, we need to study its *li*. In Kongzi's view, the kind of *li* in a society indicates its level of civilization, and we can describe the kind of society by describing how its *li* functions. Kongzi said that:

> I can speak of the *li* of the Xia dynasty, but [the Xia descendants in] Qi can no longer verify it. I can speak of the *li* of Yin [Shang], but [the Yin descendants in the state of] Song can no longer verify it. [This is because] historical records are no longer adequate. If [they were] adequate, I would be able to verify it. (*Analects* 3.9)

RITUAL AS CULTURAL GRAMMAR   85

Specific patterns of culture evolved through these dynasties. Knowing their respective *li* is an important way of knowing these patterns, and the ability to describe their *li* indicates someone's knowledge of these cultural patterns.

Fourth, grammar has an instrumental function in the learning of a language and in using a language to express themselves by its speakers. Studying grammar, either formally or informally, is necessary for linguistic competence. Grammar can be formalized; it is more about commonality than particularity in using a language. So is *li*. The rules of *li* are formalized and can be formulated in general terms.[12] For Kongzi, to establish oneself, namely, to become a functioning and contributing member of the society, a person must learn *li*. Kongzi said that "One has nothing to establish oneself on without learning *li* "[13] (*Analects* 16.13). Learning to behave appropriately in accordance with *li* is a necessary step for children to become mature members of a society. Using grammar competently is necessary for people to adequately express themselves and effectively communicate with others in society.

Fifth, grammar sets the standard for good use of language; it has regulative and prescriptive functions. Grammar issues prescriptions in the form of "Do" or "Do Not," such as, "Do not use a plural pronoun with a singular antecedent" or "[Do] Use a singular pronoun with a singular antecedent." Under normal circumstances, being ungrammatical is bad and should be avoided. Whether a person speaks grammatically or not measures whether he or she is literate. Similarly, *li* is a measure of appropriate social behavior; it has a regulative and prescriptive force and serves as the directives for people's actions. In other words, *li* possesses normativity. A violation of *li* is generally considered inappropriate or a transgression; it should be avoided (*Analects* 12.1). Kongzi explicitly criticized Zai Wo for not following the *li* of mourning his parents (*Analects* 17.21). In Confucian classics such as the *Book of Rites* and the *Zuo Commentary* there are numerous uses of the expression of *fei li* 非禮 ("contrary to *li* " or "not in accordance with *li* "), to register disapproval of certain actions.[14] When we do things, we should do them in accordance with *li*. Kongzi said:

> Respect without *li* results in futility, caution without *li* results in timidity, bravery without *li* results in disorder, and straightforwardness without *li* results in hastiness. (*Analects* 8.2)

We usually consider respect, caution, bravery, and candor to be good virtues, but they cannot be practiced appropriately without *li*. For example, when one meets with the president of the United States, she should shake hands with the president. Withholding a handshake would be disrespectful or a sign of protest. But this is not the case when meeting with the King of the United Kingdom, where acting in accordance with British *li* would require abstaining from physical contact with the King.

For Kongzi, the effective practice of *li* is an important indicator of the health of a society. One of Kongzi's major criticisms of his time was that "*li* was deteriorating and music was disintegrating."[15] He insisted that "acting not in accordance with *li* is no good" (*Analects* 15.32). He found it intolerable when the Ji family in the state of Lu used a troupe of sixty-four dancers at home for entertainment, which was considered appropriate only for the Son of Heaven (*tian zi* 天子) and it was thus a violation of *li* (*Analects* 8.1). Just as a good speaker of language follows grammar, a good person of a culture follows *li*. Without *li*, things will go awry. Kongzi considered it his mission to restore *li* in his society. He maintained that a ruler, by following the rules of *li* oneself, can make people behave (*Analects* 13.4, 14.44). Kongzi told his disciples that "[If one] broadly studies classics and regulates oneself with *li*, one will not go astray" (*Analects* 12.15; see 6.25 and 9.10 for similar remarks). When Fan Chi asked about *xiao* 孝 or filial care, Kongzi replied, "[When parents are] alive, serve them in accordance with *li*; [after parents] die, give them funerals in accordance with *li* and hold memorial services for them in accordance with *li*" (*Analects* 2.5). These rules of *li* tell us what to do with parents. Broadly speaking, *li* serves as guidance in our lives and it has a normative function.

Moreover, a culturally mature person can internalize *li* in her daily life, behaving in accordance with *li* naturally without having to constantly refer to an instruction manual of *li*.[16] This is similar to a native speaker who speaks her language naturally without having to constantly think about grammar. Internalized *li* gives its possessors a strong sense of propriety and civility in conducting herself (see Chapter 12 of this book for the connection between *li* and civility).

Sixth, rules, either of grammar or of *li*, are not absolute and, under certain circumstances, breaches can be allowed. It is thought that Shakespeare once rejected excuses by saying "but me no buts," where the first "but" is used as a verb even though "but" is not a verb.[17] Similarly, there are circumstances where moral persons may be required to depart from *li*. In Confucian philosophy, the concept of *yi* 義 plays a crucial role in moral action. *Yi* means what is morally right and appropriate. Under certain circumstances, *yi* may require us to suspend *li* to do what is right. In the *Mengzi* there is a discussion of what a man should do if his sister-in-law is drowning in water. Mengzi said that, although according to *li* there should be no physical contact between him and his sister-in-law, he still should give his hand to save her life (*Mengzi* 4A.17). This is of course different from holding her hand in normal circumstances. Just as a master of a language knows when to trump grammar to achieve extraordinary effects in the use of language, a morally mature person knows when to trump *li* for the sake of *yi*.[18]

Seventh, and finally, although grammar largely remains constant, it can also change over time. In the fifteenth and sixteenth centuries, it was grammatical in English to negate a sentence by attaching a "not" to the end of the sentence (e.g., "I see you not"). Today, it is no longer considered grammatically appropriate. While the analogy of *li* and grammar explains adequately Kongzi's general conservative attitude toward *li*, it also explains why he was not an absolutist on the rules of *li*. Although a society's rules of *li* largely remain steady, they can change, and Kongzi was not opposed in principle to all kinds of changes. For example, he said, "Using linen hats has been the [ancient] *li*, but now silk hats are used. It is economical and I follow the majority" (*Analects* 9.3). For Kongzi, certain changes in the rules of *li* can be appropriate and justified. In language, new expressions and new practices emerge, which cause adjustments in grammar. Cultures also change as society evolves; the emergence of new social practices causes *li* to change as well. However, while grammar can change, it must remain stable for the use of language to continue without too frequent disruptions. Obviously, if grammar were to change constantly, one would not be able to grasp the language, let alone master it. *Li* as the grammar of a culture must also remain stable, at least for the most part. Without a substantial degree of stability in *li*, a culture cannot sustain itself.[19]

From a contemporary perspective, however, Kongzi's own attitude toward changes of *li* may be too conservative for modern times when social changes have accelerated. In the *Analects*, Kongzi evidently was concerned more with preserving traditional *li* than reforming it (e.g., 3.9, 3.17, 6.25, 12.1, 16.2, 17.21). There is, however, resource in the Confucian tradition for a more liberal position for progressive Confucianism. For instance, the chapter *Liqi* of the *Book of Rites* states, "as for *li*, timing is the most important," suggesting that *li* has to adjust to specific times and situations. In contemporary times, a major challenge for progressive Confucianism is how to adjust its *li* to suit progressing social reality. On the one hand, many old rituals that were

88   RESHAPING CONFUCIANISM: A PROGRESSIVE INQUIRY

appropriate for slow-paced agrarian society may no longer be appropriate to the fast-paced modern life.[20] On the other hand, as social roles change in contemporary times, so should their corresponding *li* (see the next discussion in this chapter and in subsequent chapters, especially Chapters 4 and 5, for changing social roles).

These similarities provide grounds for us to understand *li* as cultural grammar.[21] David Wong has pointed out an important difference between *li* and grammar. That is, whereas *li* has the content of moral significance, linguistic grammar does not (Wong 2014, 185). How should we see this difference? I think *li* has moral significance because it plays a normative role in the Confucian moral/virtuous life. The moral significance of *li* is established on, and cannot be separate from, the moral enterprise of Confucian social life, and its normative function is moral because it engages in a moral enterprise of the good life. Language per se, on the other hand, is not a moral enterprise. What makes the analogy hold is the fact that both have a normative function in the enterprises with which they engage respectively, whether it is moral or amoral. Within each enterprise, a practitioner may do well or achieve "excellence" (ἀρετή), to borrow an Aristotelian expression. Their moral significance, or the lack thereof, depends on the enterprise in which they each play their respective roles.

Chris Fraser has raised another objection to the analogy between *li* and grammar. He writes:

> Claiming that ritual propriety [*li*] causally produces social order is analogous to claiming that grammar causally produces smooth linguistic communication, when in fact it is more likely our ability to communicate that allows us to develop shared rules of grammar. (Fraser 2012, 260)

My response is this. While Confucians hold that there is a close relationship between ritual propriety and social order, it does not mean that ritual propriety in itself causes social order. Obviously, grammar in itself does not produce smooth communication; the use or practice of grammar causes smooth communication. Similarly, *li* by itself does not cause social order; it is the use and practice of *li* that causes social order. Xunzi famously pointed to the fundamental difference between human beings and animals as the fact that human beings are equipped with the capacity of *yi* 義, the moral sense of right and wrong (*Xunzi*, chapter 19). Just like human beings have an inborn potential for formulating and using linguistic grammar for linguistic communication, human beings also have an inborn potential to develop a sense of moral propriety by developing and implementing *li* in life. Without a moral capacity, animals do not develop and implement *li*. There is a mutual efficacy between human linguistic capacities and the use of linguistic grammar; there is also a mutual efficacy between human moral capacity and the use of *li*.

3. *Li* for Contemporary Times

I have shown that, as norms, laws, protocols, etiquettes, ceremonies, etc., *li* largely constitutes the "form of life" in a culture. Although every society does not need to conceptualize all social norms under one category, *li* or otherwise, cultural grammar permeates throughout the fabric of every society, in ancient times as well as today, just as linguistic grammar is embedded in every language. Needless to say, a substantial part of what was covered under *li* in ancient times should be handled under the separate category of law through legislation in contemporary society. I suppose, nevertheless, most readers agree to the need for various norms of *li* in today's society, even though people can disagree on specific terms. Less clear, however, is whether the ritual performance component of *li* is still significant to the contemporary world.

Ritualized activities can be formal, as in swearing in a country's new president, but they can also be casual, as one says "good morning" to a stranger on the way to work. In modern times, ritualized propriety apparently has lost much of its significance. People take our ritualized lives much less seriously. Many factors contribute to its decline. We now live in a "disenchanted" world, as characterized by Max Weber. People justify actions often merely by their instrumental utility. Behaviors out of ritualized propriety often appear to value primarily "formality" rather than instrumental value, at least not directly or immediately. Furthermore, modern life is fast paced. Ritualized performance takes time away from actions which bring forth immediate outcomes. For various reasons, modern rationalizations of the world do not seem to need ritual as a significant building block. However, we modern people may have overlooked the real meaning of ritual in the good life.

In their book *Ritual and its Consequences*, Adam Seligman et al. (2008) make a strong case for the need for ritual in our times, under their general concept of ritual. They argue for the fundamental importance of ritual in a meaningful

90 RESHAPING CONFUCIANISM: A PROGRESSIVE INQUIRY

world. First, ritual creates a subjunctive realm that makes our shared social world possible. Such a realm takes place in the form of "as if" or "could be." The formality, reiteration, and constraint of ritual are all necessary aspects of the world we create together. We can see a similar view in Confucianism. Being agnostic regarding the gods, Kongzi's attitude toward worshipping is that, when you worship the gods, you should do so in a manner "as if" they exist (*Analects* 3.12). The point is not that whether you are convinced that the gods are real, when you participate in a worshipping ritual, you should act as if the gods are present. Otherwise, the pure act becomes meaningless. Similarly, when one visits the graves of deceased parents and "talks" to them, she should speak "as if" her parents are listening. That makes her "conversation" meaningful; the act enriches the meaningful world in which she lives. Without ritualized actions, our jointly created world would lose much of its significance.[22]

Second, the authors further argue that ritual pervades many realms of human endeavors, both public realms and private ones. Ritual behaviors create ways of negotiating our very existence in the world. "It occurs in myriad forms of normal everyday behavior, as well as in various forms of social and psychological pathologies" (Seligman et al. 2008, 8). Indeed, when we ask a casual acquaintance, "How are you?" without expecting a truthful answer, it is by no means a futile act but enacting a constructive move for maintaining our shared social space. This view is consistent with my understanding of the role of Confucian *li*, which is more than creating a subjunctive realm. *Li* constitutes an important part of our actual world. Our world is not a purely physical realm. Just as human relations are intrinsic to the real world in which we live, *li* also constitutes our world in substantial ways. We live through the practice of *li*. The ways in which we live our lives are constituents of our actual world.[23]

Third, ritual offers an alternative mode of human existence to what the authors call "sincerity." Seligman and his colleagues use "sincerity" to designate the attitude or sentiment that is concerned excessively with individual choice, with being authentic, and with what is "real." A very strong dose of sincerity is manifested in religious radicalism. Seligman et al. (2008) argue that the contemporary world is marked by an overwhelming concern with sincerity at the expense of ritual. Ritual stands in contrast, but not necessarily in opposition to sincerity. Ritual enables us to lead a balanced life and to create a more harmonious world.

Finally, our era needs to take ritual seriously and to employ it in dealing with contemporary challenges. Various problems brought out by

RITUAL AS CULTURAL GRAMMAR 91

globalization, struggles with religious commitments and ethnic identities, and cultural conflicts in the form of the "West and the rest," all suggest "the failure of our existing cultural resources to deal with ambiguity, ambivalence, and the gentle play of boundaries that require both their existence and their transcendence" (ibid., 10). We need to reengage with ritual as a constitutive aspect of the human project to negotiate the emergent realities of our present time. One example used by the authors to make their case is voting. We usually understand voting as participating in a political process of deciding on elections. From such a perspective, many people have argued that it is irrational to vote. In her article on "Your Vote Doesn't Count: Why (almost) everyone should stay home on Election Day," Katherine Mangu-Ward argues against voting because, in all of American history, a single vote has never determined the outcome of a presidential election (Mangu-Ward 2012). She cites a study of the 2008 election cycle by political scientist Andrew Gelman and colleagues, which shows that the chance of a randomly selected vote determining the outcome of a presidential election is about one in sixty million. In a couple of key states, the chance that a random vote will be decisive creeps closer to one in ten million, which drags voters into the dubious company of people gunning for the Mega-Lotto jackpot (ibid.). Her argument appears to be powerful if one understands the nature of voting as merely deciding on the election. Because the chance of influencing the election outcome is so small, we cannot avoid the rational conclusion of the futility of voting. There have been various arguments against this kind of anti-voting argument. Seligman et al. (2008) present an important one from the rather refreshing perspective of ritual. In their view, even though voting in many cases may have no practical value, it is nevertheless a ritual "of great significance because it allows us to re-create a social imaginary, a world where the people control the government" (Seligman et al. 2008, 11–12). In such cases, we vote not so much to decide on an election as to re-create our democracy periodically. Thus understood, at least part of the reason for voting is akin to the same reason we follow codes of etiquette and civility in our daily lives. It is hard to say that something of concrete practical value would be lost if I fail to say "How are you?" or "Good morning!" when I see a casual acquaintance on the street. But things look different if we take such utterances as participating in the creation or re-creation of our social world, strengthening its fabric, and in the meantime reinventing ourselves in well-maintained, meaningful community.

The case made by Seligman et al. (2008) makes us consider the significance of ritual in contemporary society seriously. Indeed, without the social dimension created through participating in ritual activities, our world would have been much impoverished. The main emphasis of their argument is on the formal aspect of ritual propriety, which is aligned more with the "hardware" aspect of *li* as discussed earlier than the "software" aspect. These authors show that, even in contemporary society, the formal aspect of ritual still matters greatly. However, their emphasis on the formal aspects of ritual behaviors does not imply that developing an internal sense of the importance and moral relevance of ritual is irrelevant. On the contrary, their work can be read as an earnest endeavor to urge and help readers to develop a deep sense alongside of the formal aspect of ritual practice. In this way, we can see their main argument as promoting ritual propriety as a whole that is both the internal and external dimensions of ritual propriety. Their argument suggests that, far from being an outdated concept, ritual propriety is directly relevant to constructing a meaningful world in our times (readers can see Chapter 12 of this book for the connection between *li* and civility in contemporary society).

As has been shown, while the formal aspect of Confucian *li* is undoubtedly important, so is its meaningful content, or what I have called "*li*-meaning" in this chapter. In fact, Confucian thinkers have emphasized the intended meaning of ritual propriety more than its formality. Kongzi maintained that the physical mechanism of ritual in itself does not carry the full import of *li* (*Analects* 17.11). This means that in practicing *li* we maintain and re-create our cultural world that makes life meaningful. My "*li* as cultural grammar" argument shows the importance of *li* not only for the Confucian way of life but for a meaningful life in all cultures. Without *li*, culture cannot exist, just as language collapses without grammar; without culture, meaningful life becomes impossible. Studying Confucian *li* gives us an opportunity to reflect on an essential aspect of our social lives; it helps us understand the importance of ritual propriety to a culturally rich and ethically meaningful world.[24]

Study Questions

1. What are the two origins of the Confucian *li*?
2. Explain the "hardware" and "software" of *li*.
3. Why does the author interpret *li* as ritual propriety?

4. What alternative terms you would use to designate the domain of the Confucian *li*?
5. Explain the various dimensions of the Confucian *li*.
6. Explain the two kinds of grammar discussed in the chapter. How are they related to the argument of *li* as cultural grammar?
7. In what way does the Confucian *li* resemble grammar?
8. According to Seligman et al. (2008), why is ritual important to our social world?
9. Is ritual performance meaningful in your life? If yes, how so?

SECTION II
SELF AND OTHERS

4

Filial Care

Confucian ethics requires mutual obligations of care between parents and children. It stipulates that parents should be loving and caring and that children should be filial (*xiao* 孝).[1] In the broad context of Confucian ethics, *xiao* has been associated closely with *ren* 仁 (care-centered virtue). Thus, understanding the concept of *xiao* is key to understanding *ren* and furthermore, the entirety of Confucian ethics.[2] In anglophone scholarship, *xiao* has been interpreted commonly as "filial piety," mainly on the basis of the teachings from Kongzi and, to a lesser degree, Mengzi, without taking into consideration the important contributions of the other key pre-Qin Confucian thinker Xunzi. This chapter aims to present a holistic study of *xiao*. On the basis of the historical development of the concept and in the light of today's moral sensibilities, I argue that, as far as grown children's relation to parents is concerned, the Confucian concept of *xiao* as developed by classical thinkers contains three important components: (1) children are morally obligated to care for parents materially and physically; (2) they should maintain a high degree of respect for parents; and (3) when parents are in the wrong or on the verge of wrongdoing, grown children must help parents rectify their behavior so they lead moral lives. Such a tripartite concept should be understood as filial care instead of filial piety. On the basis of Kongzi's contribution of respect as an important component of *xiao* and related teachings by classical thinkers, I expand the second component to form the psychological dimension of Confucian *xiao*. The result is a modern articulation of *xiao* that encompasses the physical, psychological, and moral aspects of filial care.

1. Beyond Material Care and toward Respect

To contextualize the main argument of this chapter, let me first explain briefly why Confucians hold *xiao* in high regard. The *Analects* states, "*xiao* and brotherly love are the foundation of (becoming) *ren*" (1.2). In the Confucian view, under normal circumstances, a person's moral growth begins in the

---

Reshaping Confucianism. Chenyang Li, Oxford University Press. © Oxford University Press 2024.
DOI: 10.1093/oso/9780197657621.003.0005

98   RESHAPING CONFUCIANISM: A PROGRESSIVE INQUIRY

family. The family is the first social environment in which one begins to receive care and learns to care for others. The first people with whom one is acquainted are one's parents. According to this perspective, to become a person of *ren* one must love first his parents and elder siblings and then love other people outside one's family. It is hard to imagine that someone who treats his parents badly at home can relate well with others in society. The *Zhongyong* states that the way to becoming a virtuous person may be compared to what takes place during travel, when, to go a distance, we must first traverse the space that is near, and to ascend a height, we must start from the lower ground (TTC, 1627; cf. Chan 1963, 102). Kongzi prescribed the way of a good person in the following order: filial when at home, respectful to elders when away from home, becoming earnest and faithful, loving all extensively, and seeking close association with those who are *ren* (*Analects* 1.6; cf. Ni 2017, 83). Confucians take the development of the self as a process of realizing one's humanity through social relationality. Our human-relatedness starts with our relationship with our parents. Therefore, becoming a filial son or daughter is a necessary part of the process of achieving humanity.[3] Thus, *xiao* occupies a key place in Confucian ethics.

The initial idea of *xiao* pre-dates Kongzi. Early variations of the character *xiao* 孝 can be traced to the late Shang dynasty (ca. 1600–1046 BCE) or early periods of the Western Zhou dynasty (1046–771 BCE).[4] In sacrificial bronze inscriptions in pre-Confucian eras, the word primarily denotes religious service to deceased parents and ancestors. Evidence also indicates that *xiao* had a broad use for service to brothers, close friends, and even relations by marriage beyond parents and ancestors.[5] Abundantly, *xiao* is a subject discussed extensively in various Confucian classics. In the *Analects*, although *xiao* is used also for serving spirits (8.21) and deceased parents (1.11; 2.5), most times it is used for serving living parents. The Confucian *Erya* lexicon, dated third century BCE, says that "being good with parents is called *xiao* 善父母曰孝" (TTC, 2591). The *Shuowen* lexicon refers *xiao* as "being good at serving parents 善事父母." In both cases, *xiao* is defined as treating parents well. Classic Confucian thinkers transformed this concept through two major steps. First, Kongzi extended *xiao* from material care to include respect for parents. Second, Xunzi reinterpreted respect so that it is aligned with moral goodness that is independent of parents' wishes.

In early times, the meaning of *xiao* is associated closely with providing materially for parents when aged parents have lost productivity and become dependent on their grown-up children. The character for *xiao* 孝 consists of two components.[6] The lower component is *zi* 子, son or child; the upper component 耂 symbolizes the old. The word thus suggests that the son supports, upholds, or is subordinate to "the old." An ancient variation of the character is 𩠽, replacing the lower component *zi* 子 with the character 食 (*shi*), namely food.[7] Such a composition specifically indicates providing food for the old, a practice commonly denoted as *yang* 養, which also carries the component 食 (*shi*).[8] The word *yang*, however, has a broader meaning than providing food. The *Shuowen* lexicon explicates *yang* in terms of *gong yang* 供養, namely to supply living provisions. Generally speaking, *yang* includes also providing other things to sustain the life of someone or something. To *yang* a plant, one provides it with water, nutrients, appropriate temperature, regular cleaning, proper trimming, etc. To *yang* an animal, one provides it with food, shelter, and due physical attention as needed. To *yang* a person, whether a child or parent, one provides her with food, shelter, clothing, physical care, etc. Understood this way, we should understand *yang* as material care in general.

Evidently, the practice of *xiao* in the sense of providing food had been the main consideration in early times. The *Book of Rites* interprets *xiao* as *xu* 畜, a word used usually for raising domestic animals.[9] Its author states that (grown-up) filial sons should do three things: to *yang* parents when they are alive, to hold funerals when they die, and to make sacrificial offerings after their death.[10] In the *Book of History*, the king ordered people to drive their wagons from home for trading business away in order to "*yang* parents."[11] The *Book of Poetry* records people's complaints against bad rulers:

> Laboring for the king never ends and we cannot attend to crops in the field.
> On what do our parents rely?
> Laboring for the king never ends and we cannot attend to crops in the field.
> On what do our parents feed?
> Laboring for the king never ends and we cannot attend to crops in the field.
> What do our parents eat?[12]

Back then, people's primary concern was mostly with having food. It is not surprising that coming up with adequate food was a struggle that occupied much of their time. It is worth noting, however, that instead of saying that they would not have food for themselves, which would be more immediate, the poem points to starving parents, indicating the importance placed on supporting parents with food in ancient times.

100 RESHAPING CONFUCIANISM: A PROGRESSIVE INQUIRY

Early Confucian thinkers inherited the conception of *xiao* with a strong connotation of *yang*, but they developed and elaborated upon the idea beyond the original meaning of material care. In the *Analects*, Kongzi converses with his disciples regarding *xiao* on multiple occasions, mostly in Chapter 2. In *Analects* 2.7, Kongzi said:

> Nowadays for someone to be *xiao* means no more than being able to provide for parents (*yang*). Even dogs and horses are, in some way, provided for (*yang*). If there is no respect (*jing* 敬), where is the difference? (Lau 1979, 64, modified)

In Kongzi's view, *xiao* goes beyond material care; it requires respect for parents. The idea of respect as a requirement of *xiao* may have appeared before Kongzi. The *Book of History* states, "when the son does not respectfully (*zhi* 祗) carry out the order of his father, he wounds his father's heart grievously."[13] The word *zhi*, here translated as "respectfully," is glossed as *jing* 敬 in the *Shuowen* lexicon. If we take this passage to be from a pre-Kongzi era as usually presumed, then we see the idea of respecting one's father (or parents) had already been recognized. However, evidently, this idea of respect did not register in people's common understanding of *xiao* so Kongzi had to bring up the issue in *Analects* 2.7. And it was Kongzi who extensively elaborated the concept of respect as indispensable to *xiao*. In the subsequent passage of the *Analects*:

> Zixia asked about being filial. The Master said, "The difficulty is with the countenance. If the young merely offer service when there is work to be done and defer to elders when there is wine and food, how can this be enough to be considered filial?" (*Analects* 2.8; Ni 2017, 101)

The passage can be read as Kongzi's example of respect for parents. Respect needs to be displayed through behavior. Keeping a cold face, even when providing physical assistance, is without respect. Kongzi's point is, *xiao* is not merely about meeting parents' material and physical needs; it also requires children to act respectfully toward parents. Thus, Kongzi included a psychological dimension to *xiao* in addition to the material and physical.

In Confucian philosophy, respect is closely connected to ritual propriety (*li* 禮). Once the prince Mengyizi asked what it means to be *xiao*, Kongzi replied, "never fail to comply" (*wu wei* 無違). When his disciple later inquired about it, Kongzi explained:

> When your parents are alive, comply with ritual propriety in serving them; when they die, comply with ritual propriety in burying them; comply with ritual propriety in sacrificing to them. (*Analects* 2.5; Lau 1979, 63, modified)

As has been explicated in Chapter 3 of this book, in the Confucian view respectful behavior is carried out by acting in accordance with ritual propriety. For instance, at a traditional Chinese family dinner, children do not start eating before their parents do, unless there is a reason otherwise.[14] Today in a courtroom, people stand up when the judge enters the room. Students raise their hands before they speak during a class. Conversely, ritual propriety would become meaningless if it is acted on without respectfulness. The *Book of Rites* states that in performing ritual propriety, having respect is the most important.[15] The *Zuo Commentary* states, "respect is the vehicle for practicing ritual propriety; without respect, ritual propriety does not work."[16] As Kongzi indicated in the *Analects*, ritual propriety requires more than merely external or physical performance with ritual instruments (17.11). Mengzi said, "those who behave with ritual propriety respect people" (*Mengzi* 4B26). The kind of practice of ritual propriety is meant to include respectfulness as a necessary component. Thus understood, treating parents with ritual propriety entails treating parents with respect.

Thus, Kongzi (and his contemporaries) formally extended the meaning of *xiao* from providing parents with material and physical assistance to respect, and further associated respect with ritual propriety. This was an important development in the evolution of the concept of *xiao* in Confucianism. Such a move raised the bar for the ethical requirement of *xiao*. The *Book of Rites* states, "providing for parents is attainable but respecting them is (more) difficult (to achieve)."[17] As Kongzi said in *Analects* 2.8, providing parents with food and undertaking their work is easy in comparison with maintaining a good countenance and demeanor while carrying out these tasks. When one serves parents with respect, one satisfies a higher requirement of Confucian *xiao*. It should be noted that such filial respect is not dependent on the moral attainment of parents, even though parents are expected to have moral attainment. In the Confucian view, children owe such respect to parents as defined in the roles of an appropriate parent–child relationship.

102   RESHAPING CONFUCIANISM: A PROGRESSIVE INQUIRY

In his enlightening study of Confucian filial ethics, Heiner Roetz combined the elements of *yang* and *jing* into the one requirement of "respectful care" and formulated a tripartite structure of *xiao* in terms of respectful care, obedience, and moral vigilance.[18] Such a formulation is inadequate when we take into consideration the views of Xunzi and the *Classic of Filial Care* (*Xiaojing* 孝經). Incorporating these developments in classic literature, I configure the components of *xiao* differently. In my view, respect as a requirement of *xiao* is not only there to provide a qualifier to material and physical care, but it is a requirement in its own right. The respect component of *xiao* is significant independently of material and physical care, and as will be shown shortly, different understandings of respect by various Confucian thinkers explain the demand for absolute obedience or the absence thereof beyond material provision. Treating respect as an element of *xiao* in addition to material and physical care not only ascribes to it the importance this concept deserves but is also crucial to placing Kongzi's emphasis of filial obedience in context. Furthermore, respect should also be understood as a reason for moral vigilance. When conducted appropriately, moral remonstration with parents is not a form of disrespect; on the contrary, it is a higher form of respect, as I will argue in the next section.

2. From Respect to Moral Vigilance

Just how central is obedience to *xiao* ? Heiner Roetz has treated obedience as the second among the three key components of his tripartite interpretation. I will argue that the historical development of the concept of *xiao* reveals that different thinkers have had varying levels of emphasis on obedience. Whereas Kongzi emphasized obedience and Mengzi softened his view on it, Xunzi and the author of the *Classic of Filial Care* (*Xiaojing*), as will be argued, emphasized the need for moral vigilance which can override obedience. For Xunzi, when parents are in the wrong, one's duty for moral vigilance requires that one help parents correct themselves rather than simply obey them blindly. Xunzi's view in this regard must be taken as a crucial component of the discourse of *xiao* in pre-Qin Confucianism.

Both Kongzi and Xunzi emphasized respect for parents, but they understood it differently. For Kongzi, respect implies to treat parents nicely and to avoid offending them. For Xunzi, under certain circumstances, respect may require one to go against parents' wishes in the name of morality. Kongzi's view was widely reflected in common uses of the word for respect, *jing* 敬 in classic literature, in which *jing* was often associated with yielding and submission and it was used in conjunction with words of such connotations. For instance, "respectful and yielding" (*jing rang* 敬讓),[19] "respectful and submissive" (*jing er shun* 敬而順),[20] and "respectful and obedient" (*jing cong* 敬從).[21] Occasionally, *jing* was even used straightforwardly in the sense of "obey" as in the case of *jing ming* 敬命,[22] namely obeying orders. In this connection, Kongzi included "to respect and not to disobey" (*jing bu wei* 敬不違) parents in one breath in his articulation of *xiao* (*Analects* 4.18). One may think that here "not to disobey" (*bu wei*) refers to the same as in *Analects* 2.5, where *wu wei* 無違 means to comply with ritual propriety. However, there is no reference to ritual propriety in 4.18 or its adjacent passages. The context of "to respect and not to disobey" suggests that "not to disobey" follows from, and is a requirement of, "respect." This close association of *jing* with a yielding or submissive attitude led ancient Confucian thinkers to inject into *xiao* a strong requirement of children's submission to parents. This submissive understanding of *jing* also made Kongzi and some of his followers reject open conflict with parents even when parents are morally corrupt.

Classical Confucian thinkers recognized that even persons of *xiao* may be at variance with parents at times. The question is how to handle their differences, especially when they disagree on moral matters. Among early Confucian thinkers, the general view on children's proper course of action when parents are in the wrong (*guo* 過) is to *jian* 諫 and to *zheng* 諍. *Jian* means to persuade superiors when they are wrong; *zheng* means candid criticism. These two words have been translated into English as "remonstrate" and "expostulate" respectively. Combined together, *jian-zheng* with parents when they are morally at fault, is a requirement of *xiao*. The idea of filial remonstration is found in major Confucian classic texts such as the *Analects*, the *Mengzi*, the *Xunzi*, the *Classic of Filial Care*, and the *Book of Rites*. Classical thinkers differ, however, on the proper extent of remonstration. In *Analects* 4.18, Kongzi said, "to serve parents *ji jian* " (*shi fumu jijian* 事父母幾諫). As explained earlier, "to serve parents (*shi fumu*)" is to practice *xiao*. The word *jian* means remonstration. *Ji* means either "slightly," "mildly."[23] Kongzi's statement can be read as "in serving parents, one should mildly remonstrate with them (when they are wrong)." Kongzi continued:

> If you see your advice is ignored, you should not become disobedient but remain respectful. You should not complain even if in so doing you wear yourself out. (*Analects* 4.18; Lau 1979, 74, modified)

104 RESHAPING CONFUCIANISM: A PROGRESSIVE INQUIRY

Evidently, Kongzi's view on the extent a person should go in helping parents correct themselves, as recorded in the *Analects*, is a conservative one. His understanding of "remaining respectful" implies obedience to parents even when parents are in the wrong. His bottom line is that one should not oppose parents at the cost of family relationships. In *Analects* 13.18, Kongzi maintained that, even if a father stole a sheep, the son should not expose him. However, what if the father has committed major crimes? The *Analects* did not discuss such extreme cases.

There is a hidden tension in Kongzi's two views related to filial duty. On the one hand, he maintained that one should not oppose parents at the cost of family relationships even when they have done wrong (*Analects* 4.18). On the other hand, he also insisted that one should always treat parents in accordance with ritual propriety (*Analects* 2.5). These two views are consistent only if we assume that parents always wish and act as ritual propriety prescribes. But that is not the case in real life. What should one do when parents violate ritual propriety? If one goes along with parents, one violates ritual propriety. Conversely, if one complies with ritual propriety, one goes against parents. Kongzi's discussion leaves out these kinds of cases. He has apparently extended the requirement of respect for parents to entail absolute submission or at least a very strong requirement of obedience in the wake of a son's failed remonstration. For Kongzi, filial submission trumps the duty of filial remonstration when the two are in conflict.

In comparison with Kongzi, Mengzi is more open to managing possible tensions between parents and children for moral reasons. In *Mengzi* 4B30, his disciple Gongduzi said to Mengzi that everyone in the country considered Zhangzi as unfilial, but "why do you, Master, not only associate with him but treat him with courtesy?" In reply, Mengzi enumerated five kinds of unfilial behavior, namely, the neglect of parents due to laziness, the neglect of parents due to self-indulgence in playing games and drinking, the neglect of parents through miserliness, indulgence in sensual pleasures to the shame of parents, and a quarrelsome and truculent disposition that jeopardizes parents' safety. Then, Mengzi said:

> Has Zhangzi a single one of these failings? In this case father and son are at odds from taxing each other over a moral issue. It is for friends to demand goodness (*ze shan* 責善) from each other. For father and son to do so seriously undermines the love between them (*zei en* 賊恩). Do you think that Zhangzi does not want to be with his wife and sons? Because of his offence,

FILIAL CARE   105

he is not allowed near his father. Therefore, he sent his wife and sons away and refused to allow them to look after him. To his way of thinking, unless he acted this way, his offence would be greater. That is Zhangzi for you! (*Mengzi* 4B30; Lau 1970, 135)

Zhangzi was a general in the state of Qi. His father supposedly killed his mother. Deep differences between Zhangzi and his father on the matter wedged them apart. Mengzi's comments reveal two important points. First, for Mengzi, if it is on moral ground, offending one's parents does not make one unfilial. Obviously, Mengzi still regarded Zhangzi as a decent person worthy of continued association. Second, regardless of the reasons, alienation between children and parents is still regrettable and should be avoided if possible; when it becomes unavoidable due to deep differences such as in this case, filial children should take action to bemoan the loss of familial love. In Zhangzi's case, he sent his wife and sons away as self-punishment.

Given that Mengzi placed a large value on filial duty, he would agree with Kongzi that one should avoid offending parents on non-moral issues or even minor moral issues. Mengzi, however, brought up an issue that Kongzi left out: namely proper action needed in addressing major moral transgressions by parents. If we are to believe the story regarding Zhangzi's father killing his mother, then Zhangzi's offense to his father is at least tolerable. Nevertheless, Mengzi drew a line between relationships among friends on the one hand and family relationships on the other. To him, friends can make the demand of correcting course back to goodness (*ze shan*) to one another as a condition for friendship, but that should not be the case for the relationship between children and parents. If a son insists on his father correcting himself from wrongdoing, the son betrays his father's kindness in raising him (*zei en*) and will ruin their family relationship. Mengzi explicitly stated that "father and son should not demand goodness (*ze shan*) from each other. To do so will estrange them" (*Mengzi* 4A18; Lau 1970, 125).

Xunzi took a major step forward in providing a more liberal guideline for resolving the conflict between a person's moral duty to society at large and one's filial duty toward parents. Like Kongzi and Mengzi, Xunzi realized that pursuing moral goodness and honoring parents' wishes do not necessarily coincide. Unlike Kongzi, however, Xunzi did not shun the issue of sometimes inevitable conflict between different kinds of obligations in question. Xunzi's solution is that, when the conflict between doing the morally right and obeying parents becomes unavoidable, one should do the morally right.

106 RESHAPING CONFUCIANISM: A PROGRESSIVE INQUIRY

Although Xunzi recognized that obeying parents reflects a virtue, he did not take it to imply absolute submission. Chapter *Zidao* of the *Xunzi* explicates "the Way of sons" as the chapter title pronounces, namely the right course of action for sons (children) in dealing with parents:

> Inside the home to be filial toward one's parents and outside the home to be properly courteous toward one's elders constitute the minimal standard of human conduct. To be obedient to superiors and to be reliable in one's dealing with inferiors constitute a higher standard of conduct. To follow the dictates of the Way [*Dao*] rather than those of one's lord and to follow the requirements of morality rather than the wishes of the father, constitute the highest standard of conduct. (*Xunzi*, chapter 29; Knoblock 1994, 251)

For Xunzi, the most important concern is to follow the Way (*Dao*) and to do the morally right, even though it may entail disobeying one's parents. Specifically, Xunzi maintains that under three conditions a filial son should not obey his parents. First, if following the mandated course would bring peril to his family whereas not following it would bring security. Second, if following the mandated course would bring disgrace to his family whereas not following it would bring honor. Third, if following the mandated course would make him act like a savage whereas not following it would cultivate and improve him (*Xunzi*, chapter 29; Knoblock 1994, 251). Under all these conditions, what is right overrides what is usually taken as required by filial duty to obey parents.

Xunzi was careful not to call such conduct "unfilial" though. Instead, he regarded it a higher form of filiality and called it "greatly filial" or "great filiality" (*da xiao* 大孝). The term implies that such an act is not only for moral goodness but also for the good of parents, not the contrary. On such a view, the good of parents is not always reflected in what they wish at the moment of action. Parents mistake sometimes. When they do, following their wishes of the moment is not in their best interest or for their own good, nor the best way to care for them. Hence, Xunzi insists that a filial son must contend with his father when the latter goes morally astray. Of course, such contentions with parents do not have to be outright rude or untactful. A mature, virtuous person would know the best course to navigate difficult situations in contending with parents to minimize the cost on their relationship, just as in other similarly touchy scenarios. Furthermore, it can be argued that, by standing firmly and consistently on moral grounds in dealing with parents, a filial person can help parents correct themselves early on before they come to the point of making large mistakes. This is also what Xunzi has called "the great filiality."

Xunzi's view on the need to act for the course of great filiality is explicitly shared in the *Classic of Filial Care* (*Xiaojing* 孝經). According to the Han historian Sima Qian, the *Classic of Filial Care* was written by Kongzi's disciple Zengzi (*Records of History*, chapter 67; Sima 1982, 2205). The fact that the phrase "Zengzi said" appears in the text several times is an indication that the text was not actually written by Zengzi, however. But the text is quoted in the *Lü's Spring and Autumn Annuals* (*Lüshi Chunqiu* 呂氏春秋), a text completed toward the end of the Warring States period (475–221 BCE). This fact indicates that the *Classic of Filial Care*, or at least part of it, was written fairly early in history, probably in the third or second century BCE, after the passing of Mengzi. As one of the Confucian *Thirteen Classics*, the *Classic of Filial Care* consists of eighteen sections, delineating various kinds of filial duty and conduct. An important feature of the *Classic of Filial Care* is that the author makes explicit that children's duty of *xiao* is for both father and mother and that, as far as *xiao* is concerned, parents should be treated in a symmetrical and balanced way, especially in Chapters 1, 5, 6, 9, 13, 16.

It is noteworthy that Section 15 of the *Classic of Filial Care* is specifically on the topic of children remonstrating with wrongful parents as a filial duty. The section is entitled "Remonstration and Expostulation" (*Jian Zheng* 諫諍). In it, Zengzi asks Kongzi whether following the father's commands is equivalent to *xiao*. Kongzi, as quoted in the text, replies:

> How could you say that? How could you say that? In the old days, the son of Heaven had seven expostulating ministers. Although he was not following the Way (*Dao*), he did not lose the country. . . . When a duke has five expostulating ministers, although he does not follow the Way (*Dao*), he will not lose the state. When a local lord has three expostulating ministers, although he does not follow the Way (*Dao*), he will not lose the estate. A scholar-official (*shi* 士) with expostulating friends will not lose his good reputation. When a father has expostulating sons, he will not become un-right. Therefore, when someone is becoming un-right, a son must expostulate with his father, and ministers must expostulate with their ruler.[24] (TTC, 2558)

108 RESHAPING CONFUCIANISM: A PROGRESSIVE INQUIRY

A similar passage is found also in Chapter *Zidao* of the *Xunzi* and in Chapters 9 and 15 of the *Recorded Sayings of Kongzi 's Family* (*Kongzi Jiayu* 孔子家語), a text dated to the early Han dynasty. Kongzi, as quoted in these texts, emphasized the importance of remonstration and expostulation in various kinds of human relationships, from superior–subordinators, to friend–friend, to father–son. A person, whether a minister, a friend, or a son, has a moral duty to help his superior, his friend, and his father to stay on or revert to the right path. The quoted Kongzi concludes his response to Zengzi as follows: "One should expostulate when things are not right. How can it be *xiao* if a son (merely) follows his father's commands?" (TTC, 2558).

We do not know how authentic these quotes of Kongzi are in the above texts. They are evidently inconsistent with pertinent quotes in the *Analects* illustrated earlier in this chapter. As far as the record of Kongzi is concerned, it is generally accepted that the *Analects* is more reliable and quotes in subsequent texts are likely to contain modifications by later authors. If, however, these quotes of Kongzi in the *Xunzi* and the *Classic of Filial Care* are authentic, then they show a different Kongzi on the matter of children's remonstration of parents from that of the *Analects*. At any rate, the above investigation shows that all these classical thinkers recognized and valued the role of the son's remonstration of the father in the ideal father-son relationship. The weight placed on remonstration increased from Kongzi in the *Analects*, to Mengzi, and to Xunzi, the *Classic of Filial Care*, and the *Recorded Sayings of Kongzi's Family*, largely in chronological order. This increased resoluteness of remonstration in filial duty brings it into direct tension with the requirement of filial obedience. Evidently, when the two requirements come into conflict, different thinkers provide varied solutions. Kongzi in the *Analects* leans more toward obedience, whereas Xunzi and the author of the *Classic of Filial Care* lean toward resolute remonstration. Mengzi, as illustrated above, seems to have provided a transition between these two views.

This difference between Kongzi and Xunzi can be explained by their different understandings of the implications of respectfulness (*jing*). To Kongzi in the *Analects*, respectfulness requires obedience to parents when there is disagreement between parents and children, as indicated in his statement, "to respect and not to disobey" parents (*Analects* 4.18). For Xunzi, however, true respectfulness requires resolute moral vigilance. Xunzi's Way (*Dao*) of sons is to become well-cultivated through respect and love.[25] However, it does not extend to unconditional submission to parents' wishes. Instead, Xunzi specifically claims that for the sake of parents' moral integrity, in certain circumstances "disobeying parents is respectfulness."[26] Thus, Xunzi's conception of respect serves as the ground for moral vigilance (see more discussion of respect in Chapter 10 of this book).

How do we make sense of Xunzi's position on this issue? Or how can Xunzi's conception of respect be justified? In Chapter *Zidao* of the *Xunzi*, the first two of Xunzi's three conditions for practicing "great filiality," i.e., not to bring peril or disgrace to the family, are on avoiding undesirable consequences. The third, i.e., not to act like a savage and to seek moral cultivation, is straightforwardly a moral requirement. It implies that treating parents with respect requires children to stick to the moral path rather than giving in to parents' wishes when the two conflict.

Today, we can give such a conception of respect a modern reading. One of the greatest modern philosophers who have contributed immensely to our understanding of respect is Immanuel Kant. If we borrow philosophical resources from modern philosophy, Kant's account of punishment and respect may help us contemporaries make better sense of Xunzi's view on "great filiality" from a modern perspective. For Kant, rationality gives the person the capacity to be moral; punishment is a form of recognition and respect for such a form of rational personhood. Hence, society punishes a person for wrongdoing out of respect for the person. It implies that, in punishment, society attributes a form of rational personhood to the wrongdoer. Indeed, in Kant's view, the wrongdoer should even claim his entitlement for appropriate punishment on the ground of the respect that society owes him as a rational being. Xunzi evidently did not develop a concept of rationality as Kant did. But today we can nevertheless justify Xunzi's account along the following line. Parents are or ought to be good persons; helping them do the morally right is to help them be true to their moral orientation. When parents are morally wrong, disagreeing with them does not mean disrespect, as filial respect does not entail unconditional submission at the cost of being morally right. On the contrary, there are times when a filial son's respect for his parents demands that he does *not* submit to the wishes of his parents. For Xunzi, great filiality requires one to be able to tell when it is appropriate to submit or not to submit to the wishes of parents and to be able to carefully practice the virtues of respectfulness, loyalty, and trustworthiness, and uprightness and diligence.[27] This difference with Kongzi in the *Analects* on the implications of respect enables Xunzi to uphold both requirements of respect and moral vigilance in the concept of *xiao*. This is a major development of the Confucian philosophy of *xiao* from Kongzi to Xunzi, a major step forward in

110 RESHAPING CONFUCIANISM: A PROGRESSIVE INQUIRY

the historical development of Confucian moral philosophy, making it more consistent with our modern moral sensitivities.

On the ground of his understanding of respectfulness for parents, Xunzi would disagree with Kongzi in *Analects* 4.18 on whether a filial son should continue to remonstrate with wrongful parents if they do not heed their son's recommendation, when the disagreement concerns serious moral choices. Xunzi would probably disagree with Kongzi regarding whether the son should help his father conceal wrongdoing when the latter steals neighbor's sheep (*Analects* 13.18). Thus, Xunzi would not insist on preserving family relationships at any cost, though Kongzi in the *Analects* apparently would. Xunzi would also disagree with Mengzi on what one should do in cases like, hypothetically, Shun's handling of his murderous father. The famous passage on this issue is in *Mengzi* 7A35:

> Tao Ying asked, "When Shun was emperor and Gao Yao was the judge, if the Blind Man killed a man, what was to be done?"
> "The only thing to do was to apprehend him."
> "In that case, would Shun stop it?"
> "How could Shun stop it? Gao Yao had authority for what he did."
> "Then what should Shun do?"
> "Shun looked upon casting aside the Empire as no more than discarding a worn shoe. He would have secretly carried the old man on his back and fled to the edge of the Sea and lived there happily, never giving a thought to the Empire." (Lau 1970, 190, modified)

Shun was a sage-king. The Blind Man was his father. Gao Yao was Shun's minister of justice. In Tao Ying's hypothetical scenario, Shun's filial duty to serve his father and his civic duty to uphold the law come to a direct clash. Mengzi suggested a twofold solution. On the one hand, Shun should not interfere with the state's prosecution of his father for murdering someone. On the other hand, Shun should give up his throne and take his father to flee to the edge of the sea so he and his father could live there happily together. In the end, filial duty overrides civic duty on Mengzi's account, though in an indirect way. Xunzi would disagree. Xunzi would see this case as one in which one must follow a higher duty in not submitting to the personal interest of Shun's father. In such circumstances, the great justice (*da yi* 大義) requires Shun not to break the law in serving his father's interest.[28] Whether he should give up his throne or not, Shun definitely should not take his father to flee from justice. Such a disagreement between Mengzi and Xunzi reveals a deeper difference in their conceptions of *xiao*.

In history, however, the requirement of moral vigilance by *xiao* has been largely suppressed from the Han dynasty onwards.[29] This tendency was made worse especially since the Song dynasty (960–1279), when Xunzi was banished from mainstream Confucianism. With the elevation of Kongzi's *Analects* and the *Mengzi* into among the Confucian canonical "Four Books," along with the *Great Learning* and the *Zhongyong*, Xunzi was pretty much taken out of the picture for Confucian teaching. Governments of various subsequent dynasties often used Confucianism as an official ideology to maintain their rule, drawing a parallel between filial obedience to parents on the one hand and people's obedience to rulers on the other. Such a submissive philosophy has been grounded on certain ideas in Confucian classic texts. For instance, in the *Analects* 1.2, Kongzi's disciple Youzi said:

> It is rare for a man whose character is such that he is good as a son and obedient as a young man to have the inclination to transgress against his superiors; it is unheard of for one who has no such inclination to be inclined to start a rebellion. (Lau 1979, 59)

In the context of the *Analects*, being a good son implies being obedient to one's father. In such an understanding, *xiao* is indeed "filial piety." Rulers subscribed to the political philosophy of ruling the country with "filial piety" (*yi xiao zhi tianxia* 以孝治天下). Thus, Confucian philosophy of *xiao* through the lens of this official ideology has emphasized children's submission and obedience to parents as a way to prepare submissive and obedient subjects for the ruler. Consequently, this may have been one of the reasons for Xunzi's philosophy to have been dismissed and discounted throughout the long history of China.[30] Today, we must take Xunzi into account in fully understanding the Confucian concept of *xiao*. For Xunzi, filial duty does not dictate blind obedience to parents, nor does it prepare for submissive subjects for the ruler.

3. Three Requirements of Filial Care

If we take Confucianism as a developing and evolving philosophy, as we should, then we have evidence to conclude that in the classical period the Confucian concept of *xiao* culminated with three major requirements, namely material provision, respectfulness, and moral vigilance. In the most developed view represented by Xunzi and the *Classic of Filial Care*, filial respect does not extend to absolute obedience to parents as held in the *Analects*; instead, filial respect is compatible with moral vigilance, which may require children to do the right thing even if at the cost of family relationships in extreme circumstances.

By now it should be clear why "filial piety" is not an appropriate interpretation of *xiao*. The primary meaning of "piety" is religious devotion. It is a way to win the favor or forgiveness from a god or gods. Although the Confucian notion of *xiao* requires children to materially support and respect parents, in parallel to a religiously pious person who is required to present offerings and to show reverence to the gods, Confucian parents are not gods. Children's relationship with parents is a kind of delicate mutuality rather than the vertical one between a pious worshiper and a god. More importantly, a religiously pious person is not supposed to go against the gods. Such a person demonstrates humility and submission and does not doubt the rightfulness of the gods. Socrates was accused of being impious precisely because he questioned the absoluteness in worshipping the gods and wanted people to think about morality independently. The developed version of Confucian *xiao* in Xunzi and the *Classic of Filial Care* requires children to place moral rightness before obedience to parents. Under normal circumstances, the moral course requires children to support their parents and attend to their wishes. When parents are in the wrong morally—and they can be because they are human—children are required to remonstrate with parents, out of respect. Therefore, interpreting Confucian *xiao* as "filial piety" is inadequate and misleading.[31]

I propose we interpret Confucian *xiao* as "filial care" to capture all three layers of its meaning. Confucian *xiao* encompasses material support (*yang*), respectfulness (*jing*), and moral vigilance (*jian-zheng*). *Yang* includes material and physical support. This aspect of *xiao* as filial care is rather straightforward. Used in this sense, care means "to protect someone or something and provide the things that that person or thing needs," as is defined in the Cambridge Dictionary.[32] Scholars like Heiner Roetz already used "care" to discuss the *yang* component of *xiao*.[33] My study further justifies it. In the context of Confucian filial philosophy, *yang* is mainly about providing parents with material and physical care. To be sure, specific terms of material and physical care may change over time. In ancient agrarian societies, *yang* was primarily about providing food, shelter, clothing, etc. In modern societies, it may be more about regularly contacting and visiting parents, accompanying

FILIAL CARE 113

and assisting them in seeking medical care, etc. The general idea, however, remains the same. It is about caring for parents in usually tangible ways.

Can we also characterize filial respect and filial moral vigilance in terms of care? I argue that we can and should. Robin Dillon has espoused a kind of respect associated with care and argued that it should be characterized properly as "care respect." Unlike other forms of respect, care respect involves "caring for others by responding to their needs, promoting their well-being, and participating in the realization of their selves and their ends" (Dillon 1992, 116). It calls for attention and appreciation of the object. It regards human selves as having intrinsic value in our everyday ordinariness and acknowledges human limitedness and imperfection. Thus, in exercising care respect, the respecting party recognizes the uniqueness of the respected and accepts the respected on their own terms. Thus, care respect comprises patience, lenience, and acceptance of frailty. Dillon writes:

> Care respect thus provides a kind of constraint on evaluative respect: it calls us to be slow to judge and generous in our evaluation, recognizing the reality of deep disagreement among morally sincere persons, our own limitations in understanding, and the profound impact of our evaluations. (Dillon 1992, 123)

Dillon's view of care respect is applicable to Confucian filial respect, especially when it is practiced along with moral vigilance. People hold different values and prioritize them in different ways. And we do not always have all the relevant facts in relation to forming a moral judgment. Care must be exercised in resolving moral differences. In interacting with parents, even when they have acted in morally problematic ways, it is important to work with them in a thoughtful and gentle way. With Confucian filial respect, parents are perceived as possessing unique value, nonfungible to any other individuals, and as calling for special care.[34] In the context of Confucian filial care, this kind of care respect is especially relevant when serving aged and infirm parents, with whom thoughtful tactics are needed to avoid the unnecessary cost to familial relationships.

Care respect for parents does not imply that children should give up moral independence. As Dillon writes:

> Care respect does not, however, require us to be uncritical, to tolerate the intolerable, to admire the despicable or the inane; rather, it seeks a kind

of acknowledgement and acceptance that does not extend to endorsement but instead provides the framework for questions of endorsement. (Dillon 1992, 123)

Dillon has provided a useful idea that can help us understand Confucian filial respect as construed by Xunzi. Care respect calls on children to care for parents in gentle ways, but it does not extend to children's unconditional submission to the wishes of parents, nor does it require children to endorse moral wrongs on the part of parents. Rather it paves the way to moral vigilance as advocated by Xunzi. This kind of moral vigilance bears some similarities to medical care. In medical care, medical personnel may recommend a proper diet to patients, as well as correct ills in them by prescribing medicine. In recommending a diet, medical personnel take into consideration of patient preferences; in prescribing medicine medical personnel propose what is best for treatment, even if the patient does not feel like taking it. Both are forms of care. In Xunzi's view, filial respect requires children to hold on the right way when parents are in the wrong. It would compel children to help parents to return to the right course when parents have gone astray. Therefore, care respect and moral vigilance are not opposed to each other; rather, the latter can be seen as an extension of care respect.

Care respect can be placed largely in the psychological aspect of filial care. Ancient Confucian thinkers may not have expounded *xiao* explicitly in terms of psychological care. However, they evidently took the psychological dimension into the consideration of filial care. The direct impact of respect or the lack thereof on parents is psychological. As quoted above, Chapter *Kanggao* of the *Book of History* already connects respect to its psychological impact as it claims that a son can wound his father's heart grievously when the son fails to carry out the orders of his father respectfully (TTC, 204). The act of respect expresses a psychological attitude and results in psychological care. Furthermore, when Kongzi extended *xiao* to include respect, he did it with other psychological considerations. In the *Analects* 2.8, Kongzi said that one should not only provide for and serve parents, but also must maintain the appropriate countenance in interaction with parents. Appropriate countenance manifests not only respectfulness but also sincerity; serving parents with a cold or resentful face is a sign of insincerity and of a lack of respectfulness. Such a requirement is psychological in nature.

Material provision alone, no matter how good it is, does not meet parents' psychological needs. In response to an inquiry about being filial, Kongzi said, "Give your father and mother no other cause for anxiety than illness" (*Analects* 2.6; Lau 1979, 64). One cannot help but fall ill sometimes; but one can and should avoid doing things that are problematic or dangerous and would make parents worry. Kongzi also said, "while your parents are alive, you should not go too far afield in your travels. If you do, your whereabouts should always be known" (*Analects* 4.19; Lau 1979, 74). In ancient times, communication over long distances was difficult, if ever possible. Traveling afar from home would inevitably cause anxiety in parents. To avoid making parents worry and to minimize their anxiety is also a practice of the psychological aspect of filial care. Moreover, Section 10 of the *Classic of Filial Care* quotes Kongzi saying, when the filial son provides for parents, he should "aim at making them happy,"[35] suggesting that care for the psychological wellbeing of parents is a higher goal than mere material provision. Mengzi also emphasized the importance of psychological care for parents. He specifically included as a requirement of *xiao* not to bring shame to parents (*Mengzi* 4B30). Mengzi discussed two kinds of care for parents. One is "looking after the mouth and belly," whereas another is "to be solicitous of the wishes (*zhi* 志) of his parent" (*Mengzi* 4A19; Lau 1979, 125–126). "Wishes" refers to the frame of mind. Mengzi argued that care for parents should go beyond mere mouth and belly; it should extend to care for their mental or psychological needs. In contemporary times, we know a lot more than the ancients about the importance of psychological wellbeing for good lives. The psychological dimension of Confucian filial care should be given more attention, especially given that more and more aged parents possess financial independence and that material provision is often no longer a priority.

Finally, moral vigilance is a kind of moral care. It requires grown children to be watchful in safeguarding parents' moral personhood. If one cares genuinely about parents and treats them as wholesome persons, one must treat them as persons capable of maintaining moral integrity. Therefore, genuine respect for parents demands moral vigilance in helping them not to fall into moral ills. When children are young, parents attend to children's moral growth as well as physical and psychological growth. All are important aspects of parental care. Such parental care often continues into children's adulthood as expected in Confucianism. When children have grown up, their duty to help parents in maintaining a moral life is also a kind of care, namely filial moral care. Filial care in the moral dimension is an integral part of Confucian *xiao*.

In conclusion, the Confucian concept of *xiao* as it has evolved should be understood as filial care. It encompasses material and physical assistance, respect, and moral vigilance. In comparison with material and physical assistance, respect as espoused by classical thinkers is mainly in the psychological domain. In addition, classical thinkers also promoted psychological care beyond respect. Considered systematically, these thinkers have laid the groundwork for us to construe the Confucian philosophy of *xiao* as a holistic filial philosophy of material care, psychological care, and moral care. On such a basis, *xiao* can be further developed in these three areas to meet contemporary needs. In earlier, economically stricken periods of history material care was understandably a primary concern. As the economic situation improves in contemporary times, more attention should be shifted to parents' psychological needs, which should go beyond a merely respecting attitude. Furthermore, in accordance with Xunzi's justification, moral care should always be an essential part of filial care as is in any intimate human relationship. Such an interpretation of Confucian *xiao* not only accurately reflects the historical development of the concept, but also makes it suitable for contemporary society.

Study Questions

1. Why is *xiao* important in Confucian ethics?
2. What is the earliest meaning of *xiao* ? What is Kongzi's contribution to the concept of *xiao* ?
3. How did Kongzi, Mengzi, and Xunzi differ on their understandings of *xiao* ?
4. According to Xunzi, under what kinds of condition should a filial son not obey his parents?
5. What kind of respect is "care respect"? How is it different from other kinds of respect?
6. According to the author, why should *xiao* be understood as "filial care" rather than "filial piety"?
7. What are the three dimensions of Confucian filial care?
8. In your opinion, is filial care still relevant in contemporary society?
9. In your view, do children have filial duty toward "bad" parents? How bad do parents have to be before children are released from filial duty, if ever?

5

Differentiated Gender Equilibrium

In a widely publicized 2015 interview, entitled "Only Confucianism Can Accommodate Women," the noted conservative Confucian thinker Jiang Qing 蔣慶 made the claim that being a good daughter, a good wife, and a good mother are the necessary requirements for being a good woman on the basis of her natural attributes and the attributes of the family. He claimed that these roles are the most fundamental values in assessing the meaning of life for Chinese women. One can only imagine what Jiang had in mind when he referred to the traditional roles of daughter, wife, and mother as prescribed in the ancient texts *Lienü Zhuan* 烈女傳 (*Biographies of Exemplary Women*) and *Nüer Jing* 女儿經 (*Classic Teachings for Girls*).[1] We can be reasonably certain, however, that he did not mean the kind of roles represented by such women as the militant Mulan 木蘭.[2] To be fair, Jiang also added that, with changes in modern society, women can pursue careers and public lives, and therefore now the list of the roles of good women should include being a good career person as well (Jiang 2015). Jiang's interview has raised lots of eyebrows, in part because of his insistence on family life as the primary arena for evaluating women. We cannot say that Jiang's remarks were without historical precedent in the Confucian tradition, as there is plenty of textual evidence from the corpus of the Confucian classics in support of his view. Confucianism has been colored by sexist ideas over the course of its long history. The issue has still not been resolved, even in the twenty-first century. A pertinent question to raise, however, is whether contemporary Confucianism should continue holding this traditional view or should it reform itself in response to new social realities. If reform is needed, how should it be done?

In this regard, the challenge for Confucianism is how to effectively adapt to social changes in modern times and yet also preserve its own valuable characteristics, and thus, contribute to the contemporary gender equality discourse. This chapter examines traditional Confucian characterizations of appropriate husband–wife relations, offering a critique as well as a defense respectively of pertinent ideas in gender relations. My focus is on spousal relations because the family has been at the core of Confucian social philosophy.[3]

Reshaping Confucianism. Chenyang Li, Oxford University Press. © Oxford University Press 2024.
DOI: 10.1093/oso/9780197657621.003.0006

118 RESHAPING CONFUCIANISM: A PROGRESSIVE INQUIRY

Specifically, this chapter explores ways for Confucians to achieve family harmony, which requires role differentiation (*bie* 別), without gender inequality. Dubbed "*differentiated differentiations*," I use a reformulated *yin-yang* conception as the guiding idea in illustrating a proposal for variously differentiated roles of husband and wife in a harmonious family.[4]

1. Spousal Relation in the Context of Family Harmony

Family harmony occupies a central place in the Confucian philosophy of the good life. Being a good family member requires self-cultivation, which paves the way for a person to become a productive member in society. In the Confucian conceptual scheme of the good life, the family is both the first school and the home of harmonious personhood, an indispensable incubator for persons to grow and mature, both physically and in virtue. Proper spousal relations should be understood in the context of the Confucian family life.

The Confucian philosophy of the family is characterized as *qijia* 齊家, often translated as "regulating the family" (e.g., Chan 1963, 86). As a key idea in the Confucian moral and social philosophy, it figures most prominently in the classic text *Great Learning*. I propose, however, that, in the context of Confucian general philosophy, *qijia* should be interpreted more appropriately as "harmonizing the family," in the sense of harmony previously discussed in Chapter 1. In classic texts, the character 齊 (*qi*) has carried various meanings. It can mean "to regulate," in the sense of placing something in order or making things uniform; it can also mean "to make equal," as will be discussed in Chapter 10 of this book. It has also been used in association with harmony (*he* 和). Etymologically, the character 齊 (*qi*) is connected with the character 劑 (*ji*), which as a verb literally means mingling herbs in processing Chinese medicine.[5] The Confucian classic of the *Rites of Zhou* 周禮 describes cooking a dish by mingling eight ingredients together in terms of *qi*.[6] Here *qi* means to bring various flavors into a good balance for a rich soup. Offering soup-making as a prototypal analogy of harmony in the *Zuo Commentary*, philosopher Yanzi states, "the cook harmonizes (*he*) the ingredients together and mingles (*qi*) them in order to make the soup tasty."[7] Here *qi* is used in parallel with *he* as harmony. The classic annotator Zheng Xuan on the *Book of Rites* 禮記 explicates *qi* in terms of the compound term *qi-he* as harmonizing ingredients in making a soup, bringing *qi* together with *he*.[8] On such an

DIFFERENTIATED GENDER EQUILIBRIUM 119

account, *qi* means harmony and thus *qijia* means "harmonizing the family." In ancient times, *qijia* is usually attributed to the role of the father. However, the discussion of some important elements of family harmony such as filial care (*xiao* 孝) and brotherly love (*ti* 悌) in the *Great Learning* indicates that harmonizing the family is a goal for all family members. Every family member plays his or her own distinct yet indispensable role in achieving family harmony. Such a goal requires developing and maintaining appropriate relations between parents and children, between older and younger siblings, and most importantly, between husband and wife.[9]

The relation between husband and wife is a cardinal relation within the Confucian family. Confucian classics place the relation between husband and wife among the most fundamental and most significant human relations. The *Xugua* Commentary of the *Book of Changes* states:

When there are Heaven and Earth, there are the myriad things; when there are the myriad things, there are men and women; when there are men and women, there are husband and wife; when there are husband and wife, there are father and son; when there are father and son, there are the ruler and the subject.[10]

Here the relation between husband and wife is placed in the context of a broad setting of the Chinese cosmology to indicate its fundamental importance. Furthermore, the relation between husband and wife comes before those between father and son, between ruler and subject. This implies that the family comes before the state. Indeed, the traditional conception of the state is modeled after the family, giving the family primacy ahead of the state. Similarly, the sixth century Confucian thinker Yan Zhitui 顏之推 (531–591) enunciated a philosophy of the family in his widely read *Yan Family Teachings*. Chapter 3 of the *Yan Family Teachings* states:

Where there are people, there are husbands and wives; when there are husbands and wives, there are fathers and sons; when there are fathers and sons, there are brothers. The affective cohesion of the family is just these three relations.[11]

Echoing the *Xugua* Commentary of the *Book of Changes*, Yan's ordering of these family relations places the husband–wife relation as the primary and most important one for a harmonious family, anticipating a prevalent view

120 RESHAPING CONFUCIANISM: A PROGRESSIVE INQUIRY

in contemporary times. On such a view, the most important relationship for family harmony is between husband and wife.

Most prominently in the Confucian tradition, Mengzi advocated a philosophy of the five fundamental relations for humanity and their respective cardinal virtues. These are:

> Affection between father and son; duty between ruler and subjects; differentiation (*bie* 別) between husband and wife; precedence of the old over the young; and trustworthiness between friends. (*Mengzi* 3A4; Lau 1970, 102 modified)

In Mengzi's formulation, three of these five fundamental relations are family relations, even though the relation between husband and wife comes after those between father and son, and between ruler and subjects. Each corresponding virtue is characteristic of a healthy and productive relationship. The proper relation between husband and wife is characterized as "differentiation (*bie* 別)." By itself, "differentiation" does not tell us anything useful as two persons can be different or differentiated in countless ways. Mengzi's characterization is meaningful only if we take the notion in the context of the Confucian philosophy of the family. That is, differentiation between husband and wife is a meaningful characterization of their relation only if it is considered in the Confucian ideal of family harmony. Therefore, the ideal of proper differentiation between husband and wife should be understood as achieving harmony between husband and wife through differentiating roles in their family life. Then, what exactly has such a differentiation been characterized? And what is a proper differentiation in contemporary society?

2. The Traditional View of Spousal Relations

Confucianism has been patriarchal for most of its long history. Its view on the relation between husband and wife is no exception. The traditional Confucian view of the relation between husband and wife is controversial and problematic today, mainly because it has deprived the wife of equal standing with her husband, as has typically been the case in many world traditions. Within the context of the ideal of family harmony, the core teachings of traditional Confucian philosophy of spousal relations have consisted of three main ideas. First, there should be differentiation between husband and wife.

Second, the appropriate kind of differentiation between husband and wife is for the husband to manage the external affairs of the family and for the wife to handle the internal affairs. Third, the husband is to take the leading role in the family.

Let us look into the first idea. The husband and wife occupy different roles in the family for it to function properly. The *Book of Rites* states, "Only when the roles of the man and woman are differentiated is the appropriate relation between husband and wife established."[12] The term for differentiation, *bie* 別, is used in the opposite of sameness (*tong* 同). Conceptually, the emphasis on differentiation is connected to the Confucian philosophy of harmony, which presupposes and requires difference, as has been explicated in Chapter 1 of this book. The same requirement applies to family harmony. Whereas differentiation within the family does not necessarily result in harmony, no harmony—of the Confucian conception—is possible without differentiation.

In promoting harmony, the *Book of Changes* seeks a balance between common grounds and differences, with a particular emphasis on differentiation. Its commentary on the hexagram *ge* 革 states:

> Water and fire extinguish each other. When two females occupy the same space, their wills do not complement each other (*bu xiangde* 不相得). This causes alteration.[13]

Hexagram *ge* ䷰ consists of two trigrams, ☱*dui* 兌 and ☲*li* 离. Traditional interpretations have associated *dui* with water (*ze* 澤) and the youngest daughter (*shao nü* 少女) of *qian* 乾 (Heaven) and *kun* 坤 (Earth), and associated *li* with fire (*huo* 火) and the middle daughter (*zhong nü* 中女) of *qian* and *kun*. When *dui* and *li* are interpreted as water and fire respectively, in Hexagram *ge* water is situated on the top of fire. Because water and fire are diametrically opposed, the commentary says that they extinguish each other. This would indicate disharmony. On the second pair of associations with females (daughters), there have been different readings. One reading holds that as the youngest daughter is situated on the top of her "elder sister," it is out of natural sequence; much like water on the top of fire, their positions symbolize disorder. Another reading is suggested by Tang commentator Kong Yingda 孔穎達 (574–648) in his classic annotation of the *Book of Changes*. Kong reads the two "daughters" as two females. He says that, unlike a male and a female who resonate with each other, "two females" are repetitious (*fu* 復) and thus symbolize sameness under the same roof. Therefore, they lack complementarity (*xiangde* 相得), and their relationship cannot be maintained.[14]

To be sure, in real life two females, or for that matter, two males, can form a harmonious unity. In the text, however, these are taken as symbols of sameness without diversity or difference. The explicit use of females in making a negative example reflects an unfair bias of its time.[15] In the context of the *Book of Changes*, nonetheless, we can understand this example of two persons of the same gender living together as suggesting that two persons of the same characteristics comprise an unusual union. The *xiang* in *xiangde* 相得 means mutuality; *de* means to acquire, to achieve. *Xiangde* literally means two subjects acquire something from each other, something that is different from one's own, to their mutual advantages respectively. Such complementary exchange presupposes two subjects possessing different things to offer each other and, in the meantime, also in need of different things from each other. It is like two things being dovetailed together. When two subjects possess the same set of things or characteristics, they fail to *xiangde*, which leads to instability and disharmony. The passage suggests that, due to a lack of differentiation between them, the two subjects do not complement each other, therefore their relationship is unstable. Just as the ancient saying of harmony suggests, merely "mixing water with water" does not make a tasty soup,[16] because they have exactly the same characteristics and there is nothing with which to harmonize. In the context of our consideration here, we should not take this statement as only concerning female persons. The philosophical point that is more relevant to my discussion, however, is that a harmonious relationship requires differentiation. This applies to the roles of husband and wife as well.

The second main idea of the traditional Confucian philosophy of spousal relations is built on the first one; it is about the appropriate kind of differentiation between husband and wife. In this regard, the traditional Confucian view on the spousal division of labor has been on the basis of a separation between affairs internal (*nei* 內) and external (*wai* 外) to the family. The *Book of Changes* states:

> The correct post for the female is the internal whereas the correct post of the male is the external. When the male and the female are in their respective correct positions, it is the great appropriateness between heaven and earth. The responsible rulers in the family are the parents. When the father acts like a father, the son like a son, the older brother like an older brother, the younger brother like a younger brother, the husband like a husband, the

wife like a wife, the family is on the right path. When the family is on the right path, it provides a foundation for society to become stable.[17]

Ancient thinkers held that husband and wife need to perform different duties in the family to complement each other for the sake of family harmony. On the basis of perceived characteristic differences between the two sexes, the husband has been assigned to external affairs for the family, whereas the wife to internal affairs. Such an assignment of gender roles was based largely on the social background of an ancient agrarian society. The *Shuowen* lexicon explicates the character for male, 男 (*nan*), as follows:

> It consists of the word 田 (*tian*, fields) and 力 (*li*, labor); it means that males labor in the fields. (Xu and Duan 1992, 698)

In agrarian societies, a natural division of labor was for the husband to work in farming fields and to handle family business, whereas the wife stayed home taking care of children and managed domestic affairs. The sociological justification for this division of labor may be found in labor efficiency. In most cases, men are physically more suitable for laboring in farming fields to grow crops, and women are physically and usually psychologically more equipped for taking care of children; families with a division of labor along these lines are likely to be more efficient.[18]

This division of labor itself may not have been necessarily problematic in agrarian societies. Today, however, such a division of labor is no longer adequate with contemporary social changes. Furthermore, even with the internal–external division of labor in agrarian societies, there is still a problem with an uneven division of power between husband and wife associated with such an established division of labor. For if both the internal and external are important to the healthy operation of the family, arguably there should be a balance of power between these spheres to achieve true harmony in the family.

Now we come to the third main idea of traditional Confucian philosophy on spousal relations. Conventionally, Confucianism has given the husband the leading role in the family, making husband and wife unequal in power distribution. The *Book of Rites* defines "the appropriate relation between husband and wife" as that "he leads and she follows."[19] It states:

> Women follow men. At home, a woman follows her father and elder brothers. When married, she follows her husband. When her husband

124 RESHAPING CONFUCIANISM: A PROGRESSIVE INQUIRY

dies, she follows her son. (Chapter *Jiaotesheng*; TTC, 1456; cf. Legge 1885 IV, 441)

"Follow" here is a literal translation of *cong* 從, which can also be interpreted as "to obey."[20] With few exceptions, the husband typically had more power than the wife did in the family. The division of power between men and women in ancient society was grounded on an ideological construction that takes men as superior to women (*nanzunnübei* 男尊女卑).

This sexist idea can also be traced back to the *Book of Changes*. In the *Book of Changes*, each of the sixty-four hexagrams consists of six lines. These lines are either solid (—) or broken (--), symbolizing the forces of *yang* and *yin* respectively. A *yang* line or a *yin* line can appear in any position of the hexagram, higher or lower, top or bottom, varied compositions of which make different hexagrams. The first two hexagrams, *qian* 乾 (䷀) and *kun* 坤 (䷁), are made of six solid lines and six broken lines, respectively. The *Xici Commentary* of the *Book of Changes* pairs *qian* with Heaven and *kun* with Earth, asserting that "Heaven is superior and Earth is inferior; in such a way the order of *qian* and *kun* is set."[21] It also pairs *qian* with *yang* and *kun* with *yin*.[22] Furthermore, it makes a parallel claim with the sexes, stating that "the way of *qian* constitutes the male and the way of *kun* constitutes the female."[23] The analogy of the duos of Heaven and Earth, *qian* and *kun*, *yang* and *yin*, male and female gets close to drawing the conclusion that male is superior and female is inferior, though without explicitly stating so.[24] Later the Han Confucian Dong Zhongshu (179–104 BCE) formally and explicitly incorporated the idea into Confucianism. In *Chunqiu Fanlu*, his *magnum opus*, Dong claims not only that *yang* is superior, and *yin* is inferior but also that husband is *yang* and wife is *yin*, defining *yin-yang* philosophy in sexist terms.[25]

This line of reasoning shares a remarkable parallel with sexist reasoning in the West as characterized by Karen Warren (2012). Warren formulates such reasoning as follows:

(1) Women are identified with nature and the realm of the physical; men are identified with the "human" and the realm of the mental.
(2) Whatever is identified with nature and the realm of the physical is inferior to ("below") whatever is identified with the "human" and the realm of the mental: or, conversely, the latter is superior to ("above") the former.

DIFFERENTIATED GENDER EQUILIBRIUM 125

(3) Thus, women are inferior to ("below") men; or, conversely, men are superior to ("above") women.

(4) For any X and Y, if X is superior to Y, then X is justified in subordinating Y.

(5) Thus, men are justified in subordinating women. (Warren 2012, 159)

Warren's formulation is made within the context of discussing environmental philosophy. Pairing women with nature or the physical and men with the mental is meant to justify both man's domination of nature and men's domination of women. A more general and commonly used argument in the West can be found in associating men with reason and women with feelings. On the assumption that reason should rule feelings, the conclusion is drawn that men should rule women.[26]

In comparison, a similar argument on the Chinese side can be constructed as follows:

(1) Heaven is superior, and Earth is inferior.

(2) *Qian* is associated with Heaven and *kun* is associated with Earth.

(3) By implication, *qian* is superior and *kun* is inferior.

(4) *Qian* is manifested in the male and *kun* is manifested in the female.

(5) Therefore, the male is superior, and the female is inferior.

On the Confucian side, if we add to this argument the idea that women (daughters and wives) should follow or obey men (fathers and husbands) as suggested in the *Book of Rites*,[27] then we arrive at a conclusion very similar to Warren's formulation, as follows:

(6) For any X and Y, if X is superior to Y, then X is justified in subordinating Y.

(7) Thus, men are justified in subordinating women.

Whereas the Chinese version uses "Heaven" and "Earth," the Western version uses "nature/body" and "the mental/mind." Both apply a logic of subordination of the "inferior" by the "superior." When it comes to relations in the family, such reasoning implies that the husband is superior and the wife inferior and that the husband is justified in subordinating the wife.

It is obvious now that the traditional uneven and unfair distribution of power between husband and wife is not conducive to family harmony, even

126   RESHAPING CONFUCIANISM: A PROGRESSIVE INQUIRY

though it may create a false sense of harmony in the form of forced conformity;[28] real harmony requires not only differences, but also equity, equilibrium, and creative tension.[29] Contemporary Confucians must adjust
their conception of the appropriate relation between husband and wife to
reflect and accommodate the reality of modern economic and social lives.
They need to treat men and women equally. This means that they need to
uphold the ideal of harmony between husband and wife without defining the
wife's role as subordinate to the husband. Of the three main ideas of the traditional Confucian philosophy of spousal relations, contemporary Confucians
should preserve the need for differentiation as a precondition for family harmony while discarding the second and third ideas, namely the restrictive division of labor between husband and wife along the internal and external
lines of the family, and the idea of the superiority of men over women. It must
redefine gender differentiation between husband and wife for achieving
family harmony in contemporary society.

3. Challenge to Differentiated Gender Relation

The demand for reexamining traditional gender roles is universal across
the globe today. While women's liberation movements have been forged
over time in the West, their focuses have been largely in public realms, especially in politics and the workplace. In the Western scholarship of the last
few decades, gender equality within the family has also become an important
goal. Susan Moller Okin (1989) has been influential for her argument that
the family must be reformed on the principle of justice. In her view, justice in
the family is primarily a matter of gender equality. Despite their differences
otherwise, Okin shares one important commonality with Confucians: both
sides reject a sharp separation between private and public spheres. For Okin,
continuity across these spheres provides a common ground for justice in
both realms. As she said, the family "must be just if we are to have a just society" (Okin 1989, 14)—something a progressive Confucian could have just
as easily said. In Confucianism, the family is inherently connected to society;
the philosophy of harmony is applicable both to the family and to society at
large. Progressive Confucian thinkers also share Okin's view that the power
structure within the traditional family needs to be changed. In the Confucian
view, however, the solution to the problem does not hinge on whether there
should be differentiation between husband and wife—there should be for the

DIFFERENTIATED GENDER EQUILIBRIUM 127

sake of family harmony—but on whether such differentiation is fair and conducive to the healthy operation of the family. In that regard, Confucians part ways with Okin.

Okin takes a hardline, egalitarian approach with no differentiation. Extending the application of the "veil of ignorance" to gender issues, Okin proposes a reformed Rawlsian strategy to "arrive at a basic model (of the family) that would absolutely minimize gender" (Okin 1989, 175). Her goal is not only to reduce and eliminate "inequalities of gender," but "ending gender itself" (Okin 1989, 17). For Okin, a just society is an androgynous one and a just family is "genderless." She maintains:

> Any just and fair solution to the urgent problem of women's and children's vulnerability must encourage and facilitate the equal sharing by men and women of paid and unpaid work, of productive and reproductive labor. We must work toward a future in which all will be likely to choose this mode of life. A just future would be one without gender. (Okin 1989, 171)

For Okin, one's sex should be regarded as a category like eye color or the length of one's toes. Personal traits like eye color or toe length are completely irrelevant to people's social roles, so should be a person's sex (ibid., 79).

Okin's call for radical reform has already met with various criticisms, including resistance from feminist thinkers. Objecting to Okin's demand for a genderless society, Martha Nussbaum argued that our experience of being sexually drawn to males or females, or both, goes much deeper than Okin has implied, and it is more intimately connected with our lives and identity (Nussbaum 1992, 46). Nussbaum's view is probably shared by a large number of people, both male and female. Most people have difficulty seeing themselves in the genderless world for which Okin aspires. Becoming genderless would drastically reduce, if not eliminate, the richness of people's lives. While it is true that people's gender identity has been and still is subject to discrimination, entirely eliminating such identity with regard to their social roles is far from a reasonable solution. Similarly, Anne Phillips argued that Okin's "equal sharing" model is too radical to be acceptable. For Phillips, "the general principle of gender equality does not carry over to the most specific contention that everyone must take equal shares" (Phillips 2007, 38). While progressive Confucians applaud Okin's effort to protect women and to promote gender equality, they will not endorse her solution for related problems. Okin's philosophy of genderlessness and "equal sharing" of

128 RESHAPING CONFUCIANISM: A PROGRESSIVE INQUIRY

housework within the family implies the elimination of differences between husband and wife. Such a move is contrary to the Confucian philosophy of difference-based harmony in the family.

In the twenty-first century, a contemporary Confucian philosophy of the family has to address three key questions. First, whether there should be differentiation between husband and wife in the family. Second, whether spousal equality can be achieved with differentiation in the family. Third, what kind of difference should exist and whether differentiation is to be associated with a person's sex. As I will argue next, progressive Confucians will give an affirmative response to the first two questions. They will maintain that some kind of differentiation between husband and wife should be preserved for the sake of family harmony, and that gender equality can be achieved through appropriate differentiation. The third question requires careful examination and calls for a nuanced and qualified response. I will do so by drawing on a new interpretation of the *yin-yang* philosophy from the *Book of Changes*.

4. *Yin-yang* Philosophy and Gender Equality

Chinese thinkers have often used the concepts of *yin* and *yang* in describing the harmonious relationship between husband and wife and their respective roles in the family. *Yin* and *yang* have been defined in various ways (see more discussion in Chapter 1 of this book). As far as the husband–wife relation is concerned, their primary meanings are that *yang* stands for active and leading roles and *yin* for receptive and adaptive roles. In the view of a reasonable *yin-yang* philosophy, the appropriate kind of differentiation between the sexes should be context-dependent and adjusted with time. Obviously, the social and working conditions for the division of labor in industrialized societies differ from ancient agrarian societies. Now forms of work are more diverse; varieties of lifestyle are far richer; there are many more ways to satisfy people's increasing kinds of needs. Contemporary social conditions call for new ways of differentiation between husband and wife. This calls for a new interpretation of *yin-yang* philosophy.

Fortunately, the sexist reading of the *Book of Changes*, as has been examined above, is not the whole story. The text is complex and compiled probably by different authors at different times. The *Book of Changes* comprises varied ideas. On the one hand, there is a discriminatorily gendered and sexist line

DIFFERENTIATED GENDER EQUILIBRIUM 129

of thinking regarding the relation between husband and wife, as can be expected in most ancient texts. On the other, the text also indicates a flexible and balanced understanding of such relations. Related directly to my discussion here, there is another theme in the text that counterbalances such a vertically subordinating model with flexible *yin-yang* equilibrium. The general motif of the *Book of Changes* is harmony out of differentiation (e.g., see Yu 2017). The text maintains that the *Dao* of Heaven encompasses both *yin* and *yang*; it calls for grand harmony through the integration of these virtues.[30] The harmony of *yin* and *yang* requires differentiation, but differentiation does not have to be in a fixed order of superiority and inferiority. On such a consideration, *yin* and *yang* are different yet equal because they each play a respective yet indispensable role. Accordingly, it is a mistake to equate differentiation with a division between husband and wife in terms of superiority and inferiority. Indeed, as will be argued next, an appropriate understanding of the *yin-yang* philosophy does not or should not come in a fixed hierarchical structure.

The *Book of Changes* claims that "the conjunction and alternation of *yin* and *yang* is called *Dao*."[31] The idea is that *yin* and *yang* are to be coordinated and that they complement each other in driving the operation of the world. In such an understanding, *yin-yang* philosophy serves as a counter-balancing force to the sexist tendency in terms of *qian* and *kun*. Alison Harley Black has argued, "we may legitimately pursue the possibility that some of the basic concerns of Chinese metaphysics and cosmology transcend questions of gender . . . . *Yin* and *yang* (do) not mean 'feminine' and 'masculine' etymologically or invariably or primarily" (Black 1989, 184). Black's study reveals that there are many fascinating reversals in the *Book of Changes*, with its typical alignment of feminine traits such as love, benevolence, and harmony with *yang* and masculine traits such as order, righteousness, and action with *yin* (Black 1989, 179–184). Her study opens doors for an alternative understanding of the *yin-yang* philosophy that can help us reconceptualize a new gendered relation between husband and wife.

In the Confucian view, harmony requires coordination among various forces, including those characterized in terms of *yin* and *yang*. Progressive Confucians can accept and retain the idea of *yin-yang* differentiation, interdependency, and complementarity without accepting the doctrine that one is systematically superior to the other. Although one thing can be superior to the other in some way or ways, it cannot be superior to the other systematically. In this context, *yin* and *yang* apply to a broad range of differentiated

130 RESHAPING CONFUCIANISM: A PROGRESSIVE INQUIRY

forces and characteristics interacting with one another in a coordinated and balanced fashion. When these forces are present and they interact appropriately, harmony can be achieved.

Robin R. Wang's extensive study shows that the paired *yin-yang* concept in Chinese philosophy demonstrates six types of relations. They are as follows:

1. Opposition and exclusion. The two are different and in contrast; something cannot be both *yin* and *yang* in the same way at the same time.
2. Interdependency. Neither can sustain itself without the other.
3. Mutual inclusion. Nothing is exclusively *yin* or exclusively *yang*. Something that is regarded as *yin* contains forces of *yang*, and vice versa.
4. Interaction and resonance. The two mutually affect each other. Each is reflected in the other.
5. Complementarity. Each side supplies what the other lacks.
6. Transformation. Neither is absolute. Both evolve and go through correlated strengthening and weakening processes. (Wang 2012, 8–11)

These six features are crucial to our understanding of the *yin-yang* relation. In addition, we can add a seventh feature: Mutual Enhancement and Growth. Mutual enhancement comes out of, yet is more than, mutual complementation and transformation. In forming a unity, *yin* and *yang* strengthen each other and promote each other in generating harmony. When this happens, the whole is greater than the sum of the two considered separately. Each side involved is enhanced and enriched. In the family, for instance, when husband and wife interact and collaborate in accordance with a flexible *yin-yang* philosophy, they will not only complement each other but also enhance each other in their existence and growth toward wholeness in life.

How does a *yin-yang* philosophy help us advance a model of the family with equality? One such solution has been proposed by Kelly Clark and Robin R. Wang (2004). Clark and Wang maintain that the Confucian case for gender equity need not depend on gender differences. They propose that women should seek to balance their *yin* and *yang*:

What follows for women, therefore, is that women with a natural preponderance of *yin* should have their own moral manuals that prescribe rituals for the cultivation of *yang*. Women, with a predominance of *yin*, are more disposed toward peace, patience, benevolence, sympathy, submissiveness, listening, and so on. Women should be granted access to role-specific

DIFFERENTIATED GENDER EQUILIBRIUM   131

activities designed for the cultivation of *yang* capacities. The Confucian *Analects* for women would include instruction in war, leading, initiating, and dominating. (Clark and Wang 2004, 415)

Clark and Wang are being cautious not to generalize their proposal to all women. Obviously, their recommendation does not apply to women who already possess plenty of *yang*, such as the ancient woman warrior Mulan and the former UK prime minister "iron lady" Margaret Thatcher (1925–2013). In the meantime, from their proposal, one can also infer that men with a natural preponderance of *yang* may need to cultivate more *yin* to achieve a similar balance as women who have cultivated *yang* adequately. One question arising here is, would such moves make men and women alike? If in modern societies, the two sexes indeed lose their traditional gender roles, how can husband and wife be differentiated today?

As we work with the Confucian *yin-yang* philosophy, I suggest that we take *yin* and *yang* as conceptual metaphors for interpreting our experience and for understanding our world rather than firmly delineated concepts, along the line of the conceptual metaphor theory developed by George Lakoff and Mark Johnson (1980). As conceptual metaphors, *yin* and *yang* are not to be defined strictly. They are cognitive tools that we can use to map our experienced world. On the basis of such an understanding, I further propose to reconceptualize a flexible *yin-yang* model of spousal relations. For such a model, one important step to take is to delink the fixed association of husband with *yang* and of wife with *yin*. This, however, is not necessarily to reverse the associations as some radical feminists might suggest. Instead, we need to understand *yin* and *yang* as relation-based qualities rather than entity-based qualities. An entity-based quality defines the quality of an entity by itself. For example, a dog has four legs. This four-leggedness as an entity-based quality goes with the dog, regardless of where it is and in what relation it is with regard to other things. In contrast, whether a dog is large is not an entity-based quality but a relative quality. A Border Collie may be large in comparison with a Chihuahua, but it may be small standing next to a Great Dane. A Chihuahua may be large in comparison with another. *Yin* and *yang* are relative qualities rather than entity-based qualities. A relative quality exists only in relation to other things; nothing is *yin* or *yang* in and by itself. A man may be *yang* in relation to his son but is *yin* in relation to his father. A woman is *yin* in relation to her mother but is *yang* in relation to her younger sister. In this reading of *yin-yang*, therefore, it is a mistake to identify

132   RESHAPING CONFUCIANISM: A PROGRESSIVE INQUIRY

the wife solely as a person of *yin* and the husband exclusively as a person of *yang*. Furthermore, even between two persons, one's *yin* or *yang* quality vis-à-vis the other is not always fixed. The author(s) of the ancient text *Chuci* 楚辭 described a kind of change called "switched positions of *yin* and *yang*."[32] Although a king is *yang* in relation to his minister and the minister is *yin*, when the minister usurps power and controls the king, their *yin-yang* relation is reversed. Similarly, a woman is typically considered as *yin* and her father as *yang* in their relation, however when her father becomes old and frail, in some aspects of their relation she becomes *yang* and he becomes *yin*. This means that within a relation, the roles of *yin* and *yang* can change, either in whole or in part. On such a flexible understanding of *yin* and *yang* as relative qualities, a person has many roles to play in life, some as *yin* and others as *yang*. When we apply this reading of *yin-yang* philosophy to the husband–wife relation, we can understand their roles not only as fluid and adjustable but also as multifaceted, namely that each person can play the role of *yin* in some aspects and *yang* in other aspects of the family life. Thus, we can achieve *differentiated differentiations* between husband and wife, as opposed to uniform differentiations either between husband being superior and wife being inferior or between husband for external affairs and wife for internal affairs of the family. Such a conception of differentiation provides more room to flexibly accommodate specific circumstances in the family.

This new understanding of *yin* and *yang* supports a theoretical framework of husband–wife relation in our times. On the basis of such a rehabilitated *yin-yang* conception, where *yin* and *yang* are relative characteristics, a flexible *yin-yang* model of spousal relations can preserve differentiated roles in a reasonable form and also accommodates gender equality in the family. In such a theoretical framework, we delink the exclusive connection of wife with *yin* and of husband with *yang*. Neither husband nor wife is exclusive *yin* or exclusively *yang*. Either spouse can be *yin* or *yang* on different aspects of family life in accordance with their relative characteristics. For instance, the wife can play a *yang* role in remodeling the home whereas the husband can play a *yang* role taking care of the family garden. One can play both *yin* roles and *yang* roles simultaneously but in different aspects of family life. In the meantime, neither *yin* nor *yang* in some respects show the inferiority or superiority of the whole person. Such a model provides a foundation for sex equality and gender equality with differentiation in the family.

Such a reformed understanding of *yin* and *yang* can accommodate family needs in contemporary societies. In his discussion of Okin's model, Richard

DIFFERENTIATED GENDER EQUILIBRIUM   133

Arneson presents a scenario where the wife is a cardiologist, and the husband is less than professionally successful (Arneson 1997). Arneson argues that, in such cases, the wife should play a leading role in the family. The traditional *yin-yang* role assignment defines the wife exclusively as *yin* and the husband exclusively as *yang*. In such a view, this "reverse" of traditional spousal roles would be an infelicitous "switch" of the positions of *yin* and *yang* in the sense that *yin* unduly overtakes *yang*. In the entity-based reading, such a "reverse" would make the family "unduly strong in *yin* and unduly weak in *yang*."[33] However, if we delink the exclusive wife-*yin* and husband-*yang* connections, we can read the situation differently. In the scenario presented by Arneson, there are still *yin-yang* role assignments in the family, where the wife is *yang* and the husband is *yin* in one important aspect of their family life. Such an arrangement would be in principle no different from having a female CEO in a company with male employees in subordination. Family life is multi-faceted, however. In Arneson's example, the cardiologist wife can be in the leading role in the family in some important ways (e.g., perhaps in deciding where to relocate the family for her professional growth). In other aspects of their family affairs, the husband may lead, in deciding what kind of house and which house to purchase for the family—if he is good at these things, and which school their children should attend or where their next family vacation trip will take place, for instance. Hence, he is *yang* in these aspects of their family life.

On the conception of *yin-yang* as relative qualities, the family becomes "unduly strong in *yin* and unduly weak in *yang*" only when neither husband nor wife takes any leading role, and both remain inactive in family activities. A family can also become "unduly strong in *yang* and unduly weak in *yin*" when both the husband and wife fight for the leading role in the same aspect of the family life and neither is willing to accommodate the other. In either case, family harmony is in jeopardy. *Differentiated differentiation* between husband and wife can avoid such problems.

Furthermore, role assignments in the family are not fixed; they do not have to be permanent. A dual-career couple, for instance, may alternate priorities and take turns in shouldering more housework, depending on career needs and family needs. Subject to family circumstances, each half of the couple can take, and alternate, a leading role at different times. By taking turns in playing the leading role in the family, the couple practices the *Dao* of "the conjunction and alternation of *yin* and *yang*."[34] As discussed above, in the family the same person can be *yin* and *yang* in different aspects of family

134   RESHAPING CONFUCIANISM: A PROGRESSIVE INQUIRY

life at the same time and be so in different ways. On this proposed theoretical model, husband and wife still play different roles in the family, without being fixed one way or another. On specific cases and in different stages of life, spouses may play reversed roles that manifest the *yin-yang* philosophy in different ways. In such an ongoing process, husband and wife achieve and maintain differentiated equilibrium.

Besides the theoretical framework in terms of a flexible *yin* and *yang* conception, there is also a practical consideration. That is, there can nevertheless be gender patterns of division of family labor between the sexes on the basis of general biological and physical characteristics, even though these can be overridden by personal interest, talents, and circumstantial needs. "Woman" in a gendered sense does not have to disappear altogether to achieve gender equality. Take childrearing as an example. In *yin-yang* philosophy, childrearing is associated with *yin* in family affairs in contrast with other family matters such as family business. *Yin* is closely associated with tenderness, patience, and subtlety, which are important traits for working with children. A key feature of *yin* is to be accommodating, which is particularly suitable for childrearing. It is reasonable to anticipate that, due to usual biological differences between men and women, the wife as a mother in most cases tends to possess more "mothering" characteristics than the husband with regard to childrearing. Having gone through a nine-month pregnancy, women are usually more inclined to care for their babies than men are. For this and other reasons, wives are more associated with childrearing in a large proportion of families. This feature makes it more natural and feasible for women to mother children. Such an arrangement is also more efficient for the family. In the meantime, the role of the husband must include responsibilities to assist the wife and to compensate for her labor in appropriate ways.

Furthermore, such an arrangement along biological lines does not have to be categorical and absolute. Husband can take a "mothering" role as well. As in Nancy Meyers' movie *The Intern*, the couple Jules and Matt switched traditional family roles for the good of the family. Whereas Jules is dedicated to "About The Fit," a fast-growing, e-commerce fashion startup in Brooklyn, Matt gave up his own career to be a stay-at-home dad to their daughter, Paige. Through ups and downs, and various adjustments, the couple complements each other by balancing a successful family business and meaningful family life. There are situations where one member of the couple may have to shoulder a larger share of less desirable tasks in the family. When this happens, appropriate arrangements should be made to compensate inequity in the family to maintain equality, even though the appropriateness of these arrangements may be family specific or even person specific.

One question may arise. Even with allowing variations, am I still holding an entity-based conception of *yin-yang* ? Am I claiming that men or women are particular ways solely due to their biological makeup? The answer is no. *Yin* and *yang* being relative qualities do not mean entity attributes are entirely irrelevant. Let me illustrate this point with an example. Imagine that in a hypothetical place most women are about 1.7 meters in height and that most men are 1.8 meters. Then it is likely that in most couples, the man is taller than his female counterpart. As an entity-quality, each person's height alone does not determine whether one is taller or shorter. But it does matter in determining one's relative quality. Likewise, because it is women who are born with female characteristics and go through pregnancy, they are likely to be more inclined to be suited for certain tasks in the family. Such a correlation between female biology and the motherly gender role in the family is a weak one, however. It does not mean that the husband cannot play a nurturing role in the family—in some cases the husband can be more motherly than his wife. Nor does it mean that the wife cannot serve an active and leading role in the family. More importantly, as far as the wife plays a leading role in childrearing, she is also *yang* rather than *yin* in making pertinent decisions on childrearing. In such an arrangement, she leads and her husband follows.

The model I propose here has two main features. The first feature is that it draws on the *yin-yang* philosophy as a theoretical framework to address an important contemporary challenge. By reinterpreting the concepts of *yin-yang* and introducing the concept of *differentiated differentiations*, we diversify differences between husband and achieve gender equality without becoming uprooted from cultural tradition. The second feature is that the model provides adequate flexibility in family role assignments without eliminating gender altogether. If the above model is feasible, we will have both family harmony on the basis of differentiation and gender equality. The former satisfies the philosophy of Confucianism; the latter meets the challenge of contemporary societies. Together, such a move establishes gender equality on a profound cultural foundation. Of course, for people outside the Confucian tradition, such a flexible scheme for gender equality does not have to be framed in Confucian *yin-yang* philosophy. As far as Confucianism is concerned, however, such a solution should prove satisfactory on both fronts.

To recapitulate, of the three main ideas of the spousal relation in traditional Confucianism, progressive Confucians can preserve the idea of differentiation and complementarity for the sake of family harmony, while rejecting the outdated division of labor along the internal–external lines and the idea that the husband is superior to wife. As times have changed, the division of labor between husband and wife must properly reflect new social realities. When appropriately reconstructed, Confucian *yin-yang* philosophy provides a good conceptual tool for family harmony on the basis of differentiation, without the traditional stereotyped view that disadvantages women. Equality between the sexes can be achieved without giving up on gender differences and without jeopardizing family harmony.[35]

Let me conclude with a response to Jiang Qing's comments about women in contemporary society. I note that the aspiration for women to become good daughters, good wives, good mothers, and good career persons must go together with the aspiration for men to become good sons, good husbands, good fathers, and good career persons. And, both men and women should aspire to play good family roles inside, and good social roles outside, the family.

Study Questions

1. What are the main ideas of gender roles in traditional Confucianism?
2. What are the parallels between traditional Confucian view of gender relations and the traditional view in the West?
3. What is your view of Susan Okin's philosophy of gender equality? Do you agree with her proposal? Why or why not?
4. Explain the difference between entity-based qualities and relation-based qualities.
5. Can you explain the Confucian *yin-yang* philosophy in your own words?
6. In the view of the author, can *yin* and *yang* actually be equated to genders? Explain.
7. What are main features of the flexible *yin-yang* model of spousal relation as proposed by the author?
8. Explain *differentiated differentiation* between the husband and wife as articulated by the author.
9. In your view, would the proposed framework work? Do you have an alternative solution, especially with regard to the relation between sex and gender?

6

Friendship

Friendship is one of the five fundamental human relationships articulated by Mengzi, along with relationships between parents and children, ruler and subjects, husband and wife, elder sibling and younger sibling (*Mengzi* 3A4). It is a relationship that has become increasingly important in modern lives as the locus of people's interactions has shifted largely from traditional rural kin-centeredness to urban settings where social networks are primarily of people of non-relations.[1] Progressive Confucianism must take friendship even more seriously than it has been treated by classic thinkers so it can appropriately reflect the important role of friendship in contemporary times. The purpose of this chapter is to present the Confucian conception of friendship as a moral ideal, rather than accounting for all types of friendship as actually practiced in society.[2] I explicate the Confucian conception by investigating its two special features. The first of these features is that Confucian friendship is based on virtue. The main purpose of friendship is to foster virtue with friends for a virtuous life. I argue that the Confucian conception for friends to share virtues does not preclude friends from possessing individuality, which is prized in modern lives. The second feature is that Confucians give friendship a special role in a person's life and friends are regarded as extended family. On the basis of these features, I also examine how this Confucian conception can respond to the fungibility problem of friendship.

1. Particularized Virtues

The Confucian conception of friendship is grounded explicitly on virtue. The *Analects* advocates the ideal of promoting *ren* 仁 (comprehensive virtue) with friendship. It quotes Kongzi's disciple Zengzi that virtuous persons (*junzi*) "advance *ren* with friendship" (*Analects* 12.24). *Ren* is the highest ideal of the good life in Kongzi's *Analects*. Friendship is meant to be achieved along with realizing the virtue of *ren*. Mengzi says explicitly that, in making friends, one should "befriend the person's virtues" (*Mengzi* 5B3). In such a

Reshaping Confucianism. Chenyang Li, Oxford University Press. © Oxford University Press 2024.
DOI: 10.1093/oso/9780197657621.003.0007

view, a good person embodies good virtues. When we find a good person as a friend, it is these virtues that endear the person to us. Xunzi explicates the meaning of the word "friend/friendship," *you* 友, with its homophone 有, to have, to possess, in a form of mutuality. He claims that "friendships are how people hold to each other" (*xiangyou* 相有; *Xunzi*, chapter 27; Hutton 2014, 313). Xunzi maintains that the foundation of such mutuality is the *Dao*, as people who do not share the *Dao* cannot be friends because they have nothing to hold each other together (ibid.). For all these thinkers, friends are people who share common values, learn from each other, and help each other develop virtues. What they mutually have serves as the foundation of their friendship. The requirement of virtue for friendship, however, does not imply that having virtue is the only condition for friendship. The formation of a friendship requires more, personality being one of them. Two virtuous persons may not make a good match for being friends. The point is, however, like in Aristotle's conception of true friendship, shared virtue is central to Confucian friendship.[3]

A question arises. Would this emphasis on common virtues make Confucian friends without individuality? I will argue that the answer is no. Not only do Confucian friends retain their own personalities aside from commonly shared virtues, but Confucian virtues are also individualized in persons.

In academic literature, two approaches have been employed to account for friendship. The particularist approach uses specific factors to explain a friendship, appealing to friends' unique qualities and the particular circumstances of the origin of a friendship. On this account, someone is a friend because of the special qualities that she possesses in a distinctive way, and due to the particular circumstances in which friends find each other. As presented in the American television sitcom *The Big Bang Theory*, Leonard and Sheldon are both unique personalities, who become friends not only because Leonard is drawn to Sheldon by the latter's exceptional brilliance, but also because at their beginning Leonard is looking for a room whereas Sheldon happens to need a roommate. In contrast, the universalist approach to friendship gives general reasons for being friends, appealing to their good qualities or virtues. On the latter account, one would say that Leonard and Sheldon become friends because they share a common interest in science, and both are curious and inquisitive, etc. Either approach, however, encounters problems. Particularist reasons seem idiosyncratic and subjective, or even arbitrary, while good reasons require a degree of generality. Universalist reasons point

FRIENDSHIP   139

to general traits shared by many, making these reasons equally good reasons for being friends with all people of the same or similar qualities.[4] Yet friends are always particularly selected persons with individuality. As a virtue-based approach to friendship, the Confucian conception appears universalistic in orientation. Virtues are presumably generic and shared. Then, how can Confucians accommodate individuality in friendship? I argue that, in the Confucian conception of virtue-building ethics, the fact that virtues are generic and shared by many does not imply that they are possessed and practiced in the same way. Confucian virtues are particularized through personal cultivation; it is in the particular ways people possess and practice virtues that Confucians find grounds for individuality.[5]

Without any doubt, traditional Chinese thought recognizes personal individuality. The classic text of *The Lüshi Chunqiu* (*Lü Annuals of the Spring and Autumn* 呂氏春秋) records a famous story of two true friends, Yu Boya 俞伯牙 and Zhong Ziqi 鍾子期. Yu was an extraordinary zither player and Zhong was his best friend and most dedicated listener; the latter was characterized as Yu's *zhiyin* 知音; that is, someone who truly understood, appreciated, and resonated with Yu's music. As the legend goes, when Zhong died, Yu was in deep sorrow and broke his own zither because he believed that no one else would be able to truly appreciate his music. His friend Zhong was unique and irreplaceable. Kongzi was attentive to people's particularities in acquiring and developing virtues. The *Records of History* (*Shiji* 史記) reports Kongzi noting that his seventy-two disciples were equipped respectively with special talents (*yi neng* 異能).[6] Yanhui, Min Ziqian, Boniu, and Zhonggong were exemplary of virtuous conduct; Zaiwo and Zigong were known for being good at using language appropriately; Ranqiu and Jilu were exceptional in attending to administrative affairs; and Ziyou and Zixia shone in literature. However, each disciple also had varied weaknesses. Shi was biased. Shen was slow. Zhai was dull. Zhongyou was careless.[7] Presumably, Kongzi's disciples all had acquired such virtues as *ren* (humaneness and care), *yi* (rightness, appropriateness), *li* (ritual propriety), and *zhi* (wisdom), which were at the core of Kongzi's teaching.[8] Yet, they achieved these in varying degrees and practiced them in different ways. In the *Analects*, Kongzi responded to numerous disciples on how to become virtuous (*ren*). Each time he gave a different answer. For him, each person was different and needed to develop virtue in accordance with one's specific circumstances. To some, Kongzi said that to be virtuous is to "care about people" (*Analects* 12.22). To others, it is about following ritual propriety (*li* 禮, *Analects* 12.1). Yet to some other people, it is about studying

140 RESHAPING CONFUCIANISM: A PROGRESSIVE INQUIRY

hard (*Analects* 19.6), being mindful in speaking (*Analects* 12.3), and being respectful toward others and being diligent with work (*Analects* 13.19). To be sure, these records themselves do not indicate directly that Kongzi advocated particularized virtues. One may even think that Kongzi merely prescribed what he perceived as lacking in these disciples and wished them to become more virtuous in respective aspects, and hence Kongzi only wanted people to make up for what is deficient in each person, and that developing respective virtues will make them alike. However, there is clear evidence to prove that Confucian philosophy subscribes to a concept of particularized virtue, as shown next. According to such a view, a person does not necessarily become generic when acquiring virtues because virtues are always instantiated in particular ways.

For Kongzi, virtues need to be practiced and developed in ways appropriate to individual persons. While it is true that each person should pay particular attention to developing the virtues that he or she lacks, such effort must be carried out in person-specific ways. Hence, shared virtues do not make people lose individuality. This can be seen in the following ways. First, even though two persons develop the same virtues, they may not have achieved the same degree of virtuousness. The excavated text *Wuxing* (*Shuo*) 五行 (說) quotes Kongzi as saying:

> [Sage king] Shun possesses the virtue of *ren*, so do I. Yet my virtue of *ren* is not as good as Shun's, because I have not accumulated as much virtue. Shun possesses the virtue of *yi*, so do I. Yet my virtue of *yi* is not as good as Shun's, because I have not accumulated as much virtue. (Wei 2005, 117)[9]

Varying degrees of achievement of the same virtue set two persons apart. Possessing the same virtue does not make people homogenous.

Second, in the Confucian view, persons in possession of the same virtue may practice it in different ways appropriate to their respective circumstances. Take the sage-king Shun as an example. Mengzi repeatedly praised Shun for being filial (e.g., *Mengzi* 4A28, 5A4, 6B4). In *Mengzi* 5A1, someone asks Mengzi whether the sage-king Shun acted in a filial way when he got married without telling his parents in advance. The background assumption of the query is that filial sons should get their parents' blessings before marriage. The inquirer refers to the Confucian classic *Book of Poetry* (*Shijing* 詩經), "when one gets married, he must tell his parents first." But in this case, Shun did not. Was Shun's act unfilial? Mengzi defends Shun by stating Shun was still treating his parents filially because marriage establishes a great human relationship and that, if he had told his parents beforehand, they would not have allowed him to marry. It would have not only undermined a great spousal relationship for Shun, but it would also have caused further antagonism between Shun and his parents. According to legend, Shun's parents were malicious toward him and did not wish him to have a good life. Had Shun told them of his upcoming marriage, they would have ruined it. In Mengzi's view, under ordinary situations, one should tell their well-meaning parents before marriage; but in Shun's case, not telling them in advance was the right thing to do because it not only allowed him to establish a family but also prevented his parents from committing more immoral acts. Seen this way, not only was Shun's act not a violation of morality, it was actually one of moral care for his parents (see my discussion of moral care in Chapter 4 of this book).

Because the same generic virtue may be practiced differently, the Confucian virtue approach to friendship does not exclude the particularity of individual persons. Two of your friends may both care about how you conduct yourself. Yet one may be more straightforward with you and the other may help you in a gentle way. Two friends can both be frugal. Yet one may be frugal to everyone whereas the other is frugal only with herself and is generous with others. Therefore, two virtuous persons in possession of the same kind of virtue may nevertheless practice them in different ways. A person may appreciate a virtue to be practiced in one way or another, but not in just any way. For example, Jennifer may appreciate her friend being very direct in pointing out her mistakes, whereas Megan may prefer a gentle course of correction. In cases like these, someone of the same virtue of honesty may make a good friend with Jennifer but not with Megan or vice versa. While the shared generic virtue is a general good, the particularized way of practicing such virtue is an additional good to the friend in question. As has been argued by Dean Cocking and Jeanette Kennett (2000), it is a constitutive feature of friendship that friends are characteristically receptive to being directed and interpreted in certain ways. In such a process, friends shape each other as they maintain their relationships. Thus, the very act of being friends may further reinforce people's particular ways of acting virtuously, and effective interactions with friends make a person particularly suitable for being friends with a certain type of people with whom she has been friends.[10]

The third and perhaps the most important reason for Confucian virtues to be particularized is that various virtues may relate to one another differently in different persons. A person possesses multiple virtues. Even in the

142 RESHAPING CONFUCIANISM: A PROGRESSIVE INQUIRY

scenario where two persons possess and practice the same virtue in the same way, it is practically impossible for them to practice *all* virtues in the same way. Moreover, the Confucian view of coordinating virtues in a person's life also makes a positive claim on a person's uniqueness in virtuousness. In explicating Confucian virtues, the excavated text *Wuxing* (*Shuo*) discusses personal uniqueness (*du* 獨). It states:

> What is to be watchful of one's uniqueness? It means to carefully keep the five virtues in one's heart. When a person reaches his uniqueness in this way, he reaches oneness. Reaching oneness this way is to be [really] virtuous.[11]

The five virtues here are *ren* 仁 (humaneness and care), *yi* 義 (rightness, appropriateness), *li* 禮 (ritual propriety), *zhi* 智 (wisdom), *sheng* 聖 (sageliness). Then, why can a person achieve uniqueness by keeping the five virtues in his heart? If every one of the five virtues is the same and people keep the same five virtues in their hearts, how is it possible for them to be unique? The author suggests that such uniqueness is achieved by harmonizing the five virtues into an appropriate configuration in one's heart and that in doing so each person coordinates these virtues in particular ways appropriate to varied circumstances. The *Wuxing* maintains that when a person harmonizes these five virtues, he is indeed virtuous in the real sense. These virtues cover different aspects of a good life. Yet they are also connected. Bringing them into good coordination makes possible a holistic yet unique virtuous life, in what the text calls oneness. The *Wuxing* states:

> When the five virtues take form, the virtuous heart arises. Harmonizing them is called virtuousness. The essence of virtuousness lies in its achieving oneness. (Liu Zhao 2003, 16)[12]

As explicated in Chapter 1 of this book, Confucian harmony (*he* 和) is a concerted unity achieved through the active coordination of various components.[13] A harmonized "oneness" of these five virtues may be configured in varied ways in different people and hence brings uniqueness to each person as each one's circumstances differ, even though people share overlapping commonalities. In this way, individuality is retained even when people share the same generic virtues.

The above three considerations of particularized virtues, namely varying degrees of moral attainment of the same virtue, different ways of practicing virtue, and harmonizing various virtues in unique ways in particular persons, jointly establish the individuality of virtuous persons for the Confucian conception of friendship. The conception of virtues as particularized in different individuals does not imply that a virtue in a generic sense is not a good. Surely it is. But it is always instantiated on individual persons in particular ways. This argument establishes, however, that particularized virtues make their possessors unique with respect to the virtues, and a person of particularized virtues may be especially suitable for being friends with a certain type of people. While Confucian virtues as generic traits are shared commonality, their attainment and practice leave ample room for particularity. The generality of virtues determines that Confucian friendship is not arbitrary or utterly subjective; particularized virtues contribute to and maintain individuality. Thus, through the particularization of general virtues, Confucian virtue-based conception provides an alternative to both universalist and particularist accounts of friendship.

2. Friends as Family

Let me begin to explicate this second important feature of the Confucian conception of friendship with two stories. The *Analects* records that one of Kongzi's friends died, without having any kin to hold a funeral. Kongzi said, "let him be given a funeral from my home" (*Analects* 10.15). Usually, only family members or close kin are expected to host funerals for the dead. Kongzi went a step further in helping his deceased friend. Chapter *Tan-Gong A* of the *Book of Rites* records that, when Kongzi died, some of his disciples wondered about what kind of clothes they should wear in mourning their teacher. A leading disciple Zigong said:

> When Kongzi was mourning Yanyuan, he did not wear special mourning clothes but mourned Yanyuan as his own son. Kongzi did the same for Zilu. Let us mourn our master as our own father without special mourning clothes. (TTC, 1284)

Yanyuan was one of Kongzi's top disciples. When Yanyuan died, Kongzi was as devastated as if he lost his own son. When Kongzi died, some of his disciples were unsure of what ritual to follow in mourning him because he was not just a usual teacher. Zigong cited Kongzi's own example to make a case that they should mourn him as if he was their father. Members of Kongzi's learning community not only learned together as teacher and students but also enjoyed one another's company. If we use one of the five fundamental human relationships to account for the relationships between Kongzi and his disciples, they belong to the category of friendship. This story along with the one of Kongzi burying his deceased friend conveys the sense that good friends are like family and should treat each other accordingly.

How should we understand the similarities between the relationship between friends and the three familial relationships in the five fundamental human relationships, namely between parents and children, between spouses, and between siblings? Sociologist Ambrose King 金耀基 has argued that in the Chinese culture, friendship is conceived in terms of family. As he observes, "the relationship between friend and friend is stated in terms of elder brother (*wu xiong* 吾兄) and younger brother (*wu di* 吾弟)" (King 1985, 58). The Confucian family is the base for distinguishing the "internal" sphere (*nei* 內) as opposed to the "external" sphere (*wai* 外) in society. The Confucian ideal is to expand the "internal" sphere to become more and more inclusive and eventually to reach the entire world, as depicted in the ideal of sagehood. King writes:

> The common expression *zi jia ren* ("our family people") can refer to any person one wants to include; the concept of *zi jia ren* can be contracted or expanded depending upon the circumstances. It can theoretically be extended to an unlimited number of people and thereby becomes what is called *tian xia yi jia* ("all the world belongs to one family"). (King 1985, 61)

We should differentiate people labeled as *zi jia ren* 自家人 out of courteousness in social settings, as it happens in China even today, on the one hand and *zi jia ren* in actual practice on the other. *Zi jia ren* in the real sense must be grounded on well-established relationships. Friends are people with whom such relationships have been established.

Classic stories provide examples of Confucian friendship modeled after family. The popular Chinese novel *Legend of Loyalty and Dutifulness by the Water Margin* (*Zhongyi Shuihu Quanzhuan* 忠義水滸全傳, Shi 1996), a story of the Northern Song Dynasty (960–1127), can be read as a manifestation of the Confucian conception of friendship and how friendship can promote such moral ideals as *zhongyi* 忠義 (Loyalty and Dutifulness) and *tiandao* 天道 (Heavenly *Dao*). It depicts outlaws gathered in a remote region fighting for justice. The 108 characters became close friends with strong bonds among them as in a large family. The novel has been translated into English under the title *All Men Are Brothers*—even though the 108 characters included women—underscoring the Confucian ideal of true friendship as family. Another influential novel, *Romance of the Three Kingdoms* (*San-guo Yanyi* 三國演義, Luo 1996), a story of second-to-third century China, portrays a legendary friendship between three men, Liu Bei, Guan Yu, and Zhang Fei. The novel begins by portraying how the three unrelated men swore broth- erhood in a peach garden. Each of the three exemplifies a Confucian car- dinal value: Liu represents *ren* 仁 (humaneness and care), Guan represents *yi* 義 (appropriateness and dutifulness), while Zhang represents *yong* 勇 (courage and bravery). Legends like these and sociological studies such as Ambrose King's provide strong evidence that, in Confucianism, friendship is conceived in terms of family relationships.[14] This conception does not mean that Confucian friendship is just one of these relationships within a biolog- ical family, nor that the relationship is without its own particular characteris- tics. When they say friends are family, it suggests that Confucian friendship is conceived as one that is included in the Confucian "internal" sphere symbolized by family.

Some Confucian texts distinguish biological family relationships from other relationships that include friendship. The excavated text *Six Virtues* (*Liude* 六德), for example, maintains a stringent notion of the "internal" sphere. It places father, son, and husband in the "internal" sphere and ruler, minister, and wife in the "external" sphere, and it explicitly prioritizes members of the ancestral clan over friends (Cook 2012, 791). Even on such stringent notions of family relationships, Confucian friends are never- theless conceived as a social circle immediately right next to family, to be differentiated from "mere acquaintances" (*suo zhi* 所知[15]) and other social relationships. To be more appropriate, we should say that, in the Confucian conception, rather than friends *being* family, friends are *like* family. To say that friends are like family implies that friends should be treated as family in relevant ways.

There is a puzzle remaining with this account of the Confucian family conception of friendship, however. Even though the idea that friends are like family has been entrenched broadly and deeply in the Confucian tradi- tion, we cannot find a formal articulation of this view in classic texts. Indeed, *Analects* 10.15, quoted earlier in this chapter, seems to be the closest passage in the text to hint at a connection between friendship and family. As Xiufen

146 RESHAPING CONFUCIANISM: A PROGRESSIVE INQUIRY

Lu has pointed out, even though Ambrose King used historical and sociological evidence in support of his claim regarding the Confucian family conception of friendship, King was unable to "draw any textual evidence from the Confucian corpus to support his claim" (Lu 2010, 226). If Confucian thinkers take friends to be like family, why didn't they articulate such a conception explicitly in classic texts? Without answering this question, the claim that Confucians model friends after the family is suspect.

I believe that this puzzle can be solved by an etymological examination of the Chinese word for friend, *you* 友. The ancient character of *you* is written in the form of 𦥑, symbolizing the two hands of a person, suggesting resemblance and close relationship. Research by numerous scholars has demonstrated that, during the Western Zhou period (eleventh century BCE to 771 BCE), *you* along with the compound term *pengyou* 朋友[16] meant kinsman or clansman. Zha Changguo's study shows that, in Western Zhou bronze inscriptions, *you* and *zu* 族 (clan) have been used interchangeably, indicating their common designation. The fact that *pengyou* appear side by side with *hungou* 婚媾 (relatives by marriage), but not with father, son, and brothers, suggests that these internal family roles were included in the category of *pengyou*. Zha concludes that *you* meant members of a clan (*zuren* 族人). Subsequently in history, *you* was used to describe affable relationships beyond kinship (Zha 1998). Maria Khayutina's research shows that those designated as *you* during the time period took part in sacrificial rituals for ancestors, further evidence to indicate that *you* were members of the same clan. The term was a common name for associates among kin relatives—members of *zongzu* 宗族 of various generations and degrees (Khayutina 1999). Zhu Fenghan also draws the same conclusion in his study of bronze inscriptions during the Western Zhou period and points out that similar usages were retained during the Eastern Zhou period ("Spring-Autumn," 770 BCE–476 BCE) (Zhu 2004). These studies show that *you* as friend in the sense in which we today understand it grew out of its earlier meaning associated with family.[17] The Confucian conception of friendship should be understood against this etymological background.

During or soon after the "Spring and Autumn" period, the early meaning of *you* as kin and clan gradually shifted to brotherhood and started explicitly to carry an affable quality. Chapter *Juncheng* of the *Book of History* (*Shang Shu* 尚書) prescribes "to *you* with brothers (*you yu xiongdi* 友于兄弟)," with *you* used as a verb.[18] The *Erya* 爾雅, one of the earliest Chinese lexicons and one of the Confucian *Thirteen Classics*, defines *you* as a characteristic of good brotherhood. It states, "treating parents well is called *xiao* (filial care); treating brothers well is called *you*."[19] In other words, *you* is fraternal love, an ideal relationship between brothers. When brothers treat each other well, with mutual love and care, they are called *you*. Such a good relationship is conceptualized in parallel with good child-parent relationships. Both are family relationships.

You as a characteristic of good brotherhood is also found in other Confucian classic texts. The *Zuo Commentary* (*Zuozhuan* 左傳) states that elder brothers become *you* by loving (younger brothers).[20] In the *Xunzi*, when asked about being a good elder brother, Xunzi said, it is about loving and becoming a *you* to younger siblings (*Xunzi*, chapter 12). On the basis of this earlier meaning of *you* as brotherhood within the family, calling a non-family person *you* already places such a person on par with family members. Thus, it would have been redundant to make an argument that a *you* is like family. This is similar to the case when we extend the use of "brother" to non-family members in close relationship with us, we do not need to say that a brother is family: saying "you are my brother" to a non-biologically related person already implies that he is like family. By placing the word *you* in its etymological context, we can explain why classic Confucian thinkers did not (need to) argue explicitly that a friend is like family. The acceptance of the use of *you* for friends already implies accepting friends as family.

Numerous classics advocate the understanding of *you* as "people who share the same aspirations."[21] According to Chapter *Jinyu* of the classic text *Discourse on the States* (*Guoyu* 國語), the expression of "people who share the same aspirations" originally refers to brothers with the same moral virtues.[22] Hence, on this understanding, regarding someone as a *you* (friend) is just to regard him (or her) as a sibling who shares with us the same moral virtues and aspirations. In this idealized notion of friend, virtue and family bond are connected. One would not take an unrelated person into one's own "internal" sphere unless that person is virtuous. On the basis of the above examination, I conclude that, in the Confucian conception of friendship, friends are non-blood related people whom we consider as family.

3. Confucian Response to Fungibility Problem

If we are asked why we are friends with someone, we usually point out some virtues or good qualities of the friend as reasons. But if these are the reasons,

148 RESHAPING CONFUCIANISM: A PROGRESSIVE INQUIRY

we should be friends with anyone with these qualities, and we can even replace our current friends with anyone in possession of these qualities without substantive loss in friendship. However, it does not feel right to say that a particular friend is replaceable by just any other person with the same qualities. After all, true friends do not betray each other; we do not trade friends for advantage as we trade commodities. No true friend can look at another friend in the eyes and say, "I am friends with you because you are virtuous, but I can replace you when I find a more virtuous person." But then, if friends are not to be replaced like that, what is the reason or reasons? Here arises the fungibility problem of friendship. In the rest of this chapter, I will explore how the Confucian conception of friendship can respond to such a challenge.

In the literature on friendship fungibility, some thinkers bite the bullet and accept fungibility in friendship. In a sense, friends are indeed replaceable. At some point in life, everyone loses friends and finds new ones. It is indeed not a problem when this happens if we talk about friends in a loose sense. You participate in a month-long summer camp and make many new friends there. You keep in touch with them for a while afterwards even when you are reunited with your other, long-time friends in school or at home. Then, gradually your summer camp friendships fade away. New friendships are formed to take their place. Thus, friends seem fungible. The fungibility problem discussed in this chapter, however, is confined to what we may call "true friends," to those whom Confucians would treat like family, rather than casual friends or "mere acquaintances" (*suo zhi* 所知). The problem is not merely about whether friends change over time but *whether one can intentionally replace a friend for one's own benefit without substantive loss*. Substantive loss can be either sentimental or moral. Losing a loved one can result in a sentimental loss. Doing things that compromise one's moral integrity brings forth a moral loss, an injury to morality. The problem is both practical and theoretical. Practically, should we treat our friends as fungible in real life? Theoretically or philosophically, if the merits of our friends are the foundation of our friendships as people often think, would that make our friends fungible?

In view of Confucian friendship, the problem of friendship fungibility can be examined in two categories. First, it is about a challenge to the virtue-based conception of friendship, namely, if friendship is justified on the ground of virtue, whether one can be justified to replace a friend with another person of the same set of virtues without substantive loss. We can call this issue "fungibility on common virtues." The second kind is more radical.

It is about whether friends are fungible irrespective of the basis of friendship, virtue-based or not. I believe either kind of fungibility is at odds with our common moral sensibilities. We usually hold that we are friends with someone for the particular individual that she is, and for *her* virtues, rather than with just anyone who happens to instantiate these common virtues. Furthermore, a friend is not a thing. Under normal circumstances, we can replace a thing with one of the same or better qualities without substantive loss, but we cannot do that with a friend. In the rest of the chapter, I argue that the two characteristics of the Confucian conception of friendship provide solid grounds for fending off the fungibility challenge.

Let us first examine possible responses to "fungibility on common virtues." One possible solution is to understand friendship on the basis of virtues *plus* a substantiated soul that grounds individuality. Commenting on his friendship with La Boétie, Montaigne said famously:

> In the friendship I speak of, our souls mingle and blend with each other so completely that they efface the seam that joined them, and cannot find it again. If you press me to tell why I loved him, I feel that this cannot be expressed, except by answering: Because it was he, because it was I. (Pakaluk 1991, 192)

On such an account, friends are two souls joined together, as this particular "he" and this particular "I." True friends are "soulmates." Even though people may share the same virtues, each person presumably has only one particular soul that is numerically distinct; hence, a friend cannot be replaced with another, who possesses a different soul. Such a solution can work, however, only if one accepts the existence of distinct souls. Without a commitment to the existence of distinct souls, this solution has no force.

Confucians do not endorse a reified self, such as a soul; hence the "soulmate" account of friendship does not work for them. There is no, or at least no explicit, notion of a reified self in ancient Chinese thought.[23] The closest Chinese counterpart of a "soul" is *po* 魄 or *hun* 魂. *Po* and *hun* are generated by the *yin-yang* forces out of *qi* 氣, the primary material force or vital energy. The *Zuo Commentary* explicates that a person's life begins with forming *po* and *hun* through transformation, and the *po* and *hun* are strong when the more quintessential material is used.[24] In ancient texts, *po* and *hun* are used to account for a person's vital capacities rather than personal identity. Individual identity is usually described by ways of people's familial and social relationships, roles, and deeds. Confucians cannot ground individuality and uniqueness on anything like a God-created soul. Without a solid concept of the soul, the Confucian virtue-based conception of friendship appears vulnerable to the fungibility challenge.

I argue, however, that the Confucian account of particularized virtues provides an effective response to the challenge of "fungibility on common virtues." In this Confucian view, virtues are particularized in individual persons. Each person may acquire, possess, and exercise virtue in a particular way appropriate to specific circumstances. Persons of the same generic virtues will nevertheless retain their respective particularity as distinct individuals with respect to virtue. People become friends and remain friends with each other because of their virtues instantiated and practiced in particular ways. When one loses a friend, there is indeed a loss of virtues as they are instantiated and practiced in that particular person. The challenge of "fungibility on common virtues" argues that friends are fungible because they are the same in terms of virtue. It is the thesis that one can replace a friend with the same virtues *because* these virtuous people are alike. The Confucian particularized virtue account can respond adequately to such a challenge. Confucians can retain a virtue-based conception of friendship without falling victim to this fungibility problem.

The fungibility problem, however, can go even deeper in a radical form. One can argue that even unique things can be fungible. A used book collector, for example, can trade a copy of *Hamlet* from John Dewey's personal library, with Dewey's autograph and annotations, for a copy of *King Lear* from Bertrand Russell's personal library, with Russell's autograph and annotations. Both copies are unique. Nevertheless, she can do so without any sentimental loss if she is not especially fond of *Hamlet* or Dewey. Likewise, she can do so without moral loss because she is not obliged to the collected books previously owned by Dewey. Cases like this suggest that whether something is fungible depends on the nature of the relationship. One needs to show that friendship is a special kind of relationship. To that end, we now look into the other characterization of Confucian friendship, namely friends are like family, and see how it can provide an effective refutation of radical friendship fungibility.

If friends are to be treated like family, then we cannot treat a friend as interchangeable with someone else and we cannot intentionally replace a friend for our own benefit. In Confucian philosophy, family members have special obligations toward one another. Parents are to care for their children

FRIENDSHIP 151

in ways that parents should do, and children are to care for their parents in ways that children should do. These special obligations are not applicable to others in the "external" sphere (e.g., in business dealings), even when others are equally virtuous or needy. On such a Confucian conception, once a friendship has been formed, friends treat each other like family. There is a special bond between friends, and they have special responsibilities toward each other.

Understood this way, there is an asymmetry between before a friendship is formed and afterwards, as one between before and after a new member joins a family. Before a child is born to a family, the child could be any of an infinite number of possible children. Once a child has been born into a family, she has come into a relationship with her parents and older siblings. Her parents can no longer abandon her, even if they could have had a more loveable child. Similarly, before a particular friendship is formed, one has a range of possibilities for making the next new friend, without the obligation to become friends with any particular person. One should choose friends carefully and choose only those with virtue, but there is nothing ethically inappropriate if one fails to become friends with anyone, including those with virtue. However, once a friendship has been formed the situation changes. Friends have duties toward each other,[25] including a duty not to abandon each other, even if other people could have been "better" friends. Just as one cannot simply trade her own child for another equally or more loveable child, one cannot replace a friend with another person with similar or even superior qualities. On such an account, Confucian friendship is not fungible.[26]

This is not to say, of course, that one can never break up with friends. In extraordinary situations, one can break off a close friendship, just as in extraordinary situations one can even disown family members. If, in these extreme circumstances, even family relationships are not absolutely inviolable, then friends, even understood as family, are also replaceable.

Confucian thinkers have differed on the extent of our obligations toward maintaining the wholeness of the family. As previously discussed in Chapter 4, Kongzi seems to have held a strong view on the inviolability of the family. For instance, in the *Analects* 13.18, he suggests that father and son should not report to authorities each other's inappropriate behaviors, presumably to maintain a strong family tie. Xunzi, however, allows moral integrity to override narrowly defined family obligations, with the former carrying greater weight in regulating moral conduct (*Xunzi*, chapter 29). Xunzi's view suggests that narrowly defined family wholeness is not absolute. Along with

152   RESHAPING CONFUCIANISM: A PROGRESSIVE INQUIRY

such a view, one may infer that Confucian friendship is not absolute either. The *Mengzi* records a conversation between Mengzi and King Xuan of Qi, as follows:

> Mengzi said to King Xuan of Qi, "Suppose a subject of your majesty's, having entrusted his wife and children to the care of a friend, were to go on a trip to the state of Chu, only to find, upon his return, that his friend had allowed his wife and children to suffer cold and hunger, then what should he do about it?"
> "Break with his friend."
> "If the Marshal of the Guards was unable to keep his guards in order, then what should be done about it?"
> "Remove him from office."
> "If the whole realm within the four borders was ill-governed, then what should be done about it?"
> The King turned to his attendants and changed the subject.
> (Mengzi 1B6; Lau 1970, 66–67, modified)

With the analogies of a case where one should break up with his untrustworthy friend and a case where an inept marshal should be fired, Mengzi hinted that a bad ruler should also be replaced. By using an analogy of a failed friend to point out the king's failure, Mengzi obviously implied that special circumstances can justify breaking up a friendship, similar to Xunzi as the latter argued that special circumstances may justify breaching narrowly defined family obligations.

We should not, however, confuse the issue of breaking up with friends under extraordinary circumstances with friendship fungibility. Friendship fungibility is about whether we can intentionally replace a current friend for another profitably without the kind of special circumstances discussed by Mengzi. To that question, the Confucian family conception of friendship gives an unmistakably negative answer.

The Confucian family-based response is different from the standard history approach to the problem of friendship fungibility. Contemporary thinkers have attempted to tackle the fungibility problem by appealing to the particular history of a friendship. Think of two persons who started hanging out together since childhood, became friends early in life, and have remained friends for a long time; a third person with the same or similar qualities, if she does not share such a history, cannot replace either of them as a friend. Thus, it is argued that friends are not fungible. Others, however, have argued that this history approach provides an explanation rather than a justification for a friendship. One may argue, for instance, from the history approach, that a friendship is built on idiosyncratic and subjective properties. These only explain why two persons have become friends rather than justify maintaining their friendship. Justification demands reasons.[27]

Jennifer Whiting has argued that history can both provide reasons for forming a friendship and for continuing to maintain it. She distinguishes reasons for beginning a friendship from reasons for continuing a friendship. The former can be fungible; the latter is not. Whiting writes:

> My friends' merits justify my concern for them in the way in which the similar merits of others would have justified my concern for them had I become friends with them instead. (Whiting 2016, 63)

However:

> Increased investment in a person or a relationship may (like increased investment in an activity) increase my sense of reward, thus strengthening my commitment and preventing me from forming other attachments and commitments I may still regard as in some sense equally worthy. (Whiting 2016, 63)

Whiting's distinction between reasons for forming a friendship and reasons for continuing a friendship is useful as it helps us focus on the fungibility problem with continuing a friendship. However, while her account may give us a prudent reason not to give up on friends, it does not make a strong case for justifying friendship non-fungibility. For one thing, obviously, not all kinds of "increased investment" demand continuing the "investment"; whether "increased investment" justifies "continued investment" has to do with not only the "return" of the investment and available alternatives, but also, more importantly, the nature of the "investment." We need to show why friendship is so special for which past "investment" indeed justifies "continued investment." That has to do with the nature of the fundamental characteristics of friendship.

The Confucian family-based argument against friendship fungibility also involves personal experiences of a shared history. After all, two friends must share a history in their relationship before they take each other as family.

The Confucian approach is nevertheless different from the history approach against friendship fungibility. The history approach argues that, because someone has had a special or unique history with her friend, she should not replace her friend with another person. For this argument to work, it needs to show why such a history justifies continuing their relationship rather than replacing it with a new one. For that purpose, shared experience alone is not enough, no matter how unique it may have been. I have had a unique and pleasant experience co-teaching a philosophy of science course with a physicist colleague. That however does not entail I should not move on to find someone else to collaborate on teaching a different and perhaps equally exciting subject. The matter has to do with the nature of the shared experience. To ground non-fungibility, the history argument needs to take a further step and to spell out why shared experience by friends is of a different nature than those like my co-teaching experience. The Confucian family conception of friendship provides such grounding. In the Confucian view, shared experiences with a friend matter constitutively, making a person like family. Thus, friendship non-fungibility is grounded on family non-fungibility; family non-fungibility is not grounded merely on a shared history.

The Confucian argument against fungibility on the ground that friends are like family may be subject to objections in two directions. On the first objection, one may contend that family members are fungible. Indeed, to some people today, families are less relevant to their lives than friends are. Hence, one may hold that the Confucian family model of friendship actually makes friends fungible, or even more rather than less fungible. To this objection, Confucians would insist on the centrality of the family to a good life. They model friendship on a healthy conception of the family rather than a disintegrated one. To Confucians, the remedy to broken families in contemporary societies is to find ways to restore and strengthen them, rather than just accepting them in deterioration. In other words, the Confucian account against friendship fungibility is grounded on a particular conception of family.[28]

On the second objection, one may argue that the Confucian model of friendship after family makes an overcommitment to friends because it is impractical to take all friends as family. Confucian responses to this objection can be twofold. First, the Confucian requirement of treating friends like family applies to what we may call "true friends," not just any casual friends or "mere acquaintances" (*suo zhi* 所知). In real life, people indeed treat good friends like family, and sometimes even more than family. Nowadays, the term "friend" has been used rather loosely, even applicable to people whom one hardly knows on Facebook. The Confucian concept of friendship is confined to much stronger relationships and therefore is limited in scope. Second, within the Confucian family, members are in different relationships and should be treated in respectively appropriate ways rather than in a uniform way. For instance, a parent–child relationship is different from spousal or sibling relationships. Treating friends like family does not mean we should treat friends just like any other family member in every way. For example, we can expect that family members live under one roof, but not friends under usual circumstances. Nevertheless, friendship comes with a bond between persons. Confucians see an analogy between a bond between friends and a bond between family members. Such a bond, either between friends or between family members, entails a commitment to maintaining the relationship. A contemporary Confucian philosophy of friendship can be further developed to account for specific obligations friends have toward each other in modern times.

Now let me recapitulate this chapter. In the Confucian view, virtues are particularized in persons and friends are like family. These two accounts are conceptually independent of each other. On the particularized virtue account, even though virtues are general traits, when they are instantiated in individual persons, they are particularized. Particularized virtues make virtuous persons unique. Virtuous people are nevertheless distinct from one another. Such an account eliminates a perceived weakness of the Confucian virtue-based conception of friendship. On the family account, friendship as a general category is analogous to family relationships, even though each individual friend, like each individual family member, can still be special in his or her own way. Taking friends as family requires us not to see friends as fungible. Jointly, the Confucian conception of friendship as family and particularized virtues provides an adequate ground against friendship fungibility. Evidently, this Confucian conception of friendship holds the bar rather high. It is an ethical ideal that sets a model for people to emulate, even though different people can achieve such a goal only in varying degrees.

Study Questions

1. What does it mean to say that the Confucian conception of friendship is virtue-based?

2. Explain particularist and universalist approaches in the philosophy of friendship. To which one do you agree?
3. What does it mean to say that virtues are particularized?
4. What does the etymology of the word *you* reveal about Confucian friendship?
5. Explain the history approach to the problem of friendship fungibility. Do you agree with it?
6. Should we treat close friends like family?
7. What does the fungibility of friends mean? In your view, are friends fungible?
8. Confucians generally hold the family to be more central to the good life than friends. Do you agree? Why or why not?

7

Virtuous Life and Longevity

Longevity (*shou* 壽) has been one of the three primary human ideals in Chinese culture, along with happiness (*fu* 福) and prosperity (*lu* 祿).[1] The traditional symbol of longevity, an old man with a long beard and a big forehead, holding a gigantic peach in one hand and a long cane in the other, has been a popular and auspicious figure in China and in Chinese communities all over the world. Philosophically, however, the ideal of longevity has been associated mainly with Daoism. The notion of *yang sheng* 養生, or nourishing a healthy life, is a prominent concept in Daoist philosophy, and has exerted a profound influence in Chinese culture at large. In comparison, Confucian contributions in this regard have not been as focused as Daoism and much less has been done in studying them. Traditionally, however, longevity has been an ideal in close connection with virtuous living in Confucianism. It is the first of the five blessings in a person's life that are enumerated in the *Hongfan* chapter of the *Book of History* (*Shangshu* 尚書), one of the Confucian *Thirteen Classics*.[2] Kongzi famously said that "virtuous people live long lives" (*ren zhe shou* 仁者壽; *Analects* 6.23).[3] As role models, Confucian sages have often lived long lives.[4] By investigating the link between the Confucian ideal of longevity and cultivating virtue, this chapter makes the case that the Confucian virtuous life is founded on the ideal of personal harmony, and in that connection, it promotes a holistic life, which tends to lead to longevity. Such longevity is healthy and virtuous longevity. I will also show that these Confucian ideas remain relevant to the modern life.

1. Harmonizing *Qi* and Cultivating Virtue

In this section, I will look into the Confucian view of the human body and show that, in this view, the moral, psychological, and physical dimensions of a person's life are not separate, and that the Confucian good life integrates all three dimensions in harmony.

Reshaping Confucianism. Chenyang Li, Oxford University Press. © Oxford University Press 2024.
DOI: 10.1093/oso/9780197657621.003.0008

158 RESHAPING CONFUCIANISM: A PROGRESSIVE INQUIRY

Chinese cosmology holds that every existence in the world, including human beings, is ultimately a form of *qi* (energy force; see Yang 2004, 12). It is a deeply rooted Chinese belief that a person's health depends on the smooth flow of *qi*, both within the body and beyond. When *qi* is obstructed, or when the balance between the forces of the *yin qi* and the *yang qi* is upset, a person falls into various forms of illness. Maintaining a good life, therefore, is to maintain a good flow of one's *qi*. Fostering and cultivating *qi* requires a person to channel it in appropriate ways and to strike an on-going active equilibrium between its forces. Thus, in a good life, a person brings the forces of *qi* into a harmony.

It is believed that at different stages of life, one's *qi* tends to carry different tendencies. Different strategies are needed to bring it into harmony. Kongzi once said:

> The virtuous person (*junzi*) exercises three cautions. When he is young, his blood-*qi* is not yet firmly formed; he needs to be watchful against sexual temptations. When he is mid-aged, his blood-*qi* is strong; he needs to be cautious in competing for posts. When he is in old age, his blood-*qi* is withering; he needs to be careful about acquisitions.[5] (*Analects* 16.7; cf. Ni 2017, 383)

Blood-*qi* is the type of *qi* that enables a being to be animate, as characteristically in a human being. The *Inner Canon of the Yellow Emperor* (*Huangdi Neijing* 黃帝內經),[6] a classic text on traditional Chinese medicine, characterizes blood-*qi* in terms of the "human spirit."[7] Given the ancient Chinese belief in *qi* as the source and constituent of everything and the absence of a sharp Cartesian mind–body distinction in ancient Chinese philosophy, "spirit" is a refined form of *qi*.[8] Blood-*qi* constitutes the human spirit or human essence, without which a person cannot live as a human being. In ancient Chinese physiology, blood-*qi* is closely connected to the concept of the "blood system" (*xuemai* 血脉). "Blood" is a form of *qi*, and the "blood system" is not confined to blood circulation channels in modern medicine. The *Inner Canon* states that "what makes a person alive is his blood-system."[9] The "blood-system" should be understood to mean the system of blood-*qi*. The text further relates the blood-system and the well-being of the human spirit to harmony: "when the blood-system is harmonized, the quintessential human spirit takes its proper position."[10] When the human spirit occupies its appropriate position, the person lives in the way he is supposed to live as a

VIRTUOUS LIFE AND LONGEVITY   159

human person; when the spirit is out of place, the person no longer lives in a normal way. Therefore, for a person to live as a healthy person, he must harmonize his system of blood-*qi*.

Kongzi suggests that the inner state of a person depends on the state of her blood-*qi*. The optimal state of the blood-*qi* is harmony rather than mere strength. The *Luyu* 11 Section of the *Discourse on the States* (*Guoyu* 國語) states, "if one's blood-*qi* is (too) strong, one may live a long life, but may not have a good ending in life; longevity without a good ending is nevertheless unfortunate."[11] Strong blood-*qi* tends to make the person too obstinate and aggressive, which leads one's life being put in jeopardy. A good life is completed with a peaceful ending. This requires blood-*qi* to be harmonized and maintained as such. This is another way of saying that a good life requires internal harmony in the person.

From Kongzi's three cautions we can draw at least two points. First, a person's natural disposition, including both the physical and psychological, is rooted in his blood-*qi*. People at different stages of life possess different levels of blood-*qi*. Second, a person's approach to cultivating virtue, which builds up the discipline to regulate his dispositions, should be chosen appropriately in accordance with his natural dispositions. It should be noted that here Kongzi prescribes different kinds of advice for a virtuous life to people with different levels of blood-*qi*. Evidently, for Kongzi, a person's action can be influenced by his blood-*qi* and the effect of his blood-*qi* can be managed through virtuous living.

In the Confucian view, a person's efficacy in managing blood-*qi* depends on the level of self-cultivation, which is primarily moral in nature. This close association between cultivating virtue and the cultivation of *qi* is consistent throughout major classic Confucian thinkers.[12] Mengzi is well-known for his comment on cultivating *qi*. He said, "I am good at nourishing my vast, flowing *qi*" (*Mengzi* 2A.2; Bloom 2009, 30). Mengzi explained it this way:

> This *qi* is consummately great and consummately strong. If one nourishes it with uprightness and does not injure it, it will fill the space between Heaven and earth. This *qi* is the companion of rightness (*yi* 義) and the Way (*Dao*), in the absence of which, it starves. (*Mengzi* 2A.2; Bloom 2009, 30).

Unlike blood-*qi*, which is morally neutral, Mengzi's "vast, flowing *qi*" is achieved through cultivating virtue. It is led by his strong will or determination (*zhi* 志) for a virtuous life (*Mengzi* 2A.2).[13] For Mengzi, the goal in life is

160 RESHAPING CONFUCIANISM: A PROGRESSIVE INQUIRY

for the person to live up to the ideal of the humane virtue (*ren* 仁) and moral rightness (*yi* 義). He said, "if I (*wu shen* 吾身) do not live through humane virtue and moral rightness, it is called self-abandonment" (*Mengzi* 4A.10).[14] The use of the word *shen* in *wu shen* in reference to his selfhood is suggestive here. The word literally means "the body," but it is often used by philosophers like Mengzi and Xunzi to mean the person, or "one's self" (*zishen* 自身). In this connection, it connotes the corporeal self. "The corporeal," in the ancient Chinese context, is constituted of *qi*. Because the cultivation of *shen* toward humane virtue and moral rightness requires fostering *qi* in the person, the moral path and the path toward a healthy physical life are thus conceptually integrated.

Xunzi followed a similar line of thinking. In the chapter of "Self-cultivation" of the *Xunzi*, he stated:

> In pursuing goodness, if a person cultivates *qi* and nurtures his life, he can follow [the long-lived] Ancestor Peng; if he makes himself known for self-cultivation, he can match [the sage kings] Yao and Yu.[15] (Yang 1971, 13; cf. Hutton 2014, 10)

Here Xunzi explicitly connected cultivating *qi* and nurturing life with longevity. Ancestor Peng is believed to have been a minister of the sage-king Yao and to have lived to seven hundred years old. For Xunzi, if a person cultivates *qi* and nurtures her life, she can live a long life, comparable to Ancestor Peng. However, cultivating *qi* as a physical exercise should not be separate from moral refinement. Xunzi put a direct link between the cultivation of *qi* and the nurturing of the heart-mind (*yang xin* 養心). He said:

> The method of cultivating *qi* and nurturing the heart-mind is as follows. When a person's blood-*qi* is strong, she needs to harmonize it with softness. When she is able to contemplate deeply, she needs to be consistently bent toward the good. When she is brave and hot-tempered, she needs to be channeled in the appropriate way . . . When she is stupid and dumb, she needs to be educated with ritual propriety and music and to be improved through reflection.[16] (Yang 1971, 15–16; cf. Hutton 2014, 11)

The first phrase can be read also as "the method of cultivating *qi* in order to nurture the heart-mind," which implies an even closer connection between cultivating *qi* and nurturing one's heart-mind. With either reading, these two exercises are closely linked, even though with different focuses. If we understand "the cultivation of the person (*xiushen* 修身)" to mean holistic personal cultivation, then it includes both the cultivation of *qi* and the nurturing of the heart-mind. As suggested in the passage of Kongzi on blood-*qi* quoted earlier, the nurturing of the heart-mind cannot be separate from cultivating one's *qi*. Xunzi continued to indicate this connection by discussing the characteristics of *qi* and the heart-mind together:

> When blood-*qi*, will, and intelligence are regulated with ritual propriety, they flow in good order. When they are not in accord with ritual propriety, they are unruly or weak. When people follow ritual propriety in handling their food, clothing, dwelling, movements, their activities are regulated harmoniously; otherwise they are falling and become sick. When they accord with ritual propriety in appearance, attitude, advancing and retreating, and walking, they are elegant; otherwise they are arrogant, boorish, and uncultured.[17] (Yang 1971, 13–14; cf. Hutton 2014, 10)

In Xunzi, as in Kongzi and Mengzi, the cultivation of a person takes a comprehensive approach. It covers what is usually taken to be a person's physical ("blood-*qi*"), psychological ("heart-mind"), as well as moral dimensions in life. Xunzi emphasized that all these must comply with ritual propriety (*li*). He was of the view that, if a person uses ritual propriety in regulating his life, he is not only ethical and elegant, but also guards against physical and psychological illness. Xunzi maintained that the best way to nurture the heart-mind is to be sincere and to be true to oneself (*cheng* 誠). When a person is sincere, she persistently practices the virtue of *ren* and demonstrates human excellence. Such an ability carries a spiritual impetus. With this spiritual impetus, she can contribute to the transformation of the world (Yang 1971, 28).[18] In this way, Confucian self-cultivation is at once physical, psychological, and moral.

On the basis of the above investigation, we can conclude that, in Confucian philosophy, a person's physical health and moral integrity are determined by the state of *qi* within the person. Health is not merely a physical matter because a person's state of *qi* is fostered through the cultivation of oneself; this cultivation has a physical, a psychological, and a moral dimension to it. A healthy person, therefore, maintains the smooth flow of *qi* by engaging in daily activities geared toward cultivating virtue and moral betterment.[19]

162   RESHAPING CONFUCIANISM: A PROGRESSIVE INQUIRY

Let me note that this ancient theory of *qi* should be read better as a philosophy rather than a scientific account. To take it as a scientific account, we will need to have empirically verifiable evidence to prove its credibility. If we instead take it as a philosophical account, we need only theoretical plausibility. *Qi* has been closely associated with energy or "vital energy" in the contemporary discourse.[20] The main idea of this theory of *qi* is that there is a flow of vital energy within a person and that maintaining its smooth flow is vital to a person's healthy existence. In the Confucian context, a smooth flow of *qi* implies internal harmony in a person, which is connected to virtuous living.

2. Virtuous Life and Healthy Longevity

On the face of it, suggesting that moral people—understood as those who follow moral principles or their conscience in action—will live long lives is simply false. We know many good people die young. However, the Confucian conception of the moral is on virtue rather than narrowly defined moral behavior.[21] In the Confucian view, a moral life is a virtuous life; that is, a good life achieved through cultivating virtue. Then, how does cultivating virtue enhance longevity in the Confucian view?

In Confucianism, the cultivation of the person, which integrates the physical, psychological, as well as moral dimensions, implies a movement toward the internal harmonization of the person. Harmony is not only a moral requirement, but is also necessary for people's physical well-being, which tends to lead to healthy longevity. Indeed, from the Confucian perspective of virtuous living, these are the two sides of the same coin.

Kongzi's and Mengzi's philosophy encompasses not only inter-personal harmony in society and harmony with nature, but also intra-personal harmony as has been shown above. Xunzi also made intra-personal harmony a key point. For Xunzi, human beings are born with a natural tendency toward self-interest. If they follow this tendency, they will seek self-interest and, they will fight with one another, which would lead to social disorder. To prevent such a deplorable prospect, early sage-kings established ritual propriety (*li* 禮) (see *Xunzi*, chapter 23 *Xing-e*). A society well-regulated by ritual propriety is a harmonious one. In the same vein, when a person follows ritual propriety in her life, she not only harmonizes with others, but also harmonizes within herself. When she harmonizes with others, she is in good relationships with other people in society; when she harmonizes within herself, she is in a good physical as well as psychological state and she does not fall into illness. Here enters the Confucian presumption that such a person is likely to live a long life.

Achieving a state of "harmonized and balanced blood-*qi*"[22] is an important Confucian ideal. Kongzi made a connection between a person's moral achievement and her peace of mind. When describing a person of *ren* 仁, Kongzi said that "the person of *ren* is not in anxiety" (*Analects* 9.30).[23] It would be an over-interpretation if we take this to mean that a person of *ren* never becomes concerned about things. A person of *ren* has a strong sense of moral responsibility and, of course, is concerned about things, such as the moral state of society as Kongzi was evidently concerned about. However, such a person is not anxious in that she has nothing to hide and feels comfortable with the way she conducts herself. Kongzi said that "the virtuous person is open and at ease, whereas the petty person is constantly apprehensive" (*Analects* 7.37).[24] Similarly, Mengzi also said that "the virtuous person has a concern to the end of his life, but he does not have a morning's anxiety"[25] (*Mengzi* 4B28; cf. Van Norden 2008, 112). To Mengzi, this means that a virtuous person is concerned with life-long cultivation but is not anxious in his daily life. We can understand this view in the sense that a moral person is not concerned about his or her own personal gains and is not worried about how others would think of him as long as she is doing things right. When asked if a person of virtue would complain, Kongzi said, "if one sought excellence in virtue and has acquired it, why should he complain?" (*Analects* 7.15).[26] A person of virtue retains a good state of mind because she enjoys a healthy internal harmony. Such harmony is not merely psychological, which is suggested by being free from anxiety; it is also physical; as we have demonstrated in the first section, in Confucian thought, the psychological and the physical are closely connected.

The classic *Chunqiu Fanlu* (*The Luxuriant Dew of the Spring and Autumn Annals* 春秋繁露), authored by the Han Confucian scholar Dong Zhongshu (Tung Chung-shu 董仲舒, 179–104 BCE), states that, "when a person is in anxiety his *qi* becomes sick."[27] When one's internal *qi* is disturbed and out of order, its regular flow is interrupted and its internal harmony is upset. Anxiety (*you* 憂) is a sign of disharmony in a person. When a person is constantly in anxiety and is without internal harmony, his psychological and physical health becomes jeopardized.

Dong was one of the ancient philosophers who made the closest connection between the moral pursuit of the *Dao*, nurturing the person (*shen* 身),

164   RESHAPING CONFUCIANISM: A PROGRESSIVE INQUIRY

and harmony. In his view, pursuing the *Dao* implies nurturing oneself (*shen*) in accordance with the *Dao*.[28] Dong said, "because the *Dao* of Heaven and Earth culminates in harmony, all living things value their *qi* and nurture it."[29] For Dong, to nurture one's *qi* is to harmonize it in accordance with the *Dao*. Dong maintained that harmony as the right path of Heaven consists in balancing the forces of *yin* and *yang*.[30] When *yin* and *yang* are balanced, they generate the best mix of *qi*. Thus, the nurturing of the person consists in balancing the *yin qi* and the *yang qi* within oneself, which in turn generates harmony. When the *yin qi* and the *yang qi* are harmonized, the person thrives.

Dong said:

> People who are great in nurturing their lives cherish their *qi*. *Qi* takes shape in accordance with a person's spirit; a person's spirit comes from his will (*yi* 意). What the heart-mind wishes is the will. One who is not at ease with his will disturbs the peace of his spirit. When the spirit is disturbed, his *qi* diminishes. When the *qi* diminishes it is difficult to maintain his person. Therefore, the morally refined person maintains his will at ease by becoming indifferent toward desires and aversions. He keeps his will at ease in order to appease his spirit, which in turn nurtures his *qi*. When he has plenty of *qi* and it is well-nurtured, he gains the most important in the nurturing of the person.[31]

For Dong, nurturing *qi* is by no means a mere physical matter. Like his Confucian predecessors, in nurturing *qi* Dong saw a direct connection to the cultivation of the heart-mind. Following Mengzi, Dong held that the heart-mind is the leading force of a person's *qi*.[32] The "spirit" stands for a psychological force that proceeds from the heart-mind's will; it exerts an influence on *qi*. For Dong, the key to nurturing one's *qi* is moral cultivation. He said:

> The heart-mind is the ruler of *qi*. How can *qi* not follow the heart-mind? This is the reason that all philosophies under Heaven maintain that the heart-mind is the foundation.[33]

In other words, when the heart-mind is so determined, a person has formed the will; following such a will she can cultivate her *qi* for a virtuous life.[34] From this point, Dong made a straightforward connection between virtuous living and longevity. He said:

VIRTUOUS LIFE AND LONGEVITY 165

Most persons of excellent virtue live long lives because they are not greedy for external things and they remain clean internally; their heart-minds are harmonious and peaceful without departing from centrality and up-rightness. They acquire the very best between Heaven and Earth to nurture themselves.[35]

Here Dong gives three reasons as to why most persons of excellent virtue live long lives. First, such persons are not desirous of things in the world, nor do they enslave themselves after material gains. Second, such persons retain peace of mind. They are unlikely to be anxious or moody. They minimize stress by avoiding selfish pursuits. Third, persons of excellent virtue are able to use the best in the universe to nurture their selves. For example, persons of excellent virtue are able to follow the four seasons and make the best use of them to remain productive and appropriate in life. For all these reasons, persons of excellent virtue tend to live long lives. But ultimately, such persons enjoy longevity because they are able to cultivate their *qi* in harmony.

Dong explained:

The constant *qi* of Heaven is active without stagnation. Hence, a person following the *Dao* does not keep his *qi* stagnant either. When *qi* is not channeled well, it overflows without leaving free space. Therefore, the morally refined person nurtures it and harmonizes it. He regulates it with standards; he rids of the isolated and accepts that which harmonizes with others. One who stands at a very high terrace is exposed to too much *yang* whereas one who stays in a very large room is exposed to too much *yin*;[36] both are distant from the harmony of Heaven and Earth. Therefore, sages do neither. They only maintain centrality.[37]

According to this understanding, *qi* in the world is naturally dynamic. As part of the interconnected world, a person needs to nurture his *qi* in ways that are consistent with the constant flow of *qi* in the world. The way to achieve this end, for Dong, is the path of centrality and harmony.[38] He said:

Those who can manage the world with centrality and harmony are those with the greatest virtues; those who can nurture themselves with centrality and harmony can live the longest lives possible.[39]

166   RESHAPING CONFUCIANISM: A PROGRESSIVE INQUIRY

He also maintained:

> Those whose persons constantly embody centrality and harmony are people who flow well with the steady interaction between Heaven and Earth. Flowing well this way enables people to live long lives. Otherwise, they live shortened lives.[40]

In Dong's philosophy, virtuous living leads to longevity because it enables the harmonious flow of *qi* in a person, which resonates with harmony in the larger world ("between Heaven and earth").

Dong's philosophy of cultivating *qi* and nurturing the person is not limited to metaphysical formulations. He developed a rather concrete program of everyday activities to achieve it. Believing that sentiments such as anger, worry, sorrow, and hatred are harmful to life, Dong insisted that, to nurture life, one needs to maintain peace of mind and remain cheerful.[41] According to Dong:

> Those who nurture their lives are good with handling *qi*; they wear seasonally appropriate clothes in spring, stay in cool places in summer, take cover from strong wind in autumn, and avoid heavy humidity in winter. They act this way so that they harmonize with [the pattern of] *qi*.[42]

Furthermore, one should often wash clothes, keep a half-full stomach (no over-eating), frequently engage in physical activities, and avoid idle living.[43] Needless to say, personal hygiene and good habits with eating food and physical activities all contribute to longevity. The ideas of being active in physical activities, avoiding living idly, together with the close association of the fostering of *qi* with the cultivation of the heart-mind, indicate that the Confucian ideal of longevity is not merely living a long time, but also living a quality life and a virtuous life. It is healthy longevity or virtuous longevity. It is longevity as a result of good health and superb virtue.

In Dong's view, a person's longevity to a large extent depends on her own effort on personal cultivation. He said:

> Longevity is like repayment (*chou* 讎).[44] Although the number of people is enormous, they each must get their due in life. The long or short span of life depends on a person's own practice. Those who follow a long-lasting way get long lives; those who follow a short-lasting way get short lives.

VIRTUOUS LIFE AND LONGEVITY   167

> Whether a person gets a long or short life depends on her practice in life. From today to the future, no one can change that. Therefore, we say, longevity is repayment.[45]

According to this understanding, how long a person lives depends on how she lives. If she lives the good way, which for Dong means the way of Confucian self-cultivation with virtuous living habits, she can enjoy longevity. Otherwise, she lives a short life. Here personal effort is emphasized as the key to longevity.

Of course, we are all aware of the fact that virtuous people do not necessarily live long lives. There are many factors in life that are out of our control. A person may suffer from a deadly disease, or she may die of an accident. A person may live a short life even if she does everything right, like Kongzi's top disciple Yan Hui, who allegedly had superb moral virtue but died at the age of thirty-three. Or a person may live a long life even if she lives badly, like some long-lived alcoholics today. Dong recognized that there are factors beyond people's control that affect people's lives and that personal efforts do not completely determine longevity. Dong qualified the correlation between virtuous living and longevity. He said:

> A person's practice corresponds with his long or short life. When someone indulges himself in practice, but lives a long life, it is his *ming* that benefits him. When someone behaves well but lives a short life, it is his *ming* that hurts him. If we take what *ming* does to people's long or short lives to be people's own doing, that is a big mistake. Therefore, when a person's *ming* of Heaven gives him a long life but he harms it, he shortens his life. When Heaven gives a person a short life, but he nurtures it, he prolongs his life. So, to prolong or to shorten a person's life depends on oneself; the person's own effort works in addition to what Heaven allocates![46]

Ming 命, often translated as "fate" or "destiny," points to forces in the universe that are beyond people's control. While emphasizing the important impact on longevity by personal effort, Dong did not rule out the impact of *ming* on people's longevity. On the contrary, he fully acknowledged its effect. He emphasized the important difference a person can make in life within the possibilities allowed by *ming*. For instance, a well-disciplined cancer patient actively cooperating with her doctor may nevertheless prolong her life. A habitually careful person has a better chance to avoid deadly accidents. For

168   RESHAPING CONFUCIANISM: A PROGRESSIVE INQUIRY

Dong, there is no doubt that, other things being equal, personal effort makes a whole world of difference in living a long life. Therefore, the Confucian idea that virtuous persons live long lives should be understood as that virtuous living promotes longevity.

We should accordingly understand the connection between virtuous living and longevity in Confucian thinkers. The *Zhongyong* quotes Kongzi saying that "those with great virtue must attain longevity."[47] This, however, should not be understood as saying that a virtuous person always enjoys longevity. "Must" here expresses "oughtness" rather than a universal fact. Sometimes, good people die young. That is unfortunate. But as Dong suggested, that is because there are forces beyond people's control. As far as what is under people's control, virtuous living can make a significant difference in people's longevity.

From the above, we can conclude that classic Confucian thinkers, Dong in particular, view cultivating virtue through harmonizing qi in the person as essential to the good life. According to their views, a well-cultivated person is in a state of harmony, whose heart-mind is in peace and whose body is sustained by a constant, smooth flow of qi. A person in such an optimal state tends to live a long life. The harmonization of qi in the person improves one's moral as well as physical life. Thus, in Confucianism, virtue cultivation, harmony, and longevity are intrinsically linked.

3. Longevity in Modern Life

The Confucian philosophy of virtue cultivation aims to achieve internal harmony in the person, not only to enhance people's moral attainment but also to promote people's overall health. Hence, it facilitates longevity. For this reason, traditionally old age in China has often been seen as a sign of virtuous living. Because of this association between the attainment of virtue and longevity, in the Confucian culture, people of old age are respected and even revered. In his once well-circulated book *The Importance of Living*, Lin Yutang wrote:

> In China, the first question a person asks the other on an official call, after asking about his name and surname is, "what is your glorious age?" If the person replies apologetically that he is twenty-three or twenty-eight, the other party generally comforts him by saying that he has still a glorious

VIRTUOUS LIFE AND LONGEVITY   169

future, and that one day he may become old. But if the person replies that he is thirty-five or thirty-eight, the other party immediately exclaims with deep respect, "good luck!"; enthusiasm grows in proportion as the gentleman is able to report a higher and higher age, and if the person is anywhere over fifty, the inquirer immediately drops his voice in humility and respect. (Lin 1937, 192–193)

Lin's report is truer in the old days than it is today; people's life expectancy is much longer today than in ancient times. In the old days in history, living conditions were harsh and longevity was hard to achieved. Once longevity was reached, it was taken to be at least a sign of having lived with virtuous habits. Thus, Lin's description reveals an important aspect of the Confucian culture regarding old age. The direct linkage between virtue cultivation and longevity in Confucianism is established on the basis of a comprehensive notion of the virtuous life. To develop good virtues, people need to start from forming good habits in everyday life, including those conducive to good health and longevity.

The connection between moral attainment and longevity, of course, is not absolute. This can be seen in two ways. First, as we discussed previously, moral attainment does not guarantee longevity. Second, a long life itself is not to be equated to a virtuous life. When Confucian thinkers talk about longevity, they do not promote longevity per se, because for them the only life worth living is the virtuous life. A person of excellent virtue first of all aims at a virtuous life rather than merely a long life. Indeed, it is hard to imagine someone could be a virtuous person if he is concerned constantly about prolonging his life.

In extreme circumstances, being virtuous may require the sacrifice of one's life. Mengzi famously said that "life is what I want; moral rightness is also what I want. But if I cannot have both, I would rather sacrifice my life in order to obtain moral rightness" (*Mengzi* 6A.9). If separated from morality, longevity is not necessarily a good thing. Kongzi once chided a friend, who was not caring to his young brother in his youth and achieved nothing after he grew up, hence having not been virtuous, that now he was "old but did not die, what a thief!" (*Analects* 14.43) It is not easy to say precisely what we can draw on this quote from Kongzi. Perhaps Kongzi was unhappy because that friend was rude to him, as the story in the *Analects* indicates. Or perhaps Kongzi was just teasing his friend. What we can learn for certain from this story, however, is that Kongzi did not believe that living a long life is necessarily a sign of good virtue, which makes a life worth living. For Confucians, longevity itself is not the ideal in life; it is longevity as a result of virtue cultivation, or longevity integrated with virtuous living, that is ideal in life. Nevertheless, if we accept the view that most people achieve some kind of moral attainment and embody virtues in life, they should have long lives. Under this consideration, longevity is generally a good thing for society to promote.

Life expectancy is now a major indicator of societal development. High life expectancy is usually correlated with prosperous societies.[48] Public health measures are credited with much of the recent increase in life expectancy (e.g., Buxbaum 2020). If we accept the Confucian philosophy of the linkage between virtue and longevity, what kind of attitude should society adopt in promoting public health and longevity? In the Confucian view, social programs of public health care should not be taken merely as a matter of physical health in separation from virtuous living, or they will not be effective even when they are instituted. Public health programs can take the form of promoting virtuous living.

As shown earlier, the Confucian notion of the good person is a comprehensive notion that encompasses virtuous living conducive to good health and longevity. For a long time, mainstream modern Western medicine has tended to remove moral considerations from its practice (Brandt and Rozin 1997, 2). In such a view, being "scientific" means being able to isolate the function of the physical body from all other socio-cultural considerations. Translated into public policy, it implies that medicine and public health policy are to be separate from people's virtue. In the Confucian view, because people's moral and psychological states affect their physical well-being, health care programs, including public health programs, must be integrated with moral education to be effective. For example, if someone gets angry easily with people around him and his frequent anger jeopardizes his health, learning to form and maintain meaningful relationships with other people should be part of his health program. If someone is depressed, helping her to adjust attitudes in life should be an important part of her recovery plan; she may find a lot of joy in helping others, for example. A harmonious mentality contributes to healthy living and longevity. Furthermore, because Confucian moral cultivation is about developing virtuous persons, it encompasses the formation of good living habits, including those good habits of healthy living. Public campaigns against unhealthy living habits can be construed as movements to promote virtuous living.

VIRTUOUS LIFE AND LONGEVITY 171

Interestingly, during the last few decades in the United States, there has emerged a trend of "secular morality"; the public has developed a strong "moral" opposition against such behaviors as smoking, behaviors that had been considered as pure personal choices. Now, in the eyes of many people, these behaviors are "sinful" and immoral. Therefore, society has placed pressure on individuals to abandon these behaviors. It is "secular morality" because these behaviors are not sins against God as in religious morality; they are behaviors against other people and bring harm to others in addition to themselves. While many people in America oppose these harmful behaviors because they harm other people (as in second-hand smoking), from a Confucian point of view, these behaviors should also be reformed so that these individuals can develop virtue. As shown in the previous section, a virtuous person does not behave in ways that disharmonize oneself. Therefore, on the ground of virtue morality, Confucians today would support public policies against "sinful" habits such as smoking now that it is known to be harmful to people's health. Such policies can be implemented via various measures, such as promoting public education on the harms of smoking, imposing "sin taxes" on cigarettes, and establishing "no smoking" zones in public spaces.

Furthermore, Confucians hold that healthy living should be fostered through moral education, even though societies today also use legal means to promote a healthy living environment. This implies that civic education, particularly in school, should be understood broadly to include virtuous living in general (I will come back to the matter of civic education in Chapter 12). Students should learn that a good person is not only one in compliance with moral rules, but also one with good living habits and virtuous behavior. For example, a virtuous person should not be a smoker or an alcoholic, should not get up late in the morning for school or for work, and should not over-indulge oneself in food. A related issue is obesity, which has been a large problem in society. Obesity-related diseases cost a huge amount of recourses in society and significantly shorten people's lives. A major cause of obesity is over-eating.[49] Millions of years of evolution simply did not prepare our bodies to be stuffed with a large amount of food readily available in today's affluent society. Toward this issue, many people today take an attitude of indifference, holding that it is purely a matter of personal lifestyle. In the Confucian view, however, obesity caused by over-eating is a sign of lack of self-discipline. Too heavy a stomach disrupts the harmonious flow of one's *qi*. A virtuous person should be able to keep his appetite under control and should be able to overcome his urge to eat more than what his body needs. Such a person would also engage in physical exercise as it is an important way of nurturing life. Therefore, the Confucian advice for combating obesity is to engage in virtuous living, rather than narrowly focusing on the stomach and body weight. In the Confucian view, of course, public policy should be geared in that direction for the good of the entire society. If people can actively pursue virtuous living, they all will be more likely to live healthy and long lives. That way, we will all be better off.

In summary, ancient Confucian thinkers developed a comprehensive view of virtuous living and longevity on the basis of their philosophy of the harmonious flow of *qi*. In their view, a good life is to be lived with virtue. Toward such a goal, people should develop good living habits in everyday life. A virtuous life promotes good health and tends to lead to longevity. Understood this way, there is a close association between virtuous living and healthy longevity. Such a philosophy can continue to inspire people in contemporary times.

Study Questions

1. In the Confucian view, how is the cultivation of virtue connected to longevity?
2. What is the role of harmony in Confucian virtuous living?
3. What is blood-*qi*? What role does it play in the world?
4. Do you agree that virtuous living, such as good habits, has moral relevance?
5. Do you think longevity itself is a good thing or only healthy longevity is a good thing? Why or why not?
6. Given that our current life expectancy is considerably higher than in ancient times, should longevity still be an important value in society as in the past?
7. A painful long life may not be desirable. But is a healthy life the longer the better? Should society maximize people's life expectancy as long as possible? If not, is there such a thing as the desirable length?
8. Do you think that smoking and alcoholism is morally problematic? Why or why not?

INTERLUDE

8

Can Sages Be Wrong?

In the previous chapters, we have encountered Confucian teachings in the form of the words or deeds of the sages (*sheng* 聖). Confucian sages have often been regarded as having perfect knowledge and utmost virtue.[1] Today, however, some of their teachings appear problematic against modern moral sensibilities. Thus, we must pause and ask: did Confucian sages sometimes get things wrong? If they have got things wrong on some issues, students of Confucianism today need to not only develop new ideas to replace erroneous or outdated ones, but also provide a reasonable account for why classic texts must be rectified. But can sages be wrong?

A common list of Confucian sages included Kongzi and Mengzi as well as early legendary rulers such as Yao 堯, Shun 舜, and Duke Zhou 周公. Later, such thinkers as Zhu Xi 朱熹 (1130–1200) and Wang Yangming 王 陽明 (1472–1529) were also added to the list, even though they have not been nearly as prominent as their forerunners. Given the high status and reverence with which sagehood was imbued, questions with regard to sages' perfection inevitably arise. For radical foes of Confucianism, such a question is not even worth raising in the first place. For them, Kongzi and his followers were hardly right on anything. All of China's ills, on their view, are to be traced to Confucianism and even to Kongzi himself. In modern times such views peaked during the May Fourth Movement in 1919 under the banner of "Down with Confucianism 打倒孔家店!" and again during the Cultural Revolution (1966–1976) under Mao Zedong. For some other people, conversely, such a question is a non-starter because Kongzi and others revered in the tradition were sages and it is simply not possible for sages to be wrong. A popular Chinese proverb says, "people are not sages, how can they be without any fault?"[2] This saying implies that sages are free from fault. According to such a view, all ancient teachings by the sages are to be inherited in their entirety, or at the very least one should defend them in all ways possible. I believe that the appropriate progressive attitude is in the middle. I argue that Kongzi and Confucian sages in general, even as sages, can be mistaken, even though they have made significant contributions to

Reshaping Confucianism. Chenyang Li, Oxford University Press. © Oxford University Press 2024.
DOI: 10.1093/oso/9780197657621.003.0009

176   RESHAPING CONFUCIANISM: A PROGRESSIVE INQUIRY

world civilization and most of their teachings are still valuable. An important task for contemporary students of progressive Confucianism is to separate the wheat from the chaff, identifying the good, valuable, interesting, and productive in this tradition to learn from it and to reform it progressively.

In this chapter, I will trace the history of the canonization of Kongzi as an example of sages and investigate related debates, argue for the fallibility of Confucian sages, and contrast it with strategies for tackling similar issues in monotheistic traditions. I will show that this fallibility of Confucian sages marks a significant difference between Confucianism and monotheistic traditions when it comes to reforming traditions in our times and that the fallibility of Confucian sages allows us to better assess the tradition and to renew Confucianism for contemporary society.

1. Issues of Confucian Sagehood

The Confucian idea of sagehood is represented by the character 聖 (*sheng*), appearing often in the compound term *sheng-ren* 聖人; that is, person of *sheng*. The character is believed to have had the meaning of intelligence and wisdom prior to Kongzi, but the ideal of sagehood as perfect wisdom and virtue was a Confucian invention (see Z. Wang 1999). Over the long history of Confucianism, various ideas have been proposed and argued for on matters of sagehood. At the center of the disagreements are two related issues. First, whether someone is a sage. Kongzi himself explicitly denied that he was a sage (e.g., *Mengzi* 2A2). Subsequent thinkers in the tradition generally regarded Kongzi as a sage and recognized him as the "Ultimate Sage" (*zhi sheng* 至聖), the first of all Confucian sages. The second issue is whether sages are perfect and are free from mistakes. Strictly speaking, being perfect and having no faults are not the same thing. For we can imagine a person who is not perfect in every aspect yet does not commit any fault in what she does. In the Confucian discourse of sagehood, however, these two characteristics have often been linked closely. Whereas some held that sages are perfect and hence cannot be wrong, others held that even sages have imperfections and therefore they can make mistakes.

Kongzi set the bar extremely high for sagehood. He once said, "I have not had a chance to meet a sage; I am satisfied to have seen virtuous persons [*junzi*]" (*Analects* 7.26). *Analects* 6.30 records a conversation that Kongzi had with his disciple Zigong regarding sagehood:

Zigong said, "If a person were able to confer benefits on the people extensively and able to aid the multitude, what would you say of the person? Might the person be called human-hearted [*ren*]?" The Master said, "Why speak only of human-heartedness? A person like this must be called a sage! Even Yao and Shun would find it difficult to accomplish." (Ni 2017, 187)

In the Confucian tradition, the legendary kings Yao and Shun have been almost always included on the list of sages. Here, Kongzi did not confirm explicitly that Yao and Shun achieved sagehood. Instead, he said even they would have found the deed of conferring extensive benevolence in society difficult to achieve, indicating the level of extreme difficulty in becoming sages.[3]

During Kongzi's lifetime, people in the street did not regard him as a sage. Once, Kongzi was lost on a journey. His disciple Zilu asked an old man if he had seen the revered teacher. The old man commented with contempt that Kongzi "did not labor with his four limbs and nor was he able to discern the five grains, how can he be a teacher?!" (*Analects* 18.7) In the eyes of the old man, Kongzi was not a worthy teacher, much less a sage.

Analects 9.6 records that Kongzi avoids considering himself as a sage even when others called him so:

The prime minister asked Zigong [Kongzi's student], "Isn't your master a sage? How come he has so many skills?" Zigong said, "It must be heaven that has set him on the course to become a sage, and, in addition, be versatile in skills." (Ni 2017, 233)

Supposedly, with an elevated status, a sage does not need mundane skills, which are for ordinary people to possess for making a tedious living. Upon hearing the prime minister's remark, Kongzi said, "I was poor when I was young, and that is why I acquired many humble skills. Does a well-cultivated person [*junzi*] need many skills? No, not many" (*Analects* 9.6). Here Kongzi changed the reference from "sage" to "*junzi*," hence another indication that he did not claim to be a sage even though others regarded him as one.

Tu Weiming has observed:

Kongzi never believed that he had attained sagehood. He was, like us, struggling to learn to be human. His self-image was that of a fellow traveler,

178 RESHAPING CONFUCIANISM: A PROGRESSIVE INQUIRY

committed to the task of realizing humanity, on the way of becoming fully human. (Tu 1985, 59)

Tu's remark provides a good summary of the issue of Kongzi and sagehood.

Similarly, Mengzi did not claim to be a sage either. In the *Mengzi*, someone called Mengzi a sage. Mengzi said:

> What an extraordinary thing for you to say of me! Zigong once asked Kongzi, "Are you, Master, a sage?" Kongzi replied, "I have not succeeded in becoming a sage. I simply never tire of learning nor weary of teaching." Zigong said, "Not to tire of teaching is wisdom; not to weary of teaching is benevolence [*ren*]. You must be a sage to be both wise and benevolent." A sage is something even Kongzi did not claim to be. What an extraordinary thing for you to say of me! (*Mengzi* 2A2; Lau 1984, 79)

Mengzi nevertheless regarded Kongzi as a sage (*Mengzi* 5B1). For Mengzi, however, sages and ordinary people are the same in kind (*Mengzi* 6A7, 4B28). He said that the ancient sage Duke Zhou 周公 also made mistakes (*Mengzi* 2B9). Mengzi described ancient sages this way: Bo Yi was the sage who was unsullied; Yi Yin was the sage who accepted responsibility; Liu Xiahui was the sage who was harmonious; "Kongzi was the sage whose actions were timely" (*Mengzi* 5B1; Lau 1984, 150). The fact that they each had respective strengths seems to suggest that, at least for Mengzi, sages were not perfect in every aspect. They were better and more cultivated than the rest of us, but they were not qualitatively different from us.

This leads us to the second issue of the Confucian discourse of sagehood, whether sages are perfect. Whereas some maintain the perfection of sages, others deny it. Section 12 of the *Zhongyong*, for instance, asserts explicitly that even the sages do not fully understand the *Dao*, nor can they fully practice it:

> The Way [*Dao*] of the superior man [*junzi*] functions everywhere and yet is hidden. Men and women of simple intelligence can share its knowledge; and yet in its utmost reaches, there is something which even the sage does not know. Men and women of simple intelligence can put it into practice; and yet in its utmost reaches there is something which even the sage is not able to put into practice. (Chan 1963, 100)

The message is clear that no one is perfect in knowledge, including the sages.[4] If we accept that good actions cannot be separate from good knowledge, then it follows that the lack of knowledge implies imperfection in action. This presumably includes sages as well as common men and women.

While not considering himself a sage, Kongzi highly valued the ability to reflect upon oneself and to remedy one's own imperfections. The *Analects* records that Kongzi said, should he be able to spend more time studying the *Book of Changes* (*Yijing*), he would be able to avoid making large mistakes (*Analects* 7.17). Commentators have varied interpretations of this remark.[5] There is no doubt here, however, that Kongzi looked to avoid serious mistakes (*da guo* 大過), implying that he was not immune from fault. The classic text *Yanzi Commentary on the Spring and Autumn Annuals* (*Yanzi Chunqiu* 晏子春秋) records Kongzi making a mistake. Kongzi went to the state of Qi to meet with Duke Jing. Yet, he did not want to see the duke's Prime Minister Yanzi. When his disciple Zilu raised the issue of possible impropriety, Kongzi said that Yanzi's character was questionable because he served three dukes in the state of Qi, suggesting a lack of the virtue of loyalty. Yanzi heard it and remarked that Kongzi did not understand his circumstances. He chided that Kongzi was like someone living in mountains who disparages those using fishing nets on the sea and like someone living by the sea who belittles those using axes in mountains. When Kongzi later realized that his allegation against Yanzi was unfounded, he repented and said:

> I commented on Yanzi privately yet failed to pinpoint his fault. It was my big mistake! I heard that a cultivated person makes friends with those who are not as good as oneself, and takes as teachers those who are better than oneself. Now I have misspoken of Yanzi. He criticized me for it. That makes him my teacher![6]

Afterwards, Kongzi sent his disciple Zaiwo to apologize on his behalf and then went to meet with Yanzi in person. The *Analects* records also a story of Kongzi mistaking in his assessment of Duke Zhao's moral conduct. When he was asked whether Duke Zhao was versed in ritual propriety, Kongzi said, "yes." Then, someone pointed out a fact to the contrary. Kongzi remarked, "I am a fortunate man. Whenever I make a mistake, other people are sure to notice it" (*Analects* 7.31; Lau 1979, 90). Kongzi was subject to making mistakes and he knew it.[7]

180   RESHAPING CONFUCIANISM: A PROGRESSIVE INQUIRY

If even Kongzi was not free from fault, other thinkers in the tradition, sages or not, cannot possibly be perfect either. The classic *Hanshi Waizhuan* 韓詩外傳 records a story when Mengzi, the secondary sage (*ya sheng* 亞聖) in the Confucian tradition, was at fault. One day, Mengzi asked his mother for permission to divorce his wife for her lack of virtue because, when he walked into her room, he saw his wife sit in an unseemly posture. His mother scolded him instead and said that it was Mengzi who acted against ritual propriety because he entered his wife's private space unannounced. Upon reflection, Mengzi realized his own fault and repented (Han Ying, Book 9, section 17).

So, it seems evident that Kongzi and Mengzi, and presumably other Confucian sages, were fallible, like the rest of us. Then why and how did the tradition of painting them as faultless arise? There has been a history of canonization of Kongzi into sagehood, which gradually made him a perfect figure; in the wake of his ascension, the process was repeated later for other Confucian sages.

Contrary to the tradition of contestation in the pre-Qin period, most Confucian classic commentators since the Han Dynasty (202 BCE–220 CE) onward have tended to establish sages as the hallmark of perfection and, along with them, Confucian classic texts as the infallible canons. Scholars of the Han period contributed significantly to the exaltation of Kongzi as a sage. The chapter on Kongzi in the *Records of History* (*Shiji* 史記), Book 17, enumerates his various accomplishments and concludes:

> From the son of heaven to kings and princes, all have taken Kongzi as their standards in understanding the Six Arts. He was indeed the Ultimate Sage.[8] (Sima Qian 1982, 1946)

The state Confucian scholar during the Han Dynasty, Dong Zhongshu 董仲舒 (179–104 BCE) claimed that "the sages parallel with heaven" (*shengren peitian* 聖人配天) (*Chunqiu Fanlu*, ch. 79; TTM, 807). Similarly, another influential Han thinker Yang Xiong 楊雄 (53 BCE–18 CE) said, "The sages' writings, speeches, and conduct are truly like heaven!" (Yang 2013, 213). For these thinkers, "heaven" stands for the ultimate moral order and moral authority. Presumably, heaven does not make mistakes. Comparing the sages to heaven gives them the highest status in the world. Claiming that their writings, speeches, and conduct are truly like heaven implies that everything that sages said and did was impeccable. The Confucian classic texts have been called *jing* 經, which means "standard teachings" or "perennial teachings," suggesting that these texts themselves are the perennial criteria of right and wrong.

Confucian classics are a vast corpus of literature, in which scrutinizing readers can always find questionable spots. Then, how can perfect sagehood be protected against these troubling words? Confucian thinkers, in canonizing these texts, have attempted to gently patch up what may have appeared problematic. The Song neo-Confucian thinker Cheng Yi 程頤 (1033–1107), for instance, took a twofold strategy in dealing with such questions while defending the infallibility of Kongzi as a sage. First, Cheng Yi regarded some sections in Confucian classics, such as Chapter *Ruxing* of the *Book of Rites*, as inconsistent with Kongzi's teaching and discredited them outright as inauthentic (Cheng and Cheng 2011, 254). Second, Cheng Yi maintained that when we read the classics, even those authored by the sages, we should not be confined to the surface meaning of their words. Instead, we should understand the personality and character of the sages and thereby draw their true teaching (Cheng and Cheng 2011, 284). In other words, once we understand the true spirit of their teachings, we can catch their real meaning beyond the language in the text, regardless of what the text says literally. Thus, to protect the impeccability of the sages, Cheng Yi did not hesitate to change the wordings and sectional sequences in the *Great Learning*. For instance, he changed *qin-min* 親民 (to love people) to *xin-min* 新民 (to renew people) in the opening passage, and in Section 6, he regarded the statement of *ciwei zhiben* 此谓知本 as superfluous words, which should be deleted.[9] Hermeneutical matters aside, Cheng Yi's goal was to defend the perfection of the sages by altering classic texts when deemed necessary for the integrity of the texts (as he understood them). His bottom line was that the sages cannot be wrong even though what we have taken to be the words of the sages can be wrong.

The strongest defender of Kongzi's fault-free sagehood was the Song neo-Confucian thinker, Zhu Xi. Zhu made a large contribution to turning Kongzi from a great thinker to a god-like sage by arguing for the perfection of sagehood. Conceptually, Zhu equated sagehood with the *Dao*, declaring that "The *Dao* is the sage without a body and the sage is the embodied *Dao*."[10] He continued with Cheng Yi's view that the sages have no faults to regret for, nor have they anything to improve upon (Zhu 1986, 903).[11] For example, Zhu claimed:

> The sages are perfect. They cannot be sages if they have even a slight deficiency . . . [Sage] Shun did not have any fault. Therefore, he was a sage. Otherwise, how could he have been Shun?! (Zhu 1986, 232)

182   RESHAPING CONFUCIANISM: A PROGRESSIVE INQUIRY

In Zhu's view, not only Kongzi but all Confucian sages have reached perfection and hence are free from fault. To justify his view, Zhu went on to argue that Kongzi was born with knowledge and that his virtuous behavior goes hand in hand with virtuous knowledge. If sages possess innate virtuous knowledge that cannot be further improved, it follows that sages are perfectly virtuous persons who are free from any fault.

The idea of some people "being born with knowledge" is traceable back to Kongzi, even though he did not attribute such a quality to himself. In the *Analects*, Kongzi asserted:

> Those who are born with knowledge are the highest. Next come those who attain knowledge through study. Next again come those who turn to study after having been vexed by difficulties. (*Analects* 16.9; Lau 1979, 140)

On Kongzi's classification, perhaps it was to be expected for Zhu Xi and others to place Kongzi in the category of the "highest," belonging to those who are born with knowledge. Zhu Xi recognized that such knowledge is moral in nature, about right and wrong rather than the empirical (Zhu 1986, 891). On his view, if Kongzi was born with knowledge, he would be able to act accordingly and would be able to avoid (moral) fault altogether.

But Zhu Xi's assertion can be challenged. Does having inborn knowledge mean that Kongzi was a sage at birth or as a child? A "yes" answer would be rather implausible. The view of perfect sages with inborn knowledge is inconsistent with Kongzi's own view of himself. Kongzi proclaimed explicitly that he was not born with knowledge and that instead, he acquired knowledge through learning, just like the rest of us. He said, "I am not one who was born with knowledge; I love ancient [teaching] and earnestly seek it" (*Analects* 7.20; Chan 1963, 32). Ancient teaching, for Kongzi, is moral knowledge. The fact that Kongzi had to actively seek it indicates that his knowledge in this regard was learned, not inborn. Kongzi was indeed keen on seeking knowledge. He set his heart on learning when he was fifteen years old (*Analects* 2.4), and he advocated "tireless learning" (*Analects* 7.2). He once studied so hard in reading that the hide string in his bamboo book broke three times (Sima 1982, 1937).

Zhu's view of sages with inborn knowledge led to a problem that had been already encountered by Cheng Yi. A disciple once asked whether the sages, who were born with knowledge, still needed to learn. In his response, Cheng said, "those who are born already with knowledge do not depend on learning,

CAN SAGES BE WRONG? 183

yet the sages must nevertheless learn" (Cheng and Cheng 2011, 253). Cheng did not explain why the sages must learn even though they already possess perfect knowledge. There is apparently a contradiction. One needs to learn because of lacking knowledge or the imperfection of knowledge. Yet, the sages are supposed to face neither deficiency on Cheng's and Zhu's accounts. If the sages already possess perfect knowledge, what is the point of learning? Evidently, Cheng said the sages still learn in an effort to reconcile the perfection of the sages with the Confucian doctrine of the necessity of learning. In the *Analects*, Kongzi said explicitly on numerous occasions that he loved learning (e.g., 1.14, 5.15, 5.28, 6.3, 8.13, 11.7, 17.8, 19.5). However, Cheng stopped short of accepting that the sages learn because they also need to improve themselves.

Difficulties such as these, however, did not prevent Zhu Xi from insisting on his claim. Zhu Xi alleged that all these sayings by Kongzi of himself, about his learning experience and his mistakes, are merely Kongzi's expressions of modesty (*qianci* 謙辭). By saying so, Zhu risked making Kongzi contradict himself yet at another level. Kongzi said, "To say that you know when you do know and say that you do not know when you do not know—that means you truly know" (*Analects* 2.17). Why would the sage need to pretend that he had no knowledge when he already knew?![12]

Furthermore, even if we grant that the sage cannot be wrong, what about his teachings before he turned into a sage? And how do we tell which sayings were made after he turned to a sage? Reflecting on his own life, Kongzi said:

> At fifteen, I had my heart-mind set on learning. At thirty, I was able to take my stand. At forty, I had no more perplexities. At fifty, I knew the mandate of heaven (*tianming* 天命). At sixty, my ears (*er* 耳) were attuned. At seventy, I could follow my heart's wishes without overstepping the boundaries. (*Analects* 2.4; Ni 2017, 97)

No matter at what age level of his life—fifty, sixty, or seventy—we attribute perfect sagehood to Kongzi, he nevertheless spent a long time before reaching it. Then we would have to conclude that Kongzi was not perfect during most of his lifetime. Because a large portion of the teachings from Kongzi, presumably, were recorded before he became a sage, it follows that these teachings are not fault-free.

With all these difficulties, the effort to make Kongzi an impeccable sage encountered resistance within the Confucian tradition along the way. As early as the first century CE, Wang Chong 王充 (27~97) stood up as one of the first to challenge the perfection of Kongzi. While accepting Kongzi as a sage (*Lunheng*, chapter 3, Section 7; Yang 1999, 22), Wang also recognized Kongzi's fallibility. Wang's major work *Lunheng* 論衡 contains a chapter on "Questioning Kongzi" (*Wen Kong* 問孔). In the seventy sections of the chapter, Wang raised a large number of challenges to the alleged perfection of Kongzi. Wang said:

> Generations of Confucian scholars placed trust in their teachers and took the ancients as correct. They think the sayings of the sages are always right. They only learn about these sayings without questioning. In fact, however, even when the sages wrote with careful deliberation, they were unable to ensure all their sayings were correct. Not to mention when they said things in a rush; how can these all be right?[13]

Wang went on to challenge numerous records of Kongzi. *Analects* 5.10 records Kongzi's student Zai Yu slept during the daytime when he was supposed to study. Kongzi said, "rotten wood cannot be carved; a wall of dung-and-mud cannot be troweled. What is the use of reprimanding Yu?" (Ni 2017, 153) Wang commented that sleeping during the daytime is a minor misconduct whereas the analogies of rotten wood and dung-and-mud are appropriate only for people of major transgressions. Therefore, Kongzi overreacted to Zai Yu's behavior (*Lunheng*, chapter 28, Section 19; Yang 1999, 297–298). In *Analects* 12.7, Kongzi said that in governing a state, one needs to have sufficient food, sufficient arms, and the trust of the people. If one of the three had to be cut down, it should be the arms. The next one to cut down if pressed should be food. The most important thing to retain, hence, is people's trust. Wang commented that, without food, people would abandon ritual propriety (*li* 禮); without ritual propriety, trust could not be maintained, implying that Kongzi got his priorities wrong (*Lunheng*, chapter 28, Section 57; Yang 1999, 306).

To be sure, these matters can be debated. There may have been justifiable reasons for Kongzi to react the way he did (see Ni 2017, 153–154); one could argue that with the people's trust, a state would be able to reacquire food and arms. The point here, however, is that Wang did not believe Kongzi was perfect, and he was willing to challenge the sage.

Zhu Xi's contemporary Lu Xiangshan 陸象山 (1139–1193) argued unequivocally that "ancient sages were not free from faults," and that "they were sages precisely because they were able to correct their faults."[14] Lu even asserted that, if we apply specific standards to measure the lives of the ancient sages, we will find that they all have unforgivable faults.[15] For thinkers like Lu, the greatness of the sages lies precisely in their ability to acquire knowledge tirelessly and to improve themselves through self-correction. Similarly, Ye Shi 葉適 (1150–1223), another contemporary of Zhu Xi, also objected to Zhu's characterization of the sages. Ye said, if the sages are faultless, "then there is no ground for [former sage kings] Yao, Shun, Yu, and Tang to cultivate themselves."[16] Yet, self-cultivation is central to the sagely teachings. Obviously, the notion of self-cultivation presupposes room for improvement. In Ye's view, if the sages were already perfect, self-cultivation would be inapplicable to them. That is contrary to the core of Confucian teachings.

In this regard, one of the foremost critical thinkers was Li Zhi 李贄 (1527–1602) of the Ming dynasty.[17] Li directly challenged the view that Kongzi's words are the absolute standards for measuring right and wrong. In his *General Commentary on Concealed Works* (*Cangshu jizhuan zonglun* 藏書紀傳總論), Li wrote:

> If we all take what Kongzi has taken to be right as right and what Kongzi has taken to be wrong as wrong, then there is really no right and wrong. However, assessing right and wrong is being human. How can it stop (with Kongzi)?[18] (Li Zhi n.d.)

For Li, right and wrong can change over time. What was regarded as right in the past may not be right in today's perspective, and vice versa. Here Li did not distinguish between what was right, on the one hand, and what was *regarded* as right on the other, hence there may be a relativist undertone in his remarks. But he said that, if Kongzi were living today, Kongzi might not hold the same view as he did during his lifetime. Then, why should we today take Kongzi's view as the ultimate truth? Li's main point is that we cannot hold ancient classic texts as infallible and that we must use our moral sensibilities to evaluate classic texts (ibid.). Li's stance is significant for students of Confucian philosophy today. Social circumstances change, and so do people's views. Studying Confucian philosophy today, we should consider what these classic thinkers would have thought if they were living today. If ancient thinkers were reasonable people as they are believed to be, they should be re-educatable as Rorty indicated (see the Introduction of this book) and should hold reasonable views if they were our contemporaries, as we have elaborated under the principle of progressive humanity in the Introduction.

186 RESHAPING CONFUCIANISM: A PROGRESSIVE INQUIRY

Let me summarize: Kongzi did not regard himself as a sage, nor did he think he was free from fault. Subsequent Confucian thinkers took Kongzi to be a sage, as one on a growing list of Confucian sages. However, Confucian thinkers have been divided on whether Confucian sages were infallible. While Cheng Yi and Zhu Xi among the most influential thinkers in subsequent dynasties maintained the infallibility of sages, others have argued to the contrary. Nevertheless, all these thinkers—including Zhu Xi and Cheng Yi—hold the view that classic texts can present wrong messages and should be treated as such.[19] This approach opens doors for us in contemporary times to read Confucian classic texts with a grain of salt when they come to be suspicious from contemporary perspectives. This characteristic, as I will show next, marks a significant difference between Confucian views of classic texts and monotheistic views of respective scriptural texts.

2. Varied Approaches to Canonical Texts

Confucianism is by no means the only tradition with historical baggage. All world cultural traditions have struggled with similar problems. Every tradition must come to terms with its ancient teachings that seem no longer appropriate today. Monotheistic traditions, too, face modern challenges to their scriptures. What monotheistic religions share is the belief that the canonical texts represent the revealed word of God, who is omnibenevolent, omnipotent, omniscient, and omnipresent. A brief comparison with monotheistic traditions of their strategies in dealing with similar problems can help us appreciate the distinctive feature of Confucian progressive approaches to classic texts.[20]

Christianity has faced challenges to its scripture in modern times. The book of *Genesis*, for instance, states that God created the world in six days, whereas modern science has indisputably demonstrated a different story. Is the Bible wrong in this regard? If one believes in science, it would seem so. Yet, believers have resisted such a conclusion. In addressing the Pontifical Academy of Sciences on the subject of cosmology and how to interpret the *Genesis*, Pope John Paul II said:

> The Bible itself speaks to us of the origin of the universe and its make-up, not in order to provide us with a scientific treatise, but in order to state the correct relationships of man with God and with the universe. Sacred

CAN SAGES BE WRONG? 187

Scripture wishes simply to declare that the world was created by God, and in order to teach this truth it expresses itself in the terms of the cosmology in use at the time of the writer.[21]

Accordingly, if *Genesis* does not aim to present the origin of the world as a scientific document, then it should not be read as literally describing the factual process of creation. This statement of the Pope implies that the world was not created in six days. Yet, the Pope stopped short of stating that the Bible is wrong in describing God's creation of the world in such a way. Instead, he wanted believers to extrapolate the true meaning, so to speak, from the text that appears literally problematic. Presumably, the scripture is sacred; it cannot be said to be mistaken. The bottom line must be upheld.

Additional examples abound. *Genesis* 7:23 indicates that God intentionally killed every man, woman, and child on the planet in the great flood, except for eight people. In *Genesis* 16:7–9, God commands Hagar to go back into slavery and bear children for her master after she had already fled and become free. In the New Testament, Jesus Christ is recorded saying that, if a woman commits adultery, not only she will be made to suffer intensely, but her children will also be struck dead (Revelation 2:22–23). Punishing the perpetrator's children is a reoccurring theme in the Bible (e.g., Hosea 13:16, Samuel 15:2–3).[22] A literal reading would make Jesus cruel rather than loving and forgiving. Sensible Christians today would find it difficult to endorse these words and to hold that the children of an adulteress deserve to be killed by an omnibenevolent God. Yet, Jesus is God and what he said cannot be wrong. Then, how do we explain the passage without denying the impeccability of the Scripture? One may say, as Pope John Paul II has suggested, that the writer of the Bible only used the language for readers at the time when the book was written. If that is the case, is the language still appropriate for today's world?

The same encounter is found in Rabbinic teachings. Judaist scholars have attempted to account for similar problems. The Zohar teaches, "the Torah, in all of its words, holds supernal truths and sublime secrets" (Fishbane 1989, 34). These supernal truths and sublime secrets are not to be confused with the narratives themselves, however. The narratives in the Torah are merely her outer "garments." Just as the wine must be kept in a jar, so the Torah must be contained in an article of outer clothing. As Michael Fishbane put it:

Its narrations which relate to things of the world constitute the garments which clothe the body of the Torah; and that body is composed of the

Torah's percepts, *gufey-torah* (bodies, major principles). People without understanding see only the narrations, the garment; those who serve the most high King and stood on mount Sinai, pierce all the way through to the soul, to the true Torah which is the root principle of all. (Fishbane 1989, 34)

Accordingly, the scripture is proclaimed sacred precisely because its teachings are not constituted by language in an ordinary sense. Radiating from the inmost center of divinity, the narratives are a species of the divine Logos; they are but a tangible exteriorization of divinity that provides the symbolic map for the human spiritual journey that may culminate in communion with the most inward truth of God (Fishbane 1989, 35). The language of the Torah is a special language which conveys the ultimate reality or truth of God.

Among early Islamic philosophers to encounter similar issues was Ibn Rushd (Averroes) (1126–1198). For Ibn Rushd, Islam is the ultimate truth, and the nature of philosophy is the search for truth. Truth, however, appears in two forms, scriptural truth and scientifically formulated truth or demonstrative truth. The latter cannot conflict with the Qur'an. Islamic theologians maintain that the scriptural text carries with it both an apparent meaning and an inner meaning. It is its inner meaning that conveys the sacred message (Hillier, n.d.). Therefore, if the scripture appears to conflict with demonstrative truth, such conflict must be only superficial, and the scripture should be interpreted allegorically. In other words, if the scripture appears wrong, it is the apparent meaning that is wrong, not its inner meaning. The real goal for readers is to discover the inner meaning, which is always right.

Generally, in dealing with problematic statements in monotheistic scriptures, the primary solution is to differentiate their inner meanings from the language used in the expression. The language itself, as troubling as it may be, however, cannot be rejected as wrong. After all, the language is part of the sacred scriptures. In this regard, these monotheistic thinkers take a different approach than Confucian thinkers such as Cheng Yi in dealing with Confucian classic texts. For Cheng Yi, the sages cannot be wrong, even though the language in the text can be wrong as it may not accurately record or represent the ideas of the sages. Thus, he took a text-fallibility approach. In taking such a stance, however, Cheng Yi in some way indirectly admitted that the recorded words of the sages—in the way presented to us—can be wrong. After all, the sages do not talk to us directly; all we contemporaries have available to deal with is the text that has been passed on to us. And that is all that matters. In this sense, we can borrow Derrida's famous slogan that "there is nothing outside the text"—replacing "nothing" with "no sage" (Derrida 1972, 148). Hence, as conservative as it is, Cheng Yi's position can nevertheless be taken to mean that the sages *as we know them through classic texts* can be wrong even though the "real" sages in antiquity cannot be wrong. It can be argued, however, that the "real" sages in actuality are just those historical figures manifested through classic texts who represent the spirit of moral rightness to us today. In comparison, other thinkers in the Confucian tradition, like Wang Chong, Lu Xiangshan, Ye Shi, and Li Zhi, took a sage-fallibility approach, asserting the fallibility of not only the classic texts but also of the sages. This is a direct fallibility approach vis-à-vis the indirect approach by Cheng Yi and Zhu Xi. Either way, these Confucian thinkers stand in sharp contrast to the upholders of textual infallibility in the monotheistic traditions.

3. Fallibility of Confucian Sages

Now to recapitulate our findings in the previous sections. On the issue of whether canonical texts can be wrong, Confucian thinkers have taken a different route in stark contrast to their counterparts in monotheistic traditions. As has been shown, their stances differed with regard to the fallibility of the Confucian sages and classic texts. One such stance is that the sages can be wrong and, therefore, so can the classic texts. Another stance is that classic texts can be wrong, but the sages are always right.[23] Although strong disagreement exists on whether sages can be wrong, Confucian thinkers in both camps share a view that classic texts can be wrong, for different reasons. For the first camp, fallible classic texts indicate that, at least in some cases, ancient sages got things wrong. For the second camp, that classic texts get things wrong when these texts fail to represent accurately the views of the sages. Thus, thinkers of both camps can agree that the recorded words of sages *as presented in classic texts* can be wrong. When we say that Confucian sages can be wrong, we take the route of such thinkers as Wang Chong, Lu Xiangshan, Ye Shi, and Li Zhi. For practical purposes, however, saying that Confucian sages can be wrong can also cover the attitude of Cheng Yi, namely the recorded words of the sages as presented in classic texts can be wrong, regardless of whether ancient sages themselves were wrong. Whereas the language of monotheistic scriptures is regarded as sacred, students of Confucian philosophy do not need to take the language of Confucian classic texts as a

190 RESHAPING CONFUCIANISM: A PROGRESSIVE INQUIRY

special language. There is an important distinction. Confucian teachings are delivered in ordinary language accessible to everyone. They can be assessed on such terms. Ultimately, Confucian thinkers, including the sages, are human and humans can be wrong. The fallibility of Confucian sages makes possible an alternative approach to dealing with canonical teachings that are problematic in contemporary perspectives.

The fallibility approach opens four possible ways for research on Confucianism today. First, it enables us to read classic texts as they are and assess them accordingly. Second, it allows us to see different views of classic thinkers and compare them to find progress in their ideas. Third, it makes it possible for us to not only correct but also improve and update Confucian teachings in a progressive manner. Fourth and finally, it opens doors for today's Confucian thinkers to debate about certain issues that do not already have clear answers, without having to take statements by previous sages as the last word.

In the first possible way, traditional Confucian teachings can be placed in three categories measured by contemporary moral sensibilities, (1) good messages delivered in appropriate language, (2) good messages in problematic language, and (3) problematic messages in plain language. The category of good messages delivered in appropriate language occupies the largest share of the three. In the previous chapters, I have cited passages discussing Confucian teachings on various topics. Most of these passages contain messages of significant value for our world today. Most Confucian teachings about a variety of moral virtues belong to this category, such as classical teachings on cultivating virtue, promoting education, and advocating caring government, as are quoted and referenced abundantly throughout this book.

In the second category, there are good messages in problematic language. This category includes valuable messages delivered with historically biased language in distorted ways. For instance, *Mengzi* 3B2 records Mengzi responding to a question about being a "great man" (*da zhangfu* 大丈夫):

> To dwell in the broadest place on earth; to stand in one's proper place in the world; to put into effect the great Way [*Dao*] of the world; to follow it with the people when one obtains one's goal; to practice the Way by oneself when one does not obtain one's goal; wealth and prestige are incapable of seducing him; poverty and low status are incapable of moving him; awe and military might cannot bend him—it is this that is called being a great man. (Van Norden 2008, 78)

Mengzi's description of the "great man" sets a good example for the ideal Confucian personhood. Such a person is upright, independent, free-minded, and with utmost dignity and integrity. This exemplary image has inspired countless people in pursuing the Confucian moral ideal throughout history. However, Mengzi used the gendered term of *da zhangfu* in expressing his ideal. That makes it problematic in contemporary perspectives. His use of such a term is not accidental. In fact, Mengzi formulated his point by specifically contrasting such an ideal with the appropriate way of womanhood:

> Just as a father instructs a man when he comes of age, so does a mother instruct a daughter when she gets married. Sending her off at the threshold, she warns her, "When you join your new family, you must be respectful and circumspect. Do not disobey your husband." Making obedience one's standard is merely the way of a wife or concubine. (*Mengzi* 3B2; Van Norden 2008, 78)

Mengzi's purpose is to promote the ideal of moral uprightness. Yet, in making his case he described it in biased gendered terms and used in contrast the prevalent view of his time that a married woman should be obedient to her husband, as the contrasting way of the "great man." Mengzi's rhetoric here reveals his gender bias against women, a view shared by almost everyone during his time. Today, we should take his message for the morally upright and discard his sexist language.

Then, there is a third category: problematic messages in plain language. Some of Kongzi's sayings regarding women belong to this category. *Analects* 8.20 records Kongzi commenting on King Wu's remark of having ten able ministers. Kongzi said, "because there was a woman among them, there were actually only nine (able ministers)." His sexist attitude here is plain and simple. A reasonable conclusion is that Kongzi indeed held sexist views toward women and such a view is no longer acceptable in contemporary times. Having accepted the fallibility of Confucian sages, for messages of this sort we do not need to hide or try to explain them away with various excuses. Instead, we should accept the fact that some messages from classic Confucian thinkers are wrong and must be rectified as we study and develop Confucian philosophy progressively as a living tradition.

Following such thinkers as Wang Chong, Lu Xiangshan, and Li Zhi, we can accept the stance that Confucian sages are human and, as such, they can be wrong. Such a realization is liberating. Confucians do not have to defend

192 RESHAPING CONFUCIANISM: A PROGRESSIVE INQUIRY

every word by Kongzi or other sages at the cost of credibility and plausibility. For example, contemporary Confucians have been troubled deeply by Section 17.25 of the *Analects*, where Kongzi is recorded as saying:

> Women (*nüzi* 女子) and petty persons are difficult to deal with. If you let them get too close, they become insolent. If you keep them at a distance, they complain. (Lau 1979, 148)

Xing Bing 邢昺 (932–1010), an influential annotator of the *Analects*, already found this passage problematic. He noted that here *nüzi* does not include virtuous and intelligent women such as the mother of King Wen of the Zhou Dynasty (TTC, 2526). For Xing, there is nothing wrong with the statement in general as long as exceptions are made for a handful of recognized virtuous women in history. Presumably, most of Xing's contemporaries would have agreed with his assessment of the female population.

Today, people have found Xing's qualifications inadequate; various attempts have been made to explain away a reading that shows Kongzi to be sexist. For instance, some have said that *nüzi* refers to young servants rather than women in general.[24] These attempts have been less than effective, however. Evidently, even prominent Confucian scholar Xing recognized that *nüzi* is a general reference for women, otherwise he would not have had to qualify it by making exceptions for King Wen's mother. One must wonder, can we really rule out that Kongzi held sexist views regarding women, given that virtually everyone else did during his times? If we cannot rule it out, why shouldn't this passage be taken as what it literally says? If we accept that Kongzi and Confucian sages can be wrong in their views, we are in a better position to deal with similar issues in a more reasonable manner.

Now I move to the second of the four ways made possible by the fallibility approach. That is, it allows us to see different views of classic thinkers and compare them in order to find progress in their ideas. As has been shown in Chapter 4 of this book, the views on children's filial duty to parents vary from Kongzi, Mengzi, to Xunzi. Whereas Kongzi's view is the most conservative of the three, Mengzi's view is more moderate, with Xunzi's view appearing most appropriate from contemporary perspectives. As we draw Confucian teachings from its ancient past, we do not need to assume that all classic thinkers share the same views. With the fallibility approach, it becomes a legitimate question to inquire, which one of these views should be upheld for today's progressive Confucianism?

The third possible way with the fallibility approach is that it enables us to not only correct but also improve and update Confucian teachings in a progressive manner. Here is an example. Kongzi was among the first in history to advocate education regardless of a person's social class. His pioneering philosophy of education has benefited countless people to this date. Yet, at the same time, out of his three thousand students, not a single one was female. By today's standard, this seems highly problematic. If he were to live in today's society where the two sexes are regarded as equal, would Kongzi teach female students? The principle of progressive humanity, as expounded in the Introduction of this book, tells us that a reasonable answer is affirmative. In such a light, the Confucian teaching of "education regardless of social classes" (*you jiao wu lei* 有教無類) (*Analects* 15.39) has now become "education regardless of social classes and regardless of sexes." We must apply this type of thinking as we examine Confucian ideas from ancient times.

Finally, the fallibility approach also paves the ways for a fourth possibility. That is, it makes it possible for today's Confucian thinkers to debate openly about certain issues that do not already have clear answers, without having to take statements by previous sages as the last word. Confucian philosophy progresses forward in such a process. Alasdaire MacIntyre said:

> A tradition is an argument extended through time in which certain fundamental agreements are defined and redefined in terms of two kinds of conflict: those with critics and enemies external to the tradition who reject all or at least key parts of those fundamental agreements, and those internal, interpretative debates through which the meaning and rationale of the fundamental agreements come to be expressed and by whose progress a tradition is constituted. (MacIntyre 1988, 12)

A cultural tradition evolves with time, and it must be able to treat its own history in ways that promote healthy growth and renewal. Within a tradition, internal debates are often carried out by reinterpreting existing views and, at times, introducing new ideas into its conceptual reservoir. In such a process, tackling issues inherited from the past to meet contemporary needs is the most important challenge in advancing a tradition.

194 RESHAPING CONFUCIANISM: A PROGRESSIVE INQUIRY

The fallibility approach allows students today to debate on whether a certain Confucian teaching still holds. For instance, *Analects* 13.18 records:

> The Duke of She told Kongzi, "In my country there is an upright man named Kung. When his father stole a sheep, he bore witness against him." Kongzi said, "The upright men in my community are different from this. The father conceals the misconduct of the son and the son conceals the misconduct of the father. Uprightness is to be found in this." (Chan 1963, 41)

Contemporary thinkers have taken various approaches to the issue raised here. By and large, we can place them in two camps. One camp holds that it is morally permissible to conceal misconduct for one another within the family (e.g., Gong 2004). The other is of the opposite view, especially with serious misconduct. The latter camp is further divided into two groups. One group holds that Kongzi was wrong in holding such a view (e.g., Liu 2007). The other group of the second camp attempts to explain away the apparent conflict with ethical conduct through novel textual readings. For example, some have come up with readings that the passage does not mean that the father stole a sheep or that family members can conceal one another's misconduct.[25] These different approaches within the second camp reflect varied attitudes toward Kongzi, even though they share the view that stealing a sheep is wrong and family members should not conceal such wrong doings for one another. Whereas some think that Kongzi can be wrong, others think otherwise. If we accept the fallibility of Confucian sages, there is little need for explaining away the problem through novel readings. Here the philosophical problem facing us is, Should the son conceal the misconduct of his father?[26] Contemporary Confucian thinkers can now openly debate about the matter and can even disagree with Kongzi on the matter. Such engagement is the nature of philosophy and should be accepted as healthy within contemporary progressive Confucianism.

In conclusion, the fallibility approach to Confucian sages is important to progressive Confucianism today. It is not my intention to show that other alternative approaches do not work. I wish to show, however, that in comparison with other approaches, this Confucian fallibility to mistakes makes it more ready to admit faults and modify itself in response to new challenges in contemporary times. Progressive Confucian thinkers should fully use this special feature of Confucianism. This is a straightforward way, and hopefully a more sensible way for moving forward.

Building on the concept of the fallibility of Confucian sages, this book argues for cases that can appeal to a broad readership, including both those within the Confucian tradition and people who are external to the tradition but nevertheless are willing to hear the argument. Inevitably, people will disagree on exactly which idea or which part of an idea should be discarded or substantially reformed. The matter is complex because it is not merely about interpretation, but it has also to do with our own values and orientations. Readers of this book will have plenty of room to judge the extent of success of such an effort.

Study Questions

1. In Confucianism, what kind of persons are sages?
2. What have been the main controversies about sages?
3. Why is the fallibility of Confucian sages a relevant issue for our study today?
4. Is there a similar fallibility in monotheist traditions or other traditions that you are familiar with?
5. In your view, what are the strengths and weaknesses of the fallibility approach?
6. According to the author, what new possible ways does the fallibility approach open? Explain these.
7. The author argues that traditional Confucian teachings can be placed in three categories. What are these? Do you agree?
8. In your view, should the son conceal the misconduct of his father? If yes, is there a limit on how far one can go along this line?
9. Besides those cited in this chapter, can you think of other examples of problematic teachings in a cultural tradition? How do you assess them?

SECTION III
SOCIO-POLITICAL RECONSTRUCTIONS

9

Freedom through Choosing

Freedom is a primary value in contemporary society. A progressive account of the Confucian view of the good life in the twenty-first century must include a reasonable conception of freedom. Yet, freedom has rarely been associated with Confucian philosophy. This unfortunate situation is due largely to two reasons. First, ancient Confucian thinkers did not take freedom as a top value. Instead, they were concerned primarily with restoring order in a chaotic society by strengthening family ties and rectifying social relationships. The second reason is that most contemporary students of Confucian philosophy take a historical approach rather than a forward-looking approach. For them, Confucian philosophy is what it has been, not what it can be or should be for the contemporary world. In this chapter, I argue that Confucianism has resources for constructing its own conception of freedom and that there is no need to transplant a Western notion of "free will" for such a purpose. I construct a commonsensical conception of Confucian freedom largely along the lines of Charles Taylor's "exercise concept." An exercise concept of freedom is concerned with exercising control over one's life. A person is free only to the extent that she has effectively determined herself and the shape of her life. Thus, "if we are free in the exercise of certain capacities, then we are not free, or less free, when these capacities are in some way unfulfilled or blocked" (Taylor 2001, 205). Thus understood, Confucian freedom is to be realized by developing personal capabilities and by creating societal conditions to achieve meaningfully chosen goals. Specifically, it is to be realized in the process of choosing the good (*zeshan* 擇善). Understood as such, Confucian freedom is both liberating and fulfilling.

1. Freedom or Free Will

In the modern West, the term "free will" is commonly used in reference to human agency and the ultimate source of freedom. The metaphysical notion of free will as the ultimate agency that determines human action, however, is

Reshaping Confucianism. Chenyang Li, Oxford University Press. © Oxford University Press 2024.
DOI: 10.1093/oso/9780197657621.003.0010

200   RESHAPING CONFUCIANISM: A PROGRESSIVE INQUIRY

a deeply problematic concept.[1] Confucians do not need to import this notion to establish human agency and to explicate human freedom.

A historical examination reveals that the original notion of free will was not necessary for explicating human freedom. While freedom was unquestionably a part of ancient Greek philosophy before the Common Era, "free will" was not. "The Greeks had no word of this kind in their language to denote will or intention as such" (Dihle 1982, 20), let alone "free will." Greek philosophers tended to see human action as a result of the two forces in the soul, appetites and intellect. For Socrates, the soul becomes free as the person masters philosophy and uses his intellect to control appetites. However, we do not have to ascribe free will to the soul to make the point. The soul in Plato's *Phaedo*, for instance, is similar to the rational part of the soul, reason, in his *Republic*. It confronts and regulates desires, far from being neutral with respect to the good as the metaphysical notion of "free will" purports to be. The notion of ἀκρασία (*akrasia*), often translated as "weakness of the will," simply means "lack of power (over oneself)." The noun is derivative from the adjective ἀκρατής (*akratēs*), powerless. Which is in turn derivative of the negative particle of *a* and κράτος (*krátos*), strength or power. Hence, ἀκρασία means "not having the power (to control oneself)." There is simply no "will" in it. Translating it in terms of the will is a later interpretation. The interpretation suggests that the soul (which Socrates affirms) somehow contains a will (which Socrates does not affirm), and that the will is not strong enough to control the soul. In doing so, an inner agency is planted inside the soul, which for Socrates is already the agency itself. Aristotle discusses freedom in terms of voluntary actions, involuntary actions, and choice. The agent of these actions is the person (*Nicomachean Ethics* Book III, Sections 1 and 2). Choice or προαίρεσις (*prohairesis*) is a purposive decision shaped by reasoning. Aristotle maintains that the person lacking self-restraint (*akrasia*) acts out of only (non-rational) desires, whereas the self-restrained person acts from choice (προαίρεσις) (*Nicomachean Ethics* 1111b14–15). The term προαίρεσις is used here in a specific way. In a study of Aristotle's use, Charles Chamberlain interprets the term as "commitment" that encompasses the entire process of rational decision-making. He writes:

> Aristotle seems to use the term *prohairesis* to refer to all parts of this process, from the selecting from deliberation to the point at which desire and reason concur. (Chamberlain 1984, 153–154)

FREEDOM THROUGH CHOOSING 201

Thence, these ancient Greek philosophers simply did not appeal to a metaphysical notion of "free will" in their accounts of human agency. This fact in itself does not prove that there is no free will. It does suggest, however, that we can make good sense of the human world and philosophize in meaningful ways about human agency without appealing to the concept of free will.

The concept of free will has a specific cultural origin. It came into prominence in the West largely due to the work of Saint Augustine,[2] whom Hannah Arendt has called the "first philosopher of the will" (Arendt 1978, 84). Augustine did not invent the concept entirely from nothing, however. Epictetus (55–135 CE) already made a major departure from Aristotle and interpreted προαίρεσις as the will. The will, for Epictetus, is an independent power and is naturally free (*Discourses* II, Ch. 15). When Epictetus stated that the good is within the power of the will (*Discourses* III, Ch. 7) and that nothing is good or bad besides the will (*Discourses* III, Ch. 10), he came close to the view that only the will is capable of committing evil. Nevertheless, it was Augustine who drove the notion to prominence. Albrecht Dihle writes:

> St. Augustine was, in fact, the inventor of our modern notion of will, which he conceived for the needs and purposes of his specific theology and in continuation of the attempts of Greek theologians, who developed their doctrine of the Trinity in terms of Neoplatonic ontology. He took the decisive step towards the concept of human will by reinterpreting a hermeneutical term as an anthropological one. This eventually led him to an adequate philosophical description of what the Biblical tradition taught about man's fall, salvation, and moral conduct. (Dihle 1982, 144)

The will for Augustine is the "free will." He was influenced deeply by Greek intellectualism, believing in the power of human intellect in directing a rational life. This view, however, appeared inadequate as he gradually realized the large impact of non-rational factors on human life. He was faced with a rather challenging task. If God is all-good and God created humans, how could humans ever fall? Developing a robust theodicy, Augustine set out to show that human wrongdoings do not affect the all-goodness of God. For that purpose and others, he had to develop a concept of free will that is sufficiently strong in order to defend the all-goodness of God. By developing his theory this way, Augustine has given free will a life of its own; no longer the soul, not even the intellect or reason, it is the "free will" that is ultimately responsible for human action. Dihle has observed, Augustine's "will" leaves out any reference to thought, instinct, or emotion as possible sources of its intention. This is a major departure from the ancient Greek, who express intention only together with one of its causes, but never in its own right (Dihle 1982, 24–25).

Augustine's move has led Western philosophy to a notion of free will that is totally stripped out of the human person. The "will" is now the independent intending agency for action. It intends its intention that is absolutely its own. When it comes to existentialist philosophy, free will has transformed into radical absolute freedom. In the ways in which the concept has been construed, free will does not depend on anything for its existence and operation; it is a completely free-standing entity, presumably a non-physical one. It is like a little man stuck in a person's head making all decisions for the person, or a soul within the soul. This little man cannot be shut off from outside. This notion of free will has been infested with a world of problems in the face of challenges from determinism. These problems cannot be resolved. An alternative is to get out of the trap set out by Augustine and his followers. Instead of conceptualizing human agency in terms of free will, we should look for a holistic notion of human freedom.

Admittedly, for many people the expression of "free will" is already commonplace in everyday life.[3] Abandoning the concept of free will in accounting for freedom should not inhibit people from using the term to mean that a person can think independently and can act freely.[4] Such uses do not have to imply the notion of "free will" as developed by Augustine and his followers, namely the "free will" rather than the person (or the "heart-mind" in Chinese philosophy) is making all decisions. As a metaphysical concept, however, "free will" should be laid to rest.

Some thinkers have attempted to introduce free will to account for freedom in Confucian philosophy. In an article entitled "A Theory of Confucian Selfhood: Self-Cultivation and Free Will in Confucian Philosophy," Chungying Cheng claims that in Confucianism *zhi* 志 is "an independent decision-making power that is absolutely free" (Cheng 2004, 132). But does *zhi* mean free will? When Confucian thinkers talk about *li zhi* 立志 and *yang zhi* 養志, they are talking about establishing (*li*) a purpose or determination (*zhi*) and nurturing (*yang*) such a determination (*zhi*). This is the case even when the word is used as a verb, as in Kongzi's famous statement, "*zhi yu xue*," in *Analects* 2.4,[5] which Wing-tsit Chan has translated as, "my mind was set on learning" (Chan 1963, 22). In his classic annotations of the *Analects*, Zhu

Xi explains this statement as meaning that *zhi* is what the heart-mind (*xin* 心) intends.[6] The Han annotator Zhao Qi interprets Mengzi's notion of *zhi* as "what the heart-mind intends and consciously considers."[7] In all these cases, it is the heart-mind that does the intending and considering, not the *zhi* itself. The *zhi* is the outcome rather than the initiator of these psychological activities. This is a major difference between *zhi* and free will. Whereas free will is supposed to lead the "heart-mind" (soul) in St. Augustine, in Confucian philosophy is the other way around: the heart-mind leads and determines *zhi*. In the Confucian view, a person should establish a goal in life for personal cultivation and orientate oneself in the right direction. After such an orientation has been set, the person needs to strengthen and re-enforce such a goal continuously so that it does not wither and continues to guide the person's life. Rina Camus writes aptly:

> *Zhi* is inextricably valenced. It is not construed as a parallel force to other faculties, superior or inferior. Instead, it is a power that ensues from the heart-mind and bears in its course and configuration that the heart-mind cherishes. (Camus 2018, 1105)

As Camus maintains, *zhi* is not purely volitional; it involves a plan or intention that one harbors in the heart-mind.[8] Kwong-loi Shun has rendered *zhi* as "directions" (Shun 2004). Similarly, Sor-hoon Tan explicates *zhi* in terms of "personal commitment" rather than "will" (Tan 2003, 50), while Stephen Angle translated *zhi* as "personal moral commitment" (Angle 2009, 55).[9] In such understandings, *zhi* is a product of the heart-mind, not its master. It is neither an independent agency nor absolutely free.

There may be a variety of reasons why Confucian philosophers did not develop a concept of free will. One of these reasons, I suggest, is that there was no such need. Confucianism does not recognize an omnipotent and omniscient god. Thus, there is no need for a theodicy. They did not, and do not, need a concept of free will to account for human agency. Attempting to locate a concept of "free will" in Confucianism as evidence for Confucian freedom is heading in the wrong direction, like climbing a tree in search for a fish, to borrow an expression from Mengzi (*Mengzi* 1A7). This is not to say, however, that ancient Confucian thinkers did not have ideas of freedom or that contemporary Confucians cannot develop a conception of human freedom on the basis of these ideas, as will be demonstrated next.

2. Freedom through Choosing

Isaiah Berlin is known for his two concepts of liberty: negative liberty and positive liberty (Berlin 2002). In *Unfinished Dialogue* (2006), Berlin saw a need to supplement these concepts with another. He proposed that there are two senses of liberty. The first sense is ordinary political liberty, which includes both negative liberty and positive liberty. These are values that we pursue, along with other values. He said, "then there is a basic sense, which is choosing" (Berlin and Polanowska-Sygulska 2006, 218). The latter sense of liberty is more basic than the first because it underlies the first and is broader than political freedom in scope. Berlin used "liberty" and "freedom" interchangeably. With regard to choosing, he said that "freedom is to do with the absence of obstacles to choice" (ibid., 152). In the rest of this chapter, I will show that a conception of freedom as choosing is deeply rooted in Confucian philosophy and that bringing it to the forefront through reconstruction will enable Confucianism to address issues of the modern world more effectively.

The Chinese term for freedom commonly used today is *ziyou* 自由. *Zi* means self. Among numerous ways in which the word *you* has been used are: (i) to follow, as in "to follow this road," and (ii) by, as in "blown away by wind," which indicates the agency of an event. Combining the two words, the compound term *ziyou* literally means "following oneself" or "acting by oneself."[10] Thus, *ziyou* has a close etymological connection with autonomy.

The term of *ziyou* does not appear in pre-Qin texts. Among the first to use it were two Han dynasty scholars of Confucian classics, Zheng Xuan 鄭玄 (127–200) and Zhao Qi 趙岐 (ca. 108–201). The *Book of Rites* discusses the appropriate protocol for meeting with a superior. It advises that one should request to be seen but not request to leave the meeting until the superior tells one to leave.[11] Zheng Xuan commented, "one does not dare to follow oneself (*ziyou*) on whether to leave or to stay."[12] In other words, it is courteous for the inferior to wait until he is dismissed by his superior; deciding on his own would be rude. Even though such a view may look over-restrictive today, this statement suggests a limit on one's freedom, indicating an unfavorable view of unrestrained freedom. Conceptually, the statement proves that *ziyou* has acquired a sense of freedom because the claim that one is not free to do something implies the issue of freedom.

Another source comes from the *Mengzi*. When he was in the state of Qi, Mengzi commented that, because he held no office there, "Why should I not have plenty of scope when it comes to the question of staying or leaving?"

(*Mengzi* 2B5; Lau 1970, 89). In his annotations on the *Mengzi*, Zhao Qi commented, "(Mengzi was) free to stay or leave; he had plenty of scope when it comes to that matter."[13] The Chinese expression of "free to stay or leave" is *jin tui ziyou*. Here *ziyou* comes with a favorable sense of freedom.[14] Because nothing held Mengzi back, it was his choice to decide on the matter; it was his freedom. In these cases, *ziyou* carries a connotation of freedom in the usual sense of the term.[15] These examples show that, although pre-Qin thinkers did not use the term *ziyou* that was used later for freedom, they did think about freedom in their own expressions, including what kind of freedom is appropriate, as explicated by later thinkers like Zheng Xuan and Zhao Qi. In both cases, the sense of freedom is conveyed and framed in terms of making choices. Evidently, in both cases the person in question could choose to stay or to leave, even though there is a matter of appropriateness involved in the decision. In these instances, freedom as suggested is rather in a minimal and crude sense, without philosophical elaboration. They can, however, serve as building blocks in constructing a philosophical conception of freedom. Research shows that Robert Morrison (1782–1834) was (among) the first to translate the Western term "freedom" to *ziyou* in Chinese (Lin 2021). This translation was popularized by Yan Fu 嚴復 (1854–1921). Yan's introduction of John Stuart Mill's work to China greatly enriched the significance of *ziyou* by connecting this term with Western concepts of "freedom" and "liberty." Unlike John Stuart Mill, however, Yan noted both positive and negative aspects of *ziyou* (Lin 2021), carrying on the Chinese traditional view. That is, freedom as *ziyou* is valuable and necessary for pursuing the good life, as in the case of Mengzi; in the meantime, it can also be improperly used as in the case discussed by Zheng Xuan.

I suggest that traces for ideas of freedom in these early thinkers can be identified in two forms. The first form is *communication without coinage*. This refers to cases where thinkers communicated ideas of freedom without explicitly coining *ziyou* or similar terms, as the above Mengzi case demonstrates. Mengzi clearly had the idea that he was free to stay or leave the state of Qi. He did not, however, coin a specific term like *ziyou* for the idea. Zhao Qi later identified the idea and explicitly assigned the term *ziyou* to it. If we agree with Zhao's interpretation as I think we should, we accept that Mengzi expressed an idea of freedom in his statement without explicitly coining the term, even though the idea is in a rather primitive form. The second form is by way of *implied concept*. By "implied concept," I mean a concept x that is logically entailed in another concept y so that y cannot make sense without presupposing an understanding of x even though x is not explicitly articulated. For example, Chapter *Tangong* B of the *Book of Rites* records a story of Kongzi conversing with a woman, who lived at the foot of Mount Tai where tigers had killed her father-in-law, her husband, and her son. When Kongzi asked why she did not leave the place, she responded that there was no cruel government. Kongzi then commented that a cruel government is more brutal than man-eating tigers (TTC, 1313). In this case, by asking why the woman did not move away, Kongzi implied that she could choose to stay or leave. Similar to the "ought implies can" relation, saying that a person ought to do x implies that the person can do x, the very fact that pre-Qin thinkers discussed whether someone should choose to do something, or how to choose, shows that they already implied logically that the person in question has the freedom to do so. Otherwise, their discussions would not have made sense. So far as their discussions make sense, we can conclude that the idea of freedom is implied regardless of its lack of sophistication and nuances. In view of this understanding, even though ancient Confucian thinkers did not use freedom as a concept to articulate their vision of the good life, progressive Confucian thinkers today can develop from these early ideas and frame Confucian philosophy in terms of freedom.

In pre-Qin Confucian classics, the idea of freedom is implied and framed in their discourse on the topic of making meaningful choices. One keyword used frequently for such a function is *ze* 擇. The *Shuowen* lexicon defines *ze* as *jian* and *xuan*, namely "to differentiate and to select."[16] It means to discriminate among options and make choices. Xunzi, for example, takes choice (*ze*) as what the heart-mind makes among one's dispositions through deliberation.[17] This meaning is also expressed by the compound term *xuanze* 選擇 in classic texts (e.g., *Mengzi* 3A3; *Xunzi*, chapter 11). In this regard, pre-Qin Confucian thinkers bear a striking resemblance with Aristotle as the latter uses προαίρεσις (*prohairesis*) to describe a person's ability to make choices as a form of freedom. Having choices implies options; choosing among options is freedom, at least in a minimal sense.

This tradition of understanding freedom in terms of making choices is reflected in the work of the prominent twentieth century Chinese scholar Qian Mu 錢穆 (1895–1990). Qian holds that an essential characteristic of the human life is being able to choose among available goals (Qian 2004, 17). In his view, there is a positive correlation between available choices and freedom. There is more freedom when there are more choices provided through more available and richer goals. Qian writes:

FREEDOM THROUGH CHOOSING 207

When there are two goals for you to choose from, you have two counts of freedom; when there are ten goals for you to choose from, you have ten counts of freedom [*ceteris paribus*]. (Qian 2004, 18)

For Qian as for his ancient forerunners, the degree of human freedom lies with the amount and the quality of available choices ("goals") in life. Freedom is enhanced when more and better choices are made available. Qian holds that culture is the human activity to create more and better choices beyond nature. Understood this way, the concept of Confucian freedom in terms of choice-making is not metaphysical in character. It does not aim to refute determinism or its likes such as a fated course of life (*ming* 命). Rather it is existential; it takes as a fact that people can choose and do choose in life and this fact proves the existence of freedom. The real question for Confucian freedom is about how to achieve meaningful freedom and to create conditions for personal and social fulfillment in achieving such freedom, rather than a metaphysical entanglement on whether human freedom is possible.

In pre-Qin texts, *ze* is often used to mean the act of choosing from available options. For instance, in *Mengzi* 1B22, Mengzi tells the Duke of Liang that, faced with external threats, the duke must choose (*ze*) between staying to fight for their land or taking his people to a safe place.[18] In the *Zuo Commentary*, Wuji asks Ziwu to show a few weapons from which he can choose (*ze*).[19] Chapter *Aigong Year 11* of the same text states that it is always that birds choose (*ze*) trees, and never that trees choose birds.[20] In all such usages, choosing means exercising the capacity to select one out of several options. Moreover, *ze* is used frequently for choosing a specific thing or a specific type of thing. In such cases, the act of choosing and the intended chosen outcome are linked. For instance, in the *Book of Rites*, Zigao in the midst of a serious illness says, "after I die, choose (*ze*) a barren land for my burial."[21] In the *Zuo Commentary*, Hun Liangfu says that Duke Wei should choose (*ze*) the talented one of his two sons.[22] Chapter *Zhaogong Year 7* of the same text states that one of the functions of governance is to choose (*ze*) appropriate people (for assignment).[23] In these cases, choosing is directed in a specific way, either choosing an infertile land for burial, choosing a gifted son for assignment, or selecting the right people for government offices.

This kind of choosing does not mean just picking anything randomly from several options. It is to choose an option with certain determinate considerations. Evidently, when deliberating on making choices, ancient thinkers not only discuss the act of choosing itself; more importantly, they consider how to choose and what to choose. In *Analects*, 4.1 Kongzi says, "it is good to live in a place of *ren* (virtue); if one chooses (*ze*) not to live in such a place, how can we say he is wise?"[24] One's choice reflects the kind of person one is, and one's choices contribute to the making of a person. In such an understanding, freedom is realized not in choosing per se, but in choosing an appropriate option. For this reason, Xunzi emphasizes the importance of *shanze* 善擇, namely being good or competent at making appropriate choices (*Xunzi*, chapters 9, 11). One should choose wisely and effectively in achieving goals.

Because the noun "choice" in English is used also to denote objects of choice (e.g., "there are two choices on the table"), and because *ze* emphasizes the act or process of making choices, I translate *ze* as "choosing" in its gerund form to register it clearly as an action concept. This is consistent with Isaiah Berlin's view that "choosing is a kind of action" (Berlin and Polanowska-Sygulska 2006, 152). In the Confucian context, "choosing" is the gate to freedom.

3. External and Internal Conditions for Choosing the Good

Berlin's second sense of liberty (freedom) as choosing, as quoted earlier, is a thin concept. He took choosing to be "simply the capacity for choice," capacity merely in a subjective sense, an ability that is given to human beings (Berlin and Polanowska-Sygulska 2006, 152). In his view, choosing is freedom, yet "the ability to realise your choice has nothing to do with it. You may not be able to realise it" (ibid., 218). Berlin illustrated with an example:

> You choose not to be tied to the tree. You can't help it if you're tied. But you enjoy being tied? No: you choose freedom. I'm sorry I can't give it to you. But you choose it. (ibid., 218)

His point seems to be that, when you choose to realize a goal, you are free even if you are prevented from realizing the goal. At this point, Confucian freedom takes a different route. Confucian freedom differs from Berlin's thin notion of choosing in two important ways. First, Confucian freedom is connected intrinsically to its realization and freedom cannot be separated from the conditions for its realization. Thus, it pays particular attention to

FREEDOM THROUGH CHOOSING 209

how freedom is to be realized. Second, for Berlin, "choosing is part of the evidence for being a human being" (ibid., 218). His notion of choosing as freedom is anthropological in nature, without any moral qualification. In comparison, Confucian freedom is not defined as just any form of choosing; it is understood as choosing to build a life that exemplifies humanity. Choosing is to choose the good for the good life. I will now address both points in turn.

On the basis of our investigation in Section 2, a Confucian conception of freedom can be constructed along the lines of freedom through choosing—not choosing per se but choosing effectively. Two sets of conditions are necessary for choosing to take place in fruitful ways. First, there must be available options from which a choice is made. Second, the choosing agent must possess relevant abilities to choose. Circumstances of these two sets of conditions affect the degrees of realizable freedom in a person and in society. Various Confucian pursuits can be construed as advancing freedom by developing these two sets of conditions. For convenience, I call them "external conditions" and "internal conditions" respectively.[25]

External conditions concern whether, and to what extent, a person is facilitated or constrained by existing factors in one's environment. These conditions can be either favorable or unfavorable for making effective choices. Unfavorable conditions also include—but are not limited to—external interference, which is the focus of Isaiah Berlin's discussion of the concept of negative liberty (Berlin 2002, 173). In the story of Kongzi's conversation on man-eating tigers (TTC, 1313), while the woman could choose between living in a harsh mountain environment or under a cruel government, her freedom was extremely limited. Her freedom would have been significantly increased if her option had included the external condition of a safe environment with a caring government. Ancient Confucian thinkers advocated for a better social environment so the range of possible choices can be expanded. For instance, they established schools and advocated education for all social classes (e.g., *Analects* 15.39), they argued against heavy taxation so people could have adequate means to live their lives (e.g., *Mengzi* 1A5), and they insisted that government should not draft labors for state projects during farming seasons so people could produce adequately for living a decent life (e.g., *Analects* 1.5). The last point later developed into an important political creed in Confucian (as well as Daoist) political philosophy that the government should not interfere with people's normal lives (*bu raomin* 不擾民).[26] According to this creed, governments should leave people alone as

210   RESHAPING CONFUCIANISM: A PROGRESSIVE INQUIRY

much as possible, except for collecting taxes and drafting people for necessary state projects and during wartimes.

Internal conditions have to do with an agent's ability for exercising available choices in meaningful ways. To use an analogy, while a bird in a cage has little freedom, a bird without a cage may not be free if it does not possess the adequate ability to fly. Similarly, when a seasoned mountain climber and an amateur get lost in deep mountains respectively, they possess the same amount of negative freedom to return home. They are provided with the same external conditions. However, they cannot achieve the same degree of freedom because a seasoned climber is equipped with the knowledge, skills, and experience to get out alive whereas an amateur may not. There is a matter of agent competency.

No one is born with competency. Developing competency requires socialization. As far as freedom is concerned, socialization is a double-edged sword. It can foster as well as frustrate freedom. Recent feminist philosophy of personal autonomy has provided useful insights into explicating agent competency in the context of socialization. Autonomy and freedom are closely related concepts. Autonomy, literally self-ruling or independent decision-making, emphasizes a person's internal capacity to make decisions for herself. Freedom is often associated with the environment of action and with the action itself. A person cannot be autonomous without a free environment, even though a free environment does not necessitate personal autonomy.[27] Strictly speaking, a non-autonomous person cannot act freely. By examining autonomy with socialization, we have much to learn about freedom in the context of social relationships.

The idea of autonomy has been associated closely with Immanuel Kant. For Kant, autonomy is the property of a rational will which establishes law for itself. In a similar vein, autonomy in John Rawls' theory of justice is manifested in free and rational agents formulating principles of justice in the "original position" (Rawls 1971). In such views, people in relationships are less autonomous than free-standing individuals. Feminist philosophers, however, hold that the human person is a relational social being, a view that is shared in Confucian philosophy (see Yao 1996). They have articulated theories of relational autonomy on the basis of the relational self (e.g., Stoljar 2018). On this feminist account, personal autonomy is not separate from socialization (Mackenzie and Stoljar 2000, 4). The pertinent question here is what kind of socialization is conducive to personal autonomy and thus to freedom. In an oppressive society, intensive socialization leaves no breathing room for people to pause, to reflect, and to think for themselves. It, therefore, suffocates freedom. However, reasonable socialization is necessary for the normal, and optimal, development of autonomous individuals. On this conception, people's relationality is not only compatible with personal autonomy, but also a necessary condition for achieving it.

Diana Meyers has argued that autonomy requires competency. She maintains that personal autonomy has a threefold structure: self-discovery, self-definition, and self-direction. That is, an autonomous person must know what she is like, must be able to establish her own standards and to modify her qualities to meet them, and must express herself in ways that she deems fitting and worthy of herself personally in action (Meyers 1989, 20, 32). In Meyers's view, personal autonomy has episodic and programmatic characteristics. It involves episodic self-direction—a person pauses at decision points to reflect and to orient her direction in that period of her life. Programmatic self-direction enables a person to establish well-meshed, long-term life plans that provide for an integrated personality. To be able to achieve these, autonomous people need to develop skills that enable them to engage in meaningful inquiries and to carry out their decisions. Meyers calls such skills "the competency of autonomy." In her view, whether a person is autonomous depends on whether the person possesses and successfully uses the skills comprised by the competency of autonomy (ibid., 53). In this conception, personal autonomy is a capacity that individuals acquire through meaningful socialization. It is an accomplished faculty, rather than something people automatically possess just by being left alone without external interference. In real life, people sometimes regret decisions they made earlier because they did not "know better." To "know better" implies not only to be more informed but also to be more competent in decision making. For instance, a graduating student with a philosophy major must decide whether she will continue to pursue a post-graduate degree in philosophy or in law. It is her decision. However, there is a huge difference between deciding on an impulse or making a deliberative decision after taking all relevant factors into consideration, such as career prospects and the likelihood of lasting interest. What counts as relevant is not arbitrary. She needs pertinent knowledge and skills to synthesize information to give herself a holistic view of the matter to make a responsible choice. She needs skills of competency for her autonomy. Thus, contemporary feminists provide a vantage point from which we can examine and frame the Confucian conception of freedom in contemporary terms.

212   RESHAPING CONFUCIANISM: A PROGRESSIVE INQUIRY

As mentioned before, the Chinese term for freedom, *ziyou*, literally means "following oneself"; it has a strong connotation of autonomy. It implies that freedom is realized through personal autonomy. Developing a well-cultivated self is at the center of Confucian moral philosophy. In the Confucian view, the self is realized through learning and appropriate socialization (see more discussion in Chapter 12 of this book). Through such a process, a person becomes more and more competent in conducting oneself and thus expands one's capacities for freedom. This aspect of Confucian freedom overlaps with Berlin's notion of positive freedom; both call for the need of mastering one's own destination. Berlin identified two forms of self-mastery. One is self-abnegation. In self-abnegation one "retreats to the inner citadel" by denying one's own desires and wishes to cope with external limitations (Berlin 2002, 181). This kind of self-mastery reduces one's scope of freedom. The other is self-realization, or self-identification with a specific ideal. The danger with the latter is that others in society may manipulate an individual to serve their purposes (Berlin 2002, 183). When interpreted in a balanced way, the Confucian philosophy of freedom avoids both drawbacks. On the one hand, while Confucian classic thinkers maintained that controlling certain desires is necessary, they also promoted the pursuit of reasonable desires. Xunzi, for instance, advocated that people should foster their *qing* 情 (feelings) so they maintain and satisfy reasonable desires (*Xunzi*, chapter 19). On the other hand, Confucian self-mastery aims to develop self-competency in preparing people to live their own lives without being subjected to manipulation by others. We find this stream of thought especially in Mengzi, who advocated self-cultivation toward the ideal of "great man" (*da zhangfu* 大丈夫), a morally cultivated person who cannot be led astray by wealth and rank, nor can he be moved by poverty and privation, nor deflected by power or force (*Mengzi* 3B2). Such a person is independent and steadfast in pursuing his goals.

To sum up the above discussion of freedom's external and internal conditions. Confucian freedom is realized neither by external conditions alone, as is often attributed to Berlin's negative liberty, nor exclusively by managing the agent's internal capacities, as targeted by Berlin's criticism of positive liberty. Rather it is realized by integrating both sets of conditions that are optimized through human effort. This marks the first major difference between the Confucian conception of freedom and Berlin's thin concept of choosing as pure subjective freedom.

The second major difference from Berlin's choosing is that Confucian choosing is not separate from pursuing the good life. In moral philosophy, freedom always comes with constraints. Different moral philosophical theories stipulate different constraints. In John Stuart Mill, for instance, people are free to do whatever they want, unless their actions harm others (Mill 1978). In Confucian social and moral philosophy, humanity is not purely an anthropological concept; it is also a moral concept. Being human implies living one's life that is virtuous in character. Hence, Confucian pursuits, in terms of choosing, are to be realized in the process of *zeshan* 擇 善, "choosing the good." The Confucian classic *Zhongyong* states, "the authentic person chooses the good and holds firmly onto it."[28] This conception of freedom as "choosing the good" is to be realized through continuous concrete acts of choosing wisely and meaningfully in daily life. The good includes good action, good personhood, good life, a good society, and the good world. In the context of Confucian philosophy, the good should not be equated with a singular choice. To be sure, when a child's life is in danger, choosing the good requires us to save the child's life—the only good choice. In everyday life, however, choosing the good often includes a wide range of options. A mother can choose to spend her savings to treat her son on a holiday, or save for his future education, or to donate to charity for more disadvantaged children. She can choose to donate to Oxfam or some other charitable organizations. She can also choose to keep her savings for other long-term purposes. All these choices can be good. Moreover, good people can disagree on what a good choice is under normal circumstances. A student may disagree with her parents on whether she should pursue a career in medicine or education. As long as she makes a well-informed and carefully deliberated choice by optimally using her external and internal conditions and takes her choice as a step toward her goal of the good life, she is exercising freedom.

This Confucian conception of freedom is a "thick" notion, in contrast with Berlin's thin notion of choosing, or a generically anthropological account of what humans are able to opt for in everyday life. This "thick" notion of freedom nevertheless logically presupposes a "thin" notion. That is to say, advocating for choosing the good entails that people are able to choose between the good and something else. From a Confucian point of view, the "thin" notion of freedom is an ontological fact to be recognized, whereas the "thick" notion of freedom is a value to be advocated. Benjamin Schwartz asks, why is that "the freedom to choose between good and evil . . . never seems to be put forth, in most Chinese thought, as a supreme value?" (Schwartz 1985, 274). A twofold response can be offered to Schwartz's question. First, Confucian moral philosophy is not framed in terms of the radical opposition

214 RESHAPING CONFUCIANISM: A PROGRESSIVE INQUIRY

of good and evil as in Christian ethics. Confucian ethics focuses primarily on moral cultivation through everyday life rather than making a series of sharp choices between good and evil. Second, freedom in the "thin" sense entails three logically possible outcomes: to choose the good, to choose the bad, and to choose neither. If only choosing the good is of positive value, why should the freedom to choose per se be given "supreme value"? The *Xunzi* records Kongzi criticizing certain people: "day by day they select and choose among things, not knowing which are valuable"[29] (*Xunzi*, chapter 31; Knoblock 1994, 260). We praise people for choosing the good, not for choosing *between* the good and the bad. Indeed, when people choose to do horrible things, we wish they did not have such choices. Thus, being able to choose is a conditionally or potentially good thing rather than a supreme good. The only supreme value of freedom is choosing the good. As such, Confucian freedom as choosing the good is not only articulated as a philosophical concept but also as a value to be promoted.

One may worry that connecting freedom with the good may unduly limit people's freedom. The Confucian strategy is to focus on expanding conditions, both internal and external, for people to choose on their own competency, as has been illustrated in this section. The good comes in plurality. Moreover, in ancient China, the good was understood mainly within the Confucian culture. Today, this notion can be interpreted in a culturally non-specific way, to accommodate culturally diverse interpretations of the good. Thus, choosing the good can be understood in either culturally specific ways or in general terms. In culturally specific ways, Confucianism advocates a kind of integration as prescribed in the context of its social-moral project. In general terms, freedom is achieved as long as there is a successful integration of personal capabilities and existing conditions, while the good can be defined in non-Confucian cultural terms.

4. From Ancient to Contemporary

My reconstruction of Confucian freedom has brought it close to Charles Taylor's exercise-concept of freedom. Taylor writes:

> Doctrines of positive freedom are concerned with a view of freedom which involves essentially the exercising of control over one's life. On this view, one is free only to the extent that one has effectively determined oneself and

the shape of one's life. The concept of freedom here is an exercise-concept. By contrast, negative theories can rely simply on an opportunity-concept, where being free is a matter of what we can do, of what it is open to us to do, whether or not we do anything to exercise these options. (Taylor 2001, 205)

Thus understood, because freedom must be realized in the exercise of certain capacities, we are not free, or less free, when these capacities are unfulfilled (Taylor 2001, 206). Taylor's exercise-concept of freedom resonates well with the Confucian conception as articulated in this chapter. Confucian freedom requires both external and internal conditions. Improvement of these conditions and effectively using them in choosing are key to freedom or to greater freedom.

Conceived this way, this concept of freedom is an edifying concept. To achieve freedom, Confucians need to be motivated in appropriate ways (*li zhi* 立志) and to create and use favorable conditions, both external and internal. Choosing the good is an enabling process. It empowers people who so choose wisely and effectively. It is substantive freedom in contrast with mere abstract, potential freedom.[30] Confucians hold that choosing the good is fundamental to the good life. It is not detached from personal daily activities. When done appropriately, good choices in everyday life contribute to the overall goal of the good, virtuous life. The Confucian classic *Great Learning* states that the Great Learning teaches how to achieve the "highest good" (*zhi shan* 至善, TTC, 1673). James Legge translated *zhi shan* as "the highest excellence" (Legge 1861, 356). For Confucians, the highest state of human excellence is also the highest state of human freedom. The *Analects* shows that, having gone through life-long striving toward the highest good, at the age of seventy Kongzi finally achieved the highest form of freedom (for his time), in which he could act in whatever way he wished without overstepping boundaries (*Analects* 2.4).[31] In such a state, Kongzi was able to integrate external conditions and his own competencies optimally in his way of life. He possessed the necessary knowledge, skills, and virtue. In such a view, *zeshan* as choosing the good is a process of solidifying and expanding one's freedom, a process from possessing less freedom to more freedom.

The Confucian philosophy of freedom takes the creation and improvement of external conditions favorable for greater freedom as a major task. People in ancient agrarian societies had little power and means for making significant improvements in their environment, either physically or politically. In the meantime, beyond taxation and draft of labor, governments imposed few restrictions on people's lives. Things have changed in contemporary times. Modern governments can be more intrusive. The Confucian creed of not interfering with people's normal lives should be expanded to cover a requirement that governments should not impose unjustifiable restrictions on people's social freedoms such as freedom of association and freedom of speech. Also, progressive Confucian philosophy should adapt to the new conditions and place adequate weight on improving external conditions. Toward that end, Confucians can come into dialogue with contemporary thinkers on freedom.

Amartya Sen, for instance, has put forth an account of freedom in terms of development. He takes development primarily as social development, in the form of growth of GNP, personal income, facilities for education and personal care, and institutions of political and civil rights (Sen 1999). For Sen, development begins with the existence of unfreedoms in society, which limit people's choices and opportunities. These unfreedoms include poverty, tyranny, poor economic opportunities, systematic social deprivation, neglect of public facilities as well as intolerance or overactivity of repressive states (Sen 1999, 3). Sen differentiates his account of freedom as human capacity from the "human capital" approach. Whereas the "human capital" approach focuses more on the improved human agency in enhancing production possibilities, the human capacity approach concentrates more on people's ability to lead the lives they have reason to value and on expanding the real choices that people have (Sen 1999, 293). Progressive Confucians can endorse Sen's account of freedom as far as developing human capacity is concerned. After all, classic Confucian thinkers have always emphasized the importance of decent material wealth for the good life (e.g., *Mengzi* 3A3). From a Confucian perspective, Sen has mainly addressed external conditions, namely social conditions for freedom. On internal conditions of human freedom, Sen turns to education, which is a Confucian priority as well. In comparison, however, Confucians pay more attention to developing human capacity for freedom by growing competency. Confucian freedom places equal weight on improving people's internal conditions for freedom.

Competency for Confucian freedom is knowledge-based. Choosing the good or *zeshan* requires one to broaden the base of knowledge, to know what the good is. Kongzi says, "I learn broadly so I can choose the good and follow up with it."[32] The *Book of Rites* states, "morally cultivated persons possess broad knowledge and choose accordingly."[33] In Confucianism, choosing and learning are not separate. One cannot choose things wisely without

FREEDOM THROUGH CHOOSING 217

knowledge. Under this conception, a person who does not know the good cannot possibly realize true freedom. He can, of course, have freedom in a thin sense, like a lost amateur wandering aimlessly in deep mountains. An ignorant superstitious parent may choose to pray for a deity to cure his baby's illness instead of going to a doctor. Making ignorant choices, however, is not the kind of freedom promoted by Confucian philosophy. This idea implies that improving our knowledge and renewing it in keeping with the progress of time is essential to pursuing Confucian freedom, especially with the rapidly advancing science and technology in contemporary times.

In conclusion, classic Confucian philosophy provides resources for constructing a composite conception of freedom for the contemporary era. Accordingly, Confucian freedom has the following characteristics. First, freedom does not imply an unencumbered "free will" as its origin and as the ultimate initiator of choice for action. Instead, the agency of freedom is the person with a heart-mind (*xin* 心). As an agent for freedom, a person is always situated in an environment that is fundamentally social in nature. Second, Confucian freedom is realized in the process of choosing. Yet it is not just any kind of choosing in life; it is realized in choosing the good for a virtuous life. As such, Confucian freedom carries a moral orientation. Third, the realization of Confucian freedom requires a set of twofold conditions. On the one hand, there is the presence of favorable conditions and the absence of unnecessary external constraints. On the other, there is the agent's capacity for using existing conditions to make meaningful choices. Such capacities require agent competency. This Confucian conception of freedom has profound social and political implications. For if freedom requires both external and internal conditions, they must be developed and maintained in society. In contemporary society, this philosophy of freedom needs to be translated into real life in the form of social and political institutions. What civil liberties should Confucian philosophy endorse and advocate? How can they become reality? These questions are beyond the scope of this chapter. However, fruitful discussions of these important questions have begun (e.g., Chan 2002, 2014). Further work lies ahead.

Study Questions

1. On what ground does the author claim that the concept of "free will" has a specific cultural origin?

2. Is it appropriate to interpret the Chinese notion of *zhi* as free will?
3. The author argues that in classic Confucian philosophy the idea of freedom was an implied concept that was communicated without coinage. Explain.
4. How does Berlin's concept of choosing differ from the Confucian concept? Does it matter?
5. What is the difference between *shanze* and *zeshan*? Can they be connected in your view? If yes, in what way?
6. What is the feminist philosophy of relational autonomy?
7. What are the conditions for Confucian freedom?
8. What is the connection between freedom and virtuous lives in Confucian philosophy?
9. Why is the freedom to choose between good and evil not regarded as a supreme value in Confucianism?

10

Two Forms of Equality

Isaiah Berlin has observed, "Belief in equality—fairness—the view that unless there is a reason for it, recognized as sufficient by some identifiable criterion, one man should not be preferred to another, is a deep-rooted principle in human thought" (Berlin 2003, 65). The importance of equality as a constitutive feature of justice can be traced throughout the history of philosophy. Aristotle said, "All men [*sic.*] think justice to be a sort of equality" (*Politics* III. 12. 1282b 16–17). Contemporary thinkers of justice, from John Rawls (1971) to Michael Walzer (1983), to Ronald Dworkin (2000), have made equality a central concept of their theories. However, equality has not drawn much attention in the mainstream study of Confucianism.[1] Is Confucianism an exception to this broadly shared principle, or have Confucian conceptions of equality been overlooked and inadequately explicated? In this chapter, I argue that equality is an important value in classic Confucianism and that ancient Confucian thinkers have offered rich resources for us to construct a progressive conception of equality today. By analyzing their views in the economic, moral, and political realms, I show that, for the most part, the Confucian notion of equality can be characterized as proportional equality, which comes with apparent inequalities yet is built on a deep sense of equality and fairness. For each area of equality, I will also explore the implications of this Confucian notion of equality for contemporary society.

1. Two Concepts of Equality

Even though few people today question the value and validity of equality, disagreements exist with respect to various related issues. For instance, Harry Frankfurt has argued, contrary to many people's belief, that equality has no moral value in itself (Frankfurt 1997). There are also different approaches to tackling the concept of equality. There are issues of moral equality, such as whether there should be equal respect, equal worth, and equal dignity for all human beings. There are issues of political equality, such as whether

Reshaping Confucianism. Chenyang Li, Oxford University Press. © Oxford University Press 2024.
DOI: 10.1093/oso/9780197657621.003.0011

220 RESHAPING CONFUCIANISM: A PROGRESSIVE INQUIRY

all people have the same civil and political rights regardless of age, race, gender and even nationality. And there are issues of economic equality, such as whether people are entitled to equal distribution of wealth in society. With distributive equality, we are encountered with equality of opportunity, equality of resources, and equality of welfare. The point I would like to make for setting the context for this chapter is that, when a particular kind of equality is promoted, it cannot be realized without resulting in some form or forms of inequality. For instance, promoting equality of opportunity will end up with inequality in outcome because people's natural endowment, effort, and fortunes vary, and opportunities do not guarantee outcomes. In this sense, "equal opportunity" comes with a license for inequality in outcome and welfare. A. T. Nuyen has put this point elegantly, "no matter what x is, in order to maintain the equality of x, the chips will have to fall unevenly, or unequally, elsewhere" (Nuyen 2001, 67). Without inequality as a consequence, no equality can be achieved. Therefore, some kind of inequality is the currency for equality; it is either the price we pay or reward we reap in pursuing equality. The inevitable questions for us, therefore, are which form of equality is more important and how to balance it with ensuing inequalities.

In examining and discussing Confucian equality, I follow Aristotle in differentiating numerical equality from proportional equality (*Nicomachean Ethics* 1130b–1132b; Aristotle 1962, 116–123). Numerical equality means treating each person indiscriminately without consideration for individual circumstances. For example, in a national census, each person counts as one, no more no less. In a general election, each voter's ballot counts one, regardless of one's gender, race, or socioeconomic status. Proportional equality means treating people in due accord to relevant aspects. In Aristotle's words, this is the principle of "to each according to his desert" (Aristotle 1962, 118). For instance, in a factory where workers are paid in accordance with their productivity, each worker is paid by the amount and the quality of her products. Person x is paid twice as much as Person y when x has produced twice as much as y has. Proportional equality as understood here, however, can extend beyond a simple "contribution-reward" model. What a person deserves or is appropriately accorded to him is not solely based on what he has contributed or earned. For example, proportional equality demands that society provide special facilities to the disabled even though they may have not done anything to earn them. This apparently unequal treatment is nevertheless equality in the proportional sense. From the perspective of numerical equality, proportional equality is a form of inequality, because it allows varied treatments and often different allocations of resources. Conceptually, however, we should not confuse proportional equality with inequality as such. While proportional equality brings about inequalities as a by-product, it is ultimately justified on the ground of equality on a deeper level. Its aim is to achieve a form of equality, rather than inequality. Certain inequalities, such as racial discrimination, are simply inequality, rather than by-products of proportional equality.

Both numerical equality and proportional equality, I argue, are present in Confucian philosophy, for different purposes.

2. Numerical Equality

Numerical equality in Confucianism can be found mainly in two areas. The first is that all human beings are endowed with the same capacity for developing humanity. Mengzi famously argued that all human beings possess the four beginnings of the moral attributes of *ren* 仁 (humaneness, care), *yi* 義 (rightness), *li* 禮 (ritual propriety), and *zhi* 智 (wisdom) (*Mengzi* 2A6). On the basis of these innate endowments in every person, Mengzi endorsed the statement that everyone has the capacity to become a sage (*Mengzi* 6B22). Although often taken to be the opposite of Mengzi on theories of *xing* 性 (human nature),[2] Xunzi also endorsed a kind of numerical equality in this regard. He not only maintained that all people, sages explicitly included, share the same *xing* but also that everyone has the same potential to become morally cultivated like the ancient sage Yu 禹 (*Xunzi*, chapter 23). Kongzi did not talk much about *xing*;[3] however, he did say that *xing* is similar across all people and that it is socialization (*xi* 習) that produces social variations (*Analects* 17.2). *Xing* in this context points primarily to the moral potential of humanity. On such a principle of numerical equality, Kongzi advocated a philosophy of "education regardless of social classes" (*Analects* 15.39). In these classic thinkers' teachings of people's equal inborn potentials, we find the roots of a Confucian idea of numerical equality.

This kind of numerical equality is taken as a "given" in Confucianism. It is rather a postulate or an "ontological commitment" to serve as the grounding of Confucian moral metaphysics. Donald Munro has called this notion of equality "natural" equality—"the common attributes or characteristics with which all men [*sic.*] are born"—and it is descriptive in nature (Munro 1969, 2). This notion of equality in moral potential is important to us today as it

222 RESHAPING CONFUCIANISM: A PROGRESSIVE INQUIRY

can serve as the foundation for a basic level of human dignity.[4] Obviously, if every person has the potential to become a moral being and if being moral is a positive human value, then, *prima facie*, every person deserves a basic level of respect and recognition.[5]

These classic thinkers' views of numerical equality in people's natural endowment should not be over-interpreted, however. For one thing, Mengzi was talking about people's capacity to become morally good, not about such technical talent as in arts or working skills. Furthermore, equal moral endowment does not necessarily translate into the same moral attainment, as potentiality does not always become actuality. In Mengzi's words, "seek and you will find it; let go and you will lose it" (*Mengzi* 6A6; Lau 1970, 163). The four potential qualities are inborn, even though one could lose them without cultivation, just as plants wither without proper nurturing. Finally, even with the same endowment, to achieve moral refinement, people of various circumstances may need different kinds of efforts. In real life, people are not equally cultivated in virtue.

As thin as it has been, this category of numerical equality can serve as a starting point for progressive Confucians to develop a concept of equal respect for all human beings and for universal suffrage for all citizens, as will be argued in Sections 5 and 6 of this chapter.

Besides equality in moral potential, the second area of numerical equality in classic Confucianism is found in people's roles in society, in the form of "same role with same responsibility." That is to say that people in the same role, such as father or husband, are given the same kind of responsibilities and entitlements. We may call such equality "role-based numerical equality." For example, Kongzi promoted his ideal of "rectification of names" and said, "Let the ruler be a ruler, the minister be a minister, the father be a father, and the son be a son" (*Analects* 12.11; Chan 1963, 39). In Confucianism, people's roles are defined precisely with respective obligations. For instance, Mengzi insisted that there should be affection between father and son, appropriateness/rightness between ruler and subject, functional differences between husband and wife, precedence between the old and the young, and trustworthiness between friends (*Mengzi* 3A4). As far as being in the same role is concerned, each role's occupant is equal to another. Unlike proportional equality where people are equal even when they are treated differently (e.g., with different amounts of reward), in role-based equality people in the same role are to be treated the same way.

In two ways this "role-based" numerical equality differs from the first area of Confucian numerical equality. First, it is role-specific and not universal to all people. The responsibility for each role is the same regardless of the person's other social roles. All parents have the responsibility to raise, educate, and care for their children; all children have the responsibility of being filial to their parents. These requirements do not change even for people who occupy special positions in society, even though they discharge these duties in varied ways according to circumstances. In the same social role, everyone is equal in entitlement and responsibility.

The second difference is that the role-based equality is a stipulation in social ethics. It is a value directive and serves as a normative requirement. It calls on all people in the same role to fulfill the same kind of responsibility. Unlike the potential to become morally cultivated, with which people are born equally, people in real life are not actually performing their respective duties equally. Ethical reinforcement of this ideal is needed.

3. Proportional Equality

In comparison with numerical equality, proportional equality plays a larger role in Confucianism. Proportional equality, or equality relative to people's due, is a fundamental Confucian principle.[6] It is the cornerstone for economic, moral, as well as political equality in Confucian philosophy.

Confucian proportional equality rests on the belief that an orderly and functional society must be one with effective divisions of labor, which leads to hierarchical social organization.[7] Divisions of labor, however, should not be arbitrary; they should be based on people's abilities. While Kongzi advocated the principle of "education regardless of social classes," he also recognized the fact that people are endowed with different kinds of talent, and they exert varying levels of effort in cultivation. A person born with natural talent but exerting no serious effort will not succeed; someone without particular talent but making serious efforts may still get ahead. That does not preclude the fact, however, that people end up with varying levels of achievement. We must recognize the reality that when people race toward a destination, there are always some who get ahead and others who lag behind. In a fair society, the successful should be rewarded, not only as a form of incentive but also as due recognition.

224   RESHAPING CONFUCIANISM: A PROGRESSIVE INQUIRY

Of all classic Confucian philosophers, Xunzi presented the most elaborate argument for the linkage between good society and reasonable social hierarchy. He regarded human beings as social beings (*Xunzi*, chapter 9; Wang 1988, 164). He also took it as a necessity for society to have a division of labor to function effectively. In his view, proper social hierarchy was initially established by ancient sage-kings for the sake of a well-organized and well-functioning society. Xunzi wrote:

> Ancient kings devised to discriminate people by making ritual and moral principles, so that there are different statuses between the noble and humble, disparities between the senior and junior, classes between the intelligent and able on the one hand, and the obtuse and incapable on the other. Thus, the ancient kings enabled people to carry on their respective work and consequently received their due. (*Xunzi*, chapter 4; Wang 1988, 70; cf. Knoblock 1988, 195)

"The noble" and "the humble" indicate people's achieved social statuses. The disparities between the senior and junior depend on age in the natural course of life. The division between the intelligent and able on the one hand, and the obtuse and incapable on the other, is based on developed abilities. Xunzi took these distinctions to be the fundamental characteristics of a fair, orderly, efficacious, and harmonious society. As he said, this is "the way to make the whole populace live together in harmony and unity" (*Xunzi*, chapter 4; Knoblock 1988, 195). Xunzi described his ideal society as follows:

> When the virtuous [persons of *ren*] occupy the highest position, farmers labor with all their energy to exhaust the potential of their fields, merchants scrutinize with keen eyes to get the utmost from their goods, the various artisans use their skills to the fullest in making utensils and wares, and the officials, from the knights and grand officers up to the feudal lords, all execute fully the functions of their offices with humanity, generosity, wisdom, and ability (*Xunzi*, chapter 4; Knoblock 1988, 195, modified).

When society institutes proper divisions of labor on the basis of people's abilities, society can operate harmoniously. When people dutifully perform their respective roles, they should be rewarded accordingly. This is Xunzi's concept of proportional equality.

Such a concept of equality is conveyed in the name of *qi* 齊. Xunzi quoted from the *Book of History* the notion of *wei qi fei qi* 維齊非齊, "there is equality only insofar as they are not equal" (*Xunzi*, chapter 9; Knoblock 1990, 96).[8] Absolute equality, treating people as numerical equals in divisions of labor and in the distribution of rewards regardless of their varied abilities and contributions, is not real equality in Xunzi's sense of fairness and justice. As discussed at the beginning of this chapter, any form of equality always comes with some form of inequality. Conversely, only when there are inequalities in some consequential ways can there be equality in the intended way. Xunzi recognized this inevitability and embraced it.

The above evidence shows clearly that equality is an important value for Xunzi. It is by appealing to a deep sense of equality that Xunzi justifies the existence of certain inequalities in society. For this reason, we should consider certain apparent inequalities as (consequences of) Confucian proportional equality rather than mere inequality as such. Xunzi called his ideal society on such equality one of *zhi ping* 至平. *Zhi* means "the fullest" or "the utmost." *Ping* means "equal," "fair,, and by extension—in the context of the ideal society—harmony. In the context in which Xunzi used the term, *zhi ping* can be understood as a harmonious society achieved by the successful implementation of proportional equality.

One important issue with social hierarchy ensued from proportional equality is social mobility. A just society must give people opportunities for moving up in the social hierarchy in ways they deserve. Kongzi's philosophy of education was meant to give people from various social classes a chance to learn and improve so they can move up in social ladders, as opposed to the earlier system based on family heredity. In real life, however, such an ideal of social mobility was as difficult to achieve as it is in contemporary times.[9] Today, continuous efforts, such as instituting high quality public schools, must be made to open up social mobility for all deserving persons.

Another major issue with proportional equality has to do with determining the proper proportion. Without proper proportion, "proportional equality" can end up as blatant inequality. In the previous example of factory workers who are paid on the basis of their productivity, would it be fair if a worker who is twice as productive gets paid one-and-a-half times or twice as much as a regular worker's wage? Furthermore, most cases of the division of labor in society are much more complex than the above example. The line between maintaining the proper proportion and being out of proportion is not easily drawn. As we will show in the following section, Kongzi and Xunzi

226 RESHAPING CONFUCIANISM: A PROGRESSIVE INQUIRY

have different views on the proper proportion of distributing social wealth. This difference is relevant to developing proper proportion in contemporary society.

4. Economic Equality

Proportional equality is realized in economic rewards to people in accordance with their due. When people perform different tasks and thereby make varied contributions, they should be rewarded accordingly. Mengzi recognized the necessity to treat different things differently. He said:

> That things are unequal is part of their natures. Some are worth twice or five times, ten or a hundred times, even a thousand and ten thousand times, more than others. If you reduce them to the same level, it will only bring chaos to the world. (*Mengzi* 3A4; Lau 1984, 119–121, modified; cf. Bloom 2009, 59)

Mengzi asked rhetorically, "If a roughly finished shoe sells at the same price as finely finished ones, who would make the latter?" (ibid.) His view that forced uniformity leads to chaos resonates with Xunzi's view discussed earlier, "there is equality only insofar as they are not equal" (*Xunzi*, chapter 9). Our sense of justice requires society to treat unequals as unequals in their appropriate proportion. In economic activities, society must reward each person in accordance with one's contribution. Otherwise, As Mengzi said, "How could one govern a state in this way?" (*Mengzi* 3A4).

Xunzi provided a conceptual justification for this kind of apparent inequality. In his view, in such a system of proportional distribution people are "inequivalent and yet equal, crooked and yet aligned, different and yet one"[10] (*Xunzi*, chapter 4; cf. Hutton 2014, 31; Knoblock 1988, 195). Equality is implied in a form of inequality. Parity is achieved through apparent disparities. This recognition of differentiation in economic distribution is consistent with the principle of proportional equality. Xunzi's proportional distribution system is supplemented by a social welfare policy that the state would provide accommodations for orphans and the childless elderly, and it would subsidize the poor and the needy (*Xunzi*, chapter 9; Wang 1988, 152). As far as economic distribution policy is concerned, Xunzi strictly promoted a principle of proportional equality in accordance with one's contribution.[11]

A question with Xunzi's view is about what kind of proportion is appropriate for proportional equality in distribution. Xunzi held:

> So though one may have as his emolument the whole world, he need not consider it excessive, and though one be only a gatekeeper, receptionist, guard, or nightwatchman, he need never think his salary too meager. (*Xunzi*, chapter 4; Knoblock 1988, 195)

This statement indicates that Xunzi would allow big gaps in economic distribution. The ruler as the "Son of Heaven" is supposed to own the entire world as his wealth, whereas ordinary workers make a meager income in comparison. In Xunzi's view, such a huge disparity in economic distribution is based on an individual's proportional contributions to society. Today, we may question whether such distributions are an appropriate implementation of the principle of proportional equality. For instance, in the twenty-first century, should CEOs of major international corporations be rewarded 254 times more than the average worker (Liu 2022)?

Kongzi seems to hold a different stance in this regard. For all we know, Kongzi did not discuss economic equality directly. The *Analects* states that he rarely talked about *li* 利, namely "benefit" or "profit" (*Analects* 9.1). When he did talk about distribution, however, he showed an egalitarian preference. Kongzi said:

> When wealth is equally distributed (*jun* 均), there will not be poverty; when there is harmony, there will be no problem of there being too few people; and when there are security and peace, there will be no danger to the state. (*Analects* 16.1; Chan 1963, 54)

This passage suggests that Kongzi was egalitarian in economic distribution. However, the word *jun* is a relative term and admits of degrees. The Chinese scholar Hsiao Kung-ch'uan 蕭公權 (Xiao Gongquan) has characterized Kongzi's view as "relatively egalitarian" (*xiangdui pingjun* 相對平均," Hsiao 1998, 61). Even though Kongzi leaned more toward an egalitarian stance than Xunzi with regard to economic rewards, he did not advocate for an absolute egalitarian distribution of wealth in society. Kongzi advocated a policy of "enriching the people" (*fumin* 富民). He believed that when people become well-to-do, they can and should be educated (*Analects* 13.9). In the Warring States period, states were troubled with under-population. A state with a large population was already an achievement. Kongzi obviously was concerned with people's livelihood as well as moral refinement. While Kongzi promoted enriching the people, he also understood that things are not the same for everyone. The *Book of Rites* records Kongzi promoting a strategy to ensure that "rich people are not pretentious and poor people are not in poverty."[12] Zhen Xuan 鄭玄 (127–200) noted in his classic annotation, "this refers to that fact that farmers possessed different kinds of land and scholar-officials held different posts."[13] Just as there are officials at various posts, farmers are better off or worse off due to different levels of productivity in their lands. Kongzi recognized that in society there are rich people and poor people, due to a variety of reasons, such as farmers possessing fertile or barren land. The *Book of Rites* records Kongzi saying that rich local lords should not have wealth worth more than the value of one hundred military wagons.[14] That amount was large; the vast majority of people at that time were not remotely close to that kind of wealth. It does suggest, however, that Kongzi recognized uneven wealth distribution and that he was not a strict egalitarian. Taking all this into consideration, we should interpret the passage in *Analects* 16.1 about "even distribution" as opposing big gaps between the poor and the rich in society, rather than advocating economic egalitarianism.

Subsequent Confucian thinkers have followed a reading of Kongzi's idea of *jun* in ways consistent with his view of proper proportion. For instance, the Han Confucian Dong Zhongshu 董仲舒 (179–104 BCE) interpreted Kongzi's saying in *Analects* 16.1 to mean that:

> Let the rich be rich enough to show their wealth yet not pretentious; let the poor have enough to take care of their lives without becoming worried. This is the standard for being equitable (*jun*). When there is no shortage of wealth and when society is stable from top to bottom, society becomes orderly with ease.[15]

An orderly society with ease is a harmonious society. The Song Confucian thinker Zhu Xi 朱熹 (1130–1200) interpreted Kongzi's idea of *jun* as "each getting its due,"[16] in the spirit of proportional equality. In view of these readings, it would be appropriate to conclude that Kongzi's view on economic inequality is to allow it while preventing huge gaps between the rich and the poor. On such a view, economic inequalities are justifiable only in terms of proportional equality, and proportional equality requires proper proportion.

TWO FORMS OF EQUALITY   229

Related to economic equality is Mengzi's proposal of a well-field system for allocating farming land to common people. A well-field is a field divided in the form of 井 (*jing*).[17] Such a field is divided into nine parcels. At the center is the public parcel, and eight families each have private holdings around it. Together these families cultivate the public field, and when the public work is done, then they each work on their own lands. Mengzi emphasized the importance of being fair in allocating well-fields. He said:

> Humane government (*renzheng* 仁政) must begin with the setting of boundaries. If the boundaries are not set correctly, the division of the land into well-fields will not be equal, and the grain allowances for official emoluments will not be equitable. (*Mengzi* 3A3; Bloom 2009, 53)

The word that Irene Bloom translated as "equal" here is 鈞 (*jun*). In ancient classics, it was used in the same meaning as its homophone *jun* 均, which was used in Kongzi's discussion in *Analects* 16.1.[18] Evidently, Mengzi held that some kind of equal distribution of public land is essential for a just society under a caring government. The arrangement of the well-field system is related directly to community-building. Mengzi said:

> When those in a village who hold land in the same well-field befriend one another in their going out and their coming in, assist one another in their protection and defense, and sustain one another through illness and distress, the hundred surnames will live together in affection and harmony. (*Mengzi* 3A3; Bloom 2009, 54)

"The hundred surnames" (*baixing* 百姓) is a common Chinese expression for the diverse population in society. Mengzi held that when people possess steady means of income, they have a steady heart for moral cultivation (*Mengzi* 3A3). Hence, when people are treated equitably in economic terms, it sets a foundation for a harmonious society.

Now, if we follow Kongzi's (rather than Xunzi's) philosophy of *jun* on economic distribution, what implications can we draw for contemporary society? I think that under two conditions progressive Confucians should accept economic inequality. The first condition is that people acquire wealth through legitimate means. Some people get richer than others because they work harder or act more intelligently or are more fortunate than others. Confucianism encourages personal effort; it also recognizes the effect of

230 RESHAPING CONFUCIANISM: A PROGRESSIVE INQUIRY

personal fortunes in real life. The latter is a matter of economic luck beyond people's control, and it inevitably affects wealth distribution in society. The second condition is that there should not be big gaps between the rich and the poor. Confucians are concerned with people's welfare and social harmony. On Confucian social philosophy, harmony is the most important goal in society. Big gaps between the rich and the poor not only violate proportional equality, undermine people's welfare but are also detrimental to social harmony, and therefore should be limited.[19] Proportional equality must maintain proper proportion in economic distribution.

5. Moral Equality

In discussing Chinese philosophy, the English word "moral" is usually used to cover both *dao-de* 道德 and *lun-li* 倫理 in Chinese. In such a use, it is broader in scope than the narrow sense of "moral" as in Kantian ethics. *Dao-de*, literally "*dao* and virtue," emphasizes the subjective aspect of moral practice. *Lun-li* refers to a reasonable social order based on human relationships, pointing mainly to established social norms for human relations. Following *lun-li* is to cultivate and maintain such an order. In this understanding, Confucian *lun-li* in the broad sense of "moral" includes maintaining appropriate relationships. In the Confucian view, a person's obligations toward his parents, for example, are unequivocally moral obligations.

The matter of moral equality primarily concerns two important issues. The first is whether every person deserves the same respect; the second is whether every person exerts an equal ethical pull on us.

Respect is a major Confucian moral value, as reflected in the idea of *jing* 敬. *Jing* has a range of meanings broader than respect. It can mean reverence (e.g., toward ancestors) as well as respect toward people in general. The *Analects* records that, when Kongzi's disciple Zilu failed to demonstrate superior music skills, other disciples did not *jing* Zilu (*Analects* 11.15). It means that Zilu lost respect among his peers. Also, in the sense of respect, the *Book of Rites* records that Kongzi advised people to *jing* their wives and children.[20] He held that care and *jing* are the foundation of good government. He also said that the most important element in practicing ritual propriety (*li*) is *jing*.[21] Kongzi maintained that morally cultivated persons *jing* everyone, including people in inferior as well as superior positions. In all these instances, *jing* conveys the meaning of respect.[22]

TWO FORMS OF EQUALITY 231

The principle of equal respect for all human beings is now widely accepted in the world. It is, however, undeniable that we do not feel that all people deserve respect in equal doses. Some people are more respectable than others. Stephen Darwall distinguishes two kinds of respect: recognition respect and appraisal respect. Recognition respect consists in giving appropriate consideration to some feature of its object and it is due to every person equally, whereas appraisal respect consists in an assessment of a person or her qualities and it admits of degrees (Darwall 1977, 38–39). Darwall's view can be supported from a Confucian perspective. As far as moral respect is concerned, Confucians provide a ground for endorsing a basic level of respect for everyone. All human beings possess the same potential to become morally cultivated. Moral qualities, whether potential or actual, are to be respected. Therefore, all human beings deserve at least a basic level of respect on the basis of their moral potential. However, the Confucian principle of differentiated statuses between the morally cultivated and petty persons entails that people in real life do not deserve the same respect. Morally cultivated people deserve additional respect; people of varied moral achievements should receive appropriately differentiated degrees of respect. We can say that these are two kinds of respect: respect on the basis of inborn moral potential and respect on the basis of moral achievement. The former can be labeled as "heavenly endowed respect" and the latter as "earned respect." Earned respect is a reflection of proportional equality in the moral realm.

Respect involves inevitably a value judgment. To respect a person is to recognize the value in the person, at least in normal circumstances.[23] Confucians see human value as existing in the form of potential or realized moral quality. A person's human value increases as he becomes morally advanced and cultivated in virtue. It also can diminish when he loses his moral potential and thus becomes a "beast" (*Mengzi* 4B19).[24] In the Confucian view, insisting on *equal* respect regardless of people's moral worth achieved through cultivation is to neglect proportional equality in the moral realm, and hence to treat people without equal consideration. In this regard, the Confucian view differs fundamentally from both traditions of reincarnation and traditions of the heavenly afterlife. Traditional Hinduism, for instance, holds the belief that a moral life will be duly rewarded in one's future incarnations even if not in the current life. Traditional monotheistic teachings tell us that God ensures that a moral person will live in heaven in the afterlife. For example, Kant in his *Critique of Practical Reason* famously argued that only God can

232 RESHAPING CONFUCIANISM: A PROGRESSIVE INQUIRY

ensure that virtue leads to happiness. Accordingly, if people of virtue do not attain happiness in this life, they will be rewarded in heaven. In both cases, people's moral achievements will be duly recognized and rewarded after their current life. In comparison, Confucians focus on this life on earth. Moral achievements should be recognized in this life. Thus, a society where the worthy and unworthy are accorded with equal respect in recognition is an unjust society. Such a society is neither fair to worthy people, nor conducive to promoting moral advancement. Therefore, Confucians hold that the appropriate approach should let people earn additional respect above and beyond the basic level in this life.

One may wonder how we can determine whether someone has achieved more moral attainment and hence deserves more respect. If this cannot be determined, then the Confucian notion of differentiated respect becomes vacuous. However, this question is not as difficult to answer as it may appear. Just look at people around us in everyday life. Don't we have a good sense as to those who are more trustworthy, more dedicated, more virtuous (at least in some aspects of life)? Don't these qualities indicate moral attainment?[25] Reflecting on this fact, don't we know who deserves more respect? Don't people earn respect by being hardworking and acting morally in everyday life? The answer is affirmative, at least to a great extent. Admittedly, we may make mistakes in judgment, as in anything else. That does not, however, invalidate the philosophy in question. In the Confucian context, whether one can offer respect to other people appropriately is an indication of one's moral sensibility. Whether one can respect others in accordance with proportional equality is a way to gauge one's moral maturity.

Besides respect, the other issue of moral equality concerns whether a moral agent is subject to the same ethical pull from all people equally. "Ethical pull," according to Robert Nozick, stands for "the moral claim on us exerted by others so that, in virtue of what they are like, we ought to behave toward them in certain ways and not in others" (Nozick 1981, 451). In Confucian literature, this refers to the issue of whether we should care about all human beings equally. Confucianism promotes "care with distinctions" (*ai you cha deng* 愛有差等). A person should care about his own family and people in close relationships more than he cares about others. In terms of moral consideration, this means that people in different relationships do not exert a moral pull on us equally. For example, under usual circumstances the ties between a mother and her child is much stronger than those between regular friends,

TWO FORMS OF EQUALITY   233

not to mention strangers. This, of course, does not mean that people further away are not good people, nor that people close to us are necessarily morally superior. Confucians regard human beings as essentially social beings whose existence and identity are rooted in social relationships. These relationships constitute a large part of our identity and are the home base of our existence, including moral existence. Therefore, people close to us command more of our moral obligation. In this sense, our moral obligations to all people are not equal. This sense of moral consideration is aligned more with proportional equality than numerical equality.[26]

As far as moral equality is concerned, Confucians would accept a basic level of universal respect for humanity. They would maintain, however, that some people deserve more respect than others. Universal respect for humanity is grounded on numerical equality. Differential respect is grounded on proportional equality. Every person exerts a moral pull on us, at least potentially; yet beyond that basic level, we owe additional obligations, in variable degrees, to people in close relationships.

6. Political Equality

Besides economic and moral equality, a third area is political equality. Confucians advocate proportional political equality in the form of political meritocracy.[27] Public administration and legislation require virtues, knowledge, and talent. Because people vary in possessing these qualities, they are not equally suitable for serving in important government posts. This fact calls for proportional equality in distributing public offices. As in other realms, proportional equality in the political realm comes with inevitable inequalities in consequences. It is important to realize, however, that this is not a matter of political inequality for the sake of inequality. Some inequalities are appropriate because they are not only inevitable for proportional equality on a more fundamental level, but also because they are grounded on the reality of varied human capacities and are justified on the basis of individual desert and the overall good of society. In the Confucian view, political inequalities as consequences of proportional equality are justified if they allow the virtuous, knowledgeable, and talented to make governmental decisions, and consequently make wise decisions for the common good of the society.

234   RESHAPING CONFUCIANISM: A PROGRESSIVE INQUIRY

Ancient Confucian thinkers not only recognized the necessity of the division of labor in society, but also attempted to provide a justifiable basis for such division. Mengzi said:

> People work either with their minds or with physical labor. Those working with minds govern others. Those working with physical labor are being governed. (*Mengzi* 3A4)

In his view, some people are suitable for office work, which includes people who hold government posts, whereas others are suitable for manual work. An appropriate division of labor is needed for effective and fair operations of the world (*Mengzi* 3A4). If we borrow Mengzi's descriptions in examining proportional political equality with respect to acquiring political offices today, Mengzi's characterization appears oversimplified. People working with mental power are not necessarily governing people of physical labor; people working with physical labor can nevertheless participate in politics. However, even though today's division of labor has become more complex, and justification has become more nuanced, Mengzi's general rationale remains relevant. No matter how a society is organized, it always ends up with people in different social stations, doing various tasks, and engaging in uneven participation in political processes. The real issue is not about having or not having political inequality, but what kind of political inequality, and whether political inequalities are based on a more fundamental principle of political equality at a deeper level.

In Confucian terminologies, virtuous, knowledgeable, and talented people are called *xian* 賢 (the virtuous and talented). Under the tenet of "elevating the worthy" (*juxian* 舉賢), the Confucian ideal of getting the virtuous and talented to serve in government has been a hallmark of Confucianism. Arguing in favor of meritocracy against the ancient hereditary political system, Xunzi maintained:

> Those lacking virtue shall be without honored status. Those with no ability shall be without office. Those who lack accomplishment shall go unrewarded. Those do not transgress shall not be rebuked. In the royal court none shall occupy positions out of mere good fortune. Among the people none shall gain a living by mere good fortune. The worthy shall be honored and the able employed, each assigned a position of appropriate rank, with none overlooked. (*Xunzi*, chapter 9; Knoblock 1990, 101, modified; cf. Hutton 2014, 73)

TWO FORMS OF EQUALITY 235

Xunzi argued specifically, as descendants of commoners accumulate culture and learning, cultivate their character and conduct, and become capable of upholding social norms and justice, they should be brought to the ranks of a prime minister, knight, or grand officers. Conversely, as descendants of people from these high ranks fail to accomplish themselves, they should be relegated to the position of commoners (*Xunzi*, chapter 9; Knoblock 1990, 94). The goal of a just society, for Xunzi, is to establish a system where the ranks and official posits are assigned on the assessment of people's virtue and abilities, "so that the worthy and unworthy each obtain their proper places, and the capable and incapable each receive their proper offices, the myriad thing all get what is appropriate for them" (*Xunzi*, chapter 8; Hutton 2014, 56; cf. Knoblock 1990, 72).

On such an account, successfully recruiting the worthy to work in government is a requirement for a good society. The *Book of History* promotes the ideal for rulers to recruit talents so thoroughly that "no virtuous and talented people are left outside government."[28] The belief is that when these people all work in government, society will be well-managed and all states will be in peace.[29] In today's view, such a goal is not only too idealistic but also flawed. First, it assumes the scope of knowledge and talent is confined to managing society; it does not include people who are otherwise knowledgeable and virtuous, such as farmers and artisans. Today, it should be made clear that, as far as selecting people is concerned, virtue, knowledge and talent are sector-specific for working in government; it does not imply that people doing non-government jobs are ignorant and unvirtuous for the kind of work that they do. Second, while society needs virtuous and talented people in government, it also needs virtuous and talented people outside government. A society in which all virtuous and talented people are to work within the government is not a good one. Conversely, a government infested with ignorant and even crooked people cannot be good either. Confucians hold that government policies must be made intelligently and beneficial to the overall good of society. For that purpose, ignorance and moral incompetence have no place in making governmental policies, and those who work in government as political leaders should be virtuous and talented.

Understood this way, the goal of Confucian meritocracy is not at odds with the goal of modern democracy. In a democratic society, citizens cast votes to select people for government offices. Candidates compete for their suitability by demonstrating their qualifications in knowledge, experience,

236　RESHAPING CONFUCIANISM: A PROGRESSIVE INQUIRY

talent, and moral character.[30] After all, who wouldn't want only people with moral character, knowledge, and talent to be elected for public offices?!

Democracy requires some forms of numerical equality. Then, to what extent does Confucian proportional political equality accommodate numerical equality among citizens? Numerical equality in the political realm includes at least three areas. First, Confucian proportional political equality presupposes a fundamental conviction that everyone is to be given opportunities to develop their virtue, knowledge, and talent. Only in this way, can political division of labor be established solidly on fundamental equality. That is to say, the Confucian pursuit of equality in political arenas is to be realized mainly by creating opportunities for people to become educated, to cultivate virtues, and to develop talents, so everyone has an equal chance to become prepared for government posts if one so chooses, and when successful, people come to be well equipped to serve in public offices and to participate in government decision-making.

Second, while Confucians maintain that government should be staffed with virtuous, knowledgeable, and talented people, employment in government does not exhaust such people in society. People without public offices also have a say in political affairs. Furthermore, it does not mean that the ignorant, the unvirtuous, and the untalented should have no voice in society. On the contrary, their voices should be heard because they are part of the social reality and therefore should, and indeed must, be considered in governmental decision-making processes as well as in governmental operations. Even though the ignorant, the unvirtuous, and the untalented are likely not to make wise decisions, they are nevertheless legitimate members of society and should be considered as political decisions are made.

Third, and most importantly, Confucian proportional political equality does not preclude citizens at large from participating in determining who are virtuous, knowledgeable, and talented enough for public office. On the basis of the Confucian view on political equality, contemporary progressive Confucians should promote a general participation principle in politics. Such a principle reflects numerical equality and is to be implemented via a "one person one vote" political system. On this principle, all political offices—state leaders and legislators—at all levels should be elected, directly or indirectly, by citizens. All citizens should have the opportunity to participate in general elections. This principle can be supported on the ground of basic respect for humanity, which Confucians endorse on the basis of the universal moral potential of humanity. The right to vote signifies a form of recognition of people's dignity as members of their communities.

Admittedly, ancient Confucian thinkers of pre-modern societies did not propose or advocate such a system. However, a "one person one vote" political system is consistent with Mengzi's view that "Heaven sees with the eyes of its people; Heaven hears with the ears of its people" (*Mengzi* 5A5; Lau 1970, 205–207). On the basis of this idea, a contemporary Confucian justification can go as follows. No single person on earth can adequately prove to the entire society who are the virtuous, knowledgeable, and talented people suitable for government offices. One can suppose an omniscient divine power knows who these people are. Yet, such a power never reveals it to citizens directly (and most of us today no longer believe in divination). So, the next best thing is to let people, as imperfect in judgment as they are, decide who should be selected to make political decisions for society (see more discussion in Chapter 11 of this book). Furthermore, a "one person one vote" political system can be justified in terms of representation. State leaders and legislators not only make political decisions for society but also represent citizens; the represented should have a say on who is to represent them. With all these considerations, we can echo Winston Churchill and say that the general election is the worst form of politics except all those other forms that have been tried from time to time.[31]

Contemporary Confucian thinkers have debated on various models for the institutionalized implementations of the Confucian ideal of "elevating the worthy," by disqualifying unvirtuous, ignorant, and incompetent people from being elected (see Bell 2006; Li 2012a; J. Chan 2014a). Here I suggest that, in a mature and well-nurtured democratic society, such a goal can be achieved by non-institutional means. That is, it should be exercised by voters using their own assessment of candidates' qualifications with regard to moral character, knowledge and talent. In the political realm, the goal of Confucian proportional equality is to be achieved on the basis of numerical equality.

How to achieve such a goal is perhaps the most challenging for Confucian political philosophy today.[32] But, it is not impossible. Take Singapore as an example. Over three-quarters of Singapore's population is ethnic Chinese, who are largely Confucian in cultural heritage. In its 2020 general election, the ruling People's Action Party recommended twenty-seven new candidates. One of them was criticized on social media for being arrogant, cold, hypocritical, and uncaring by numerous self-identified neighbors, co-workers, and former colleagues. Under pressure, he withdrew his candidacy

238　RESHAPING CONFUCIANISM: A PROGRESSIVE INQUIRY

(Lim 2020). This case shows that the candidate's character can make a difference if it is taken seriously in society. And it was taken seriously during the Singapore 2020 general election. A survey by YouGov shortly before the election day asked voters what the most important qualities or traits were for a political candidate. It found that the most important quality in a political candidate according to Singaporeans is possessing integrity, with almost one-quarter (23 percent) picking it as the most important. This is closely followed by a passion to serve (22 percent). Competence (11 percent) and honesty (10 percent) were in third and fourth place respectively.[33] If we combine integrity with honesty, as both concerns personal character, the percentage adds to 33 percent.

A society in which citizens take candidates' moral character as a serious consideration does not exist by itself without effective community-building. Contemporary Confucian thinkers have argued that a key element of contemporary Confucian society is to build an efficacious community. Drawing on John Dewey's idea of communicating community, David Hall and Roger Ames have argued that the idea of democracy "is the idea of community life itself" (Hall and Ames 1999, 124), and that for Confucians today, "the question is how one might secure the dominance of moral suasion as the primary means of securing harmonious community life" (ibid. 214). Sor-hoon Tan also takes the community as a critical link in building Confucian democracy (Tan 2003, chapter 3). Confucian virtuous leadership depends on efficacious communities. A strong community is the soil for a viable Confucian philosophy of political equality, both in the form of numerical and proportional equality.[34]

In conclusion, this chapter has investigated Confucian equality in the economic, moral, and political realms. The above investigation and analysis demonstrate that Confucianism embraces both numerical equality and proportional equality, on different dimensions, and that Confucians also accept consequential inequalities necessitated by proportional equality. Believing in the inevitability of variations in individual moral refinement as well as potential and realized talent, and therefore the necessity and efficacy of division of labor, Confucians promote proportional equality, in economic, moral, and political realms, as a key notion in building a good society.

Let me add a final note. In his influential book *Spheres of Justice: A Defence of Pluralism and Equality*, Michael Walzer (1983) argued that justice requires society not to let people carry their advantage in one social sphere into another. Some people can achieve economic success, for example, but they should not use their economic advantage to benefit politically. Such a philosophy is especially important for a Confucian society that allows proportional equality. As has been argued in this chapter, Confucian proportional equality is justified on the ground of sphere-specific reasons, be these economic, moral, or political. It is valid only in its particular sphere. Carrying over into another sphere results in corruption. Using the power of a political office to benefit oneself economically, for example, is using what may be legitimate proportional equality in the political realm to achieve inequality in the economic sphere. This should be prohibited in a good society. In promoting legitimate proportional equality, Confucians must guard especially against its misuse as warmed pointedly by Michael Walzer.

Study Questions

1. The author claims that some kind of inequality is the currency for equality. What does it mean? Do you agree?
2. What is the difference or differences between numerical equality and proportional equality? ·
3. In which area or areas do Confucians recognize numerical equality?
4. How did Kongzi and Xunzi differ on economic proportional equality? In your opinion, which view is right?
5. In what ways do Confucians recognize moral proportional equality? Do you agree with the Confucians?
6. What is the difference, if any, between understanding social stratification as simple inequality on the one hand and proportional equality on the other?
7. The author argues that Confucians especially need to guard against misuse of proportional equality. Why so? Do you agree?

11

Kingliness without Kings

The overall ideal of Confucian philosophy has often been characterized in the slogan "inner sageliness and outer kingliness" (*neisheng waiwang* 內聖外王). "Inner sageliness" signifies personal moral cultivation toward the goal of sagehood, as has been explored in various chapters in this book. It is primarily about personal ethics. "Outer kingliness" prescribes political participation to achieve the Confucian good society with a caring government (*ren zheng* 仁政). The Confucian concept of "kingliness" is called "*wang dao* 王道," the Way of true kings, as opposed to "*ba dao* 霸道," the way of hegemons. In ancient times, the proper "Way" was closely associated to kings because of the belief that it could be achieved only through sage kings; today, however, the focus of this inherited phrase is on the "Way," on how to construct and maintain a good society. It is the central question of Confucian political philosophy.

The ideal of "outer kingliness" has been typically pursued in the form of service in government. Since antiquity, Confucians have not only attempted to influence rulers to provide kingly leadership in society, but also sought to work with rulers to implement Confucian philosophy through state sponsorship. And yet, whenever Confucians sought state sponsorship, the state always selectively adopted Confucian philosophy to serve its own purposes, at the expense of the integrity of Confucianism. Throughout Chinese history, countless Confucian officials attempted to help rulers do the right thing for society. They always failed, however, when their advice went against rulers' fundamental interest to stay in power. On reflection, this outcome should not be unexpected. The primary goal of rulers is to solidify power and to protect their reign; the primary concern of Confucian philosophy is the well-being of the people. When the two come to conflict, it is highly unlikely for rulers to prioritize Confucian social ideals.

In this chapter, I investigate this problem by sorting out different threads of thought in Confucian classic texts. I will first reflect on the history of the Confucian ideal of "outer kingliness" in practice, analyze its fatal flaws in the traditional approach, and then draw on various Confucian ideas to make

Reshaping Confucianism. Chenyang Li, Oxford University Press. © Oxford University Press 2024.
DOI: 10.1093/oso/9780197657621.003.0012

a case for pursuing democratic activism as an effective means to achieve Confucian social ideals in contemporary society. Accordingly, in a democratic era, progressive Confucians must discard the ideal of "sagely politics," and "outer kingliness" must be realized by active participation in democratic political processes. Thus, the political goal for Confucianism should be "kingliness without kings," or "politics without (depending on) political leaders."

1. The Dilemma of Politics and Ethics

Despite a strong emphasis on personal ethics, the state has always had a special place in Confucianism. From its beginning, serving the state has been one of its most important themes. The *Great Learning*, one of the Confucian classic "Four Books," advocates the sequential goals of "cultivating one's person (*xiushen* 修身)," "regulating/harmonizing one's family (*qijia* 齊家)," "managing the state (*zhiguo* 治國)," and finally "bringing peace to the world (*ping tianxia* 平天下)."[1] Under the banner of "inner sageliness and outer kingliness," generation after generation of Confucians have tirelessly engaged in self-cultivation and promoted their social ideals through the operation of the state.

Attempts to join the operation of the state began early in the Confucian tradition. Kongzi himself sought a post in government that would give him a chance to put his philosophy into practice. The *Analects* records a conversation Kongzi had with his disciple Zigong:

> Zigong said, "Here is a beautiful gem—Should one wrap it up and store it in a cabinet? Or should one seek a good price and sell it? The Master said, "Sell it! Sell it! I am one waiting for the right offer." (*Analects* 9.13; Ni 2017, 237)

Here Kongzi expressed his wish to be offered a government post so he could realize his political ambitions (see the annotation in Ni 2017, 237).

At times, Kongzi's fondness for government affairs puzzled his disciples. Once, in an effort to promote his political agenda, Kongzi went to see Nanzi, the notorious wife of the ruler of Wei. His act was so unseemly that even his disciple Zilu found it troubling (*Analects* 6.28). Another case in point is his evaluation of the ancient scholar-official Guan Zhong 管仲.[2] Guan was one of the two teachers of Prince Jiu in the state of Qi. Jiu was killed by his

242 RESHAPING CONFUCIANISM: A PROGRESSIVE INQUIRY

younger brother and the killer became Duke Huan of Qi. Out of loyalty to the prince, the other teacher of Jiu committed suicide. Guan Zhong, however, not only continued to live but later even became Duke Huan's prime minister, assisting Duke Huan in establishing a strong Qi state. Guan's behavior appeared contrary to Kongzi's teachings on loyalty and integrity. In *Analects* 14.16 and 14.17, his disciples Zilu and Zigong respectively questioned Guan's moral character. Apparently, they had expected Kongzi to feel the same way. However, it turned out that Kongzi gave Guan a very positive assessment and called Guan "virtuous" (*ren* 仁). Kongzi's justification for his appraisal seems entirely consequentialist, on the ground that Guan later achieved something good with his political office. Kongzi explained his view of Guan to Zilu as follows:

> Duke Huan assembled the Lords of the states together nine times, and did it without using military force. It was all through the influence of Guan Zhong. How virtuous (*ren*) he was! How virtuous (*ren*) he was! (*Analects* 14.16; Ni 2017, 332, modified)

In this passage, Kongzi praised Guan for assisting Duke Huan's political success without bloody military means. In the following passage (14.17), Kongzi further explained:

> Guan Zhong became prime minister to Duke Huan, made him leader of the lords of states, and united and rectified the whole kingdom. Even today, the people still benefit from what he conferred. Had there not been Guan Zhong, we would be wearing our hair unbound with our clothes fastened on the left. How could this be compared to the petty fidelity of common men and women, which would have him strangle himself in a stream or ditch, without anyone knowing who he was? (Ni 2017, 333)

The description of "wearing our hair unbound with our clothes fastened on the left" connotes backwardness and the lack of culture. Here Kongzi seems to have taken such political success as an indication of virtue. The passage suggests that acts which appear less than virtuous are justified to achieve greater purposes in politics.

These remarks by Kongzi, however, seem inconsistent with what is recorded in *Analects* 3.22, where Kongzi criticized Guan Zhong for having no sense of ritual propriety (*li* 禮). Because, in Kongzi's view, one becomes virtuous (*ren*) by observing ritual propriety (*Analects* 12.1), having no sense of ritual propriety would imply that Guan Zhong was not virtuous. In 3.22, Kongzi also regarded Guan Zhong as a person of "small capacity." Such remarks concern Guan's moral character, but obviously Kongzi thought highly of Guan's political capacity and achievements. The contemporary scholar Li Zehou 李澤厚 sees such a discrepancy as exposing a tension and conflict between ethics and politics in the Confucian ideal of "inner sageliness and outer kingliness" (Li 2004, 102). Whereas ethics requires one course of action, politics demands another. If we accept Li's reading, then Kongzi's assessment of Guan Zhong as being virtuous suggests that Kongzi was so concerned with political success, that when ethics and politics conflicted, he opted for politics.[3]

The case of Guan Zhong is not the only case of Kongzi's fondness in politics. In the *Xunzi* and the *Recorded Sayings of Kongzi's Family* (*Kongzi Jiayu* 孔子家語), we find the same record that Kongzi served as the minister of justice and acting prime minister in the state of Lu. According to these texts, on his seventh day on the job, Kongzi executed Shaozheng Mao 少正卯, a prominent resident in the state. The act gave his students enough concerns to question Kongzi. The *Xunzi* records a student's question as follows:

> Shaozheng Mao was a well-known person in Lu. For the Master to conduct government and begin by executing him, is this not an error? (*Xunzi*, chapter 28; Hutton 2014, 318)

Kongzi defended his act by listing various moral ills committed by Shaozheng. The accuracy of this story cannot be ascertained. It nevertheless suggests at least a possible scenario where Kongzi would have been caught in a quandary if he had become a government official. As a minister, his primary duty would be to serve the interest of the ruler, even though in doing so he would have to compromise his moral principles. This very possibility would lead him astray from his own moral path. The uneasiness of his disciple over his actions in the story demonstrated the troubling aspect caused by the tension between politics and ethics.[4]

Subsequent Confucians followed Kongzi's lead in pursuing their ideal of "outer kingliness" by providing service in government. Chapter *Wangzhi* (Kingly System) of the *Book of Rites*, for instance, stipulates a process of identifying learned people through multi-layered selections to serve in government. In a large part of Chinese history, such an ideal was carried out mainly through the imperial examination system. With its early beginning in the Sui dynasty (581–618) and largely formalized in the Tang (618–907) and Song (960–1279) dynasties, the imperial examination system was designed as the means to identify men of talent and to select officials for government service. In droves, Confucian students studied assiduously from young ages in preparation for the imperial examinations, with the goal of becoming the select few who would acquire government posts. Once selected, they were on their way to become government officials and to realize the Confucian aim of managing the state, at least purportedly.[5]

The partial success of Confucianism in gaining state sponsorship came at a high cost. The Han emperor Wudi 武帝 made Confucianism the state ideology but also made Confucianism a tool for the state, analogous to the view that *philosophia ancilla theologiae* (philosophy is the handmaiden of theology) in the medieval West. For instance, by strongly aligning filiality 孝 with loyalty 忠, Confucianism was made to serve the interest of rulers in producing submissive subjects for the state. This kind of involvement with state power has inevitably undermined Confucianism.

One could, of course, uphold ethics at the expense of politics. An opposite example can be found in the case of the Confucian scholar-official Sima Guang 司馬光 (1019–1086). Sima was an accomplished scholar and writer. At the peak of his political career, he served as prime minister in the Song royal court and had its full trust. Yet, he was deeply dedicated to Confucian moral values. In his post as the prime minister, Sima acted as a moral practitioner rather than a politician. He did not engage in making political calculations as he advanced the political goals of the royal court. He did not seek political allies and had no political friends; he even avoided private communication with his potential allies, in keeping literally with Kongzi's teaching that virtuous persons "do not form cliques" (*Analects* 15.22). Aspiring for a life of high moral integrity, Sima tried to influence others toward the moral path by regulating his life with strict ethical requirements. He even posted rules in his own guest room that required visitors not to talk about office-related matters at his home. In the end, he stood between political fractions in isolation, without political clout to implement his political agenda (Zhao 2019, 31–32). His failure was not due to a lack of political experience. Sima became a government official at the age of eighteen in 1038 and subsequently served in a variety of government posts. It was his moral idealism that failed him miserably as a politician. Yes, he may have lived a moral life as a good Confucian scholar. It was recorded that when he died, tens of thousands of people came for his funeral and people wept as if they lost a family member

(Su 1090). However, Sima was by no means a successful politician. In that capacity, he failed not only to live up to the expectations of the royal court but also arguably to the society which needed his political success.[6]

Sima, of course, was the exception rather than the rule. Most Confucian scholar-officials in history, however, were not as determined as Sima in upholding ethical principles at the expense of political success. They compromised ethics for the sake of success in politics. A contemporary example of the failure of Confucians in politics is Fung Yulan 馮友蘭 (Feng Youlan, 1895–1990), an eminent Confucian scholar and a professor of philosophy at Peking University. Fung was never satisfied with being a mere scholar, however. He wanted to put his Confucian philosophy into practice by becoming a teacher-counselor of rulers. During the republic era, Fung joined the Chinese Nationalist Party (KMT) and attempted to advise Chiang Kai-shek. In the wake of KMT's defeat toward the end of 1940s, Fung turned to the Chinese Communist Party (CCP) and used every opportunity to get Mao Zedong's attention. In early 1960s, Fung started to openly criticize Confucianism, including Kongzi and Fung's own previous work on Confucianism. He was among the first to cheer for Mao Zedong's "Cultural Revolution." He seized every opportunity to extol Mao, presumably in order to get Mao's recognition and approval. In 1973, Fung was invited by Mao's wife Jiang Qing to serve as the counselor to the political writing team Liangxiao 梁效. Throughout his affiliation with the CCP, Fung was used entirely as its tool without any chance to provide counsel from his own point of view. Fung's story is an extreme case; it is nevertheless a tragic example of a disastrous maneuver for a Confucian scholar to become the ruler's counselor when the ruler is a sheer political animal.[7]

It should be noted that such inconsistency between moral goals and political goals is not unique to Confucians. In the West, commentators of the sixteenth century writer Niccolò Machiavelli (1469–1527) have read his work as exposing such an unbridgeable gap between these two pursuits. While some have seen Machiavelli simply as the teacher of evil who reveals the worst part of humanity, others have interpreted Machiavelli as an anguished humanist, who "laments the vices of men which makes such wicked courses politically unavoidable" (Berlin 1979, 28–9). In the latter view, Machiavelli divorces politics from ethics. The pursuit of politics and that of ethics lead in opposite directions. Ethics requires good virtues such as humility, love, and kindness, whereas politics demands the art of success and the skills of getting what one wants. If one chooses to strive toward political success, which possesses its own value, one cannot uphold the ethical. In this view, ethics is about idealism, whereas politics is about realism. Confucians, however, wanted both political success and ethical integrity. That makes their situation more challenging.

Such a tension is reflected in what has been called the "dirty hands" problem in contemporary political philosophy. "Dirty hands" is used in political philosophy to describe the necessity to sometimes engage in morally problematic acts to achieve greater goods in politics. The term is taken from Jean-Paul Sartre's play by the same name. In the play, the communist leader Hoerderer, who intends to collaborate with fascist groups to form a coalition government, defends himself with a rhetorical question:

> I have dirty hands right up to the elbows. I've plunged them in filth and blood. Do you think you can govern innocently? (Sartre 1955, 224)

The implied answer is that no one can govern innocently. Michael Walzer explicates the concept of "dirty hands" as follows, in a more or less affirmative light:

> No government can put the life of the community and all its members at risk, so long as there are actions available to it, even immoral actions, that would avoid or reduce the risk. . . . That is what political leaders are for; that is their first task. (Walzer 2004, 42)

The first or primary task of political leaders is to succeed in achieving their political goals. Being able to find ways to achieve such goals is the first virtue in politics. Walzer thus declares, "No one succeeds in politics without getting his hands dirty" (Walzer 1973, 164).

The necessity of "dirty hands" in politics compels politicians to compromise ethics. One such contemporary example can be found in the Nobel Peace Prize laureate and former Myanmar's State Counsellor Aung San Suu Kyi. From 2016 to 2021, when she was in power, the international community was profoundly disappointed with her failure to stop, or at least alleviate, the persecution of Rohingya people in Myanmar (Ellis-Petersen 2018). Her inaction can be explained by her political needs. The Rohingya do not have voting rights and they receive little sympathy from general voters in the country. Supporting the Rohingya, or even appearing sympathetic to them, would have jeopardized Aung San's political agenda. Aung San had to choose between either taking a moral stand for the Rohingya and consequently losing popular support from voters or turning her back to the Rohingya to consolidate her political power. She chose the latter. She was certainly not unique in that regard. Politicians in the United States, for instance, have often to deal with similar issues. During the years when Donald Trump occupied the White House, some Republican politicians faced their own dilemmas. Many of them did not agree with some of Trump's policies and his conduct. But few were willing to openly criticize him, except for a small number who mostly were not seeking re-election, such as Jeff Flake, U.S. senator of Arizona, and Bob Corker, U.S. senator of Tennessee. One reason for this was that politicians seeking re-election could not afford to lose the support of Trump hardliners. To keep their political careers alive, Republican politicians had to bite their tongues and not offend voters whose primary loyalty was to Trump. So, they went along with Trump.

People outside politics may not agree with the way in which politicians pursue their ambitions. But we do not necessarily have to condemn them *as politicians*. This is political realism. This is in the nature of politics. Political realism does not imply that politics is always the opposite of ethics. Indeed, politics can advance ethical ideals. It is just that the two goals can come to conflict, and when they do, politics often trumps ethics in the realm of politics.

So, this has been the predicament for Confucians in working with the state. On the one hand, if Confucians did not get involved with state power, they would become marginalized and risk ending up in irrelevance. Then, they could not achieve their goals of constructing a good society. On the other hand, working with the state sooner or later but inevitably jeopardized the integrity of Confucian moral ideals and rendered it a tool used by state power for political purposes. The reality is that when rulers are non-Confucian but make use of Confucianism, they use Confucianism selectively and distort Confucianism to serve their own political purposes. Even when rulers are otherwise Confucian themselves, they are often forced to commit "dirty hands" acts in violation of Confucian teachings to succeed in politics.[8] This kind of practice is diametrically opposed to Confucian moral ideals. Both Mengzi and Xunzi, for example, held the ideal explicitly that one should never commit an immoral act even if by doing so one could acquire the empire (*Mengzi* 2A2; *Xunzi*, chapters 8 and 11). But then, such a conviction is simply not a formula for successful politics.

We may call this problem "the dilemma of politics and ethics." The need for success in politics sooner or later will compromise Confucian moral ideals; maintaining the ethical integrity of Confucianism will hinder political success at one point or another. In this sense, there can be no such thing as "sagely politics," if it means that sageliness and political rule can be integrated in the same person seamlessly, as in the legends of sage-kings propagated by the ancient Confucian thinkers.[9] In such a sense, "sagely politics" is not only unrealistic but also a contradictory term; politicians cannot be sages; sages cannot be politicians.

This tension between ethics and politics was noted early in the history of Confucianism. In the writing of the Han scholar Yang Xiong 楊雄 (53 BCE–18 CE), we find an interlocutor puzzled over why no rulers employed sagely Kongzi. Yang explained:

> Because to use him properly, they would have had to follow him. And had they followed him, they would then have had to abandon their customary ways, go against what they had acceded to. . . . It would have caused a great ruckus! Who except for the very best in heaven's realm would have been able to employ him? (Yang 2013, 123)

Here Yang was talking about the Kongzi as commonly portraited, who upheld his moral ideals. Yang's point is that, had a ruler employed Kongzi and followed Kongzi's moral way, the ruler would have had to change his way of ruling the state and hence cause big changes in the court. Rulers' way and Kongzi's moral way were not congruent. Consequently, unless Kongzi had chosen to compromise his ideals, he would not be able to find a ruler willing to employ him.

The contemporary Confucian thinker Mou Zongsan 牟宗三 (1909–1995) seems to have recognized such a necessity for politicians to do certain things that may not be appropriate for the highly virtuous and thus the impossibility of sagely politics. Mou writes:

> Being a sage is different from being a country's president. If a sage wants to be a president, he will have to depart from his identity as sage and to follow the protocol of a president engaging in politics. This is the sage's self-restriction.[10]

Even though Mou understands that sages cannot be acting as sages when they are engaged in politics, he stops short from holding that sages should not engage in politics. For Mou, the democratic transformation of Confucianism and Confucian participation in politics are not to be separated. Holding on to the traditional idea of "outer kingliness," Mou sees political participation in the form of serving as political leaders in society. In his view, becoming political leaders in public offices is so important that it even justifies Confucian sages in putting their sagehood aside, at least for the period they are in political office. Hence, Mou's model is not "sagely politics" in the full sense of the term. Similarly, the prominent Confucian thinker Tang Yijie 湯一介 (1927–2014) said, "had Kongzi become a king, we would not have had Kongzi."[11] In other words, had Kongzi become a ruler, he would have adopted a different philosophy than what we know as Confucianism.

The above investigation set the stage for me to argue that progressive Confucians today should let go the ancient ideal of sagely politics. Sages have no place in twenty-first century politics. In totalitarian states, sages, even if they exist, cannot possibly play a decisive role in making political decisions against rulers. In democratic societies, as I will argue next, Confucians should turn to democratic activism and grassroots participation in advancing their political agendas. Either way, contemporary progressive Confucians should keep the concept of sage out of Confucian political philosophy. They must wake up from the dream of sagely politics.

2. Politics without Depending on Politicians

Without sagely leaders, how can ordinary people promote the "kingly Way" (*wang dao* 王道)? This question can be addressed with a twofold answer. First, from early on, Confucian thinkers have indicated that people can advance the "kingly Way" on the grassroots level in society. Second, in contemporary times, democracy opens a new and effective way to promote the Confucian political ideals. Let us take a look at these in turn.

First, we must understand that the Confucian idea of "kingliness" or *wang dao* has never meant to be exclusively about serving in government. *Analects* 2.21 records:

Someone said of Kongzi, "Why is the master not engaged in government?" The Master said, "The *Book of Documents* [*Shangshu* 尚書] says: 'Filial, simply in being filial, and befriending your brothers, the influence will extend to government.' This is also engaging in governing. Why must there be any extra 'engagement in government' "? (Ni 2017, 110)

"Engagement in government" is a translation of *wei zheng* 為政. In today's expression, it means "doing politics." Kongzi understood *zheng* in terms of its homonym 正, getting things right (*Analects* 12.17). Namely, the government is about getting things right in society. Evidently, for Kongzi, one can engage in such affairs without actually holding a post in government. Serving in government in ancient times was a way to realize the Confucian ideal of the good society, the kingly way. It was a means to an end, the end being the Confucian good society. This idea of Kongzi's points to a way for us to rethink how ordinary people can influence government, especially in contemporary times.

Second, the twenty-first century is an era of democracy. The Confucian ideal of "outer kingliness" can be pursued through democratic activism. Ancient Confucian thinkers operated within a societal system in which their philosophy could not exert direct influence on society at large without state sponsorship. Serving in government was seen as the most effective way, and to some even the only effective way, for Confucians to achieve their social ideals through political means. Caught in the dilemma of politics and ethics, they had either to seek state sponsorship at the expense of compromising moral principles or to become marginalized in society. But times have changed. We are now in a democratic era. In a society that is less than democratic, Confucians should, first of all, advocate democracy to create conditions for democratic participation.[12] In democratic societies, politics is not merely about working in government; it can be effectively pursued from outside of government. In modern times, Confucianism can shape society through democratic participation. Through democratic activism, Confucianism can affect government policy without having to solicit favor from the government. This makes it possible for Confucianism as a political force to play an effective role in shaping social policies.

On this matter, my view draws on numerous contemporary Confucian thinkers and is congruent with many of their ideas. In the meantime, it also differs from them in many ways. First, my Confucian approach to democratic politics offers an alternative to existing theories of Confucian democracy. "Confucian democracy" stands for various attempts in recent decades, by political philosophers and political theorists, to design a form of democracy that reflects Confucian values and is suitable for societies whose citizens are largely of the Confucian cultural heritage. The field has now become fairly crowded. Here I will mention a few representative trends and indicate how my approach differs from them.

One pioneering group of thinkers in this movement takes a communitarian approach to Confucian democracy. Representatives of this group include David Hall and Roger Ames (1999) and Sor-hoon Tan (2003). These thinkers advocate Confucian democracy mainly on the basis of John Dewey's notion of democracy as a way of life; they emphasize the need for community-building as the primary approach to democracy. These thinkers are vague, however, on the institutional structure of democracy.[13] I hold that progressive Confucians must straightforwardly address issues of political institution and unambiguously advocate an electoral system of democracy. Although I share the view of these thinkers on the need for community-building, I differentiate community-building in a democratic society on the one hand and community-building as part of institutionalizing democracy as a political framework on the other hand. The view of community-building in the case of Hall and Ames, and of Tan, as I understand it, includes the latter. In my view, community-building in a democratic society can coincide with democratic political institutions in the physical realm. Conceptually, however, it is distinct from democratic political institutions. Community-building can take place either in a democratic or non-democratic society. Confucians have advocated community-building in the past and in present China.[14] They should continue advocating community-building in democratic societies. However, Confucian community-building is not and should not be part of the political institution of democracy.[15]

Another influential group is that of Confucian meritocrats. This group of thinkers, as diverse as their views are, share a conviction that democracy with Confucian characteristics must prioritize political meritocracy. This group includes such thinkers as Jiang Qing (2013), Joseph Chan (2014a), Daniel Bell (2016), and Bai Tongdong (2020). Among these thinkers, Jiang is the most conservative, even though the political system that he designed also includes a democratically elected lower chamber.[16] Chan is perhaps the most "liberal" in the group. His political arrangement includes a democratically elected lower chamber and a meritocratically selected upper chamber (Chan 2014a). While I am sympathetic to the Confucian ideal of meritocracy (i.e., people with appropriate merits should lead and play a large role in society), I do not believe it can be achieved through political institutions that secure political offices for the meritorious, as I have discussed in Chapter 10 of this book. I take meritocracy in contemporary society as a value orientation, which must be realized through democratic processes by promoting

252   RESHAPING CONFUCIANISM: A PROGRESSIVE INQUIRY

meritorious candidates in general elections rather than by political institutional arrangements.

Sungmoon Kim has proposed a theory of "pragmatic Confucian democracy" (Kim 2018). Kim argues that Confucians should pursue democracy "because of its practical capacity, in comparison with other types of political arrangements, for social coordination and its legitimate authority in achieving this critical political goal effectively, if not perfectly" (Kim 2018, 37). I am largely in agreement with Kim in this regard. However, my primary justification for democratic institutions is grounded on the fact that Confucians do not have a more reliable way to identify meritorious leaders and it lies with the practical necessity for contemporary Confucians to participate in democracy (see my discussion in Section 6 of Chapter 10 in this book).

Moreover, Kim aims to prioritize what he calls "second-order value" of democracy. He writes:

> In a pragmatic Confucian democracy, democratic institutional mechanisms do not function merely as an instrument for achieving Confucian goods; rather, they are deeply penetrated by Confucian values and programmed to produce rights, justice, and citizenship that are harmonious with such values. (Kim 2018, 14)

By infusing values into democratic institutional mechanisms, Kim wishes to make democracy not only instrumentally valuable, but also intrinsically valuable to Confucians (Kim 2018, 7). In contrast, my approach takes democracy as merely a political institution in the sense Joseph Schumpeter understands it. Schumpeter defines democracy primarily as a political "method," as an "institutional arrangement for arriving at political decisions in which individuals acquire the power to decide by means of a competitive struggle for the people's vote" (Schumpeter 1947, 269).[17] In this sense, I take democracy to possess only instrumental value, when it is used by citizens to promote the good life through electoral competition by a "one person one vote" arrangement on the basis of their political numerical identity as I have argued in Chapter 10 of this book.[18]

In my view, Confucian democratic citizens need to compete with non-Confucian citizens to promote their values through electing their representatives and through processes of democratic legislation. Thus, in contemporary societies where a majority of citizens are Confucian, the ideal arrangement is a combination of a formal democratic institution with democratically generated social policies infused with Confucian values. I have dubbed such an arrangement "democratic form with Confucian content" (Li 2012b). In such a view, democratically generated social policies, infused with Confucian values or otherwise, are not part of democratic political institutions; rather they are achieved by actively participating in the operation of democratic political institutions.

More recently, Shaun O'Dwyer has argued for a model dubbed "Confucian democrats, not Confucian democracy," to which I am more sympathetic than other views discussed in this section. O'Dwyer argues that in contemporary times, any form of Confucian democracy—a democratic institution significantly embedded with Confucian values and metaphysical convictions—is no longer feasible. Instead, he advocates the alternative model of "Confucian democrats." This is a model grounded on "democratic Confucian conviction politics." O'Dwyer defines "conviction politics" as "the conduct of political campaigns, policy, and an overall political career in accordance with deeply held principles and values, rather than in response to a perceived consensus or majoritarian sentiment" (O'Dwyer 2020, 222–223). He writes:

> Conviction politics is typically exemplified in the careers of elected officials and heads of state, although it could be used to characterize the conduct, and career, of a civil society organization leader. (O'Dwyer 2020, 223)

Specifically, he cites as an example Kim Dae-jung (1924–2009), who served as South Korea's president from 1998 to 2003. A career politician and democracy activist, Kim drew on Confucian values in carrying out his political convictions. For O'Dwyer, Kim set a good example for Confucian conviction politics in action.

I agree with O'Dwyer (2020) that there is no need for any particular form of "Confucian democracy," in the sense of a democratic institution with specific Confucian characteristics. I believe that the period of exploration for "Confucian democracy" is over. Progressive Confucian thinkers need to move on. However, O'Dwyer seems to have placed too much hope on career politicians to promote Confucian social and political ideals. If we look for influential "Confucian democrat" politicians like Kim Dae-jung in the real world, such examples are rare. They can hardly be relied on for fulfilling Confucian social ideals, which requires sustained rather than sporadic endeavors in society. In my view, Confucian citizens are the main force

254 RESHAPING CONFUCIANISM: A PROGRESSIVE INQUIRY

in contemporary East Asian societies; politicians are to serve the need and aspiration of voters. In real life, it is more likely that the politicians whom Confucians can support are ordinary people. If Confucians rid of the ideal of sages in contemporary politics, including its various reincarnated forms such as "great wise leaders" as their saviors, they can stand more solidly on realistic grounds when engaging in democratic politics. And they must do so.

Now to summarize my view on Confucian democratic politics. I take democracy as a political institutional mechanism, which is neutral toward different cultural traditions. There is no need for Confucian democracy as a political institution, just as there is no need for Christian democracy or Islamic democracy. Progressive Confucians must participate in democratic processes and promote their values through democratic activism. In a society where the majority of citizens are inclined toward Confucianism, the ideal arrangement is a combination of "democratic form with Confucian content," namely Confucian citizens can successfully promote and implement their values through effectively participating in democratic processes.

My proposal is a bottom-up model, shifting the focus of the discourse to democratic Confucian citizenship at the grassroots level. The primary aim of my approach is to establish and maintain a democratic society and to guide society through democratic participation by fostering a politically active Confucian citizenry. Accordingly, the current Confucian project for democracy is not about institutionalizing a democratic system with specific Confucian characteristics; it is rather about building strong Confucian citizenship for operating effectively in a democratic institution that works for all citizens.

Today, the Confucian ideal of "sage-kings" is dead; "outer kingliness" must be realized without "kings." With democratic activism available as an effective way to influence politicians, Confucian scholars must wake up once and for all from the long-held dream of relying on sages or becoming ruler's counsellors, which did not work and will not work due to the inherent dilemma of politics and ethics.

Democratic participation comes in a variety of forms. Confucians can even form political parties in an effort to shape public policy. However, it would be naïve to think that all Confucians belong to the same political block in a democratic society. Just as Christians can belong to opposite political parties, so too can Confucians. They may share substantive moral values and moral sentiments, but they may nevertheless opt for different routes as far as political issues are concerned. After all, people sharing the same moral values may nevertheless diverge on implementing these values. People who share the same ethics may nevertheless opt for different approaches in politics.

A pertinent question is, if Confucians must advance social ideals through democratic participation, can they have enough political clout in society? Who are Confucians anyway? Throughout history, Confucianism has never maintained a list of official members. It is a cultural tradition. While its main social ideals have been articulated and rearticulated by Confucian thinkers and activists, Confucianism exists in people's ways of life. Sungmoon Kim has argued, East Asian societies are "Confucian" not because East Asians subscribe to Confucianism by holding it as their self-chosen philosophy or faith, but because "they nevertheless live their lives largely in accordance with Confucian mores and habits, mostly informed by Confucian rituals and the ethical values associated with them" (Kim 2014, 118). In other words, people in these societies are Confucian because their lives are shaped by, and hence exemplify the Confucian cultural tradition. In such an understanding, Confucianism has a large base in East Asian societies. What is needed is political activism by self-conscious Confucians to mobilize citizens to promote political agendas in society that are consistent with Confucian values.

In conclusion, today the Confucian ideal of "outer kingliness" must be carried out through democratic participation and social activism. Confucians can achieve their goal of "outer kingliness" without being "kings" or in the service of "kings." The old dream of sagely politics must die. The new dream of "kingliness" in the form of social activism lives in the democratic era.

Study Questions

1. What does *zheng* mean for Kongzi?
2. Explain the Confucian slogan "Inner Sageliness and Outer Kingliness."
3. What is the dilemma of politics and ethics? Does this dilemma exist in other cultures and societies?
4. Who are Confucians in contemporary East Asian societies?
5. The author argues that the old Confucian dream of "outer kingliness" is dead. Explain.

256 RESHAPING CONFUCIANISM: A PROGRESSIVE INQUIRY

6. Explain the author's proposal of "politics without depending on political leaders"? How is it different from alternative models of "Confucian democracy"?
7. In the author's view, what kind of democratic institution is appropriate for Confucians today?
8. What does the author mean by "democratic form with Confucian content?" In your opinion, is this a viable solution for a modern Confucian society?
9. Do you agree with the author's view? Why or why not?

12

Education for Humanity

Historically, there is a direct link between the school of Confucianism and education. The Chinese word that we use today for "Confucian," *ru* 儒, originally denotes teachers of religious rituals. Before ancient *ru* became a philosophical school, they were teachers by profession. Education was their mission (Hu 1998, 676). Since its early conception, the Confucian social project has been educational in character, with its primary purpose to prepare people for virtuous and productive lives. In the Confucian view, the goal of becoming a caring, responsive, and responsible person is to be achieved through educational processes. This final chapter explicates the Confucian philosophy of education. I first elaborate on the Confucian concept of education and its role in making well-rounded persons, and then examine it in the context of civic education as a collaborative social effort in contemporary times, and finally argue for the role of Confucian moral education in a democratic society.

1. Education through Teaching and Learning

Education is at the center of the Confucian ethic-social project. The Confucian concept of humanity is not merely a biological concept. It is also a social and moral concept. In the Confucian conception, one is not born a human in the full sense of the word; rather, one becomes human through learning and cultivation. The process of such a transformation is through education. The theme of the 2018 World Congress of Philosophy, "Learning to Become Human" (*xue yi cheng ren* 學以成人) captures such a Confucian ideal well. Mengzi held that we are all born with the sprouts of humanity, but it is through cultivation that we foster these sprouts into full growth (*Mengzi* 2A6). This is a process of realizing our potential in becoming human in the full sense, namely a person with virtues, not only moral virtues narrowly defined, but virtues for a productive and fulfilling life in a well-rounded way.

Reshaping Confucianism. Chenyang Li, Oxford University Press. © Oxford University Press 2024.
DOI: 10.1093/oso/9780197657621.003.0013

258 RESHAPING CONFUCIANISM: A PROGRESSIVE INQUIRY

Confucian thinkers take education as a top priority in society. Kongzi was among the first in history to advocate "education regardless of social classes" (*you jiao wu lei* 有教無類; *Analects* 15.39). His view challenged the previous educational system that was monopolized by the government in exclusion of common people, a practice called *xue zai guanfu* 學在官府. For Kongzi, everyone has the potential to grow intelligently and to become a virtuous and productive member of society, and everyone should be given an opportunity to receive education as a necessary means to thrive in life.

In Confucian classics, we find abundant discussions on the importance of education. The *Analects* records a conversation between Kongzi and his disciple, Ranyou:

> Accompanied by Ranyou, Kongzi arrived in the state of Wei. He said, "this state is populous." Ranyou asked, "now that there is a large population, what should be done?" Kongzi said, "make the people rich." Ranyou asked again, "what else should be done when people become rich?" Kongzi said, "educate them (*jiao zhi* 教之)." (*Analects* 13.9)

In Kongzi's view, when people's living conditions are satisfied, society should provide education to help them grow to become productive members of a cultured society.

Xunzi also maintained that education makes a fundamental difference in people. Xunzi said:

> The children of Hann and Yue and of the tribes of Yi and Mo are all born making the same sounds, but they grow up having different customs because the process of education has effected such changes in them. (*Xunzi*, chapter 1; Knoblock 1988, 136)

Hann, Yue, Yi, and Mo were four primitive tribes. No matter to which tribe a child was born, he cried with the same sound. However, if he learned ritual propriety (*li*), he became a cultivated person; without understanding *li* as cultural grammar, he remained "barbarian." Hence, Xunzi assigned a central role to learning ritual propriety (*li*). "Barbarian" here is not a racist designation, but a term for all those who have not become civilized, namely having not acquired *li* through education, including those within our own community.[1]

EDUCATION FOR HUMANITY   259

Confucian education is usually framed in terms of *jiao-xue* 教學. *Jiao* mainly means teaching or educating others; *xue* means learning or educating oneself. Teaching is mainly the responsibility of society to provide a suitable environment for learning and it is a social calling for the able to impart knowledge and experience to learners. Mengzi once said that one of the greatest pleasures is to get to teach people with talent (*Mengzi* 7B20). Evidently, for him being a teacher is the most rewarding profession in the world. Mengzi said:

> A gentleman [*junzi* 君子] teaches in five ways. The first is by a transforming influence like that of timely rain. The second is by helping the student to realize his virtue to the full. The third is by helping him to develop his talent. The fourth is by answering his questions. And the fifth is by setting an example others not in contact with him can emulate. These five are the ways in which a gentleman teaches. (*Mengzi* 7A40; Lau 1970, 191)

Confucian teaching is holistic, aiming to cultivate well-rounded students. By transforming influence, helping students become virtuous, developing their talent, dispelling their confusion, and setting good examples, teachers help students become responsible and productive members of society. In such a process, particular attention is made to suit the student's specific circumstances (*yincai shi jiao* 因材施教). Without effective education, neither virtue nor talent is possible regardless of people's inborn capacity to be good.

As the two sides of the same coin, teaching and learning go hand in hand. Kongzi is well-known for emphasizing the importance of learning. *Xue* 學 (learning) is the first word in the *Analects*. In Kongzi's view, people are similar by nature, but they differentiate themselves by putting learning into practice (*Analects* 17.2). The *Book of Rites* contains a chapter specifically called *Xueji* 學記 (On Learning). The text states, "Jade does not become a product without carving; people do not understand the *Dao* without learning"[2] (TTC, 1521). For Confucians, the primary purpose of learning is to improve oneself to become a good person (*Analects* 14.24). In summarizing his major life stages, Kongzi placed learning at the first, saying that "at fifteen I set my heart-mind on learning" (*Analects* 2.4). This of course does not mean that Kongzi did not learn anything before he turned fifteen. Rather, earlier learning had prepared him well so that he established learning as a mission in life and pursued it with determination. Kongzi takes "love of learning" (*hao xue* 好學) as a primary virtue and discusses it repeatedly in the *Analects* (e.g.,

260 RESHAPING CONFUCIANISM: A PROGRESSIVE INQUIRY

1.14, 5.15, 5.28, 6.3, 8.13, 11.7, 17.8, 19.5). Commenting on his own strength, Kongzi said:

> In a hamlet of ten households, there are bound to be those who are my equal in doing their best for others and in being trustworthy in what they say, but they are unlikely to love learning as much as I do. (*Analects* 5.28; Lau 1979, 80, modified)

"Love of learning" is taken as a primary virtue because it is the key to cultivating other virtues. In connection with other virtues, Kongzi said:

> To love benevolence [*ren*] without loving learning is liable to lead to foolishness. To love cleverness without loving learning is liable to lead to deviation from the right path. To love trustworthiness in word without loving learning is liable to lead to harmful behavior. To love forthrightness without loving learning is liable to lead to intolerance. To love courage without loving learning is liable to lead to insubordination. To love unbending strength without loving learning is liable to lead to indiscipline. (*Analects* 17.8; Lau 1979, 144–145)

All these other virtues are important in fostering Confucian personhood. Kongzi's point is that no matter how much one is fond of these virtues, one cannot acquire them adequately or practice them properly without being attentive to learning.

We can note a few important features of Confucian learning. First, while learning includes skill acquisition to earn a living, the primary purpose of education from a Confucian perspective was to create a well-rounded person capable of a productive and morally good life. Kongzi said:

> The virtuous person [*junzi* 君子] does not seek fulfillment of his appetite nor comfort in his lodging. He is diligent in his duties and careful in his speech. He associates with people of moral principles and thereby realizes himself. Such a person may be said to love learning. (*Analects* 1.14; Chan 1963, 21, modified)

Kongzi takes learning to be a cardinal virtue for people to develop humanity and to become productive in life. To love learning is to develop one's humanity.

EDUCATION FOR HUMANITY   261

Second, Confucian learning is not merely about book-learning to acquire pure knowledge; learning must be integrated with practice. Kongzi's philosophy of education prescribes "to learn and to practice what is learned repeatedly" (*Analects* 1.1). He said, "what worries me is that people do not cultivate virtues, they learn without exchanging ideas, they learn the right things without following it, and they do not change even though they are not good" (*Analects* 7.3). In his view, learning is not merely about enriching the mind; it is more about improving practice.

Third, learning is not a passive process of being indoctrinated; it is an active endeavor to pursue knowledge, acquire experience, and develop skills. In his teaching, Kongzi encouraged students to come up with three similar cases on their own after they were shown one case (*Analects* 7.8). Taking initiatives and being proactive are essential to effective learning.

Fourth, learning is not a unidirectional process from teacher to student; everyone should learn from one another mutually. The domain of one's knowledge is like a circle. As one learns more, the circle expands. The larger the circle becomes, the more one is exposed to the unknown. This calls for more learning. In teaching, one may find that one's knowledge is not as solid and thorough as one may have thought to be and may feel the need to learn more. Thus, learning and teaching augment each other. Such a mutual dependency can be found in the same person as one both learns and teaches. It can also be between different people, between students and teachers. In learning, students not only improve themselves; they can also help their teachers to improve. The same can be said of teachers. Kongzi said:

> Walking along with two others, I am certain there is my teacher among them. I select their good qualities to follow, and their bad qualities to rectify. (*Analects* 7.22; Ni 2017, 203)

If one is serious about learning and is dedicated to learning, one can always learn from others.

Now we see what it means for teaching (*jiao*) and learning (*xue*) to be the two aspects of the Confucian philosophy of education. Teaching is for those with knowledge, virtue, and experience to help others grow, and for themselves to become more advanced in these regards. Learning is for individual persons to absorb knowledge, to develop social skills, and to become virtuous. Of the two aspects of education, teaching, and learning, Kongzi

262 RESHAPING CONFUCIANISM: A PROGRESSIVE INQUIRY

advocated that one should "learn insatiably and teach others tirelessly" (*Analects* 7.2). Chapter *Xueji* (On Learning) of the *Book of Rites* asserts:

> In learning one knows one's own inadequacies; through teaching one sees one's difficulties (*kun* 困). After one knows inadequacies one can reverse them; when in difficulties, one can improve oneself. This is the process of mutual enhancement between learning and teaching.[3] (TTC, 1521)

For Confucians, education as teaching and learning is vitally important for the good life. Individuals need to get educated to develop humanity so that they live good lives. Society needs to implement education, through teaching and learning, to prepare all-rounded and productive members for building a prosperous world.

2. Education and Virtuous Persons

In ancient times, the Confucian educational curriculum consisted of mainly the "six arts" (*liu yi* 六藝), which were rites (*li* 禮), music (*yue* 樂), archery (*she* 射), charioteering (*yu* 御), literacy and calligraphy (*shū* 書), and mathematics (*shù* 數). Along with these skills, are the Six Classics: *Book of Poetry*, *Book of History*, *Book of Changes*, *Book of Rites*, *Book of Music*, and the *Spring and Autumn Annals*. Kongzi reportedly edited and revised these classic texts to make them appropriate for educational purposes.

Kongzi himself made a career as a teacher. He had seventy-two disciples and over three thousand students. In *Analects* 7.25, Kongzi's disciples categorized his teaching under four themes: cultural refinement (*wen* 文), proper conduct (*xing* 行), dedication (*zhong* 忠), and trustworthiness (*xin* 信). Commentators have read this record in different ways. The first theme of *wen* may be understood as referring to studying classics (Ni 2017, 206). However, the study of classics was intertwined with the teachings of proper conduct, dedication, and trustworthiness. The *Analects*, especially in Chapter 10, presents Kongzi as a culturally refined person. He understood how to act at court (10.2, 10.3, 10.4), and how to wear proper clothes to suit the occasions (10.6, 10.7). He did not mind his food being elegantly prepared, displaying an attitude that can only be described as "classy" (10.8). He had an extraordinary appreciation for good music. Legend has it that once he listened to the *Shao* music and found it so enjoyable that for three months

EDUCATION FOR HUMANITY   263

he could not notice the taste of meat (*Analects* 7.14). Proper conduct (*xing*) has to do with ritual propriety. Kongzi is known for his profound knowledge of ritual propriety and for his ritual observance. The *Analects* is full of his teachings related to this topic (e.g., 1.12/3, 1.15, 2.3, 2.5, 2.23). Dedication (*zhong*) and trustworthiness (*xin*) are among the most important virtues for Kongzi. Taking one's mission seriously and having perseverance in pursuing it is a personal trait that makes it possible for one to succeed. Trustworthiness is a fundamental quality for interacting and working with other people in society. Thus, these four themes—cultural refinement, proper conduct, dedication, and trustworthiness—are interconnected in producing virtuous students. Being culturally refined implies being knowledgeable about ritual propriety, which in turn entails proper conduct. Practicing ritual propriety can help people become dedicated and dependable (see Chapter 3 of this book). Dedication enables one to see a task to its completion when entrusted by others and hence, makes oneself trustworthy. These four themes may not cover all subjects of Kongzi's teachings, but they are undoubtedly among the most important things that Kongzi taught his students. The *Analects* records that Kongzi's students excelled in various areas of education: virtuous conduct, eloquence, administrative affairs, and cultural learning (11.3).[4]

Now it would be informative to briefly compare this Confucian view of education with ancient Greek philosophers on whether virtue can be taught. In Plato's dialogue *Meno*, Socrates famously raised this very question without reaching a definitive conclusion. If we follow Socrates's view that real learning is a special kind of remembering, a view that is further developed in the *Republic*, we come to think that virtue is a form of knowledge, knowledge is innate, and one can have knowledge only by recollection, then it follows that virtue can neither be learned from outside nor be taught by others. Aristotle has a different answer to the question. For Aristotle, whereas intellectual virtue is acquired through learning and teaching, moral virtue is formed through the habituation of behavior. On achieving moral virtue, Aristotle held that we learn virtue by doing virtuous acts and by forming a habit of doing them. Aristotle said:

> Some people believe that it is nature that makes men good, others that it is habit, and others again that it is teaching. Now, whatever goodness comes from nature is obviously not in our power, but is present in truly fortunate men as the result of some divine cause. Argument and teaching, I am afraid, are not effective in all cases: the soul of the listener must first have been

264   RESHAPING CONFUCIANISM: A PROGRESSIVE INQUIRY

conditioned by habits to the right kind of likes and dislikes, just as land must be cultivated before it is able to foster the seed. (*Nicomachean Ethics* 1179b20–28; Ostwald 1962, 296)

In Aristotle's view, teaching is less effective than habituation in forming certain virtues. This is so because a person without a good character will be led by passion rather than reason and hence will not be persuaded by argument and teaching. Aristotle concluded, "Therefore, there must first be a character that somehow has an affinity for excellence or virtue, a character that loves what is noble and feels disgust at what is base" (*Nicomachean Ethics* 1179b29–31; Ostwald 1962, 296). How can one acquire a good character without being taught so? For Aristotle, children do not have the rational capacity to reason, but they can be made to do appropriate acts that are conducive to forming good habits for virtue.

Whereas Aristotle makes *loving the good* ("noble") a paramount priority in children, Kongzi makes the *love of learning* a top priority. The Confucian notion of learning, however, is broader than that of Aristotle. It is more than merely book learning or making rational argument. Imitating adults, for instance, is also a form of learning. Hence Confucian learning overlaps with Aristotle's habituation but is more than that. In ancient times, reciting classic texts at an early age was a form of learning, even though children had to wait till later to better understand the contents. Children learn from adults by following them as examples in life.[5] It is not that young children cannot be taught, but that teaching for children must be conducted at a level that is appropriate to children's learning capability. Confucians emphasize the need to foster a heart of the love of learning in children so that they are oriented toward learning from early on.

When such a philosophy of education is put effectively into practice, everyone strives to realize one's potential and people work together toward building a flourishing society. One important outcome is that such education gives people social mobility. Those who had performed well in learning were eligible for moving up the social ladder. In ancient times, this primarily meant becoming government officials, described by Kongzi's disciple Zi Xia as *xue er you ze shi* 學而優則仕, those who are superior in learning (should) serve as government officials (*Analects* 19.13). According to Chapter *Wangzhi* of the *Book of Rites*, in ancient China, scholars were evaluated and ranked according to their scholarly achievements. The selection process included argumentation (*lun* 論) and analysis (*bian* 辨) (TTC, 1327). Beginning at the level of local villages, winners at that entry level were selected as "Excellent Scholars" (*xiu shi* 秀士). Further up they were chosen as "Select Scholars" (*xuan shi* 選士). After that, they were given the responsibility to teach others. "Select Scholars" were further educated to become "Outstanding Scholars" (*jun shi* 俊士). At the most advanced level, there were "Accomplished Scholars" (*zao shi* 造士) (TTC, 1342).

In theory, the process was open to everyone.[6] However, the reality was more complicated. People's economic and social environment inevitably affected their mobility. Socially disadvantaged people could not possibly have a fair chance to ride on the selection system, in ancient times as well as today. This practical difficulty, however, does not invalidate the value of the Confucian philosophy of education through learning. The Confucian ideal of equal opportunity for education should be practiced together with another philosophy in Confucianism, namely "enriching the people" (*fu min* 富民), making people materially adequate for receiving an education. Furthermore, contemporary societies are more diversified in social advancement than in ancient times. Becoming a government official is no longer the sole or main career prospect for most people (as discussed in Chapter 10 of this book). There are a variety of ways to advance social mobility. As far as the Confucian philosophy is concerned, however, everyone should have the same opportunity to move up in the social ladder if they excel in learning. Thus, in Confucian philosophy, education and a flourishing society are intrinsically connected.[7]

3. Civic Education

To what extent is the Confucian philosophy of education still relevant today? In this section, I examine issues of civic education in contemporary societies and then present a Confucian perspective on it.

As a means for society to reproduce itself, education has always been connected to ways for society to shape, sustain or reform its way of life. In that regard, education in this general sense—more or less, directly or indirectly—has always been *civic* education. Civic education aims to produce competent citizens for society, citizens with knowledge, attitudes, and skills necessary for acting as responsible and productive members of society. From early on, Confucian education has been a form of civic education in the sense similar to the Greek idea of *paideia*. The Greek term refers to the rearing and education of the ideal member of society, the *polis*. For ancient Greeks, *paideia* was a formative process aiming for a person to become a valuable member of one's family and of one's community. *Paideia* "included education in the arts, philosophy and rhetoric, history, science, and mathematics; training in sports and warfare; enculturation or learning of the city's religious, social, political, and professional customs and training to participate in them; and the development of one's moral character through the virtues" (Crittenden and Levine 2018). It is a form of holistic education as it was understood for future citizens of the *poli*. Today in democratic societies, civic education prepares citizens to be independent-minded, deliberative, and participatory in self-governance. Successful civic education in a democratic society should produce citizens not only with a good understanding of social institutions, people's political and civil rights and responsibilities, but also adequate knowledge of the world, citizens who are equipped with the right values and dispositions, and who can competently work together with others in achieving shared goals in society.

Civic education is a life-long process. Yet the most crucial stage of civic education is in people's formative years. School education is an important part, perhaps the most important of civic education. In the philosophy of education, among the most important issues of discussion are the purpose of school education in association with the formation of virtue and character, and along with it, the question of who should control and shape such a process. These two parts are linked because the purpose of education should bear on the proper authority to manage and deliver it.

In her influential book *Democratic Education*, Amy Gutmann examines three contending theories in responding to these questions. The first is "the family state" theory. Traceable to Plato, this theory holds that the purpose of education is to produce suitable members for the state who share a common purpose identified by and with the state. In this theory, the state is the sole authority of education, aiming to cultivate "a level of like-mindedness and camaraderie among citizens" that most people would expect only in families (Gutmann 1999, 23). "Citizens of a well-ordered family state learn that they cannot realize their own good except by contributing to the social good, and they are also educated to desire only what is good for themselves and their society" (ibid.). Gutmann argues that this theory constrains people's choices among ways of life and hence is not appropriate to contemporary societies. The second theory, associated with John Locke and Thomas Aquinas, is that of "the state of families." This theory places the authority for education solely in the hands of parents and lets parents perpetuate their own values in children through family-controlled education. Gutmann argues, however, that children are not exclusively the property of their parents, and that a democratic society has a significant stake in shaping its future citizens. Therefore, leaving education entirely to parents does not serve well the reproduction of good citizens for democratic societies. The third theory is called "the state of individuals." This is a liberal theory that champions "the dual goals of *opportunity* for choice and *neutrality* among conceptions of the good life" (ibid., 34). It gives educational authority to professional educators who are motivated solely, or at least predominantly, by the interests of children in learning and unconstrained by parental or political authority (ibid., 34). According to this theory, through education, the state should not tell students what kind of good life they should pursue. Students should be left free to choose their way of the good life. Gutmann argues that this view goes too far in framing liberty and virtue as opposites. The two do not have to be mutually exclusive. Besides, liberty itself is also a value and, therefore, this liberal theory itself is not value-neutral as it purportedly to be.

Gutmann's own theory is called "the democratic state of education." It draws on the strengths of each of the above three theories and at the same time aims to overcome their weaknesses. Gutmann writes:

> Like the family state, a democratic state of education tries to teach virtue—not the virtue of the family state (power based upon knowledge), but what might best be called *democratic* virtue: the ability to deliberate, and hence to participate in conscious social reproduction. Like the state of families, a democratic state upholds a degree of parental authority over education, resisting the strong communitarian view that children are creatures of the state. But in recognizing that children are future citizens, the democratic state resists the view, implicit in the state of families, that children are creatures of their parents. Like the state of individuals, a democratic state defends a degree of professional authority over education—not on grounds of liberal neutrality, but to the extent necessary to provide children with the capacity to evaluate those ways of life most favored by parental and political authorities. (ibid., 46)

In Gutmann's democratic state of education, the state, parents, and professional educators all have important roles to play in civic education for cultivating children's character. The educational authority is a shared

268 RESHAPING CONFUCIANISM: A PROGRESSIVE INQUIRY

responsibility by all three stakeholders. They work together toward the goal of "*conscious* social reproduction," as Gutmann calls it (ibid., 14). An important feature of Gutmann's theory is that it avoids the extremes of each of the three traditional theories and preserves their reasonable elements in a balanced manner. Her theory does not leave the power and responsibility of education exclusively in the hands of either the state or families, or the individual. Instead, it integrates legitimate claims from all three sources.

Even though progressive Confucianism has yet to develop a theory for civic education in a democratic society, the tradition's vast intellectual resources have much to offer a modern philosophy of education, toward a goal compatible with that of Gutmann's theory. Of the interests and goals of education among state, parents, and individuals, classic Confucian thinkers saw and emphasized their congruity. Mengzi said:

> There is a common expression, "the world, the state, and the family." The world has its basis in the state, the state in the family, and the family in one's own self. (*Mengzi* 4A5; Lau 1976, 120, modified).[8]

Mengzi's vision is not confined to one's own state, even though his view of the world was not the same as contemporary cosmopolitanism.[9] As with most ancient theories, classic Confucianism did not envision society as multicultural in the world today. In contemporary multicultural societies, families of different cultural and religious traditions live side by side. There are competing visions of the good life. The state cannot possibly endorse all visions and ways of the good life. Taking into consideration our multicultural world and competing conceptions of the good life in it, contemporary Confucians can endorse Gutmann's proposal for an alliance of the state, parents, and teachers working together to determine the course of civic education. They may see congruity among the state, parents, and educational professionals projected in ancient times as a reflection of a partial overlap of the interests of all parties in the triadic coalition, and they may take it as the basis for promoting common goals that are to be negotiated by the three parties interested in the good of the children and of society. This will involve a process of negotiation, compromise, and accommodation for the purpose of social harmony.

In this regard, Confucianism has a strong ground for making professional educators an equitable partner in the triadic alliance, which has been largely absent in its Western counterpart until recently. Teachers enjoy a very high status in the Confucian tradition, unmatched in many other traditions. Xunzi was among the first to elevate the status of teachers to a height comparable to rulers in society largely because of their role in carrying on the cultural tradition. For him, both of teachers and rulers jointly provided the foundation of ritualized order in the world. Xunzi's version of "civic education" was mainly education of ritual propriety (*li*) in society. He argued for three foundations of ritual propriety. The first is "heaven and earth" (*tian di* 天地). The second is ancestry. And the third is rulers and teachers (*Xunzi*, chapter 19; Knoblock 1994, 58). There can be varied interpretations of "heaven and earth." One interpretation most relevant to our discussion is the fundamental ways in which the world operates, as Xunzi used "heaven" to refer to the natural order of the world. Understood this way, "heaven and earth" refers to the objective way of the world's operation. The practical locus of "ancestry" is in families; "rulers" stand for the state. It is significant for our discussion here that Xunzi placed teachers on a par with rulers on their status in providing the foundation for ritual propriety (*li*) in society. He emphasized the importance of educators for a good society:

> A state that is going to flourish is sure to honor teachers and give great weight to instructors. If one honors teachers and gives great weight to instructors, then proper models and measures will be preserved. (*Xunzi*, chapter 27; Hutton 2014, 312)

Subsequently in the tradition, Confucian thinkers have upheld the five authorities in the world in terms of "heave-earth-ruler-parents-teacher" (*tian di jun qin shi* 天地君親師). This doctrine places teachers as one of the highest authorities, side-by-side with rulers and parents in education. In this understanding, as far as education is concerned, Confucians would place rulers—today it is political authorities—and professional educators at a comparable level of importance.

Obviously, if the purpose of civic education is to produce competent and responsible citizens for democratic societies, the proper mechanism of its operation, including the authority for managing and delivering it, depends on what means can best achieve that purpose successfully. Although all three parties, the state, families, and educational professionals, have a stake in a democratic society, each holds only one perspective.[10] None of the three parties involved can claim a monopoly on pertinent knowledge and authority. It follows that the only reasonable way is to have all three parties

270 RESHAPING CONFUCIANISM: A PROGRESSIVE INQUIRY

involved in a collaborative social effort toward achieving the goal of civic education. In this regard, Confucians can embrace Gutmann's theory of civic education; the tradition's strong emphasis on teachers' role in education is especially conducive toward such a goal.

Furthermore, Confucians will agree with Gutmann that children should not be left to themselves to decide on the formation of their values and virtues. Nevertheless, because Confucian learning promotes learner's active engagement (as elaborated in the first section), students, particularly after their initial stages, also help the shaping of civic education in important ways. They can give feedback on teaching strategies and pedagogies, they can participate in experiments, and they can learn from one another. Moreover, they also shape the values they receive in their education. After all, they are participating in the creation of a future that belongs to them in due course.

4. Confucian Values for Civic Education

I have explicated the Confucian philosophy of education and have discussed how it can give positive responses to Gutmann's theory of education for contemporary societies. In the rest of the chapter, I argue that the secular nature and this-worldly orientation of Confucian philosophy makes it suitable for civic education in the contemporary world. It can play an active role in promoting education that aims at equipping citizens with civic knowledge, civic skills, and civic disposition, preparing them to be effective citizens in a democratic society.

Responsible citizens must possess not only scientific knowledge and technical skills but also good values. In today's civic education, what kind of values should be taught? This is a contentious issue. Liberal thinkers draw a line between "private morality" and "public morality," and confine civic education only to "public morality." They also differentiate moral virtue from civic virtue. Moral virtue is considered "desirable for its own sake" and "for all individuals"; civic virtue is "valued instrumentally, for its contribution to sustaining a political community" (Galston 2007). As far as education is concerned, Confucian philosophy rejects a sharp separation of the public from private spheres, or of moral virtue from civic virtue. In the Confucian view, moral education and civic education are congruent; virtues are constitutive of good personhood and morality carries with it a dimension of social relationality. So-called private virtues directly or indirectly affect a person's social participation. One way or another, a person's "private life" affects her communal and social life. Hence, moral virtues are conducive to productive community life as civic virtues. Where some virtues, such as respect and tolerance, are more directly relevant to civic participation, other virtues are either related to them or socially relevant in indirect ways. For instance, even the virtue of personal hygiene, which is usually considered a straightforwardly personal virtue, can interfere with a person's participation in public life. Therefore, civic education should not leave out so-called private virtues even though these are not its primary focus.

The teaching of moral virtues does not have to be heavy-handed, however. The sixth century Confucian thinker Yan Zhitui 顏之推 (531–591), whom we have encountered in Chapter 5 of this book, characterized an effective way of fostering virtues in young people through *qianyi anhua* 潛移暗化, namely to be influenced by a positive environment gradually and naturally (Wang 2002, 128). Building such an environment is vital to educating young people for developing both civic virtues and moral virtues.

In contemporary multicultural societies, a major obstacle for integrating "private virtues" and "public virtues" in civic education comes from religious divergence. Private morality is often associated with religion. People in multicultural societies practice different religions. Religions, especially monotheistic religions, are often mutually exclusive. For this reason, drawing on religious traditions for civic education can be divisive. In this regard, Confucian philosophy of education has its relative advantage in that Confucianism is not a religion, at least not in the usual sense.[11] Although attempts have been launched in history to make Confucianism a religion, it has never fully made such a conversion. Taking largely an agnostic attitude toward supernatural forces, Kongzi never made a religious commitment. He adopted an attitude of keeping a distance from the gods (*Analects* 6.22). When his student inquired about serving the gods and afterlife, Kongzi responded, "we cannot even serve people well, how can we serve the gods?" and "we cannot even know the present life, how can we know afterlife?" (*Analects* 11.12). Ancient Confucian thinkers sometimes referred to *tian* 天 (heaven) as a supernatural force, but it is a rather vague idea and by no means refers to a personal god. Generally speaking, Confucianism has an overall orientation for the present world. It is not religious in character, and it is not exclusivist toward other religions. For example, a Confucian can be also a Daoist, a Buddhist, or even a Christian.[12] A good contemporary example is Robert Neville. Neville is an ordained elder in the Missouri East Conference of the

United Methodist Church and has pastored in Missouri and New York. He is also renowned as a "Boston Confucian."[13] This feature of non-exclusiveness of Confucianism makes it particularly suitable for contributing to civic education in contemporary societies.[14]

Now, I will examine Confucian values and show how they may be incorporated into civic education in multicultural societies. Speaking of civic education in contemporary democratic societies, one important value to be promoted is civility. Civility is considered among the first or primary virtues of social life, especially in democratic societies. John Rawls has argued that citizens have a "duty of civility," namely a moral duty "to be able to explain to one another on those fundamental questions how the principles and policies they advocate and vote for can be supported by the political values of public reason" (Rawls 1996, 217). His use of "civility" in naming this duty is appropriate in part because such an engagement requires a willingness to listen to others and a fair-mindedness in deciding when accommodations to their views should be made with public reason. Without civility, democracy could become blatant contests for special interest groups rather than a cooperative effort toward building a just society. In an important sense, civility makes the difference between true democracy to which we aspire, and mob rule as warned by classic thinkers. Civility as a virtue, however, is more than just using public reason in political justification and persuasion. It is also more than merely following recognized protocol in participating in political activities. Furthermore, civility is not merely the exercise of tolerance, respect, and considerateness toward other fellow human beings. Cheshire Calhoun has argued that, unlike such virtues as tolerance, respect, and considerateness, civility is an essentially communicative form of moral conduct. She explains:

> Civility always involves a *display* of respect, tolerance, or considerateness. By "displaying" respect, tolerance, and considerateness, I have in mind acts that the target of civility might reasonably interpret as making it clear that I recognize some morally considerable fact about her that makes her worth treating with respect, considerateness, and tolerance. (Calhoun 2000, 259, italics original)

On this understanding, communicating moral attitudes is central to civility. Unlike being genuinely considerate or sincerely tolerant toward others, being genuinely civil requires us to follow the socially established norms in showing people considerateness, tolerance, or respect for others (ibid., 260).

EDUCATION FOR HUMANITY 273

In other words, civility necessitates discernable acts in accordance with social norms to achieve such purposes.

In this regard, the Confucian concept of ritual propriety (*li* 禮) is directly linked to civility. At the root of Confucian ritual propriety is the idea of deference or "mutual deference," to borrow a term from David Hume (*An Enquiry into the Principles of Morals*, Section VIII). Mengzi maintains that the heart of deference (*cirang* 辭讓) is the beginning of ritual propriety, indicating its central ingredient (*Mengzi* 2A6). Kongzi's student Zigong described his teacher as being warm (*wen* 溫), kind (*liang* 良), respectful (*gong* 恭), moderate (*jian* 儉)[15], deferential (*rang* 讓) in interacting with people (*Analects* 1.10). It should be noted that deference here does not equate to docility; rather it is a considerate regard for the wishes and status of other people. Confucian ritual propriety is practiced through its performance in everyday life. To borrow Cheshire Calhoun's apt expression, we can say that ritual propriety requires *display* in discernable acts. In his article on "Confucian Civility," Joel Kupperman (2010) discusses how Kongzi valued civility. In the *Analects*, not only was Kongzi warm, kind, respectful, moderate, and deferential in approaching people (1.10), he was also willing to converse and to learn from even people of humble social status (9.8). He displayed a disposition "of not trying strenuously to overpower other people's views (even ones that are clearly faulty), and of being a good listener and being responsive in discussion" (Kupperman 2010, 18). Kongzi advised people "to be patient when others do not understand" (*Analects* 1.1). Kupperman notes that, even when coming to ethical issues, Kongzi would be gentle. Kongzi advised his disciple, "reprove your friend, when dutifulness requires, but do so gently. If your words are not accepted, then desist" (*Analects* 12.23). Kongzi cautioned that being overbearing with friends and companions will lead to estrangement (*Analects* 4.26). In a similar vein, Robert Neville has rendered Confucian *li* 禮, which I have rendered as ritual propriety, straightforwardly as "civility" in some contexts (Neville 2000, 26). All these show that civility is a fundamental dimension of ritual propriety. Specific rituals of Confucian ritual propriety change over time; they may or may not suit people of other cultures. But the spirit and the concept of ritual propriety, especially civility, is broadly appliable across the entire society. As far as civic education must include civil education, Confucian philosophy of education is right on target.

Value education is at the core of Confucian education. Confucian thinkers did not believe that a good society could be achieved on the basis of

274 RESHAPING CONFUCIANISM: A PROGRESSIVE INQUIRY

institutional establishments without virtuous people. Kongzi once spoke of working with people in society:

> Guide them with edicts, keep them in line with punishments, and the common people will stay out of trouble but will have no sense of shame. Guide them by virtue, keep them in line with the ritual propriety (*li*), and they will, besides having a sense of shame, reform themselves. (*Analects* 2.3; Lau 1979, 63, modified)

We should not understand this statement as saying that there is no need for law or punishment. Its point is rather that a good society needs people who behave for the sake of virtue rather than for fear of punishment, and that such a goal can be achieved via successful virtue education. In today's language, we would say it is about good citizenship, even though ancient Confucian thinkers did not have a concept of citizenship in the modern sense. As far as its philosophy of producing valuable and responsible members of society is concerned, the Confucian emphasis on value education as a form of civic education is still very much applicable today.

Confucianism shares a broad spectrum of values with other cultural and religious traditions. In considering the suitability of Confucian values in civic education, we should make a conceptual distinction between "Confucian values" in the sense of values that Confucians endorse on the one hand, and "Confucian values" in the sense of values possessed exclusively by Confucians. The latter hardly exist. The value system we call "Confucian values" is not of values unique to Confucianism. One does not have to be Confucian to uphold these values. "Confucian values" can include values that Confucianism has held in the past and values that it continues to espouse today. Some values as interpreted, and even practiced in the past may no longer be appropriate in contemporary societies. For instance, ancient Confucians held sexist views on gender, which have been denounced by most people today, including Confucian thinkers (see my discussion in Chapter 5 of this book). Some other values, even though their historical interpretations or practices are no longer acceptable, are nevertheless subject to reinterpretation for new times. One such example is the Confucian value of filial care (*xiao* 孝). Often translated as "filial piety," *xiao* has been interpreted to the extreme in history. However, if we take the view of Xunzi, *xiao* does not mean children's absolute obedience to parents; on the contrary, it requires adult children to exercise moral vigilance to help parents when parents commit moral wrongs (see Chapter 4 of this book). It is safe to say, however, that most values from the Confucian tradition are still valid today.

The *Great Learning*, one of the canonical Confucian *Four Books*, sets the general goals for Confucian learning. Its author articulates eight aims toward which people strive to become a productive member of society. They are as follows:

1. To investigate things (*gewu* 格物)
2. To extend knowledge (*zhizhi* 致知)
3. To solidify one's intention (*chengyi* 誠意)
4. To set one's heart right (*zhengxin* 正心)
5. To cultivate one's person (*xiushen* 修身)
6. To harmonize one's family (*qijia* 齊家)
7. To manage the state (*zhiguo* 治國)
8. To achieve world peace (*ping tianxia* 平天下)[16]

Beginning with learning about things in the world, people acquire knowledge and cultivate themselves to become good members of families and society, and eventually to contribute to humanity as a whole. As the text is meant for rulers as well as commoners, "managing the state" is not only for rulers. Today, it is not even only about working in government; active participation in democratic social lives is also a way to realize this goal (see Chapter 11 of this book). In this vision of education, learning is not merely for professional training, not merely for the purpose of drawing a salary. Nor is it for the sake of one's own family. It is to achieve well-rounded growth and to become a full person in society. Thus understood, all eight aims articulated in the *Great Learning* can be promoted as universal goals that can be achieved with common social values.

In his book *Thick and Thin: Moral Argument at Home and Abroad*, Michael Walzer argues that moral concepts have two layers of meaning. The meaning of a concept can be understood in a thick way as the concept is embedded in a specific historical, cultural, religious, and political context. Its meaning can also be understood in a thin way to extend beyond specific historical-cultural-religious-political orientation and to reach globally shared understandings (Walzer 1994, 2–3). As Walzer elaborates, when Prague demonstrators in 1989 demanded "justice," they had in mind justice that was embedded "thickly" in their specific social and historical context, which we as outsiders did not fully comprehend. Yet, we could immediately identify with them and support their cause. This is so because we share with the demonstrators the value of justice in a thin sense, which does not require specific knowledge of their social and cultural circumstances. The thick and the thin admit of degrees within a spectrum, of course, rather than being categorical distinctions. Similarly, in promoting Confucian values in civic education in contemporary times, an approach can be thick or thin. Taken thickly, Confucian values are deeply and richly embedded in its specific cultural traditions. On the thin approach, however, Confucianism takes its values in their more general sense and seeks for the lowest common denominator with other cultural traditions. Taking the latter approach, as argued by Fung Yulan 馮友蘭 (1957), we "abstract" a value from its concrete historical reference framework and apply it in new social contexts. For instance, Confucian thinkers since the Han dynasty onward have interpreted the concept of loyalty (*zhong* 忠) as dedication to rulers. Today, loyalty should be detached from rulers and be applied toward one's country and people. With the thin approach, Confucian values find a large share of "overlapping consensus" with values in other cultural traditions as well as in contemporary societies.

Consider some moral principles and personal traits that the local school district of Talawanda, Ohio has attempted to help their students learn and practice:

a. Achieving self-discipline, defined as the strength to do what we believe we should do, even when we would rather not do it.
b. Being trustworthy, so that when we say we will or will not do something, we can be believed.
c. Telling the truth, especially when it hurts us to do so.
d. Having the courage to resist group pressures to do what we believe, when alone, that we should not do.
e. Using honorable means, those that respect the rights of others, in seeking our individual and collective ends.
f. Conducting ourselves, where significant moral behavior is involved, in a manner which does not fear exposure.
g. Having the courage to say, "I'm sorry, I was wrong."
h. Treating others as we would wish to be treated; recognizing that this principle applies to persons of every class, race, nationality, and religion.
i. Doing work well, whatever that work may be.

EDUCATION FOR HUMANITY   277

j. Respecting the democratic values of free speech, a free press, freedom
   of assembly, freedom of religion, and due process of law. Recognizing
   that this principle applies to speech we abhor, groups we dislike, persons we despise. (Sher and Bennett 1982, 666)

Contemporary Confucians can endorse all these values. Confucian thinkers
have had much to say about self-discipline (*keji* 克己), about trustworthiness
(*xin* 信), about truthfulness (*cheng* 誠), about the "golden rule" (*Analects*
12.2), and pretty much about everything else on the list.

The only one that seems alien to Confucianism is the last item on free
speech. However, the idea is not without precedence in the tradition. The
Introduction to the *Book of Poetry* (*Shijing* 詩經), an article that has been
attributed to Kongzi's disciple Zi Xia, advocates the idea that "speaking does
not commit any crime."[17] In ancient times, people used street poems to register their dissatisfaction and complaint against their ruler. The author held
that they should be allowed to say how they felt and should not be punished
for it. Admittedly, such a view was much reserved in the beginning as the author indicated that people's remonstration of their ruler was gentle and indirect so that it did not get them into trouble. However, the statement was read
later to mean outright that people should not be punished because of their
speeches. For instance, in a famous article "Letter to Yuan Zhen" (*Yuyuan
Jiushu* 與元九書), the Tang author Bai Juyi 白居易 (772–846) wrote:

Speaking does not commit any crime and the listener should take note (of
what has been said) as precaution. Thus, both sides live up to their hearts.[18]

The Confucian view on free speech may be construed as being twofold. For
the speaker, one should be careful with one's words. Kongzi advised his disciples to be "cautious with words" (*shen yan* 慎言; *Analects* 2.18) and to not
say things contrary to ritual propriety (*Analects* 12.1). For the listener, one
should let people speak their minds and be tolerant toward others. Although
this Confucian idea is not the same as the idea of free speech today, it evidently advocated a similar value. It can be reformulated for progressive
Confucianism to suit today's needs in society.

The thick approach advocates traditional values in a more embedded
sense, to the extent that contemporary Confucians deem appropriate. Take
for example the Confucian value of filial care (*xiao* 孝) again. The Confucian
idea somewhat overlaps with the Judeo-Christian idea of "honoring thy

father and thy mother." In contemporary times, the requirement of filial obligations is fading. From the Confucian perspective, however, filial care should be promoted for two main reasons. First, filial care is important to family cohesion and family harmony. Second, in today's increasingly aging societies, promoting filial care also enhances social cohesion and social harmony (see Chapter 4 of this book). In countries like Singapore, this Confucian value still exerts a good amount of influence. Singapore is a multi-cultural and multi-religious society. Its government has been very diligent in maintaining a good balance and harmony among various religions and cultural traditions. Nevertheless, the government has been openly promoting the value of filial care ("filial piety") through its ministries, not on the ground of Confucianism alone but on the ground that it is good for society at large, drawing on values from other traditions as well. Government policies have been made in favor of promoting this value. For instance, in the "Character and Citizenship Education Syllabus" published by the Ministry of Education for primary and secondary schools, filial responsibility is characterized as "Singapore family value."[19] This is an example of personal virtues and social values that have been dear to Confucianism to be promoted as a common value for society at large.

The thick and thin approaches to value education have respective strengths and weaknesses. The thin approach is more conducive to working with other cultural traditions in finding common grounds for promoting values in civic education. It may risk detaching specific cultural heritage from the values it promotes. The thick approach retains cultural specificities with values, yet other cultural traditions may be put off as they find the values in question too culturally specific. A good balance of these two approaches should be reached through reflection and negotiation. In the end, such a balance depends on internal dialogues within Confucianism as well as external dialogues with other cultural traditions. Both dialogues are on-going processes in multicultural societies, for Confucianism as well as other cultural traditions.[20]

In conclusion, Confucian education has been civic education in its own form. Times have changed. Both the form and content of Confucian civic education will have to change as well. Nevertheless, its basic ideas and values remain relevant to contemporary societies. Progressive Confucianism should continue to advocate the integration of learning and teaching as two indispensable components of effective education. It should support an alliance of the state, families, and educational professionals, and when appropriate, student participation, for managing and delivering civic education programs. In addition, it should promote Confucian values in contributing value education to society at large.

Study Questions

1. What are the two aspects of the Confucian concept of education?
2. Why is the love of learning so important for Kongzi?
3. Explain the four categories of Kongzi's curriculum.
4. What status has been attributed to teachers in Confucianism?
5. In your view, is Confucian education consistent with civic education? Why or why not?
6. How is Confucian education connected to the virtue of civility?
7. Explain Michael Walzer's analysis of values in terms of "the thick and thin."
8. How should we understand "Confucian values" today?
9. Do you think Confucian values are consistent with the values in your cultural tradition or a tradition of which you are knowledgeable?

Notes

Introduction

1. To avoid misunderstandings of this school as exclusively of Kongzi, some scholars writing in Western languages have used its *romanized* Chinese name and called this tradition "Ruism" to be more faithful to its Chinese expression of "*rujia*," instead of "Confucianism." For instance, see Robert Eno (1990) and Bryan Van Norden (2007). I continue to use "Confucianism" in this book mainly because the term has been widely used and is easily recognized.

2. I will not get into the debate of whether there is such a thing as Chinese philosophy. Here suffice it to say that, cross-culturally, I take philosophy as a functional concept, denoting activities by thinkers in a culture to address questions of deep human concerns, as demonstrated in the chapters throughout this book. As a functional concept, philosophy is to be defined primarily by its role in a culture rather than any particular conceptual content or methodology. Various schools of Chinese philosophy have undeniably played similar functions in Chinese societies as Western philosophy has done in Western societies. For a good analysis of the meanings of "Chinese philosophy," readers can see Defoort (2001).

3. Stephen Angle has also brought progressive Confucianism to cover various issues such as gender (see Angle 2022).

4. Reality, however, may not be ideal. Post-moderns may even argue that we can never find out what ancient thinkers meant. I believe that in many cases we know with reasonable certainty what ancient thinkers meant. I will not engage in this argument here.

5. In his insightful book *Origins of Moral-Political Philosophy in Early China*, Tao Jiang discusses a somewhat parallel divergence between sinologists and philosophers in the context of studying Chinese philosophy. A dilemma of contemporary scholars of Chinese philosophy arises due to having to deal with both disciplines of sinology and philosophy, each with its own disciplinary norms. He writes:

    > On the one hand, they have to defend the philosophical nature, or even the philosophical worthiness, of classical Chinese texts to contemporary Western philosophers who are more interested in the philosophical integrity of ideas than in their historicity. At the same time, scholars of Chinese philosophy, when dealing with Sinologists, need to justify the basic premise of their philosophical approach to the classics due to the historical ambiguity and compositional instability of these early texts. (Jiang 2021, 2)

    Satisfying two disciplinary norms is never easy, if not impossible. This difficult situation has led to an unfortunate consequence of the contemporary discourse of classical Chinese philosophy in the Western academy, i.e., for the most part it remains a

282 NOTES

marginalized field in both sinology and philosophy (Jiang 2021, 3). As will be made clear toward the end of this section, my strategy in this book for avoiding or at least minimizing such a dilemma is to prioritize philosophy as the focus of my study and to use the historical approach when it is needed, to serve the main purpose of developing Confucian philosophy.

6. As far as researchers study the history of philosophy, their work can be regarded as philosophical in that they reconstruct the philosophy of ancient thinkers, as compared with reconstructing, say, the personal lives of ancient thinkers. However, as long as their purpose is to rediscover or reconstruct ancient thinkers' philosophy as it was rather than developing a new philosophy, their work is historical in nature in my classification.

7. For a discussion of this matter, readers can see Li (2022b).

8. The passage that I discuss here reads: 凡為古文辭者, 必敬以恕. 臨文必敬, 非修德之謂也; 論古必恕, 非寬容之謂也. 敬, 非修德之謂者, 氣攝而不縱, 縱必不能中節也. 恕, 非寬容之謂者, 能為古人設身而處地也. 嗟呼！知德者鮮, 知臨文之不可無敬恕, 則知文德矣... 是則不知古人之世, 不可妄論古人文辭也; 知其世矣, 不知古人之身處, 亦不可以遽論其文也 (Zhang 1832). The *wen* of *wende* has a broad range of meanings, from literature to culture. Here it denotes mainly the study of literature, history, philosophy. I use "scholarship" to approximate such a general idea.

9. Broadly speaking, though, one can study thinkers through intracultural comparison too. Such examples include Bryan Van Norden's study of the two theories of human agency in Mengzi and Xunzi (Van Norden 1992) and Sungmoon Kim's more recent study of these philosophers' theories of virtue politics (Kim 2019).

10. For a thorough analysis of "harmony" in English, see Oxford (2022).

11. For recent studies of different ideas of harmony in various traditions, see Li and Düring (2022).

12. For my discussion of this alternative, readers can see Li (2021c).

Chapter 1

1. The character 和 is pronounced similarly to the syllable "ho" (hə) in "horizon."

2. The importance of the concept of harmony in metaphysics, social-political philosophy, and ethics is evident in the Confucian classics, as shown in this chapter. The relevance of harmony to Confucian epistemology is less salient, but by no means absent. For instance, Bo Mou has argued that the *Book of Changes* "gives a harmoniously balanced-changing-pattern-capturing perspective elaboration of people's pretheoretic understanding of truth" (Mou 2019, 87).

3. See John Sisk (1977) as an example.

4. In this chapter, I present a philosophical reconstruction of *he* out of the classical texts from a perspective of progressive Confucianism. It does not mean that word *he* was not used and interpreted in other ways. For a historical account of different uses of the word, readers can see Gentz (2019).

NOTES 283

5. 聲應相保曰和.

6. Shi Bo lived about two hundred years before Kongzi. He held the post of state historian toward the end of the Western Zhou dynasty (1046–771 BCE) and is known for developing a theory of *yin* and *yang*.

7. 夫和實生物, 同則不繼. 以他平他謂之和, 故能豐長而物歸之; 若以同裨同, 盡乃棄矣. I here translate "*ji* 繼" as "advance growth." See *Analects* 6.3, "the virtuous person helps those in emergency but does not advance the cause of the rich" (*junzi zhouji bu jifu* 君子周急不繼富) (TTC 1980, 2478).

8. 聲一無聽, 物一無文, 味一無果, 物一不講. "Color" is my translation of "物 *wu*" in its first occurrence, which literally means "thing" or "item." In his annotation of *Zhouli:Chunguan:Baozhangshi* 周禮·春官·保章氏, Zheng Xuan writes, "*wu* means color" (*wu se ye* 物, 色也) (TTC 1980, 819). I follow the *Shuowen's* definition and interpret *jiang* 講 as "harmonizing 和解也" (*Shuowen* 1992, 95).

9. 故先王以土與金木水火雜, 以成百物. 是以和五味以調口, 更四支以衛體, 和六律以聰耳, 正七體以役心, 平八索以成人, 建九紀以立純德, 合十數以訓百體 … 夫如是, 和之至也.

10. In the *Analects*, Kongzi mentioned Zuo and said he shared Zuo's sense against shameful behaviors (5.25).

11. *Junzi* generally denotes morally well-cultivated persons. The closest counterpart in single-word English is "gentleman." "Gentleman" seems no longer appropriate not only because of its sexist bias but also because it is outdated for contemporary society, whereas the ideal of *junzi* in contemporary Confucianism remains alive. A more recent translation is "exemplary person." I opt not to use it because "exemplary person" is a higher order expression when compared to "virtuous person" and hence lacks in substantive content (see discussion of a similar issue with *ren* in Chapter 2). Someone is regarded as exemplary in Confucianism because she is virtuous, not vice versa.

12. 和如羹焉, 水火醯醢鹽梅, 以烹魚肉, 燀之以薪, 宰夫和之, 齊之以味, 濟其不及, 以洩其過, 君子食之, 以平其心.

13. 聲亦如味, 一氣, 二體, 三類, 四物, 五聲, 六律, 七音, 八風, 九歌, 以相成也, 清濁大小, 長短疾徐, 哀樂剛柔, 遲速高下, 出入周疏, 以相濟也, 君子聽之, 以平其心.

14. The idea that sounds mutually respond in *he* is also found in the *Zhuangzi*, chapter 2, that gentle breeze results in mild *he* and strong wind results in great *he* (泠風則小和, 飄風則大和 *lengfeng ze xiaohe; piaofeng ze dahe*).

15. Youruo's statement can also be interpreted as meaning that, when practicing *li*, we must not violate harmony. For additional discussion of *li* in relation to harmony, readers can see Li (2014, ch. 4).

16. 由禮則和節.

17. 大哉乾元, 萬物資始, 乃統天 … 乾道變化, 各正性命, 保合大和.

18. For a lucid explication of Confucian harmony between humanity and heaven (*tian* 天), readers can see Yao (2000, 173–178).

19. For more discussion of this text in connection to harmony, readers can see Li (2004).

20. 德莫大于和.

21. 天地之道, 雖有不和者, 必歸之於和.

22. 有象斯有對, 對必反其為; 有反斯有仇, 仇必和而解 (Zhang Zai 1076). The *Shuowen* lexicon defines *chou* 仇 as *chou ye* 讎也 and further explicates that *chou you*

284 NOTES

ying ye 䚄猶應也 (Xu and Duan 1992, 382, 90). Namely, the one that responds. The word has usually been used to mean antagonistic opposition.

23. For an insightful discussion of Zhang's philosophy of "harmony as substance," see Ziporyn (2015).

24. For a study of this issue, see chapter 2 of Li (2014).

25. In this chapter, "metaphysics" is understood broadly as a branch of philosophy that studies being and becoming in their general senses as well as their operation (for a discussion of both being and becoming as subjects of metaphysical study, see Li and Perkins, 2015, Introduction, 1–15). In this broad scope, metaphysics as a subject of study is traceable to Aristotle's theory of the four causes, namely, the material, the formal, the efficient, and the final causes (*Metaphysics* V.2). For Aristotle, these four causes explain how things in the world operate in fundamental ways. Along these lines of understanding metaphysics, my discussion of how harmony takes place and of its general function in the world also falls into this branch of philosophy.

26. 夢夢墨墨, 亡章弼弼. *Mengmeng* suggests cloudiness (understood as its homonym term 朦朧); *momo* indicates murkiness. *Wangzhang* means "without patterns." Like *momo*, *bibi* here signifies boundless depth.

27. 恒无之初, 迵同太虛, 虛同為一, 恒一而已.

28. 一者其號, 虛其舍也, 無為其素也, 和其用也.

29. 無晦無明, 未有陰陽. 陰陽未定, 吾未有以名. 今始判為兩, 分為陰陽. 離為□四 (時).

30. 柔剛相成, 牝牡若刑(形). 下會於地, 上會於天. 得天之微, 時若□□□□□□□□□寺(待)地氣之發也, 乃夢(萌)者夢(萌)而茲(滋)者茲(滋), 天因而成之. Chen Guying explains, "*yin* and *yang* join forces; the firm and the soft complement each other. Through mutual compensation and mutual promotion of the firm and the soft, the integration and penetration of *yin* and *yang*, the myriad things are generated (阴阳聚合, 刚柔相济; 刚柔的相辅相成, 阴阳的融会贯通, 便成就了万物)" (Chen 2007, 216).

31. Here I use the Big Bang theory as an example of a scientific attempt to account for the formation of the universe, forgoing other alternative theories.

32. The author acknowledges his indebtedness to Wim Hordijk for his discussion of this theory.

33. Scientists do not investigate the metaphysical issue of the origin of the update rules in these processes. For living organisms, the rules could be explained scientifically in terms of evolution. Rules could be random at first and only those with a certain type of rules could have survived. From the perspective of the Confucian harmony, the update rules must be explained by the generative processes of prior harmonious cycles. The universe was not equipped with these fixed rules from day one.

34. For more discussion of the importance of a harmony outlook, readers can see Li (2014, 166–169).

35. 理在氣先 (Zhu Xi 1986, Vol. 1, Sections 11, 12). Chen Lai has argued that Zhu's view on the priority of *li* over *qi* evolved from a temporal sense to a non-temporal sense. (Chen 2000, 97). Yong Huang noted that the Cheng Brothers' concept of *li* is "creativity" (Huang 2014, 201). More recently, Eiho Baba (2015) has attempted to interpret

Zhu's *li* as emergent patterns of *qi*, bringing it closer to a harmony account of the generation of patterns in the world. For a recent study reaffirming the interpretation of Zhu Xi's *li* as a pre-set order, see Zhang (2020).

36. For a careful discussion of harmony and intrinsic value, see Löschke (2020).
37. For a discussion of Nussbaum's and Popper's accounts of harmony, see Li (2014, 7–8).
38. A similar idea is found in the *Zhong* 衷 text of the Mawangdui Silk Manuscript of the *Zhouyi*. The text records Kongzi's statement that harmonious practice is fundamental for the five virtues 和〔之〕, 此五言之本也." For an informative discussion of the idea and the specific contents of the five virtues, see Liu and Liu (2021).
39. For a fruitful discussion of a harmony approach to community-building in contemporary society, see Wong (2020).
40. For more discussion, see Li (2014, 17).
41. See Li (2021b) for more discussion of this point in the *Xunzi*.
42. For a fuller account of Confucian philosophy of personal, familial, social, and environmental harmony, readers can see Li (2014, ch.6–10).

Chapter 2

1. Some later Confucian thinkers, from the eleventh century onwards, have expanded the meaning of *ren* to also denote a cosmic quality. I will not discuss these thinkers here as they have departed too far from its original meanings as an ethical concept.
2. 洵美且仁; 洵美且好; 洵美且武. 其人美且仁;其人美且鬈; 其人美且偲.
3. Tu Weiming has read Fang's findings of early meanings of *ren* as "an altruistic concern for others." See Tu (1985, 84).
4. 仁者人也.
5. For my initial discussion of the connection between *ren* and care, see Li (1994), and more recently, Li (2022a).
6. For various definitions of virtue, see Snow (2018), especially Chapters 1, 2, and 3.
7. Similarly, Tang Junyi said that Kongzi "uses *ren* to connect various virtues 以仁統貫諸德" (Tang 1986, 73).
8. 孔子而后, 以爱言仁者, 其旨亦最切近易见 (Tang 1986, 73).
9. 以仁与他德相对, 则以爱说仁, 最为源远流长, 如《国语·周语》谓"仁, 文之爱也,"爱人能仁," "仁以保民,"《楚语》言"明之慈爱, 以导之仁." (Tang 1986, 73). The ancient lexicon *Shuowen* explicates *bao* 保 as *yang* 養, namely, to raise or foster (someone or something). The character's oracle form is a person embracing a child. The connection of *bao* with caring for a child is also found in the *Xunzi* (chapter 15), "長養之, 如保赤子," which Eric Hutton has translated as "Nurture and raise them [the people], as though caring for a newborn" (Hutton 2014, 160). I translate *bao min* 保民 as "caring for the people" here.
10. For instance, Mengzi said, "in antiquity, King Tai was fond of women and *ai*'ed his concubines 昔者大王好色, 愛厥妃" (*Mengzi* 1B4). Here "*ai*" should be translated as "love." However, it is far from clear whether *ai* as used here is *ren*.

286 NOTES

11. In the first chapter of *The Robust Demands of the Good* (2015), Philip Pettit develops an account of love as robust care. On his account, if *x* loves *y*, then *x* provides care for *y* not only in all actual scenarios, but also over a certain range of hypothetical scenarios, with reasons to do so. In accordance with Pettit's account, *ai* as care would include love as a subspecies.

12. Mengzi also described the proper attitude toward family (parents) as *qin* 親, and toward people in general as *ren* 仁 (*Mengzi* 7A45). To *qin* a family member is to be affectionate toward the person; it requires a high degree of love. To *ren* someone is to care deeply about the person, up to a degree at which we can use "love" in a mild sense. In comparison, *ai wu* requires gentle treatment with a minimum level of positive feelings. To *ren* other people encompasses the requirement of gentle treatment but extends beyond *ai wu* as *ren* requires the agent to care about people with a higher level of positive feelings. To *qin* family members requires the highest level of intense feelings and it encompasses not only care in the general sense but also affection. Thus, *ai*, *ren*, and *qin* can be understood in this context as three types of care, with intensity increasing in degrees.

13. The word *shu* 恕 consists of the word "*xin* 心" or "heart" at the bottom and "*ru* 如," or likening or likeness on the top. The word is glossed directly as *ren* 仁 in the *Shuowen* lexicon (Xu and Duan 1992, 504).

14. For additional similarities between Confucian ethics and care ethics, readers can see Li (1994).

15. 仁者無不愛也,急親賢之為務 (*Mengzi* 7A46).

16. Such a tendency was later carried so far by Song thinker Zhang Zai 張載 (1020–1077), as to care so much about everything in the world that such a person forms a oneness with the world.

17. Given that not all feminists insist on the necessity of personal relations for exercising care, this difference on the requirement of personal relations may not be a categorical difference between Confucian care and feminist care.

18. 君子之愛人也以德,細人之愛人也以姑息 (Chapter *Tangong A* of the *Book of Rites*; TTC, 1277).

Chapter 3

1. This statement is a modified translation of 使欲必不窮乎物, 物必不屈於欲, 兩者相持而長. Hutton's translation of the first part is, "They caused desires never to exhaust material goods." Accordingly, it stands for the same idea as the following part: "material goods never to be depleted by desires." This translation does not reflect Xunzi's original statement and is problematic both grammatically and logically. In these sentences, the expressions of *bu qiong hu* 不窮乎 and *bu qu yu* 不屈於 are synonymous, whereas their subjects and objects are reversed in order. Hence, they cannot possibly say the same thing. Furthermore, only the modified translation as presented here can support the concluding sentence that human desires and natural

resources should *mutually* support each other and grow together. Ivanhoe (1991) insightfully argued for "a happy symmetry" between human desires and resources in Xunzi, which is consistent with my interpretation. Ivanhoe, however, quoted Burton Watson's (1963) erroneous translation of the statement in question, similar to Hutton's, without correcting it, which weakens the symmetry interpretation. For a detailed argument for my interpretation, see Li (2021b).

2. Kongzi nevertheless remained agnostic about gods and spirits (*Analects* 11.12). For an interesting and insightful discussion of Kongzi's view in this regard in terms of "as-if-ism," see Ni (2017, 121).

3. 古之為政, 愛人為大; 所以治愛人, 禮為大.

4. Before this change, peasants paid taxes in the form of labor in public land (*gong tian* 公田) while keeping their own harvest from land allocated to themselves (*si tian* 私田). This change meant that they now had to pay additional taxes from income made in their *si tian* (see Jian 1988, 309; Yang 1981, 766). According to the historian Zhang Yinling 张荫麟, the statement refers to a change of tax policy from previously taxing by the unit of the family to taxing by the acreage (*mu*) of a family's land, aiming to raise income for the government. Confucians opposed it as the change increased working people's burden. See Li Hongyan (2005, 238).

5. Kongzi did not exclude penal laws entirely. It is recorded that, when he served as the prime minister in the state of Lu, he instituted penal laws but did not have to use them because people conducted themselves well (*Kongzi Jiayu*, chapter 1).

6. For a detailed discussion of the relation between *li* and *ren* in the *Analects*, readers can see Li (2007).

7. In Singapore, for instance, swimming pool regulations in places are still articulated in terms of *li*(*you yong chi liyi* 游泳池礼仪).

8. I benefited greatly from conversations with Randy John LaPolla on functionalist grammar.

9. I will discuss the views of David Wong and Chris Fraser on differences between *li* and grammar toward the end of this section.

10. For discussion of these conceptions of grammar, see James Williams (1998, 122–129).

11. See Chapter 8 of this book for the issue of whether Confucian sages can be wrong.

12. My approach in this regard differs from Roger Ames, who emphasizes the particularity and uniqueness of *li* actions (Ames 2002). Also see Hall and Ames (1987, 97).

13. This is an indirect quote from Kongzi's eldest son Boyu. In *Analects* 20.3 there is a similar quote directly from Kongzi, but the word used there is *zhi* (to know) rather than *xue* (to learn). Some commentators have interpreted *li* here as referring to the *Liji* (*Book of Rites*). *Analects* 20.3 suggests otherwise because there the sentence parallels with *bu zhi ming*, namely not knowing the *ming* 命 (destiny), which is not a text. However, even if the word refers to the *Liji*, it does not undermine my interpretation of *li* because the *Liji* is mainly about *li*.

14. For example, in Chapter *Tangong B* of the *Book of Rites*, sections 39 and 45, Chapter *Zengzi Wen*, section 18, and in numerous places of the *Zuo Commentary*, Chapters *Yin-gong Year One* (5), *Yin-gong Year Five* (1), and *Yin-gong Year Eight* (4).

15. This expression is traceable to *Analects* 17.21.

288 NOTES

16. Kongzi is recorded as being able to behave in whatever way he wished without overstepping boundaries after he reached the age of seventy (*Analects* 2.4). For more discussion, see Chapter 9 of this book.

17. This expression was first used probably by the English playwright Susanna Centlivre (c.1667 to 1670–December 1, 1723), even though the contemporary English journalist Bernard Levin included it in his collection of famous Shakespeare quotes.

18. For an insightful discussion of the Confucian concept of *yi*, see Tan (2014).

19. Another important similarity is that, just like the grammars of different languages can influence one another, the *li* in different cultures can also influence one another. One culture may adopt another culture's *li* in its own practice. This is so especially in modern times. I thank Ruiping Fan for raising this point in our private communication.

20. Traditional ritual can also be revived. During the COVID-19, for example, many people opted out of shaking hands to avoid physical contact and instead adopted the traditional Buddhist greeting ritual by placing the palms together at the level of the heart, with the fingertips pointed upward, or the traditional Chinese greeting ritual of making a bow with hands folded in front.

21. Some of these parallels were first drawn in Li (2007), where my main focus was on the relation between *ren* and *li* in the *Analects*.

22. For a lucid account of the "as-if" approach to Confucian ritual, readers can see chapter 3 of Puett and Gross-Loh (2016).

23. For an argument on the "metaphysical" function of *li* in constructing social reality, readers can see Puett (2015).

24. For a recent argument of the relevance of the Confucian ritual to the modern life, see Sigurdsson (2021). Michael Puett has provided an alternative account of the Confucian *li*. According to Puett, *li* provides the metaphysical infrastructure for constructing reality in the human world (Puett 2015).

Chapter 4

1. The *Liyun* chapter of the *Book of Rites*, for example, promotes the tenet of *fu ci zi xiao* 父慈子孝 as the first out of a list of human morality (*ren yi* 人義; TTC, 1422). Literally, *fu* refers to fathers and *zi* refers to sons even though *zi* sometimes also includes daughters. *Ci* (loving and caring) has been commonly used to refer to mothers in ancient times. This tenet should be understood as covering both father and mother even though it is expressed in androcentric language typical of its time. A related question often arises as to children's filial duty when parents do not care well for children. Confucian classic texts describe the exemplary son Shun as remaining filial even in extreme circumstances, when his father, stepmother and stepbrother were all malicious, even attempting to kill him (e.g., *Mengzi* 5A2). The moral of the story is apparently to teach people to affect others positively through virtuous actions. For discussions of parental duty toward children, readers can see Li (2014, 104–107) and Liang (2008).

NOTES   289

2. For a collection of studies of *xiao* in Chinese philosophy and history, see Chan and Tan (2004).
3. For additional justifications of *xiao*, readers can see Ivanhoe (2004) and Li (1997a), among others.
4. See Holzman (1998, 186).
5. See Holzman (1998, 186–187) and Knapp (1995). In practice, the domain of *xiao* has also included other people of earlier generations in the extended family such as grandparents.
6. Its bronze inscription appears in the form of 夆.
7. Its pictograph is 耂. See https://www.zdic.net/hans/%E5%AD%9Dand http://www.mebag.com/index/main/list.asp?key3=s125-005&key4=entry.
8. See Knapp (1995, 200).
9. 孝者, 畜也 (Chapter *Jitong*; TTC, 1602).
10. 孝子之事親也, 有三道焉: 生則養, 沒則喪, 喪畢則祭 (TTC, 1603).
11. 肇牽車牛, 遠服賈用. 孝養厥父母 (Chapter *Jiugao*; TTC, 206).
12. 王事靡盬, 不能蓺稷黍, 父母何怙....王事靡盬, 不能蓺黍稷, 父母何食....王事靡盬, 不能蓺稻粱, 父母何嘗 (Chapter *Tangfeng*; TTC, 365).
13. 子弗祇服厥父事, 大傷厥考心于父 (Chapter *Kanggao*; TTC, 204). Chapter *Yixun* of the *Book of History* states that one should *jing* seniors 立敬惟長, without specifying parents.
14. Traditional family rituals can change over time. Old ones may disappear while new ones merge, as explicated in Chapter 3 of this book.
15. 禮, 敬為大 (*Book of Rites*, chapter *Aigongwen*; TTC, 1611).
16. 敬, 禮之輿也. 不敬則禮不行 (*Zuo Commentary*, chapter *Xigong 11*; TTC, 1802).
17. 養可能也, 敬為難 (*Book of Rites*, chapter *Jiyi*; TTC, 1598).
18. Roetz (1993, 53).
19. *Book of Rites*, chapter *Biaoji* (TTC, 1640).
20. *Zuo Commentary*, chapter *Zhaogong 26* (TTC, 2115).
21. *Book of Rites*, chapter *Zaji* (TTC, 1558).
22. *Zuo Commentary*, chapter *Zhaogong 1* (TTC, 2020).
23. *Shuowen* lexicon defines *ji* as *wei* 微, i.e., mildly or barely.
24. 是何言與, 是何言與! 昔者天子有爭臣七人, 雖無道, 不失其天下; 諸侯有爭臣五人, 雖無道, 不失其國; 大夫有爭臣三人, 雖無道, 不失其家; 士有爭友, 則身不離於令名; 父有爭子, 則身不陷於不義. 故當不義, 則子不可以不爭於父, 臣不可以不爭於君.
25. 請問為人子? 曰: 敬愛而致文 (*Xunzi*, chapter *Jundao*; Wang 1988, 232; cf. Knoblock 1994, 178).
26. 孝子不從命乃敬 (*Xunzi*, chapter *Zidao*; Wang 1988, 529).
27. 明於從不從之義, 而能致恭敬, 忠信、端愨、以慎行之, 則可謂大孝矣 (*Xunzi*, chapter *Zidao*; Wang 1988, 529).
28. The concept of "great justice" (*da yi* 大義) appears in chapter 8, *Ruxiao*, of the *Xunzi*. It is a parallel concept with "great filiality" (*da xiao* 大孝) referred to earlier. Xunzi advocates the ideal of "understanding the great justice (*da yi*) that safeguards the altars of soil and grain 明於持社稷之大義." The altars were the sites for important sacrifices for the god of soil (*tushen* 土神) and the god of grain (*gushen* 谷神),

290   NOTES

symbolizing the very livelihood of ancient people. These did not represent only the ruling house, but also the people and the land on which they lived. Thus understood, Xunzi's point of great justice (*da yi*) is not merely about what is just or right for the ruling house, but also for the entire society.

29. The fact that *Recorded Sayings of Kongzi's Family* shares Xunzi's view suggests such a view was still upheld in early Han dynasty.

30. Another reason commonly cited for degrading Xunzi is that two of his students, Han Fei 韓非 (280–233 BCE) and Li Si 李斯 (?–208 BCE), later became leading thinkers in the Legalist school (*Fa Jia* 法家), which Confucians have traditionally opposed.

31. This criticism of the interpretation of *xiao* as filial piety can also apply to Roger Ames' interpretation of *xiao* as "family reverence" (see Ames 2011, 78). Like "piety," "reverence" also fails to capture the important meaning of moral vigilance in Confucian *xiao*.

32. https://dictionary.cambridge.org/dictionary/english/care.

33. See Roetz (1993, section of "Filial Piety as Care.")

34. For an interesting argument that healthy parent–child relationships constitute distinctive kinds of goods, readers can see Keller (2006).

35. 養則致其樂 (*Classic of Filial Care*, chapter 10; TTC, 2555).

Chapter 5

1. *The Biographies of Exemplary Women* includes 125 biographical accounts of exemplary women in ancient China. It is believed to have been compiled by the Han dynasty scholar Liu Xiang 劉向 (77–6 BCE). The *Nüer Jing* was written during the Ming dynasty (1368–1644), by unknown authors.

2. A legendary heroine from ancient China, Mulan, or Hua Mulan花木蘭, disguised herself as a male warrior and joined the imperial army to prevent her sick father from being forced to enlist as he had no son. The story was made popularly known outside China by a 1998 Disney animated film, and more recently a 2020 Disney live-action movie by the same title.

3. For a steadfast argument for the critical role of the family in contemporary Confucian moral philosophy, readers can see Fan (2010).

4. I leave aside issues of gender relations outside families and issues related to LGBT, families with special arrangements and single persons without a family life, even though ideas developed here can be extended and applied to these issues in various ways. For recent innovative discussions of feminist approaches to Confucianism, see Foust and Tan (2016).

5. For instance, the *Dingfa* chapter of the *Hanfeizi* states, "A medical doctor is to mix (herb) medicine ingredients (*yi zhe, qi yao ye* 醫者, 齊藥也)," where 齊(*qi*) means 劑(*ji*), namely, mixing in appropriate proportions (TTM, 1177). In this connection, 齊 is usually pronounced as *ji*.

6. "*Bazhen zhi qi* 八珍之齊," in Chapter *Tianguan-Shiyi* of the *Rites of Zhou*周禮·天官·食醫 (TTC, 667).

7. 宰夫和之, 齊之以味. See more discussion of the metaphor in Chapter 1.

NOTES 291

8. 齊, 謂食羹醬飲有齊和者也 (Chapter *Shaoyi*; TTC, 1515). Additional such compound uses can be found in such texts as the *Yiwenzhi* 藝文志, "hundreds of (herb) medicine ingredients are mixed (*qi*) and harmonized (*baiyao qi he*) 百藥齊和 (https://ctext.org/han-shu/yi-wen-zhi/zh).

9. For an elaborate discussion of Confucian family harmony, readers can see Li (2014, ch. 7).

10. 有天地然後有萬物, 有萬物然後有男女, 有男女然後有夫婦, 有夫婦然後有父子, 有父子然後有君臣 (TTC, 96).

11. 夫有人民而後有夫婦, 有夫婦而後有父子, 有父子而後有兄弟: 一家之親, 此三而已矣 (Wang 2007, 23).

12. 成男女之別, 而立夫婦之義也 (*Book of Rites*, chapter *Hunyi*; TTC, 1681; cf. Legge 1885 IV, 430).

13. 水火相息, 二女同居, 其志不相得, 曰革 (*Book of Changes, Tuan Commentary*; TTC, 60).

14. 一男一女, 乃相感應. 二女雖復同居, 其志終不相得. 志不相得, 則變必生矣 (TTC, 60).

15. In comparison, commentaries on hexagrams made up of two trigrams that symbolize sons (males), however, do not mention similar problems.

16. Chapter *Zhaogong 20* of the *Zuo Commentary*; TTC (1980, 2094).

17. 女正位乎內, 男正位乎外, 男女正, 天地之大義也. 家人有嚴君焉. 父母之謂也. 父父, 子子, 兄兄, 弟弟, 夫夫, 婦婦, 而家道正; 正家而天下定矣 (*Tuan Commentary* on Hexagram 37: Family Members 家人; TTC, 50).

18. This was not always the case. Frequently, women labored in the fields alongside or instead of men. But it appears that in ancient China such a reverse division labor was uncommon. It is reported that the division of labor between the two sexes in the Sani ethnic group of the Yi people 彝族撒尼人 in Southern China, for instance, is in the reverse. For the Sani, women handle external affairs and men are primarily engaged in affairs inside family. It is not clear, though, how long the Sani tradition has been, largely due to lack of written records. For a study of the Sani people, readers can see Zhang (2014).

19. 男帥女, 女從男, 夫婦之義由此始也 (Chapter *Jiaotesheng*; TTC, 1456).

20. It can be argued, however, that the last item—that she follows her son after her husband's death—has never been enforced. In reality, the Confucian notion of filial care often overrides it. For more discussion of this issue, see Li (1999, ch. 4).

21. 天尊地卑, 乾坤定矣 (TTC, 75). It is commonly accepted that the *Xici Commentary* was written later than the hexagrams. It presents a particular interpretation of the hexagrams, which may or may not have been the original meanings by the author(s) of the hexagrams.

22. 乾, 陽物也; 坤, 陰物也 (TTC, 89).

23. 乾道成男, 坤道成女 (TTC, 76). *Nan* 男 and *Nü* 女 primarily denotes the male and female sexes, even though typically in gendered ways.

24. By analyzing the *Xian* 咸 and other hexagrams in the *Book of Changes* along with their classical commentaries, Jinhua Jia has reached a similar conclusion. Jia has argued that ancient Chinese cosmology advocates a gendered view of husband and wife. She writes:

The *Xian* hexagram describes the sexed bodies and gendered relation of husband and wife, and determines as auspicious the joyful and harmonious interaction and union between the two sexes/genders in both body and mind. Here the focus is on the harmonious working of husband and wife, and the hexagram affirms both sexes' contribution to an auspicious marriage. (Jia 2016, 287)

In this gendered view, Jia further shows, the resonant gendered relation of husband and wife is built on the hierarchically defined division between man/husband as being superior and woman/wife as being inferior, even though such a relation is also reversible (Jia 2016, 289).

25. Chapter 43 of Dong's *Chunqiu Fanlu* (TTM, 797). It should be noted that, prior to Dong, the Daoist text *Liezi* (dated during the Warring States period) already claims that males are superior and females are inferior (*nanzunnübei* 男尊女卑, TTM, 196). There have been mixed views on the relation between *yin* and *yang* in Daoism. The *Daodejing* values *yin* more than *yang*, whereas the *Four Classics of the Yellow Emperor* (*Huangdi Sijing* 黃帝四經) associates superiority with *yang* and inferiority with *yin* (*gui yang jian yin* 貴陽賤陰, Chen 2007, 394).

26. For example, Aristotle states, "as regards the sexes, the male is by nature superior and the female inferior, the male ruler and the female subject" (*Politics*, 1254b13–14).

27. Chapter *Jiaotesheng* states that wife should follow her husband (TTC, 1456; cf. Legge 1885 IV, 441).

28. For an example of such forced conformity that is disguised as harmony, see my discussion of the ruler of Qi and his minister Ju in Chapter 1 of this book.

29. For more discussion of these requirements for the Confucian philosophy of harmony, see Li (2014).

30. 立天之道曰陰與陽 (TTC, 93). 陰陽合德 (TTC, 89).

31. 一陰一陽之謂道 (*Xici Commentary*; TTC, 78).

32. *Yin-yang yiwei* 陰陽易位. Its author pointed out this can happen without endorsing such a move. Today we can recognize that at least some of such changes can be beneficial and justified. https://ctext.org/chu-ci/she-jiang/zh?searchu=%E9%99%B0%E9%99%BD%E6%98%93%E4%BD%8D&searchmode=showall#result. The *Chuci* 楚辭, or *Verses of Chu*, is an anthology of Chinese poetry traditionally attributed mainly to Qu Yuan and Song Yu from the Warring States period (475?–221 BCE).

33. *Yin sheng yang shuai* 陰盛陽衰. This expression first appeared in the *Tai Xuan Jing* 太玄經 by Yang Xiong (53–18 BCE). In his view, such a change will make the myriad things wither (*wanwu yi wei* 萬物以微). https://ctext.org/taixuanjing/jian/zh.

34. *Book of Changes, Xici Commentary*; TTC, 78.

35. This reformed Confucian view on gender bears some resemblance with family complementarianism in monotheistic traditions in that both emphasize the good of the family as a whole. But they are also different in important ways. Aside from having different philosophical or theological bases, the new Confucian approach does not assign primary headship roles to men while it maintains a weak correlation between female biology and the gender role of motherhood. For defense of Christian complementarianism, see Piper and Grudem (2012).

Chapter 6

1. For an insightful discussion of this matter, see Friedman (1989).
2. Kongzi, for instance, recognizes that friendships come in different types; some are good, and some are not good (e.g., *Analects* 16.4).
3. For Aristotle's notion of friendship based on virtue, see his *Nicomachean Ethics* Book VIII. Also see Yu Jiyuan's comparative study of Aristotle and Kongzi on friendship (Yu 2007, 206–215).
4. For more discussion, see Elder (2013).
5. For the sake of space, I do not defend a particular Confucian notion of personal identity. Rather, I take it as a given that Confucians hold that two persons can be friends over time. For various views of Chinese personal identity, see Ames (1994) and Yao (1996), among others.
6. *Yi neng* can also mean "extraordinary talent." The literal meaning of *yi* is "separate" or "different." The ancient *Shuowen* Lexicon defines the word as *fen* 分, namely separate or independent.
7. Chapter 67 of the *Records of History*. Overlapping passages can also be found in *Analects* 11.3 and 11.18.
8. Traditionally, Kongzi's seventy-two disciples have been called the seventy-two *xianren* 賢人, namely "(morally) worthy persons."
9. Also see https://ctext.org/wiki.pl?if=gb&chapter=992610&remap=gb.
10. There is a qualified parallel between this view and Neera Badhwar's view on pleasures people derive from friends. Badhwar writes, "the pleasure I get from [friend] *x* is different from the pleasure I get from the new friend, even if the latter is greater" (Badhwar 1987, 15). Badhwar argues, even though irreplaceable values, including pleasures, can be comparable, they nevertheless can be *experienced* differently and can have different meanings to valuers. The Confucian view presented here implies that the difference in virtuous practice is not only phenomenological but also actual. In other words, not only friends' virtuous conduct can be experienced differently, but they are also practiced differently in the first place.
11. 慎其獨也者, 言舍夫五而慎其心之謂也. 獨然後一. 一也者, 夫五夫為〔一〕心也, 然後德之. 一也, 乃德也 (https://ctext.org/wiki.pl?if=gb&chapter=992610&remap=gb). A usual interpretation of the first statement is "being watchful with one's solitude." Here I follow Tai Lian-Chang 戴璉璋, who interprets it as "being watchful in maintaining one's uniqueness and autonomy" 謹慎於內心的獨一自主 (Tai 2003, 213). Tai's research shows that the phrase first appeared in the *Wuxing* in the sense he interprets it and was adopted in later texts with a different meaning.
12. 五行形, 德心起, 和謂之德, 其要謂之一 (https://ctext.org/wiki.pl?if=gb&chapter=992610&remap=gb).
13. See Li (2011) for more discussion of this philosophy of the harmony of virtues.
14. For more discussion of this view, readers can see Wang (2017).
15. In Chapter *Tangong A* of the *Book of Rites*, Kongzi explicates how one should use different forms in mourning one's brothers, friends, and "mere acquaintances" (*suo zhi*), indicating varying degrees of relationship (TTC, 1282).

294 NOTES

16. Literally, *peng* 朋 means "one of the same kind" or "one who can assist." When coupled with *you*, the compound noun means the same as *you*. Unlike *you* though, *peng* is a value-neutral word. When used alone or with certain words, *peng* can have a negative connotation, as in *peng dang* 朋黨 (clique) and *peng mou* 朋謀 (to co-conspire). Whalen Lai noted, *you* was a preferred word for close friends than *peng* (Lai 1996, 219). My argument does not require *peng* to have a similar origin as *you*.

17. Aat Vervoorn has disputed the above interpretation. He insists that the fact that some of these Western-Zhou sources use *you* primarily in relation to kin membership does not prove that the term did not or could not apply to other social groups or other sorts of social bonds. He argues that the root meaning of *you* was "to help or assist, to work together for a common purpose" (Vervoorn 2004, 5). However, Vervoorn is unable to provide evidence for his claim other than citing post-Western Zhou texts whereas the research by Zha, Khayutina, and Zhu are based on evidence from an earlier period. For the sake of argument, we can grant Vervoorn's point that *you* referred to "a type or quality of a relationship rather than a relationship with a particular category of person" (Vervoorn 2004, 6). It however can still be consistent with the findings made by Zha, Khayutina, and Zhu, that such an affable relationship was attributed (primarily) to members of a kin during the Western Zhou period and was expanded to apply to non-kins later. After all, many terms possess both designative and normative meanings. For instance, words like "father" and "family" can be used with both layers of meanings. When we say "a father should be like a father," the first use is a biological designation whereas the second a normative description. Findings by Zha, Khayutina, and Zhu are about the earlier period and the work by Vervoorn is based on texts of a later period when the word had acquired additional meanings such as an affable quality of a relationship.

18. Following Li Xueqing 李學勤, I take it that there is a comma before this statement (惟孝, 友於兄弟). See Li (2001, 578).

19. 善父母為孝, 善兄弟為友 (TTC, 2591).

20. *Xiong ai er you* 兄愛而友 (TTC, 2115).

21. 同志曰友. For instance, this statement can be found in the ancient lexicon *Shuowen* 說文. The *Baihutong* 白虎通, a text of the first century, attributes the statement to (an ancient version of) the Confucian classic *Book of Rites*. Similar references can also be found in commentaries of such Confucian classics as the *Analects* and the *Book of Changes*.

22. Those who have the same surname are brothers . . . they (should) share the same virtues; when they share the same virtue, they share the same heart; when they share the same heart, they share the same will 同姓為兄弟 . . . 同姓則同德, 同德則同心, 同心則同志 (https://ctext.org/guo-yu/jin-yu-si/zh).

23. For a discussion of this issue, see Roger T. Ames and Henry Rosemont Jr. (2014).

24. 人生始化曰魄, 既生魄, 陽曰魂, 用物精多, 則魂魄強 (*Zuozhuan: Zhao Year 7*; TTC, 2050) https://ctext.org/chun-qiu-zuo-zhuan/zhao-gong/zh.

25. For an argument for duty between friends, see Elizabeth Telfer's article "Friendship," in Pakaluk (1991, 248–267).

NOTES 295

26. One may argue that good friends establish strong sentimental ties and their strong emotions for each other make friendships non-fungible. There is some validity to this argument. We simply cannot transfer their emotional ties with friends to any other equally virtuous people. However, as Elizabeth Telfer has argued, even good friends can temporarily lose good will and lose concern for each other (Telfer 1971, 231). Hence, positive emotions are not always reliable for maintaining friendship. The sense and requirement of duty—in our case (quasi-)family duty—provides a more reliable ground when emotions fail.

27. For more discussion of this matter, see Helm (2017).

28. For a strong interpretation of the Confucian philosophy of the family, see Xiao (2010).

Chapter 7

1. *Lu* 祿 has often been associated with having a good career.

2. 五福: 一曰壽, 二曰富, 三曰康寧, 四曰攸好德, 五曰考終命 (TTC 193). Namely longevity, wealth, good health, good virtues, and a good ending of life. The last item is usually understood as a peaceful and painless death after having lived in longevity.

3. For an informative study of this statement, readers can see Jiao (2022).

4. By the traditional Chinese way of calculation, Kongzi lived to seventy-three years old (551–479 BCE), which was a very high age in his time. Mengzi lived even longer, to eighty-four years old (372–289 BCE). Records on Xunzi vary between seventy-five to ninety years old (313–238 BCE or 310–220 BCE).

5. 孔子曰, 君子有三戒.少之時, 血氣未定, 戒之在色. 及其壯也, 血氣方剛, 戒之在鬪. 及其老也, 血氣既衰, 戒之在得.

6. This book was compiled during the Han dynasty (206 BCE–220 CE), with chapters likely written earlier. The text is clearly under the influence of several major philosophical schools of earlier times. While the text has a strong Daoist affiliation, it also contains thoughts with Confucian connections. In this work there are traces of such thoughts as *yin-yang* similar to that in the *Book of Changes*, "five processings" (*wu xing* 五行) similar to that in the *Book of History*, and "centrality-harmony" similar to that in the *Zhongyong*.

7. 血氣者, 人之神也 (TTM, 907). It further defines the "human spirit" as "the upright *qi*" (神者, 正气也; TTM, 999).

8. For a systematic study of the mind and body relation in ancient China, readers can see Slingerland (2019). Slingerland's study shows that there is differentiation between the mind and the body in ancient Chinese thought, against a strong holistic interpretation. The Chinese differentiation between the mind and the body, however, is far from Cartesian dualism. For Descartes, the mind and the body are fundamentally distinct substances, and one cannot be converted into the other. In Chinese thought, *qi* can become coarse or refined, in analogy with water becoming steam or ice. In either form, it is the same stuff in nature. Slingerland writes:

> In the case of universal "folk" mind-body dualism, the early Chinese conceptions of mind-body (and mind-body-soul) relations can help us think

296 NOTES

more clearly about the nature of this dualism. ... What the early Chinese case suggests, in contrast, is that we are not Cartesians, and moreover not necessarily even dualists, since the body is often contrasted in early Chinese texts with both the soul and the mind. (Slingerland 2019, 17)

9. 人之所以成生者, 血脉也 (TTM, 1035).

10. 血脉和利, 精神乃居 (TTM, 1017).

11. 若血氣強固, 將壽寵得沒; 雖壽而沒, 不為無殃 (Lai 2000, 225).

12. Robin Wang has characterized this Confucian idea as caring for one's physical body as a moral virtue (Wang 2012).

13. 夫志, 氣之帥也; 氣, 體之充也.

14. 吾身不能居仁由義, 謂之自棄也.

15. 扁善之度—以治氣養生, 則後彭祖; 以修身自名, 則配堯禹.

16. 治氣養心之術: 血氣剛強, 則柔之以調和; 知慮漸深, 則一之以易良; 勇膽猛戾, 則輔之以道順....愚款端愨, 則合之以禮樂, 通之以思索.

17. 凡用血氣、志意、知慮; 由禮則治通, 不由禮則勃亂提僈; 食飲, 衣服、居處、動靜, 由禮則和節, 不由禮則觸陷生疾; 容貌、態度、進退、趨行, 由禮則雅, 不由禮則夷固、僻違、庸眾而野.

18. 君子養心莫善于誠, 致誠則無它事矣....誠心守仁則形, 形則神, 神則能化矣.

19. This philosophy is still practiced in traditional Chinese medicine today. For a general introduction of fundamental concepts in traditional Chinese medicine, including *qi*, readers can see Sun et al. (2014).

20. See Perkins' (2019) discussion of *qi* as vital energy. In her well-articulated article, Jeeloo Liu has argued that "even though this whole tradition of *qi*-naturalism falls outside of the scope of contemporary natural sciences, it is nonetheless a rational, coherent, and respectable view of nature" (Liu 2015, 33).

21. Readers can see more discussion of a broad Confucian concept of "moral" in Chapter 10 of this book.

22. 血氣和平 (TTC, 1536). See more discussions in the *Jundao* Chapter of the *Xunzi* and the *Yueji* Chapter of the *Book of Rites*.

23. 仁者不憂.

24. 君子坦蕩蕩, 小人長戚戚.

25. 君子有終身之憂, 無一朝之患也.

26. 求仁而得仁, 又何怨?

27. 憂則氣狂 (TTM, 805). 狂 *kuang* literally means "unruly" or "insane." It also means sickness (狂, 病也, Zong 2004, 1412).

28. 循天之道以養其身, 謂之道也 (TTM, 805).

29. 舉天地之道, 而美於和, 是故物生皆貴氣而迎養之 (TTM, 805).

30. 和者, 天之正也, 陰陽之平也 (TTM, 805).

31. 故養生之大者, 乃在愛氣, 氣從神而成, 神從意而出, 心之所之謂意, 意勞者神擾, 神擾者氣少, 氣少者難久矣; 故君子閑欲止惡以平意, 平意以靜神, 靜神以養氣, 氣多而治, 則養身之大者得矣 (TTM, 806). *Yi* 意 can also be translated as "intention" or "determination." It is not an entity in itself but what the heart-mind sets as a goal to accomplish.

32. 凡氣從心 (TTM, 805).

NOTES 297

33. 心, 氣之君也. 何為而氣不隨也, 是以天下之道者, 皆言內心其本也 (TTM, 805).

34. For more discussion of the Confucian concept of *yi* 意 as will, see Chapter 9 of this book.

35. 故仁人之所以多壽者, 外無貪而內清淨, 心和平而不失中正, 取天地之美, 以養其身 (TTM, 805).

36. *Yang* has been often associated with high whereas *yin* with low. Hence, Dong held that one who stands at a very high terrace is exposed to too much *yang*. "One who stays in a very large room is exposed to too much *yin*" because, presumably, one person standing in a very large room leaves too much empty space around him, which has been associated with *yin*.

37. 天之氣常, 動而不滯, 是故道者亦不宛氣. 苟不治, 雖滿不虛, 是故君子養而和之, 節而法之, 去其群泰, 取其眾和, 高台多陽, 廣室多陰, 遠天地之和也, 故聖人弗為, 適中而已矣 (TTM, 805–806).

38. In Confucianism, centrality (*zhong* 中) is closely connected to harmony. For a detailed discussion of this connection, readers can see Li (2014, ch. 5).

39. 是故能以中和理天下者, 其德大盛; 能以中和養其身者, 其壽極命 (TTM, 806).

40. 此中和常在乎其身, 謂之得天地泰. 得天地泰者, 其壽引而長. 不得天地泰者, 其壽傷而短 (TTM, 806).

41. 氣意和平, 居處虞樂, 可謂養生矣 (TTM, 806).

42. 凡養生者, 莫精於氣... 是故春襲葛, 夏居密陰, 秋避殺風, 冬避重漯, 就其和也 (TTM, 806).

43. 衣欲常漂, 食欲常饑, 體欲常勞, 而無長佚居多也 (TTM, 806).

44. The literal meaning of *chou* 儔 is "to match."

45. 壽之為言猶儔也, 天下之人雖眾, 不得不各儔其所生, 而壽夭於其所自行, 自行可久之道者, 其壽儔於久, 自行不可久之道者, 其壽亦儔於不久, 久與不久之情, 各儔其生平之所行, 今如後至, 不可得勝, 故曰: 壽者, 儔也 (TTM,806).

46. 然則人之所自行, 乃與壽夭相益損也; 其自行佚, 而壽長者, 命益之也, 其自行端, 而壽短者, 命損之也, 以天命之所損益, 疑人之所得失, 此大惑也. 是故天長之, 而人傷之者, 其長損; 天短之, 而人養之者, 其短益; 夫損益者皆人, 人其天之繼歟! (TTM, 806).

47. 故大德,...必得其壽 (*Zhongyong*, ch.17; TTC, 1628).

48. See recent World Data (https://www.worlddata.info/life-expectancy.php).

49. Obesity is a complex issue, involving various factors. I will not discuss all these factors here.

Chapter 8

1. A sage is supposedly different from a saint. In common understandings, a saint is a member of the Christian church who is sanctified or made holy after death because his or her life has been a perfect example of the Christian life. A sage is often associated with philosophical wisdom. David Hume, for instance, said that "we aspire to the magnanimous firmness of the philosophic sage" (Hume 1992, 26).

298 NOTES

2. 人非聖賢, 孰能無過? This saying is attributed to the Song Confucian scholar Cheng Duanmeng, a student of Zhu Xi (Cheng Duanmeng n.d.).

3. The last sentence is *yao shun qi you bingzhu* 堯舜其猶病諸. Although *bing* usually stands for sickness or illness, here it means being inadequate or defective. *Zhu* here serves as a pronoun, standing for the deed of conferring extensive benevolence in society. Wing-tsit Chan translated the sentence as "even (sage-emperors) Yao and Shun fell short of it" (Chan 1963, 31). In comparison, Ni's translation is charitable as it does not suggest that Yao and Shun failed in achieving sagehood.

4. The authorship of the *Zhongyong* is attributed to Kongzi's grandson Zisi 子思 (483–402 BCE). Mengzi later inherited and further developed Zisi's philosophy, forming the influential Si-Meng School 思孟学派 within Confucianism. The similar view of the sages between Zisi and Mengzi reflects the continuity of their ideas. For a good study of the Si-Meng School, readers can see Liang (2008b).

5. Huang Kan 皇侃 (488–545) said that Kongzi made this comment when he was forty-six years old and therefore he said he would study the *Yijing* at fifty. Zhu Xi, however, said Kongzi was already seventy years old at the time, and therefore he could not have said at "fifty years old." For a detailed discussion of this controversy, see Guo Yi (1997).

6. 吾竊議晏子而不中夫人之過, 吾罪幾矣！丘聞君子過人以為友, 不及人以為師. 今丘失言于夫子, 譏之, 是吾師也 (*Yanzi Commentary*, Outer Chapter B; TTM, 581–582).

7. According to the *Records of History*, after Kongzi admitted his fault, he also added, "a subject should not talk about the fault of his ruler. Not to talk about it is in accordance with ritual propriety" (Sima 1982, 2218). Zhu Xi took this statement to mean that Kongzi was not mistaken. Zhu insisted that, in such a scenario, Kongzi had to say that the duke was versed in ritual propriety because pertinent ritual propriety forbade Kongzi from pointing out directly the duke's wrongdoing. Therefore, Kongzi as a loyal subject took the blame for the duke's fault (Zhu 1985, *Lunyu* Section 31). For Zhu, Kongzi was not at fault even though Kongzi explicitly admitted fault. See more discussion of Zhu's view later in this chapter.

8. 自天子王侯, 中國言六藝者折中於夫子, 可謂至聖矣! "The Six Arts" (*Liu Yi*) may also be interpreted to mean the Six Classics (*Liu Jing* 六經) during Kongzi's time, namely the *Book of Poetry* (*Shijing* 詩經), *Book of History* (*Shangshu* 尚書), *Book of Rites* (*Liji* 禮記), *Book of Music* (*Yue Jing* 樂經), *Book of Changes* (*Yijing* 周易), *The Spring and Autumn Annuals* (*Chunqiu* 春秋).

9. See Zhu Xi's annotations of the *Great Learning* (https://ctext.org/si-shu-zhang-ju-ji-zhu/da-xue-zhang-ju/zhs).

10. 道便是無軀殼底聖人, 聖人便是有軀殼底道 (Zhu Xi 1986, Book 130, 3117).

11. 無過可悔, 無善可遷.

12. For a good discussion of this and related matters, see Lee Kwai Sang (2015).

13. 世儒學者, 好信師而是古, 以為賢聖所言皆無非, 專精講習, 不知難問. 夫賢聖下筆造文, 用意詳審, 尚未可謂盡得實, 況倉卒吐言, 安能皆是？(*Lunheng*, chapter 28, Section 1; Yang 1999, 293)

14. 過者, 雖古聖賢有所不免, 而聖賢之所以為聖賢者, 惟其改之而已 (Lu 1992, 49).

NOTES 299

15. 以銖稱寸量之法繩古聖賢, 則皆有不可勝誅之罪 (Lu 1992, 139–140).

16. 則堯舜禹湯之所以修己者廢矣 (Ye 1997, 24).

17. Scholars disagree on whether or to what extent Li Zhi was Confucian. For instance, Pauline Lee holds that Li was a neo-Confucian thinker (Lee 2000). Wu Zhen argues that Li's view was eclectic even though he was heavily influenced by neo-Confucian thinker Wang Yangming and, more directly, Wang's two students (Wu 2020).

18. 咸以孔子之是非為是非, 故未嘗有是非耳. 然則予之是非人也, 又安能已?

19. For instance, Zhu Xi accepted Cheng Yi's corrections in the *Great Learning*.

20. Monotheistic traditions are enormous with massive literature. Some of their canons have also been subjected to debates internal to each tradition. I focus on mainstream thinkers and the core texts of these traditions.

21. https://ncse.ngo/pope-john-paul-ii-creationism.

22. A similar idea, though unusual in Chinese classics, can also be found in the Confucian classic *Book of History* (*Shangshu* 尚書). In Chapter *Penggeng Zhong*, King Penggeng threatens to punish disobedient subjects by killing them and their offspring. Penggeng is considered one of the *xian-wang* (early sage kings) in the Confucian tradition, although presumably a lesser one not comparable to Yao and Shun.

23. There is another possible category, which is that neither sages nor classic texts can be wrong; they both are always correct. I will not discuss such a fundamentalist view here.

24. Peimin Ni translates it as "girls" to make the statement less sweeping (Ni 2017, 406). For a discussion of various interpretations of this passage, see Goldin (2000).

25. For a collection of essays of the debate, see Guo (2004).

26. Interestingly, a similar case was found in Plato's *Euthyphro*, on whether it is ever appropriate for a son to prosecute his father.

Chapter 9

1. For detailed discussion of related problems, see Pereboom (2001).

2. Here I present Augustine as commonly interpreted. For different readings of Augustine, see Schindler (2002) and Knuuttila (1999).

3. In their recent cross-cultural studies, Renatas Berniūnas et al. (2021) show that, whereas "choice" and "agency" can be used to investigate universal aspects of how humans think about constrained and un-constrained action, "free will" has no cross-culturally universal conceptual content and that it has been mainly a belief by the WEIRD (Western, Educated, Industrialized, Rich, Democratic).

4. To avoid confusions, I prefer using "free consciousness" (自由意識) instead of "free will" (自由意志) to express a person's desire for and self-awareness of freedom.

5. 吾十有五而志于學 (TTC, 2461).

6. 心之所之謂之志 (Zhu Xi 1986, 卷五·性理二, 96).

7. 志, 心之所思慮也 (TTC, 2685). Here I use Schwartz's translation (Schwartz 1985, 273). Despite this statement, Schwartz evidently reads too much modern Western mentality into Mengzi when he goes on to write, "one must make a choice between

300 NOTES

good and evil and this is a deliberate act of the intentional will" (ibid., 273). For Zhao Qi as well as Mengzi, however, the choice is a matter of a deliberate act of the intentional heart-mind, not of the "will."

8. As a comparative sidenote, here let me quote American philosopher Susan Wolf: "our wills are not just psychological states in us, but expressions of characters that come from us, or that at any rate are acknowledged and affirmed by us" (Wolf 1987, 49). In other words, our wills are not Augustine's self-standing "free will."

9. Jiyuan Yu's (2007) comprehensive and meticulous study of Aristotle and Confucian ethics did not treat the "will" as a subject, presumably for similar reasons. Joseph Chan has discussed *zhi* as the Confucian "moral will" instead of "free will," while insisting that "the moral will is not the free expression of an individual's arbitrary will" (Chan 2002, 290). The same can be said of other similar Chinese terms like *yi* 意 (intention). The *Shuowen* lexicon mutually glosses the two words of *zhi* and *yi* (Xu and Duan 1992, 502). The title of chapter 15 of the *Zhaungzi*, *ke yi* 刻意, for example, means sharpening the *zhi* (determination) rather than the "free will."

10. The term of *youji* 由己 in the *Analects* (12.1; TTC, 2502) expresses a similar meaning, even though the expression was not subsequently used to express the concept of freedom.

11. 請見不請退 (Chapter *Shaoyi*; TTC, 1512).

12. 去止不敢自由 (TTC, 1512).

13. 进退自由, 岂不绰绰然舒缓有餘裕乎? (TTC, 2693).

14. In his well-researched article, Feng Tianyu concludes that *ziyou* in history has been used to mean self-indulged action (Feng 2019). It may be true in many cases, but not always as evidenced here.

15. The term clearly continued with this positive sense when the Tang poet Liu Zongyuan 柳宗元 (773–819) used the term in his poem, 春风无限潇湘意, 欲采蘋花不自由 (The Xiao River is full of spring wind; I wish but do not have the freedom to gather flowers).

16. 擇, 柬選也. 柬者, 分別也 (Xu and Duan 1992, 599).

17. 情然而心为之择, 谓之虑. Eric Hutton translates this statement as "When there is a certain disposition and the heart makes a choice on its behalf, this is called 'deliberation'" (Hutton 2014, 236). Compare it with John Dewey's view: "Choice is not the emergence of preference out of indifference. It is the emergence of a unified preference out of competing preferences" (Dewey 1922, 193).

18. 君請擇於斯二者 (TTC, 2682).

19. 子出之, 吾擇焉 (Chapter *Zhaogong Year 27*; TTC, 2116).

20. 鳥則擇木. 木豈能擇鳥 (TTC, 2167).

21. 我死, 則擇不食之地而葬我焉 (Chapter *Tangong A*; TTC, 1292).

22. 召之, 而擇材焉 (Chapter *Aigong Year 16*; TTC, 2178).

23. 擇人 (TTC, 2049).

24. 里仁為美. 擇不處仁. 焉得知? (TTC, 2471).

25. I am not concerned with how exactly to draw the line between external and internal conditions. For instance, is the physical state of a person's body an external or internal condition? Because it has been traditionally held that the heart-mind (*xin* 心) makes

the choosing, we can place the physical state of a person's body as an external condition, even though it could be argued otherwise. However, either way it needs to be fulfilled to realize a person's freedom.

26. For a discussion of this creed, see Liang (2005, ch. 9).
27. Joseph Raz (1988), for example, sees a very close connection between autonomy and freedom. To be autonomous, Raz holds, a person must meet three conditions. She must possess certain mental capacities, must have an adequate range of valuable options, and must enjoy independence from coercion and manipulation. Robert Audi (1991) holds a different conception of autonomy when he argues that a prisoner forced to make a false confession to save his loved ones may be autonomous but unfree. I do not intend to engage in a study of the relation between autonomy and freedom. My purpose here is to show that if relationality does not necessarily undermine autonomy, then it does not have to undermine freedom either.
28. 誠之者, 擇善而固執之者也 (TTC, 1632).
29. 曰選擇於物, 不知所貴.
30. David Hall and Roger Ames differentiate abstract freedom from effective freedom. They hold, "in the abstract sense we are free when there are minimal constraints precluding any particular action. In the effective sense of freedom, an individual is free only when conditions promoting a given action are present" (Hall and Ames 2003, 142).
31. Social boundaries may change over time. Some of the social boundaries in Kongzi's time may no longer to appropriate for contemporary times. What remains unchanging is that freedom always comes within boundaries, such as Mill's harm principle or other restraints.
32. 多聞, 擇其善者而從之 (TTC, 2483).
33. 君子多知而擇焉 (Chapter *Zengzilishi* of the Senior Dai edition; http://ctext.org/da-dai-li-ji/ceng-zi-li-shi/zh).

Chapter 10

1. A few exceptions include Nuyen (2001), Herr (2010), and Tan (2016).
2. *Xing* 性 is subject to different interpretations. I use the label of "human nature" because it is a common translation.
3. In *Analects* 5.13, his disciple Zigong said that they did hear Kongzi talking about human nature (夫子之言性與天道, 不可得而聞也; TTC, 2474).
4. Ranjoo Herr has called this notion "the Confucian idea of equality" (Herr 2010, 266). I here expound a broader Confucian conception of equality.
5. For a discussion of issues regarding people without a minimum level of moral potential or mental capacity, see note 24 in this chapter.
6. A. T. Nuyen has called such a conception of equality "vertical equality" (Nuyen 2001).
7. For a recent argument for justifiable social hierarchy, see Bell and Wang (2020).
8. A different but logically equivalent interpretation of this phrase is that "pure equality is not equality." I thank P. J. Ivanhoe for bringing this alternative interpretation to my

302 NOTES

attention. While the meanings of both interpretations are consistent, the phrase itself is ambiguous in the *Book of History*. Ivanhoe's interpretation goes in parallel with two preceding statements in the same paragraph in the *Xunzi*. Xunzi said, "*shi qi ze bu yi, zhong qi ze bu shi* 執齊則不壹, 眾齊則不使" (*Xunzi*, chapter 9; Wang 1988, 152), namely "when all social positions are equalized, society has no unity; when all people are equal, no one can command another." In both sentences, *bu* is a negation term as *fei* in *wei qi fei qi*.

9. For a discussion of this issue in imperial China, readers can refer to Elman (2013).

10. *Zhanerqi, wangershun, butongeryi* 斬而齊, 枉而順, 不同而一. *Zhan* 斬 literally means cutting, which makes the phrase difficult to decipher. Various commentators have read *zhan* 斬 as 儳 *chan*, namely variable or unequal (see Knoblock 1988, 292, note 94). The *Shuowen* lexicon defines *shun* 順 in term of *li* 理, namely "aligned" or "making something orderly." *Yi* 一, translated as "one" here by Hutton, also means being consistent. Thus, the last statement can be read as "different and yet consistent."

11. Sungmoon Kim claimed that my view is "inconsistent" in holding that Xunzi's economic distribution principle on the basis of contribution is to be supplemented by a social welfare policy for the poor and the needy (Kim 2018, 139). Kim's own solution is "Confucian democratic sufficientarianism," in which "public equality is programmed to step in with its normative or regulative force only when there are severe inequalities between the rich and the worse-off in terms of wellbeing" (Kim 2018, 161). Kim's concept of "public equality" is broader than the economic realm as it covers people's "public status." As far as consistency between Xunzi's economic distribution principle and social welfare policy for the poor is concerned, I do not see substantive difference between the former being "supplemented" by the latter on the one hand, and Kim's public equality to "step in" under certain conditions such as severe inequalities, on the other hand. In both cases, the latter are to maintain a bottom line of a decent living for the disadvantaged. Hence, I hold that both formulations are consistent.

12. 故聖人之制富貴也, 使民富不足以驕, 貧不至於約 (Chapter *Fangji*; TTC, 1618).

13. 謂農有田里之差, 士有爵命之級 (Chapter *Fangji*; TTC, 1618).

14. 家富不過百乘 (Chapter *Fangji*; TTC, 1618).

15. 使富者足以示貴而不至於驕, 貧者足以養生而不至於憂. 以此為度而調均之, 是以財不匱而上下相安, 故易治也 (TTM, 785).

16. 均, 謂各得其分 (Zhu 1985, 70).

17. It is often translated as "well-field" because the word *jing* 井 means well, a deep hole in the ground.

18. In Zhao Qi's annotation of this passage, Zhao used the word *jun* 均 in his interpretation of Mengzi's statement (TTC, 2707).

19. For discussions of how economic inequalities may undermine the healthy operation of other aspects of society, readers can see Tan (2016) and Angle (2012).

20. 昔三代明王之政, 必敬其妻子也, 有道 . . . 君子無不敬也 (Chapter *Aigongwen*; TTC, 1611–1612).

21. 所以治禮, 敬為大 (Chapter *Aigongwen*; TTC, 1611).

NOTES **303**

22. For more detailed studies of the Confucian notion of *jing*, readers can see Sin Yee Chan (2006) and Kwong-loi Shun (2013).

23. Sin Yee Chan has argued that *jing* can also refer to mere behavior without a respectful attitude as when one *jings* someone due to fear (Chan 2006). It could be argued, however, such *jing* is merely in appearance rather than substantive. One can appear to respect someone to avoid bad consequences without a sense of respect from the heart.

24. It can be argued that when someone becomes a "beast," he still has the potential to regain his humanity by recovering his "lost heart" (*per* Mengzi), and therefore still warrants a basic level of respect. Even if a person has lost his humanity for good, we could still accord him certain respect on what I call "residual effect." A residual effect takes place when we accord respect to people who have deserved respect in the past, as to the corpse of the dead out of consideration that it had been (a part of) a human. Parallel to this is what may be called "marginal effect." A marginal effect takes place when we accord value to someone or something due to one's close association with legitimate value-bearers. For instance, even though/if we justify human rights or dignity on the basis of rationality or cognitive ability, someone without these capacities may nevertheless be accorded equal rights and dignity due to his species membership in humanity. In this regard, Confucians disagree with Peter Singer, who has argued that we should accord some animals with higher moral status than some humans because moral status depends on aspects of cognitive ability and some animals possess higher levels of cognitive ability than humans with severe and profound cognitive disability (Singer 2009; a related discussion can also be found in Singer 2002, ch. 6: Speciesism Today, especially 236–245).

25. The concept of virtue (*de* 德) is a cornerstone for Confucian philosophy. I will not get into the debate on the reality of virtue or character traits. Numerous writers have argued powerfully for the existence of virtue, including Kupperman (1991), Snow (2010), and Peterson and Seligman (2004).

26. For more discussion, readers can see Li (1994).

27. For more discussions of this subject, readers can see Bell and Li (2013).

28. 野無遺賢 (TTC, 123).

29. 萬邦咸寧 (TTC, 123).

30. For an interesting discussion of the compatibility of meritocracy and democracy in the case of the United States, see Macedo (2013).

31. For more discussion of the matter, readers can see Li (2012b). Recently, Bai Tongdong argued for an unequal approach to political power in his *Against Political Equality: The Confucian Case* (2020). In comparison, numerous contemporary New Confucians of the twentieth century, such as Mou Zongsan, Xu Fuguan, and many more, have proposed various versions of modern Confucian democracy on the basis of political equality (see Angle 2012, Elstein 2015). I will come back to this issue in Chapter 11 of this book.

32. For more discussion of this issue, see Li (2009).

33. https://sg.yougov.com/en-sg/news/2020/07/12/cost-living-top-concern-singaporean-voters/.

304 NOTES

34. I will argue in Chapter 11 of this book that, as important as it is, community-building should not be confused with democracy as a political institutional arrangement.

Chapter 11

1. For an examination of this sequence, readers can see Li (2023).
2. There have been varied interpretations of related passages in the *Analects*. For a good discussion, see Gu (2021).
3. There is, however, another line of thought in Confucian classics to the contrary, as will be discussed shortly.
4. The credibility of this story was not questioned until the Song Confucian thinker Zhu Xi (Zhu's *Hui-an Ji*, chapters 67 and 68). Subsequently, repeated attempts have been made to defend Kongzi by discrediting the story of Kongzi's execution of Shaozheng Mao. These efforts, however, provide further evidence of the discomfort felt of the conflict between realist politics and Confucian ethics.
5. For a study of this practice, see Xiao and Li (2013).
6. A contemporary example can be found in the late CCP leader Hu Yaobang 胡耀邦 (1915–1989), who held the title of the CCP chairman in 1981–1982 and then the CCP secretary general in 1982–1987. Hu is credited with his moral uprightness in rectifying millions of unjust, false, or wrong cases during the CCP's anti-rightist movement and the Cultural Revolution, and in giving minorities regions more freedom in self-governance. However, he was regarded as being too liberal and politically too naïve by his CCP peers and was in the end forced out by the hardliners of Deng Xiaoping's political realism. Caught in various political forces, Hu faced tremendous difficulties. In a touching poem written after his ouster, Hu revealed his political quandary between what was right and what was politically necessary in regard to building the Three Gorges Dam on the Yangtse River:

> 妾本禹王女,
> 含冤侍楚王.
> 泪是巫山雨,
> 愁比江水长.

> (Man Mei, n.d.)
> (I was the humble daughter of Empire Yu,
> but had to be King Chu's mistreated maid.
> My tears run like the rain of Mountain Wu,
> My sorrow is longer than the Yangtse River.)

   In his heart, Hu opposed—or at least was sympathetic to people who opposed—the project. Yet, he was unable to stand up openly due to political reasons. Today Hu is remembered by many in China as a kind and moral leader, even though people disagree on to what extent he was culturally Confucian. For a claim that Hu was Confucian, see Wan (2015).
7. For a detailed account of Fung's performance throughout his time, see Guo (2020).

NOTES 305

8. The revered late Singaporean leader Lee Kuan Yew was probably one of the most "Confucian" among all national leaders across the world in the second half of the twentieth century, even though he should be more accurately described as an eclecticist. In the 1980s, he attempted to implement a "Confucian ethics" program in Singapore. Under his leadership, Singapore was transformed from a poor backward seaport city to a widely respected prosperous country. Lee has been criticized for being ruthless toward his political opponents. In an interview with *New York Times* in 2010, Lee defended himself with brutal honesty. He said, "I'm not saying that everything I did was right, but everything I did was for an honorable purpose. I had to do some nasty things, locking fellows up without trial" (Mydans 2010). At least Lee had the courage to admit that he used "dirty hands" in advancing his political agendas. And no one can deny that he did it successfully in a political sense. Without appealing to political "dirty hands," Lee's Singapore success story would have been much different.

9. Stephen Angle discusses "sagely politics" in his influential 2009 book *Sagehood*, especially in chapter 11. Rather than taking "sagely politics" as politics by sages, Angle takes it as a project to build a moderate perfectionist society through participatory politics (Angle 2009, 212). For a critique of Angle's political philosophy of progressive Confucianism espoused in his 2012 book, readers can see Chan (2014b).

10. 作聖人不同於作總統, 聖人若要作總統, 也必須離開聖人的身份而遵守做總統辦政事的軌則法度, 這就是聖人的"自我坎陷" (Mou 2002, 278). *Ziwo kanxian* 自我坎陷, here translated as "self-restriction," literally means to move oneself to a lower position.

11. http://news.sina.com.cn/c/sd/2011-01-20/145121847192.shtml.

12. In a society where state power is maintained without democratic politics, progressive Confucians need to maintain independence from state power. In recent years, the PRC government has signaled its support for Confucianism. State leaders have sometimes adopted Confucian phrases in policy documents and speeches. Such a trend has generated an appearance of a state sponsorship of Confucianism. Some have even offered a Confucian reading of the current PRC leadership in an attempt to nudge the state to adopt more Confucian philosophy in its policies. It may also be argued, however, that the PRC leaders are merely providing a facade to make the government more palatable to a Confucian-leaning population. Other Confucian thinkers have been suspicious of the government's intention and have worried about working too closely with the state in an effort to realize Confucian ideals. Prominent Confucian thinker Tang Yijie 湯一介 (1927–2014) has warned that "the politicization of Confucianism may undermine the precious spirit of Confucianism" (Tang 2011). Zhang Xianglong 張祥龍 (1949–2022), another prominent Confucian thinker has openly expressed his reservation about state sponsorship of Confucianism. For Zhang, the change in the PRC government's attitudes from demonizing Confucianism during the Cultural Revolution (1966–1976) to accepting Confucianism as a reasonable cultural and moral heritage is an improvement. However, Zhang worries about how Confucianism can preserve its independence under state sponsorship. In his view, losing its independence, Confucianism will no longer be what it is and will become a mere tool

306 NOTES

for the state to consolidate its power of control (Zhang 2014). For similar reasons, Princeton scholar Yu Yingshih 余英時 (1930–2021) has declared that today's state sponsorship of Confucianism is "the kiss of death" (Yu 2015).

The views of these contemporary thinkers can be grounded in classic Confucian ideas, despite previously mentioned anecdotes to the contrary. Kongzi famously said that, if the *Dao* failed to prevail, he would take a raft to sail on the ocean (*Analects* 5.7). If the ruler was no good and society was corrupt, not only would Kongzi not serve the state, but he would also not even deign to live in the country, indicating the incorruptibility of his moral principle. *Mengzi* 2B5 records a story about serving the state by giving advice to rulers. Mengzi encouraged Chi Wa to serve as the Marshal of the Guards in the state of Qi so Chi could advise the ruler. Then the ruler did not take Chi's advice. Chi quit his official post and left Qi. Mengzi commented:

> One who holds an office will quit it if he is unable to discharge his duties, and one whose responsibility is to give advice will resign if his advice is not followed. (Lau 1970, 89, modified)

In Mengzi's view, Confucians can work with the state when their advice is adopted. They should not cling to government posts when their advice is ignored. That is, if one is faithful to the Confucian cause, one cannot continue working for a government when it goes against Confucian moral and social ideals. For Mengzi, retaining such independence is the bottom line for maintaining his moral integrity and for upholding his social philosophy. We should understand this view in the context of moral consideration. A ruler's (or political leader in general) action can be morally right or wrong. The responsibility of Confucian scholars is to advise the ruler to do morally right things. When the ruler refuses and does the opposite, it is a matter of moral principle not to remain on board with the ruler by continuing to serve him.

Following these ideas from Kongzi and Mengzi, we can derive the Confucian imperative that, while Confucians can work in or with the government for the good of society, they should refrain from collaborating with state power at the expense of moral principles. To maintain its moral integrity, Confucianism must not unconditionally collaborate with state power. It must maintain its independence from state power in an authoritarian society. For more discussion, see Li (2019b).

13. For a critique of the approach of this cluster of thinkers, readers can see the introduction of Kim (2018).

14. In ancient China, various efforts were made for building community through establishing "villagers' covenant 鄉村民約," by such Confucians as Lü Dajun 呂大均 (1029–1080) and Zhu Xi (1130–1200) during the Song dynasty. Contemporary Confucian activists in China have keenly engaged in reviving and building their cultural communities in rural areas (Yan 2020; Zhao 2016). Even though these activities have been mainly of cultural and ethical education in character rather than politics, these grassroots movements can be turned into political activities once the society becomes democratic.

15. We can say the same about cultivating virtues through participating in democratic activities. People can cultivate virtues when they engage in democratic activities, just as they can also cultivate virtues when they go to the gym. However, that does not

NOTES 307

make the gym as a social institution intrinsically virtuous, nor does it make demo-cratic institutions intrinsically virtuous by cultivating virtues through engagement in democratic activities.

16. For a critique of Jiang's political theory, readers can see Li (2013). I have also offered a critique of Daniel Bell's hybrid institutional model (Li 2019a).

17. Democratic institutions may also come in various forms. I will not advocate any par-ticular form of democracy here. I maintain, however, that a necessary element of a democratic institution is selecting government leaders through general elections, as required by Confucian citizen numerical equality that has been argued for in Chapter 10 of this book.

18. This represents a change of views from my previous position articulated in the chapter 7 of Li (1999).

Chapter 12

1. As Robert Neville has properly noted:

    The Confucian problem with barbarians was not that they had the wrong cul-ture but that they hardly had culture at all, and the reason was that they had no or inadequate behaviors of ritual propriety by means of which to embody the higher excellences of civilization. (Neville 2000, 9–10)

2. 玉不琢，不成器；人不學，不知道.

3. 學然後知不足, 教然後知困. 知不足, 然後能自反也; 知困, 然後能自強也, 故曰: 教學相長也.

4. The *Records of History* (*Shiji* 史記) records the same items, but they are put in the form of Kongzi's praise of his students (Section of *Record of Kongzi's Disciples* 仲尼弟子列傳). See Sima (1982).

5. For a good discussion of learning from exemplars in the Confucian tradition, readers can see Lai (2014).

6. The text does not specify that candidates must be male. In ancient times, "male-only" was an unspoken assumption, and therefore there was gender inequality. Today, how-ever, it is no longer an issue as females are widely accepted as are males in educational systems.

7. Elsewhere I have argued that from a contemporary Confucian point of view, educa-tion is a human right. See Li (2017).

8. 人有恆言, 皆曰 "天下國家." 天下之本在國,國之本在家,家之本在身. *Tianxia* 天下, literally "all under heaven," referred to the ancient civilized world. D. C. Lau translated it as "the empire."

9. Gutmann's theory of education does not explicitly bring in a global perspective, even though it can accommodate some sort of cosmopolitan education. In her 1994 article on educating children in the United States, Martha Nussbaum argued that children in the United States should be taught that "they are above all citizens of a world of human beings, and that, while they themselves happen to be situated in the United

States, they have to share this world of human beings with the citizens of other countries." Nussbaum called such a vision "cosmopolitan education" (Nussbaum 1994).

10. For instance, my experience working at a state university in the United States was that state legislators often emphasize the need for producing skilled workers for economic development, whereas educators tend to stress the value of all-rounded education.

11. Anna Sun (2013) has argued that Confucianism is a religion on the basis of its ritual performance. On such an account, Confucianism would be a very different religion than God-based religions. Also, her study is based on social practices that are identified and associated with Confucianism. These social practices are mixed with folk religions in China. My study of Confucianism is on Confucian philosophy, teachings that are traceable to classic Confucian thinkers.

12. For more discussion of this matter, see Li (1996).

13. See Neville (2000). For a discussion of the phenomenon of people being both Christian and Confucian, see Xie (2009).

14. In the 1980s, Singapore government launched an initiative for a "Confucian ethics" education. It failed. The late prime minister Lee Kuan Yew described it this way:

> Unfortunately, this led to an outburst of Christian missionary zeal, seeking conversions. This provoked a reaction from Buddhists and Muslims who also increased their missionary fervour. So we had to stop all formal teaching of Confucianism and religions. We now only teach civics and good citizenship from Primary One to Secondary Four i.e., age six to age 16. (Lee 1994)

Taking Confucian ethics as a religion makes it inappropriate for the state to promote it in a multicultural society even if it is beneficial to society. Today, Singapore government still promote family values and uphold pro-family public policies, but it does so as common values rooted in all cultural traditions. I will return this matter shortly.

15. *Jian* 儉 is usually interpreted as "frugal." The *Shuowen* lexicon glosses *jian* as *yue*, namely restrained (約也. 約者, 纏束也; Xu and Duan 1992, 376). James Legge translated the word as "temperate" (Legge 1971, 142). Because the context is about how Kongzi approached other people, "moderate" is more apt than "frugal."

16. For a detailed explanation of these items, readers may refer to Li (2023).

17. 言之者無罪 *yan zhi zhe wu zui* (TTC, 271).

18. 言者無罪, 聞者足誡, 言者聞者莫不兩盡其心焉. (https://www.arteducation.com. tw/shiwenv_4f5e854b1169.html).

19. https://www.moe.gov.sg/education/syllabuses/character-citizenship-education. For a recent study of Confucian thinking in Singapore's civic education, readers can see Sim and Lee (2019).

20. For more discussion of this matter, readers can see Li (2016b).

References

Ames, Roger. 2002. "Observing Ritual 'Propriety (*Li* 禮)' as Focusing the 'Familiar' in the Affairs of the Day." *Dao: A Journal of Comparative Philosophy* 1, no. 2: 143–156.

Ames, Roger. 2011. *Confucian Role Ethics: A Vocabulary*. Honolulu: University of Hawai'i Press.

Ames, Roger. 2020. *Human Becoming: Theorizing Persons for Confucian Role Ethics*. Albany: State University of New York Press.

Ames, Roger, and David Hall. 2001. *Focusing the Familiar: A Translation and Philosophical Interpretation of the Zhongyong*. Honolulu: University of Hawai'i Press.

Ames, Roger T., with W. Dissanayake and T. Kasulis, eds. 1994. *Self as Person in Asian Theory and Practice*. Albany: State University of New York Press.

Ames, Roger, and Henry Rosemont. 2014. "From Kupperman's Character Ethics to Confucian Role Ethics: Putting Humpty Together Again." In *Moral Cultivation and Confucian Character*, edited by Chenyang Li and Peimin Ni, 17–46. Albany: State University of New York Press.

Angle, Stephen C. 2009. *Sagehood: The Contemporary Significance of Neo-Confucian Philosophy*. New York: Oxford University Press.

Angle, Stephen C. 2012. *Contemporary Confucian Political Philosophy: Toward Progressive Confucianism*. Cambridge, UK: Polity Press.

Angle, Stephen C. 2022. *Growing Moral: A Confucian Guide to Life*. New York: Oxford University Press.

Arendt, Hannah. 1978. *The Life of the Mind (vol. 2): Willing*. New York: Harcourt Brace Jovanovich, 84–110.

Aristotle. 1962. *Nicomachean Ethics*. Translated with introduction and notes by Martin Oswald. Indianapolis and New York: The Bobbs-Merrill Company, Inc.

Arneson, Richard. 1997. "Feminism and Family Justice." *Public Affairs Quarterly* 11, no. 4: 345–363.

Audi, Robert. 1991. "Autonomy, Reason, and Desire." *Pacific Philosophical Quarterly* 72, no. 4: 247–271.

Augustine. 1972/1467. *City of God*. New York: Penguin Book.

Baba, Eiho. 2015. "*Li* [理] as Emergent Patterns of *Qi*: A Nonreductive Interpretation." In *Returning to Zhu Xi: Emerging Patterns within the Supreme Polarity*, edited by David Jones and He Jinli, 197–229. Albany: State University of New York Press.

Badhwar, Neera K. 1987. "Friends as Ends in Themselves." *Philosophy & Phenomenological Research* 48: 1–23.

Bai, Tongdong. 2020. *Against Political Equality: The Confucian Case*. Princeton, NJ: Princeton University Press.

Bell, Daniel. 2006. *Beyond Liberal Democracy: Political Thinking for an East Asian Context*. Princeton, NJ: Princeton University Press.

Bell, Daniel. 2016. *The China Model: Political Meritocracy and the Limits of Democracy*. Princeton, NJ: Princeton University Press.

310   REFERENCES

Bell, Daniel, and Chenyang Li, eds. 2013. *The East Asia Challenge for Democracy: Political Meritocracy in Comparative Perspective*. Cambridge, UK and New York: Cambridge University Press.

Bell, Daniel, and Wang Pei. 2020. *Just Hierarchy: Why Social Hierarchies Matter in China and the Rest of the World*. Princeton, NJ: Princeton University Press.

Berlin, Isaiah. 1979. "The Originality of Machiavelli." In *Against the Current*, Isaiah Berlin, 25–79. New York: The Viking Press.

Berlin, Isaiah. 1991. *The Crooked Timber of Humanity: Chapters in the History of Ideas*. Edited by Henry Hardy. New York: Alfred A. Knopf.

Berlin, Isaiah. 2002. *Liberty*. Edited by Henry Hardy. Oxford, UK: Oxford University Press.

Berlin, Isaiah. 2003. "Equality." In *Equality and Justice: The Demands of Equality*, edited by Peter Vallentyne, 41–66. Vol. 2 of *Equality and Justice*. New York and London: Routledge.

Berlin, Isaiah, and Beata Polanowska-Sygulska. 2006. *Unfinished Dialogue*. Buffalo, NY: Prometheus Books.

Berniūnas, Renatas, A. Beinorius, V. Dranseika, V. Silius, and P. Rimkevičius. 2021. "The Weirdness of Belief in Free Will." *Consciousness and Cognition* 87: 103054.

Black, Alison. 1989. "Gender and Cosmology in Chinese Correlative Thinking." In *Gender and Religion: On the Complexity of Symbols*, edited by Caroline Walker Bynum, Stevan Harrell, and Paula Richman, 166–195. Boston, MA: Beacon Press.

Bloom, Irene, trans. 2009. *Mencius*. New York: Columbia University Press.

Brandt, Allan M., and Paul Rozin, eds. 1997. *Morality and Health*. New York: Routledge.

Britannica, The Editors of Encyclopaedia. 2021. "Huang Zongxi." *Encyclopedia Britannica*. https://www.britannica.com/biography/Huang-Zongxi.

Buxbaum, Jason D., M. E. Chernew, A. M. Fendrick, and D. M. Cutler. 2020. "Contributions of Public Health, Pharmaceuticals, and Other Medical Care to US Life Expectancy Changes, 1990–2015." *Health Affairs (Project Hope)* 39, no. 9: 1546–1556. https://doi.org/10.1377/hlthaff.2020.00284.

Calhoun, Cheshire. 2000. "The Virtue of Civility." *Philosophy & Public Affairs* 29, no. 3: 251–275.

Camus, Rina. 2018. "I am Not a Sage but an Archer: Confucius on Agency and Freedom." *Philosophy East and West* 68, no. 4: 1042–1061.

Caplan, Bryan. 2007. *The Myth of the Rational Voter: Why Democracies Choose Bad Policies*. Princeton, NJ: Princeton University Press.

Chamberlain, Charles. 1984. "The Meaning of *Prohairesis* in Aristotle's Ethics." *Transactions of the American Philological Association* 114: 147–157.

Chan, Alan. 2011. "Harmony as a Contested Metaphor." In *How Should One Live?*, edited by R. A. H. King and Dennis Schilling, 37–62. Berlin and Boston: De Gruyter.

Chan, Alan, and Sor-hoon Tan. 2004. *Filial Piety in Chinese Thought and History*. London and New York: RoutledgeCurzon.

Chan, Joseph. 2002. "Moral Autonomy, Civil Liberties, and Confucianism." *Philosophy East & West* 52, no. 3: 281–310.

Chan, Joseph. 2007. "Democracy and Meritocracy: Toward a Confucian Perspective." *Journal of Chinese Philosophy* 34, no. 2: 179–193.

Chan, Joseph. 2014a. *Confucian Perfectionism: A Political Philosophy for Modern Times*. Princeton, NJ: Princeton University Press.

Chan, Joseph. 2014b. "Self-Restriction and the Confucian Case for Democracy." *Philosophy East and West* 64, no. 3: 785–795.

REFERENCES 311

Chan, Joseph. 2019. "Public Reason Confucianism Without Foundation?" *Journal of Social Philosophy* 50, no. 2: 134–144.

Chan, Sin Yee. 2006. "The Confucian Notion of *Jing* (Respect)." *Philosophy East & West* 56, no. 2: 229–252.

Chan, Wing-Tsit. 1963. *A Source Book in Chinese Philosophy*. Princeton, NJ: Princeton University Press.

Chan, Wing-Tsit. 1964. "The Evolution of the Neo-Confucian *Li* as 'Principle'." *Tsing Hua Journal of Chinese Studies* 4, no. 2: 123–149.

Chan, Wing-Tsit. 1975. "Chinese and Western Interpretations of *Jen* (Humanity)." *Journal of Chinese Philosophy* 2:107–129.

Chen, Guying 陳鼓應. 2007. 黃帝四經今註今譯 *An Annotation, Interpretation and Commentary on the* Four Classics of the Yellow Emperor. Beijing: Shangwu Yinshuguan 商務印書館.

Chen, Lai 陈来. 2000. 朱子哲学研究 *A Study of Master Zhu's Philosophy*. Shanghai: East China Normal University Press 华东师范大学出版社.

Chen, Lai 陈来. 2014. 仁学本体论 *On Ren as Substance*. Beijing: Sanlian Shudian 生活·读书·新知三联书店.

Chen, Qitai 陈其泰, Guo Weichuan 郭伟川, Zhou Shaochuan 周少川, eds. 1998. 二十世纪中国礼学研究论集 *The Twentieth Century Essays of Chinese Studies of* Li. Beijing: Xueyuan Chubanshe 学苑出版社.

Cheng, Chung-ying. 1991. *New Dimensions of Confucian and Neo-Confucian Philosophy*. Albany: State University of New York Press.

Cheng, Chung-ying. 2004. "A Theory of Confucian Selfhood: Self-Cultivation and Free Will in Confucian Philosophy." In *Confucian Ethics: A Comparative Study of Self, Autonomy, and Community*, edited by Kwong-loi Shun and David Wong, 124–147. Cambridge and New York: Cambridge University Press.

Cheng, Duanmeng 程端蒙. n.d. 性理字训 *Xing-Li Zixun/Teachings of Human Nature and Reasonable Order*. https://ctext.org/wiki.pl?if=gb&chapter=473294&remap=gb.

Cheng, Hao 程顥, and Cheng Yi 程頤. 2011. 二程集 *Collected Works of the Cheng Brothers*. Beijing: Zhonghua Shuju 中華書局.

Cheng, Lin 成林, and Cheng Zhangcan 程章燦. 1993. 西京雜記 *Collected Records of the Western Capital*. Guiyang 貴陽: Guizhou Renmin Press 貴州人民出版社.

Christman, John. 2021. *Positive Freedom: Past, Present, and Future*. Cambridge and New York: Cambridge University Press.

Clark, Kelly, and Robin Wang. 2004. "A Confucian Defense of Gender Equity." *Journal of the American Academy of Religion* 72, no. 2: 395–422. https://doi.org/10.1093/jaarel/lfh035.

Cocking, Dean, and Jeanette Kennett. 2000. "Friendship and Moral Danger." *The Journal of Philosophy* 97, no. 5: 278–296.

Connolly, Tim. 2015. *Doing Philosophy Comparatively*. London and New York: Bloomsbury.

Crittenden, Jack, and Peter Levine. 2018. "Civic Education." In *The Stanford Encyclopedia of Philosophy* (Fall 2018 Edition), edited by Edward N. Zalta. https://plato.stanford.edu/archives/fall2018/entries/civic-education/.

Darwall, Stephen. 1977. "Two Kinds of Respect." *Ethics* 88: 36–49.

Davis, Kingsley, and Wilbert Moore. 1944. "Some Principles of Stratification." *American Sociological Review* 10, no. 2: 242–249.

Defoort, Carine. 2001. "Is There Such a Thing as Chinese Philosophy? Arguments of an Implicit Debate." *Philosophy East and West* 51, no. 3: 393–413.

312 REFERENCES

Dennett, Daniel C. 1989. *The Intentional Stance* (6th printing). Cambridge, MA: The MIT Press.

Derrida, Jacques. 1976. *Of Grammatology*. Translated by Gayatri Chakravorty Spivak. Baltimore & London: Johns Hopkins University Press.

Dewey, John. 1922. *Human Nature and Conduct*. New York: Modern Library.

Dihle, Albrecht. 1982. *The Theory of Will in Classical Antiquity*. Berkeley, CA: University of California Press.

Dillon, Robin S. 1992. "Respect and Care: Toward Moral Integration." *Canadian Journal of Philosophy* 22, no. 1: 105–132.

Ding, Sixin 丁四新. 2015. "本體之道的論說——論帛書《道原》的哲學思想" (A Theory of the Dao of Reality: Philosophy in the Silk Text *Dao-Yuan*). In 先秦哲学探索 *Explorations in Pre-Qin Philosophy*, 330–355. Beijing: Shangwu Yinshuguan.

Dong, Chuping 董楚平. 2002. "中國上古創世神話鉤沉" (Exploring the Chinese Early Ancient Genesis Myths). *Social Sciences in China* 中國社會科學 5: 151–163.

Dong, Zhongshu 董仲舒. 1986. 春秋繁露 *Chunqiu Fanlu* (*The Luxuriant Dew of the Spring and Autumn Annals*). In 二十二子 *Twenty-two Masters*. Shanghai 上海: Shanghai Guji Chubanshe 上海古籍出版社.

Dubs, Homer H. 1973. *The Works of Hsuntze*. Taipei: Ch'eng-Wen Publishing Company 程文出版社有限公司.

Dworkin, Ronald. 2000. *Sovereign Virtue: The Theory and Practice of Equality*. Cambridge, MA: Harvard University Press.

Ebrey, Patricia. 2000. "Foreword." In *The Sage and the Second Sex: Confucianism, Ethics, and Gender*, edited by Chenyang Li, ix–xiii. Chicago: Open Court.

Elder, Alexis Melissa. 2013. "Metaphysics of Friendship." PhD diss., University of Connecticut. https://opencommons.uconn.edu/cgi/viewcontent.cgi?article=6478&context=dissertations.

Ellis-Petersen, Hannah. 2018. "From Peace Icon to Pariah: Aung San Suu Kyi's Fall from Grace." *The Guardian*, November 23. https://www.theguardian.com/world/2018/nov/23/aung-san-suu-kyi-fall-from-grace-myanmar.

Elman, Benjamin. 2013. "A Society in Motion: Unexpected Consequences of Political Meritocracy in Late Imperial China." In *The East Asia Challenge for Democracy: Political Meritocracy in Comparative Perspective*, edited by Daniel Bell and Chenyang Li, 203–231. Cambridge, UK and New York: Cambridge University Press.

Elstein, David. 2015. *Democracy in Contemporary Confucian Philosophy*. London and New York: Routledge.

Eno, Robert. 1990. *The Confucian Creation of Heaven: Philosophy and the Defense of Ritual Mastery*. Albany: State University of New York Press.

Falkenhausen, Lothar von. 1993. "Issues in Western Zhou Studies: A Review Article." *Early China* 18: 146–152.

Fan, Ruiping. 2010. *Reconstructionist Confucianism: Rethinking Morality after the West*. Dordrecht: Springer.

Fan, Wenlan 范文瀾. 1990. 群經概論 *A General Commentary on Chinese Classics*. Shanghai: Shanghai Shudian 上海書店.

Fang, Ying-hsien 方穎嫻. 1976. "原仁論——自詩書至孔子時代觀念之演變" (On the Origins of *Ren*: Its Evolution from the *Shi-Shu* Era to Confucius). *Dalu Zazhi* 大陸雜誌 52, no. 3: 22–34.

Fedock, Rachel, Michael Kühler, and Raja Rosenhagen, eds. 2021. *Love, Justice, and Autonomy: Philosophical Perspectives*. New York and London: Routledge.

REFERENCES 313

Feng, Bing 馮兵. 2016. "儒家「敬」論的三個發展階段——以《尚書》、《曲禮》和程朱理學為例" (Three Phases of the Conception 'Awe' in Confucianism). *Philosophical Trends* 哲學動態 11: 61–68.

Feng, Tianyu 冯天瑜. 2019. "自由概念之演绎" (The Evolution of the Concept of *Ziyou*). The Center of Traditional Chinese Cultural Studies, Wuhan University. http://ric.whu.edu.cn/info/1006/2760.htm.

Fingarette, Herbert. 1972. *Confucius: The Secular as Sacred*. New York: Harper & Row Publishers.

Fishbane, Michael A. 1989. *The Garments of Torah: Essays in Biblical Hermeneutics*. Bloomington: Indiana University Press.

Foust, Mathew, and Sor-hoon Tan, eds. 2016. *Feminist Encounters with Confucius*. Leiden: Brill Publishers.

Frankfurt, Harry. 1971. "Freedom of the Will and the Concept of a Person." *Journal of Philosophy* 68: 5–20.

Frankfurt, Harry. 1997. "Equality and Respect." *Social Research* 64, no. 1: 5–15.

Fraser, Chris. 2012. "The Limitations of Ritual Propriety: Ritual and Language in Xúnzǐ and Zhuāngzǐ." *Sophia* 51, no. 2: 257–282.

Friedman, Marilyn. 1989. "Feminism and Modern Friendship: Dislocating the Community." *Ethics* 99, no. 2: 275–290. https://doi.org/10.1086/293066.

Fu, Yazshu 傅亚庶. 2011. 孔叢子校釋*An Annotated Interpretation of the* Kong Congzi, Beijing: Zhonghua Shuju 中華書局.

Fung, Yulan. 1957. "中国哲学遗产底继承问题" (On Inheriting the Legacy of Chinese Philosophy). Guangming Daily 光明日报, January 8.

Galston, William A. 2007. "Pluralism and Civic Virtue." *Social Theory and Practice* 33, no. 4: 625–635.

Garfield, Jay, and William Edelglass, eds. 2011. *Oxford Handbook of World Philosophy*. Oxford, UK and New York: Oxford University Press.

Garnett, Michael. 2021. "Unity and Disunity in the Positive Tradition." In *Positive Freedom: Past, Present, and Future*, edited by J. Christman, 8–27. Cambridge and New York: Cambridge University Press.

Ge, Zhaoguang 葛兆光. 2015. "对"天下"的想象——一个乌托邦想象背后的政治、思想与学术" (The "Tianxia" Imagery: Politics, Thought and Scholarship Behind a Utopian Imagination). http://www.aisixiang.com/data/92884.html.

Gentz, Joachim. 2019. "Chinese *He* 和 in Many Keys, Harmonised in Europe." In *Keywords in Chinese Culture*, edited by Li Wai-yee and Yuri Pines, 37–84. Hong Kong: Chinese University of Hong Kong Press.

Gilligan, Carol. 1982/1993. *In a Different Voice: Psychological Theory and Women's Development*. Cambridge, MA: Harvard University Press.

Girardot, N. J. 1984. *Myth and Meaning in Early Taoism: The Theme of Chaos (hun-tun)*. Berkeley, LA and London: University of California Press.

Goldin, Paul R. 1999. *Rituals of the Way: The Philosophy of Xunzi*. Chicago and La Salle, IL: Open Court.

Goldin, Paul R. 2000. "The View of Women in Early Confucianism." In *The Sages and the Second Sex: Confucianism, Ethics, and Gender*, edited by Chenyang Li, 133–162. Chicago and La Salle, IL: Open Court.

Gong, Jianping 龔建平. 2004. "親親爲大是腐敗? 抑或血親倫理?" (The Service of Parents is the Greatest: Is it Corruption or Consanguineous Affection?). In 儒家伦理争鸣集 *A Collection of Contentions about Confucian Ethics*, edited by Guo Qiyong, 117–133. Wuhan: Hubei Jiaoyu Chubanshe 湖北教育出版社.

314 REFERENCES

Gosepath, Stefan. 2019. "Equality." In *The Stanford Encyclopaedia of Philosophy* (Spring 2011 Edition), edited by Edward N. Zalta. https://plato.stanford.edu/archives/spr2011/entries/equality/.

Gu, Jianing 顾家宁. 2021. "事君与内外：《论语》管仲评价发微" (Serving the Ruler and the Internal-External: An Investigation of Evaluations of Guan Zhong in the *Analects*). *Confucius Studies* 孔子研究 6: 32–42.

Guo, Luoji 郭羅基. 2020. 梁效顧問馮友蘭 *Feng Youlan as Counselor to Liangxiao*. Austin, TX: Remembering Publishing, LLC.

Guo, Ping 郭萍. 2017. "自由儒学纲要——现代自由诉求的儒家表达" (Freedom Confucianism: A Confucian Endeavor for Modern Freedom). *Lanzhou Academic Journal* 兰州学刊 7: 91–104.

Guo, Qi 郭齊. 2000. "中國歷史上哲學範疇「和」的形成" (The Formation of the Philosophical Category *He* in Chinese History). *Bulletin of the Institute of the Chinese Literature and Philosophy* 中國文哲研究集刊 16: 451–466.

Guo, Qiyong郭齐勇, ed. 2004. 儒家伦理争鸣集 *A Collection of Contentions about Confucian Ethics*. Wuhan: Hubei Jiaoyu Chubanshe 湖北教育出版社.

Guo, Yi 郭沂. 1997. "孔子学易考论" (A Study of the Issue of Confucius Learning the *Yijing*). *Confucius Studies* 孔子研究 2: 3–13.

Gutmann, Amy, ed. 1994. *Multiculturalism: Examining the Politics of Recognition*. Princeton, NJ: Princeton University Press.

Gutmann, Amy. 1999. *Democratic Education* (revised edition). Princeton, NJ: Princeton University Press.

Hahm, Chaibong. 2006. "Confucianism and the Concept of Liberty." *Asia Europe Journal* 4, no. 4: 477–489.

Hall, David, and Roger Ames. 1987. *Thinking Through Confucius*. Albany: State University of New York Press.

Hall, David, and Roger Ames. 1998. *Thinking from the Han*. Albany: State University of New York Press.

Hall, David, and Roger Ames. 1999. *The Democracy of the Dead*. Chicago and Lasalle, IL: Open Court.

Hall, David, and Roger Ames. 2003. "A Pragmatist Understanding of Confucian Democracy." In *Confucianism for the Modern World*, edited by Daniel A. Bell and Hahm Chaibong, 124–160. New York and Cambridge, UK: Cambridge University Press.

Halliday, M. A. K., and C. Matthiessen. 2004. *An Introduction to Functional Grammar*. 3rd ed. London: Arnold.

Hansen, Chad. 1972. "Freedom and Moral Responsibility in Confucian Ethics." *Philosophy East & West* 22, no. 2: 169–186.

Han, Ying 韓嬰. n.d. 韓詩外傳 *Hanshi Waizhuan*. https://ctext.org/han-shi-wai-zhuan/juan-jiu/zh.

Hawking, Stephen. 2018. *Brief Answers to the Big Questions*. New York: Bantam Books.

Held, Virginia. 2004. "Taking Care: Care as Practice and Value." In *Setting the Moral Compass: Essays by Women Philosophers*, edited by Cheshire Calhoun, 59–71. Oxford and New York: Oxford University Press.

Helm, Bennett. 2017. "Friendship." In *The Stanford Encyclopedia of Philosophy* (Fall 2017 Edition), edited by Edward N. Zalta. https://plato.stanford.edu/archives/fall2017/entries/friendship/.

Herr, Ranjoo S. 2010. "Confucian Democracy and Equality." *Asian Philosophy* 20, no. 3: 261–282.

REFERENCES   315

Hillier, H. Chad. n.d. "Ibn Rushd (Averroes)." *Internet Encyclopedia of Philosophy* (https://www.iep.utm.edu/ibnrushd/).

Ho, Li-Ching, and Keith C. Barton. 2020. "Critical harmony: A Goal for Deliberative Civic Education." *Journal of Moral Education* 51, no. 2: 276–291. https://doi.org/10.1080/03057240.2020.1847053.

Holzman, Donald. 1998. "The Place of Filial Piety in Ancient China." *Journal of the American Oriental Society* 118, no. 2: 185–199.

Hordijk, Wim. 2018. "The Evolution of Emergent Computation." https://evolution-institute.org/the-evolution-of-emergent-computation/.

Hsiao, Kung-ch'uan 蕭公權. 1998.中國政治思想史 *A History of Chinese Political Thought*. Shenyang 瀋陽: Liaoning Education Press 遼寧教育出版社.

Hsieh, Yu-wei. 1967. "The Status of the Individual in Chinese Ethics." In *The Chinese Mind: Essentials of Chinese Philosophy and Culture*, edited by Charles Moore, 307–322. Honolulu: The University of Hawai'i Press.

Hu, Shih 胡適. 1998. "说儒" (On *Ru*). In 释中国 *Interpreting China*, edited by Wang Yuanhua. Shanghai: Shanghai Wenyi Chubanshe 上海文艺出版社.

Huang, Kan 黄侃. 1998. "礼学略说" (A Preliminary Study of *Li*). In 二十世纪中国礼学研究论集 *The Twentieth Century Essays of Chinese Studies of* Li, edited by Chen Qitai et al., 13–38. Beijing: Xueyuan Chubanshe.

Huang, Yushun 黄玉顺. 2017. 爱与思: 生活儒学的观念 *Love and Deliberation: Ideas of Life Confucianism*. Chengdu: Sichuan Renmin Chubanshe 四川人民出版社.

Huang, Yong. 2014. *Why Be Moral? Learning from the Neo-Confucian Cheng Brothers*. Albany: State of New York University Press.

Hume, David. 1957. *An Enquiry into the Principles of Morals*. Indianapolis, IN and New York: The Liberal Arts Press, Inc.

Hume, David. 1992. *An Enquiry Concerning Human Understanding; [with] A Letter from a Gentleman to His Friend in Edinburgh; [and] An Abstract of a Treatise of Human Nature*. Indianapolis, IN: Hackett Publishing.

Hursthouse, Rosalind, and Glen Pettigrove. 2019. "Virtue Ethics." In *The Stanford Encyclopedia of Philosophy* (2019 Edition), edited by Edward N. Zalta. https://plato.stanford.edu/entries/ethics-virtue/.

Hutton, Eric L., trans. 2014. *Xunzi: The Complete Text*. Princeton: Princeton University Press.

Ivanhoe, Philip J. 1991. "A Happy Symmetry: Xunzi's Ethical Thought." *Journal of the American Academy of Religion* 59, no. 2: 309–322. A revised version, "A Happy Symmetry: Xunzi's Ecological Ethic," was published in *Ritual & Religion in the Xunzi*, edited by T. C. Kline III and Justin Tiwald, 43–60. Albany: State University of New York Press (2014).

Ivanhoe, Philip J. 2004. "Filial Piety as a Virtue." In *Filial Piety in Chinese Thought and History*, edited by A. Chan and S. Tan, 189–202. London and New York: RoutledgeCurzon.

Jaworska, Agnieszka. 2007. "Caring and Full Moral Standing." *Ethics* 117: 460–497.

Jia, Jinhua. 2016. "Gender and Early Chinese Cosmology Revisited." *Asian Philosophy* 26, no. 4: 281–293.

Jian, Bozan 翦伯贊. 1988. 先秦史 *A Pre-Qin History*. Beijing: Peking University Press 北京大学出版社.

Jiang, Qing. 2013. *A Confucian Constitutional Order: How China's Ancient Past can Shape its Political Future*. Princeton, NJ: Princeton University Press.

316 REFERENCES

Jiang, Qing 蔣庆. 2015. "只有儒家能安頓現代女性" (Only Confucianism Can Settle Women). *The Paper.cn*. http://cul.qq.com/a/20150813/010233.htm.

Jiang, Tao. 2021. *Origins of Moral-Political Philosophy in Early China: Contestation of Humaneness, Justice, and Personal Freedom*. New York: Oxford University Press.

Jiao, Guocheng 焦国成. 2022. "孔子仁者寿发微" (A Study of Kongzi's Statement of "Ren zhe Shou"). *Academic Journal of Zhongzhou* 中州学刊 6: 77—84.

Jones, David, and He Jinli, eds. 2015. *Returning to Zhu Xi: Emerging Patterns within the Supreme Polarity*. Albany: State University of New York Press.

Kang, Xiaoguang 康晓光. 2005. 仁政—中国政治发展的第三条道路 *Renzheng—Zhongguo zhengzhi Fazhan de Disantiao Daolu* (Caring Governance—The Third Road for Political Development in China). Singapore: World Scientific Publishing Co Pte Ltd.

Keller, Simon. 2006. "Four Theories of Filial Duty." *The Philosophical Quarterly* 56, no. 223: 254–274.

Khayutina, Maria. 1999. "Friendship in Early China." Paper presented at the 13th Conference of the Warring States Working Group, October 13–14, 1999, Lehigh University, Bethlehem, PA. https://www.academia.edu/3435695/Friendshipin_Early_China.

Kim, Sungmoon. 2014. *Confucian Democracy in East Asia: Theory and Practice*. New York: Cambridge University Press.

Kim, Sungmoon. 2016. *Public Reason Confucianism: Democratic Perfectionism and Constitutionalism in East Asia*. New York: Cambridge University Press.

Kim, Sungmoon. 2018. *Democracy after Virtue: Toward Pragmatic Confucian Democracy*. Oxford, UK: Oxford University Press.

Kim, Sungmoon. 2019. *Theorizing Confucian Virtue Politics: The Political Philosophy of Mencius and Xunzi*. New York: Cambridge University Press.

King, Ambrose Y. C. 1985. "The Individual and Group in Confucianism: A Relational Perspective." In *Individualism and Holism: Studies in Confucian and Taoist Values*, edited by Donald Munro, 57–70. Ann Arbor: University of Michigan Press.

Knapp, Keith. 1995. "The *Ru* Interpretation of *Xiao*." *Early China* 20:195–222.

Knoblock, John. 1988, 1990, 1994. *Xunzi: A Translation and Study of the Complete Works* (I, II, III). Stanford, CA: Stanford University Press.

Knuuttila, Simo. 1999. "The Emergency of the Logic of Will in Medieval Thought." In *The Augustinian Tradition*, edited by Gareth B. Matthews, 206–221. Berkeley and Los Angeles: University of California Press.

Kongzi. 1980. 論語 *Analects*. In 十三經注疏 *Thirteen Classics with Commentaries*. Beijing: Zhonghua Shuju 中華書局.

Kongzi Jiayu 孔子家语. 2003. *Confucius' Family Teachings*. Beijing: Zhongguo Wenshi Chubanshe 中國文史出版社.

Kupperman, Joel. 1991. *Character*. Oxford and New York: Oxford University Press.

Kupperman, Joel. 2000. "Feminism as Radical Confucianism: Self and Tradition." In *The Sage and The Second Sex: Confucianism, Ethics, and Gender*, edited by Chenyang Li, 43–56. Chicago and La Salle: Open Court.

Kupperman, Joel. 2010. "Confucian Civility." *Dao: A Journal of Comparative Philosophy* 9:11–23.

Lai, Kehong 來可弘. 2000. 國語直解 *The Guoyu Explicated*. Shanghai: Fudan University Press 復旦大學出版社.

Lai, Karyn. 2008. *An Introduction to Chinese Philosophy*. Cambridge and New York: Cambridge University Press.

REFERENCES   317

Lai, Karyn. 2014. "*Ren* 仁: An Exemplary Life." In *Dao Companion to the* Analects, edited by Amy Olberding, 83–94. New York and London: Springer.

Lai, Karyn. 2016. "Confucian Reliability and Epistemic Agency: Engagements with Feminist Epistemology." In *Feminist Encounters with Confucius*, edited by Matthew Foust and Sor-hoon Tan, 101–126. Leiden: Brill Publishers.

Lai, Whalen. 1996. "Friendship in Confucian China: Classical and Late Ming." In *Friendship East and West: Philosophical Perspectives*, edited by Oliver Leaman, 215–250. Richmond, Surrey: Curzon Press.

Lakoff, G., and M. Johnson. 1980. *Metaphors We Live By*. Chicago: The University of Chicago Press.

Lau, D. C. 1970. *Mencius: Translated with an Introduction*. New York and London: Penguin Books.

Lau, D. C. 1979. *The Analects: Translated with an introduction*. New York and London: Penguin Books.

Lau, D. C. 1984. *A Translation of the Mencius*. Hong Kong: The Chinese University Press.

Lee Kuan, Yew. 1994. "Speech at the Inauguration of the International Confucianism Association." Beijing, October 5. Singapore: National Archives (https://www.nas.gov.sg/archivesonline/speeches/record-details/743163cd-115d-11e3-83d5-0050568939ad).

Lee Kwai, Sang. 2015. "Inborn Knowledge and Expressions of Modesty: On Zhu Xi's Sacred Imagination of Confucius and his Hermeneutical Strategies." *Monumenta Serica: Journal of Oriental Studies* 63, no. 1: 79–108.

Lee, Pauline. 2000. "Li Zhi and John Stuart Mill: A Confucian Feminist Critique of Liberal Feminism." In *The Sage and the Second Sex: Confucianism, Ethics, and Gender*, edited by Chenyang Li, 113–132. Chicago: Open Court Publishing Company.

Legge, James. 1970. *The Ch'un Ts'ew with the Tso Chuen*. Hong Kong: Hong Kong University Press.

Legge, James. 1971/1893. *Confucius: Confucian Analects, The Great Learning and the Doctrine of the Mean*. New York: Dover Publications, Inc.

Legge, James. 1885. *The Sacred Books of China Part III/IV—The Li-Ki*. Oxford, UK: The Caldron Press.

Li, Chenyang. 1994. "The Confucian Concept of *Jen* and the Feminist Ethics of Care: A Comparative Study." *Hypatia: A Journal of Feminist Philosophy* 9, no. 1: 70–89.

Li, Chenyang. 1996. "How Can One Be A Taoist-Buddhist-Confucian?—An Illustration of Chinese Multiple Religious Participation." *International Review of Chinese Religion & Philosophy* 1: 29–66.

Li, Chenyang. 1997a. "Shifting Perspectives: Filial Morality Revisited." *Philosophy East & West* 47, no. 2: 211–232.

Li, Chenyang. 1997b. "Confucian Values and Democratic Values." *Journal of Value Inquiry* 31, no. 2: 183–193.

Li, Chenyang. 1999. *The Tao Encounters the West: Explorations in Comparative Philosophy*. Albany: State of New York University Press.

Li, Chenyang. 2000. "Confucianism and Feminist Concerns: Overcoming the Confucian 'Gender Complex." *Journal of Chinese Philosophy* 27, no. 2: 187–200.

Li, Chenyang. 2004. "*Zhongyong* as Grand Harmony: An Alternative Reading to Ames and Hall's *Focusing the Familiar*." *Dao: A Journal of Comparative Philosophy* 3, no. 2: 173–188.

Li, Chenyang. 2006. "The Confucian Ideal of Harmony." *Philosophy East & West* 56, no. 4: 583–603.

318 REFERENCES

Li, Chenyang. 2007. "Li as Cultural Grammar: The Relation between *Li* and *Ren* in the *Analects*." *Philosophy East & West* 57, no. 3: 311–329.

Li, Chenyang. 2008a. "The Concept of Harmony in Pre-Qin Confucian Philosophy." *Philosophy Compass* (3.3): 423–435.

Li, Chenyang. 2008b. "The Ideal of Harmony in Ancient Chinese and Greek Philosophy." *Dao: A Journal of Comparative Philosophy* 7, no. 1: 81–98.

Li, Chenyang. 2009. "Where does Confucian Virtuous Leadership Stand?—A Critique of Daniel Bell's *Beyond Liberal Democracy*." *Philosophy East & West* 59, no. 4: 531–536.

Li, Chenyang. 2010. "Confucian Moral Cultivation, Longevity, and Public Policy." *Dao: A Journal of Comparative Philosophy* 9, no. 1: 25–36.

Li, Chenyang. 2011. "竹帛《五行》關於德性和諧的思想研究Harmony of Virtues in the *Wuxing* Bamboo Text." 國學學刊 *Journal of Chinese Studies* (December): 59–66.

Li, Chenyang. 2012a. "Equality and Inequality in Confucianism." *Dao: A Journal of Comparative Philosophy* 11, no. 3: 295–313.

Li, Chenyang. 2012b. "民主的形式和儒家的內容——再論儒家與民主的關係" (Democratic Form with Confucian Content: Confucianism and Democracy Revisited). *Chinese Philosophy & Culture* 中國哲學與文化 10: 131–146.

Li, Chenyang. 2013. "A Critique of Heaven in Jiang Qing's System." In *A Confucian Constitutional Order: How China's Ancient Past can Shape its Political Future*, edited by Daniel Bell, 129–138. Princeton, NJ: Princeton University Press.

Li, Chenyang. 2014. *The Confucian Philosophy of Harmony*. London and New York: Routledge.

Li, Chenyang. 2015a. "Confucian Ethics and Care Ethics: The Political Dimension of a Scholarly Debate." *Hypatia: A Feminist Journal* 30, no. 4: 897–903.

Li, Chenyang. 2015b. "比较的时代：当代儒学研究的一个重要特点" (The Age of Comparison: An Important Characteristic of Contemporary Confucian Philosophy). *International East-West Studies* 东西方研究学刊 4: 33–40.

Li, Chenyang. 2016a. "Comparative Philosophy and Cultural Patterns." *Dao: A Journal of Comparative Philosophy* 15, no. 4: 533–546.

Li, Chenyang. 2016b. "The Evolution and Identity of the Confucian Tradition." In *Chinese Thought as Global Theory*, ed. Leigh Jenco, 163–180. Albany: State University of New York Press.

Li, Chenyang. 2017. "Education as a Confucian Human Right." *Philosophy East and West* 67, no. 1: 37–46.

Li, Chenyang. 2019a. "Missing Links in *The China Model*." *Philosophy East and West* 69, no. 2: 568–576.

Li, Chenyang. 2019b. "Declare the Independence of Confucianism from the State: Rethinking 'Outer Kingliness' in a Democratic Era." *Journal of Confucian Philosophy and Culture* 32: 7–16.

Li, Chenyang. 2021a. "帝王師夢的徹底破滅:《梁效顧問馮友蘭》書評" (The Final Annihilation of Ruler's Teacher Dream: Fung Yulan and Liangxiao). *Mingbao Monthly* 明報月刊 (Hong Kong) (March).

Li, Chenyang. 2021b. "荀子物-欲关系新解" (A New Interpretation of Goods-Desires Relation in Xunzi). *Academic Journal of Zhongzhou* 中州学刊 10: 101–107.

Li, Chenyang. 2021c. "Harmony and *Ren*: A Response to Leung Yat Hung's Critique of *The Confucian Philosophy of Harmony*." In *Confucian Political Philosophy: Dialogues on the State of the Field*, edited by Robert A. Carleo III and Yong HUANG, 53–71. Switzerland: Springer.

Li, Chenyang. 2022a. "The Confucian *Ren* and Care Debate: Reassessment, Development, and Future Directions." *Philosophy Compass*. 2022: e12868. https://doi.org/10.1111/phc3.12868.

Li, Chenyang. 2022b. "Chinese Philosophy as a World Philosophy." *Asian* Studies 10, no. 3 (September). https://doi.org/10.4312/as.2022.10.3.39-58.

Li, Chenyang. 2023. "The Sequential Problem of Human Aims in the *Great Learning*." *Philosophy East & West* 73, no. 2. Project MUSE's Early Release (April 2022). doi:10.1353/pew.0.0231.

Li, Chenyang, and Dascha Düring, eds. 2022. *The Virtue of Harmony*. New York: Oxford University Press.

Li, Chenyang, and Franklin Perkins, eds. 2015. *Chinese Metaphysics and Its Problems*. Cambridge, UK and New York: Cambridge University Press.

Li, Hongyan 李洪岩. 2005. 素痴集 *Suchiji*. Tianjin: Baihua Wenyi Chubanshe 百花文藝出版社.

Li, Xueqin 李學勤, ed. 2001.尚書正義 (周書) *Shangshu Zhengyi* (*Book of Zhou*), originally by Anguo Kong 孔安国 et al. Taipei: Guji Press 古籍出版有限公司.

Li, Zehou 李泽厚. 2004. 论语今读 *Lunyu Jindu* (*Reading the* Analects *Today*). Beijing: Sanlian Shudian 生活·读书·新知三联书店.

Li, Zhi 李贄. n.d. 藏书*Cangshu*, or *Concealed Book*. https://ctext.org/wiki.pl?if=gb&chapter=185874.

Liji (*Book of Rites*) 禮記. 1980. In 十三經注疏*Thirteen Classics with Commentaries*. Beijing: Zhonghua Shuju 中華書局.

Liang, Shuming 梁漱溟. 2005. 中国文化要义 *Elements of Chinese Culture*, published as 梁漱溟全集 (第三册) *Collected Works of Liang Shuming* (III). Jinan 济南: Shandong Renmin Chubanshe 山东人民出版社.

Liang, Tao 梁涛. 2008a. "上博简 《内礼》 与 《大戴礼记·曾子》" (The Inner Rules of Ritual Propriety of the Shanghai Museum Excavated Chu Texts and the *Zengzi* Chapter of *Book of Ritual* by Greater Dai). 中国思想史研究通讯 *Bulletin of Studies of History of Chinese Thought* 6: 21–23.

Liang, Tao 梁涛. 2008b. 郭店竹简与思孟学派*The Guodian Bamboo Texts and the Si-Meng School*. Beijing: Zhongguo Renmin Daxue Chubanshe中国人民大学出版社.

Lim, Min Zhang. 2020. "Singapore GE 2020: PAP new face Ivan Lim Withdraws from Election Following Allegations about His Past Behaviour." *Straits Times*. https://www.straitstimes.com/singapore/singapore-ge-2020-pap-new-face-ivan-lim-withdraws-as-a-candidate.

Lin Anwu 林安梧. 2021. 當儒家走進民主社會：林安梧論公民儒學*When Confucianism Enters Democratic Society: Lin Anwu on Citizenship Confucianism*. Taiwan: Shangzhou Press 商周出版.

Lin Laifan 林来梵. 2021. "自由概念移植史中的中国立场——以严复为个案" (The Chinese Stance in Transplanting the Concept of Freedom—Yan Fu as Example). 中国社会科学报 *Zhongguo Shehui Kexue Bao* no. 2270 (October 21).

Liu, Jeeloo. 2015. "In Defense of Chinese *qi*-naturalism." In *Chinese Metaphysics and its Problems*, edited by Chenyang Li and Franklin Perkins, 33–53. New York: Cambridge University Press.

Lin, Yutang. 1937. *The Importance of Living*. New York: Quill.

Liu, Bin 刘彬, and Liu Yongkun 刘永昆. 2021. "帛书《衷》篇子曰'五行'段申论" (Kongzi's Commentary on the Five Virtues in Chapter *Zhong* (Impartiality). 周易研究 *Studies of Zhouyi* 6: 73–97.

REFERENCES

Liu, Jennifer. 2022. "CEOs Made a Median $20 Million Last Year—254 Times More Than the Average Worker." *CNBC Make It*. April 18. https://www.cnbc.com/2022/04/18/ceos-made-a-median-20-million-last-year254-times-more-than-the-average-worker.html.

Liu, Qingping. 2007. "Confucianism and Corruption: An Analysis of Shun's Two Actions Described by Mencius." *Dao: A Journal of Comparative Philosophy* 6: 1–19.

Liu, Zhao 劉釗. 2003. 郭店楚简校釋 *Annotated Guodian Chu Bamboo Texts*. Fuzhou福州: Fujian People's Press 福建人民出版社.

Liu, Shu-hsien, and R. E. Allinson. 1988. *Harmony and Strife: Contemporary Perspectives, East & West*. Hong Kong: Chinese University Press.

Löschke, Jörg. 2020. "Harmony and Intrinsic Value." *Journal of East-West Thought* 10, no. 2: 27–44.

Lu, Xiangshan 陆象山. 1992. 陆象山全集 *Collected Works of Lu Xiangshan*. Beijing: Zhongguo Shudian 中国书店.

Lu, Xiufen. 2010. "Rethinking Confucian Friendship." *Asian Philosophy* 20, no. 3: 225–245.

Luo, Guanzhong 羅貫中. 1996. (First published in the 14th century). 三國演義 *Romance of the Three Kingdoms*. Nanjing: Jiangsu Guji Chubanshe 江苏古籍出版社.

Macedo, Stephen. 2013. "Meritocratic Democracy: Learning from the American Constitution." In *The East Asia Challenge for Democracy: Political Meritocracy in Comparative Perspective*, edited by Daniel Bell and Chenyang Li, 232–256. Cambridge, UK and New York: Cambridge University Press.

MacIntyre, Alasdair. 1988. *Whose Justice? Which Rationality?* Notre Dame, IN: University of Notre Dame Press.

Mackenzie, Catriona, and Natalie Stoljar. 2000. *Relational Autonomy: Feminist Perspectives on Autonomy, Agency, and the Social Self*. New York and Oxford: Oxford University Press.

Man, Mei 满妹. n.d. "想对父亲说" (I Wanted to Say to My Father). https://freewechat.com/a/MzU5NjU0NDU1OA==/2247553358/2.

Mangu-Ward, Katherine. 2012. "Your Vote Doesn't Count: Why (almost) everyone should stay home on Election Day." *Reason: Free Mind and Free Market*. https://reason.com/archives/2012/10/03/your-vote-doesnt-count/print.

Mengzi 孟子. 1980. In 十三經注疏 *Thirteen Classics with Commentaries*. Beijing: Zhonghua Shuju 中華書局.

Meyers, Diana T. 1989. *Self, Society, and Personal Choice*. New York: Columbia University Press.

Mill, John Stuart. 1978. *On Liberty*. Indianapolis, IN: Hackett Publishing.

Mou, Bo. 2019. *Semantic-Truth Approaches in Chinese Philosophy: A Unifying Pluralist Account*. Lanham and New York and London: Lexington Books.

Mou, Zongsan 牟宗三. 2002. 中國哲學十九講 *Nineteen Lectures on Chinese Philosophy*. Taipei: Xuesheng Shuju 臺灣學生書局.

Munro, Donald. 1969. *The Concept of Man in Early China*. Palo Alto, CA: Stanford University Press.

Mydans, Seth. 2010. "Days of Reflection for Man Who Defined Singapore." *New York Times*. September 10. https://www.nytimes.com/2010/09/11/world/asia/11lee.html.

Neville, R. C. 2000. *Boston Confucianism: Portable Tradition in the Late-modern World*. Albany: State University of New York Press.

REFERENCES   321

Ni, Peimin. 2002. "The Confucian Account of Freedom." In *The Examined Life: Chinese Perspectives*, edited by Xinyan Jiang, 119–140. Binghamton, NY: Global Academic Publishing.

Ni, Peimin. 2016. *Confucius: The Man and the Way of Gongfu*. Lanham, Maryland and London UK: Rowman & Littlefield.

Ni, Peimin. 2017. *Understanding the* Analects *of Confucius: A New Translation of* Lunyu *with Connotations*. Albany: State University of New York Press.

Noddings, Nel. 1984. *Caring: A Feminine Approach to Ethics and Moral Education*. Berkley and Los Angeles: University of California Press.

Noddings, Nel. 2002. *Starting at Home: Caring and Social Policy*. Berkeley: University of California Press.

Noddings, Nel. 2010. *The Maternal Factor: Two Paths to Morality*. Berkeley: University of California Press.

Nozick, Robert. 1981. *Philosophical Explanations*. Cambridge, MA: Harvard University Press.

Nussbaum, Martha. 1986. *The Fragility of Goodness*. New York: Cambridge University Press.

Nussbaum, Martha. 1990. *Love's Knowledge: Essays of Philosophy and Literature*. New York: Oxford University Press.

Nussbaum, Martha. 1992. "Justice for Women." *The New York Review of Books* 39: 43–50.

Nussbaum, Martha. 1994. "Patriotism and Cosmopolitanism." *The Boston Review* (October 1).

Nuyen, A. T. 2001. "Confucianism and the Idea of Equality." *Asian Philosophy* 11, no. 2: 61–71.

O'Dwyer, S. 2020. "Confucian Democrats, Not Confucian Democracy." *Dao: A Journal of Comparative Philosophy* 19: 209–229. https://doi.org/10.1007/s11712-020-09719-y.

Okin, Susan Moller. 1989. *Justice, Gender, and the Family*. New York: Basic Books.

Oxford, Rebecca L. 2022. "Seeking Linguistic Harmony: Three Perspectives." In *The Virtue of Harmony*, edited by Chenyang Li and Dascha Düring, 279–301. New York: Oxford University Press.

Pakaluk, Michael, ed. 1991. *Other Selves: Philosophers on Friendship*. Indianapolis, IN: Hackett Publishing.

Pereboom, Derk. 2001. *Living Without Free Will*. Cambridge, UK: Cambridge University Press.

Perkins, Franklin. 2019. "Metaphysics in Chinese Philosophy." *The Stanford Encyclopedia of Philosophy* (Summer 2019 Edition), edited by Edward N. Zalta. https://plato.stanf ord.edu/archives/sum2019/entries/chinese-metaphysics/.

Peterson, Christopher, and Martin E. P. Seligman. 2004. *Character Strengths and Virtues: A Handbook and Classification*. New York: Oxford University Press.

Pettit, Philip. 2015. *The Robust Demands of the Good: Ethics with Attachment, Virtue, and Respect*. New York: Oxford University Press.

Phillips, Anne. 2007. *Multiculturalism without Culture*. Princeton, NJ: Princeton University Press.

Piper, John, and W. Grudem, eds. 2012. *Recovering Biblical Manhood & Womanhood: A Response to Evangelical Feminism*. Wheaton, IL: Good News Publishers.

Popper, Karl. 1945. *The Open Society and Its Enemies* (2 Vols). London: Routledge.

322 REFERENCES

Puett, Michael. 2015. "Constructions of Reality: Metaphysics in the Ritual Traditions of Classical China." In *Chinese Metaphysics and Its Problems*, edited by Chenyang Li and Franklin Perkins, 120–129. Cambridge, UK and New York: Cambridge University Press.

Puett, Michael, and Christine Gross-Loh. 2016. *The Path: What Chinese Philosophers Can Teach Us About the Good Life*. New York: Simon and Schuster.

Qian, Mu 钱穆. 2004. 人生十論 *Ten Commentaries on the Human Life*. Guilin 桂林: Guangxi Shifan Daxue Chubanshe 广西师范大学出版社.

Quante, Michael. 2021. "Positive Liberty as Realizing the Essence of Man." In *Positive Freedom: Past, Present, and* Future, edited by J. Christman, 28–44. Cambridge and New York: Cambridge University Press.

Randall, Cassidy. 2020. "A Rewilding Triumph: Wolves Help to Reverse Yellowstone Degradation." *The Guardian*. January 25. https://www.theguardian.com/environment/2020/jan/25/yellowstone-wolf-project-25th-anniversary.

Rao, Zongyi 饒宗頤, and Zeng Xiantong 曾憲通, eds. 1985. 楚帛書 *Chu Silk Manuscripts*. Hong Kong: Hong Kong Zhonghua Shuju 香港中華書局.

Rawls, John. 1971. *A Theory of Justice*. Cambridge, MA: Harvard University Press (rev. ed. 1999).

Rawls, John. 1996. *Political Liberalism*. New York: Columbia University Press.

Raz, Joseph. 1988. *The Morality of Freedom*. New York: Oxford University Press.

Ritzer, George. 1975. "Professionalization, Bureaucratization and Rationalization: The Views of Max Weber." *Social Forces* 53, no. 4: 627–634.

Roetz, Heiner. 1993. *Confucian Ethics of the Axial Age*. Albany: State University of New York Press.

Rorty, Richard. 1984. "The Historiography of Philosophy: Four Genres." In *Philosophy in History: Essays in the Historiography of Philosophy*, edited by Richard Rorty, Jerome B. Schneewind, and Quentin Skinner, 49–75. New York: Cambridge University Press.

Rorty, Richard. 1989. *Contingency, Irony and Solidarity*. New York: Cambridge University Press.

Rousseau, Jean-Jacques. 1986. *The First and Second Discourses and Essay on the Origin of Languages*. Translated by Victor Gourevitch. New York: Harper & Row Publishers.

Sartre, Jean-Paul. 1955. *No Exit and Three Other Plays*. Translated by Lionel Abel. New York: Vintage Books.

Schindler, D. C. 2002. "Freedom Beyond Our Choosing: Augustine on the Will and Its Objects." *Communio: International Catholic Review* (Winter): 619–653.

Scholem, Gershom. 2011. *Zohar: The Book of Splendor: Basic Readings from the Kabbalah*. New York: Random House.

Schumpeter, Joseph A. 1947. *Capitalism, Socialism and Democracy*. (2nd edition 1987). New York: Harper.

Schwartz, Benjamin. 1985. *The World of Thought in Ancient China*. Cambridge, MA: Harvard University Press.

Seligman, Adam, Robert P. Weller, Michael Puett, and Bennett Simon. 2008. *Ritual and its Consequences: An Essay on the Limits of Sincerity*. New York: Oxford University Press.

Sen, Amartya. 1999. *Development as Freedom*. New York: Random House.

Shani, Itay. 2020. "The Lure of Beauty: Harmony as a Conduit of Self-Transcendence." *Journal of East-West Thought* 10, no. 2: 9–26.

Shen, Vincent. 2003. "Some Thoughts on Intercultural Philosophy and Chinese Philosophy." *Journal of Chinese Philosophy* 30, no. 3 & 4: 357–372.

REFERENCES 323

Sher, George, and William J. Bennett. 1982. "Moral Education and Indoctrination." *Journal of Philosophy* LXXIX, no. 11: 665–677.

Shi, Naian 施耐庵. 1996. (First published in the 14th century). 水滸傳*Legend of Loyalty and Dutifulness by the Water Margin*. Nanjing: Jiangsu Guji Chubanshe 江苏古籍出版社.

Shun, Kwong-loi. 1993. "*Ren* and *Li* in the *Analects*." *Philosophy East & West* 43, no. 3: 457–479.

Shun, Kwong-loi. 1997. *Mencius and Early Chinese Thought*. Stanford, CA: Stanford University Press.

Shun, Kwong-loi. 2004. "Conception of the Person in Early Confucian Thought." In *Confucian Ethics: A Comparative Study of Self, Autonomy, and Community*, edited by Kwong-loi Shun and David Wong, 183–199. Cambridge, UK and New York: Cambridge University Press.

Shun, Kwong-loi. 2013. "On *Jing* 敬: Thinking Through Tang Junyi on Chinese Culture in Diaspora." 漢學研究 *Chinese Studies* 31, no. 2: 35–62.

Shun, Kwong-loi. 2018. "Methodological Reflections on the Study of Chinese Thought." In *Chinese Philosophy Methodologies*, edited by Sor-hoon Tan, 57–74. London and New York: Bloomsbury Academic.

Shun, Kwong-loi, and David Wong, eds. 2004. *Confucian Ethics: A Comparative Study of Self, Autonomy, and Community*. Cambridge, UK and New York: Cambridge University Press.

Sigurdsson, Geir. 2021. "Can Ritual be Modern? Liquid Modernity, Social Acceleration and Li-Inspired Ritual." *European Journal for Philosophy of Religion* 13, no. 2: 65–89.

Sim, Jasmine B. -Y., and Lee Tat Chow. 2019. "Confucian Thinking in Singapore's Citizenship Education." *Journal of Moral Education* 48, no. 4: 465–482. https://doi.org/10.1080/03057240.2018.1556155.

Sima, Qian 司馬遷. 1982. 史記 *Records of History*. Beijing: Zhonghua Shuju 中華書局.

Singer, Peter. 2002. *Animal Liberation*. New York: HarperCollins Publisher.

Singer, Peter. 2009. "Speciesism and Moral Status." *Metaphilosophy* 40, no. 3–4: 567–581.

Sisk, John. 1977. "The Tyranny of Harmony." *The American Scholar* 46, no. 2: 193–205.

Slingerland, Edward. 2003. *Confucius Analects: With Selections from Traditional Commentaries*. Indianapolis, IN: Hackett Publishing Company.

Slingerland, Edward. 2019. *Mind and Body in Early China: Beyond Orientalism and the Myth of Holism*. New York: Oxford University Press.

Slote, Michael. 2001. *Morals from Motives*. New York: Oxford University Press.

Slote, Michael. 2007. *The Ethics of Care and Empathy*. New York: Routledge.

Snow, Nancy. 2010. *Virtue as Social Intelligence: An Empirically Grounded Theory*. New York: Routledge.

Snow, Nancy, ed. 2018. *The Oxford Handbook of Virtue*. New York: Oxford University Press.

Sources of Terms (Ci Yuan) 辭源 1995. Beijing: Shangwu Yinshuguan 商務印書館.

Stoljar, Natalie. 2018. "Feminist Perspectives on Autonomy." *The Stanford Encyclopedia of Philosophy* (Winter 2018 Edition), edited by Edward N. Zalta. https://plato.stanford.edu/archives/win2018/entries/feminism-autonomy/.

Su, Shi 苏轼. 1090. 司马温公神道碑 (Epitaph at Sima Guang Tome). https://zh.wikisource.org/zh-hans/司馬溫公神道碑.

Sun, Anna. 2013. *Confucianism as a World Religion: Contested Histories and Contemporary Realities*. Princeton, NJ: Princeton University Press.

324 REFERENCES

Sun, Guangren, Douglas Darwin Eisenstark, and Qingrong Zhang. 2014. *Fundamentals of Chinese Medicine*. Beijing: People's Medical Publishing House.

Tai, Lian-Chang 戴璉璋. 2003. "儒家慎獨說的解讀" (An Interpretation of the Confucian Doctrine of *Shendu*). 中國文哲研究通訊 *Newsletter of the Institute of Chinese Literature and Philosophy* 23: 211–234.

Tan, Christine A. 2020. "A Wei-Jin Philosophy of Freedom: Re-Visiting Guo Xiang's Ontology of *Zide*." PhD diss., Nanyang Technological University.

Tan, Sor-hoon. 2003. *Confucian Democracy*. Albany: State University of New York Press.

Tan, Sor-hoon, 2014. "The Concept of *Yi* (义) in the *Mencius* and Problems of Distributive Justice." *Australasian Journal of Philosophy* 92, no. 3: 489–505. DOI:10.1080/00048402.2014.882961.

Tan, Sor-hoon. 2016. "Why Equality and Which Inequalities? A Modern Confucian Approach to Democracy." *Philosophy East & West* 66, no. 2: 488–514.

Tang, Junyi 唐君毅. 1986. 中國哲學原論 (原道篇一) *An Original Study of Chinese Philosophy*. Taipei: Xuesheng Shuju 學生書局.

Tang, Yijie 汤一介. 2011. "不要把儒家意识形态化" (Don't Make Confucianism an Ideology). An interview with Zhang Jianfeng章剑锋. http://news.sina.com.cn/c/sd/2011-01-20/145121847192.shtml.

Taylor, Charles. 2001. "What's Wrong with Negative Liberty?" In *Freedom: An Introduction with Readings*, edited by Nigel Warburton, 203–217. New York: Routledge.

Telfer, Elizabeth. 1971. "Friendship." *Proceedings of the Aristotelian Society* 71: 223–241.

Thirteen Classics with Commentaries ("TTC"). 1985. 十三經注疏 *Thirteen Classics with Commentaries*. Beijing: Zhonghua Shuju 中華書局.

Tu, Weiming. 1979. *Humanity and Self-Cultivation: Essays in Confucian Thought*. Berkeley, CA: Asian Humanities Press.

Tu, Weiming. 1981. "*Jen* as a Living Metaphor in the Confucian *Analects*." *Philosophy East and West* 31, no. 1: 45–54.

Tu, Weiming. 1985. *Confucian Thought: Selfhood as Creative Transformation*. Albany: State University of New York Press.

Twenty-two Masters ("TTM"). 1986. 二十二子 *Twenty-two Masters*. Shanghai 上海: Shanghai Guji Chubanshe 上海古籍出版社.

Valmisa, Mercedes. 2019. "The Happy Slave isn't free: Relational Autonomy and Freedom in the *Zhuangzi*." *Philosophy Compass* 14, no. 3: e12569.

Van Norden, Bryan. 1992. "Mengzi and Xunzi: Two Views of Human Agency." *International Philosophical Quarterly* 32, no. 2: 161–184.

Van Norden, Bryan. 2007. *Virtue Ethics and Consequentialism in Early Chinese Philosophy*. Cambridge, UK and New York: Cambridge University Press.

Van Norden, Bryan. 2008. *Mengzi: With Selections from Traditional Commentaries*. Indianapolis, IN and Cambridge: Hackett Publishing Company.

Van Norden, Bryan. 2011. *Introduction to Classical Chinese Philosophy*. Indianapolis, IN and Cambridge: Hackett Publishing Company.

Verba, Sidney. 2001. "Thoughts about Political Equality: What Is It? Why We Want It?" https://www.russellsage.org/sites/all/files/u4/Verba.pdf.

Vervoorn, Aat. 2004. "Friendship in Ancient China." *East Asian History* 27: 1–32.

Waltham, Clae. 1972. *Shu Ching: Book of History—A Modernized Edition of the Translations of James Legge*. London: George Allen & Unwin LTD.

Walzer, Michael. 1973. "Political Action: The Problem of Dirty Hands." *Philosophy and Public Affairs* 2, vol. 2: 160–180.

REFERENCES 325

Walzer, Michael. 1983. *Spheres of Justice: A Defence of Pluralism and Equality*. New York and London: Basic Books.

Walzer, Michael. 1994. *Thick and Thin: Moral Argument at Home and Abroad*. Notre Dame and London: University of Notre Dame Press.

Walzer, Michael. 2004. "Emergency Ethics." In *Arguing About War*, 33–50. New Haven: Yale University Press.

Wan, Mu 万沐. 2015. "胡耀邦无关共产主义和无产阶级" (Hu Yaobang Had Nothing to Do with Communism and Proletarian). 世界日报 *The World Journal*. May 19.

Wang, Li 王力. 1981. 古代漢語 (一、二、三冊) *Ancient Chinese* (I, II, III). Beijing: Zhonghua Shuju 中華書局.

Wang, Liqi. 王利器 2002. 顏氏家訓集解 *Collected Interpretations of the Yan Family Teachings*. Beijing: Zhonghua Shuju 中華書局.

Wang, Ping. 2017. "The Chinese Concept of Friendship: Confucian Ethics and the Literati Narratives of Pre-Modern China." In *Conceptualizing Friendship in Time and Place*, edited by Carla Risseeuw and Marlein van Raalte, 1–25. Leiden: Brill.

Wang, Robin R. 2003. *Images of Women in Chinese Thought and Culture*. Indianapolis, IN: Hackett Publishing Company, Inc.

Wang, Robin R. 2010. "The Virtuous Body at Work: The Ethical Life as Qi 氣 in Motion." *Dao: A Journal of Comparative Philosophy* 9: 339–351.

Wang, Robin R. 2012. *Yinyang: The Way of Heaven and Earth in Chinese Thought and Culture*. Cambridge and New York: Cambridge University Press.

Wang, Tianhai 王天海. 2009.荀子校釋 *Annotations of the Xunzi*. Shanghai: Shanghai Guji Chubanshe 上海古籍出版社.

Wang, Xianqian 王先謙. 1988. 荀子集解 *Collected Interpretations of the Xunzi*. Beijing: China Books 中華書局.

Wang, Zhongjiang 王中江. 1999. "儒家'圣人'观念的早期形态及其变异" (Early Confucian Conception of Sagehood and its Variations). 中国哲学史 *History of Chinese Philosophy* 4: 27–34.

Warren, Karen J. 2012. "The Power and the Promise of Ecological Feminism." In *Environmental Ethics: What Really Matters, What Really Works*, 2nd ed., edited by David Schmidtz and Elizabeth Willott, 157–169. Oxford, UK and New York: Oxford University Press.

Watson, Burton, trans. 1963. *Hsün Tzu: Basic Writings*. New York and London: Columbia University Press.

Weber, Max. 1951. *The Religion of China*, edited by Hans H. Gerth. New York: Free Press.

Wei Qipeng 魏啟鵬. 2005. 簡帛文獻《五行》箋證 *Jianbo wenxian Wu Xing jianzheng*. Beijing: Zhonghua shuju 中華書局.

Whitehead, Alfred North. 1979. *Process and Reality*. New York: Free Press.

Whiting, Jennifer E. 1991. "Impersonal Friends." *Monist* 74: 3–29.

Whiting, Jennifer E. 2016. *First, Second, and Other Selves: Essays on Friendship and Personal Identity*. New York: Oxford University Press.

Williams, Bernard. 2001. "Liberalism and Loss." In *The Legacy of Isaiah Berlin*, edited by Mark Lilla, Ronald Dworkin, and Robert Silvers. New York: The New York Review of Books.

Williams, James. 1998. *Preparing to Teach Writing*. 2nd ed. Mahwah, NJ: Lawrence Erlbaum Associates Publishers.

Wittgenstein, Ludwig. 2009. *Philosophical Investigations*. 4th ed. Edited and translated by P.M.S. Hacker and Joachim Schulte. Oxford: Wiley-Blackwell.

326 REFERENCES

Wolf, Susan. 1987. "Sanity and the Metaphysics of Responsibility." In *Responsibility, Character, and the Emotions: New Essays in Moral Psychology*, edited by Ferdinand Schoeman, 46–62. Cambridge, UK: Cambridge University Press.

Wong, David. 2014. "Cultivating the Self in Concert with Others." In *Dao Companion of the Analects*, edited by Amy Olberding, 171–197. New York and London: Springer.

Wong, David. 2020. "Soup, Harmony, and Disagreement." *Journal of the American Philosophical Association* 6, no. 2: 139–155.

Wu, Zhen 吴震. 2020. "名教罪人抑或启蒙英雄?——李贽思想的重新定位" (Destroyer of Ritual Teaching or Enlightenment Hero?—Reassessing the Thought of Li Zhi). 现代哲学*Modern Philosophy* 3: 118–129.

Xiao, Hong, and Chenyang Li. 2013. "China's Meritocratic Examinations and the Ideal of Virtuous Talents." In *The East Asia Challenge for Democracy: Political Meritocracy in Comparative Perspective*, edited by Daniel Bell and Chenyang Li, 340–362. Cambridge, UK and New York: Cambridge University Press.

Xiao, Si 笑思. 2010. 家哲学：西方人的盲点*The Philosophy of the Family: Westerners' Blind Spot*. Beijing: Shangwu Yinshuguan 商务印书馆.

Xie, Wenyu 谢文郁. 2009. "建构和解构：耶儒在张力中互动" (Construction and Deconstruction: Tension and Interaction between Christianity and Confucianism). 云南大学学报 *Journal of Yunnan University* 4: 37–52.

Xu, Fuguan 徐復觀. 1993. 兩漢思想史 (第一卷) *A History of the Han Thought* (I). Taipei: Taiwan Xuesheng Chubanshe 台灣學生出版社.

Xu, Shen 許慎, and Duan Yucai 段玉裁. 1992. 說文解字注 *The Annotated Shuowen Jiezi* ("*Shuowen*"). Shanghai: Shanghai Shudian 上海書店.

Xunzi 荀子. 1986. In 二十二子*Twenty-two Masters*. Shanghai上海: Shanghai Guji Chubanshe 上海古籍出版社.

Yan, Binggang 颜炳罡. 2020. "乡村儒学"的由来与乡村文明重建" (The Origin of Rural Confucianism and the Reconstruction of Rural Civilization). 深圳大学学报(人文社会科学版). *Journal of Shenzhen University* (Humanities and Social Science) 37, no. 1: 5–13.

Yang, Baozhong 楊寶忠. 1999. 論衡校箋 *Lunheng Jiaojian* (Volume 1). Shijiazhuang 石家庄: Hebei Jiaoyu Chubanshe 河北教育出版社.

Yang, Bojun 楊伯峻. 1981. 春秋左傳注 *An Annotated Commentary of the Chunqiu Zuozhuan*. Beijing: Zhonghua Shuju 中華書局.

Yang, Liang 楊倞. 1971 荀子集解*Collected Interpretations of the Xunzi*. Taipei: Wenguang Press 文廣出版社.

Yang, Rubin 楊儒賓. 2004. 儒家身體觀 *The Confucian View of the Person*. Taipei: Academia Sinica 中央研究院/中國文哲研究所.

Yang, Xiong 楊雄. 2013. *Exemplary Figures* (法言). Translated by Michael Nylan. Seattle: University of Washington Press.

Yao, Silian 姚思廉. 1986. 陳書*Chen Shu*, in 二十五史*Twenty-Five Histories* (Vol. 3). Shanghai: Shanghai Classic Press 上海古籍出版社.

Yao, Xinzhong. 1996. "Self-construction and Identity: The Confucian Self in Relation to Some Western Perceptions." *Asian Philosophy* 6, no. 3: 179–195.

Yao, Xinzhong. 2000. *An Introduction to Confucianism*. Cambridge, UK and New York: Cambridge University Press.

Ye Shi 叶适.1977. 习学记言序目 (上下卷) *Records of Learning* (A&B). Beijing: Zhonghua Shuju.

Yijing (Book of Changes) 易經. 1980. In 十三經注疏 Thirteen Classics with Commentaries. Beijing: Zhonghua Shuju 中華書局.

Yu, Dunkang 余敦康. 2017. "中国智慧在《周易》，《周易》智慧在和谐" (Chinese Wisdom lies with the Yijing; the Wisdom of the Yijing lies with Harmony). A Guangming Forum Lecture. https://m.aisixiang.com/data/105116.html.

Yu, Jiyuan. 2007. The Ethics of Confucius and Aristotle: Mirrors of Virtue. New York and London: Routledge.

Yu, Ying-shih. 2015. "The Chinese Communists Are Not Confucianists." https://chinachange.org/2015/07/01/the-chinese-communists-are-not-confucianists/.

Yuan, Lijun. 2002. "Ethics of Care and Concept of Jen: A Reply to Chenyang Li." Hypatia 17, no. 1: 107–129.

Zha, Changguo 查昌國. 1998. "友与两周君臣关系的演变" (The Evolution of the connection between Friendship and the Ruler-Minister Relationship in the Zhou Period). 历史研究 Lishi Yanjiu 5: 94–109.

Zhang, Hongping 張紅萍. 2014. "阿詩瑪"的母系之家——少數民族性別關係考察札記" (Ashima's Matriarchal Family: A Report on a Fieldwork of Sexual Relationships of an Ethnic Group). http://blog.sina.com.cn/s/blog_b673dd9d0102uwgu.html.

Zhang, Liwen. 2015. "Zhu Xi's Metaphysics." In Returning to Zhu Xi: Emerging Patterns within the Supreme Polarity, edited by David Jones and He Jinli, 15–50. Albany: State University of New York Press.

Zhang, Xianglong 張祥龍. 2014. "儒家真正的大复兴在未来" (The Real Revival of Confucianism Lies in the Future). An interview with Ren Zhong 任重. http://www.pku.org.cn/people/rwft/85370.htm.

Zhang, Xinguo 張新国. 2020. "朱熹的形上学：解释性的还是基础主义的？" (Zhu Xi's Metaphysics: Hermeneutical or Foundationalist?). 孔子研究 Confucius Studies 180: 48–55.

Zhang, Xuecheng 章學誠. 1832. "文德 Virtues of Scholarship." 文史通義 Wenshi Tongyi. https://ctext.org/wiki.pl?if=gb&chapter=427494.

Zhang, Zai 張載. 1076. 正蒙 Correcting Ignorance. https://ctext.org/wiki.pl?if=gb&res=485300&remap=gb.

Zhao, Dongmei 赵东梅. 2019. "和解的破灭：司马光最后18个月的宋朝政治" (The Bankruptcy of Reconciliation: A Study of the Song Court Politics during the Last 18 Months of Sima Guang 1019–1086). 文史哲 Literature, History, and Philosophy 374: 24–40.

Zhao, Fasheng 赵法生. 2016. "何谓乡村儒学？" (What is Rural Confucianism?). ThePaper.cn, January 23. (http://www.thepaper.cn/baidu.jsp?contid=1423787).

Zhao, Tingyang. 2006. "Rethinking Empire from a Chinese Concept 'All-under-Heaven' (Tian-xia)." Social Identities 12, no. 1: 29–41.

Zhu, Fenghan 朱鳳瀚. 2004. "朋友考" (A study of peng you). In 西周家族型態研究 A Study of the Clan Forms of the Shang-Zhou Period, 292–297. Tianjin: Tianjin Guji Chubanshe 天津古籍出版社.

Zhu, Xi 朱熹. 1964. 四書集註 The Four Books Annotated. Hong Kong: Taiping Books 太平書局.

Zhu, Xi 朱熹. 1985. 四書五經 Four Books and Five Classics (vol. A, B, C). Beijing: Zhongguo Shudian 中國書店.

Zhu, Xi 朱熹. 1986. 朱子語類 Collected Sayings of Master Zhu. Beijing: Zhonghua Shuju 中华书局.

328 REFERENCES

Zhu, Xi 朱熹. n.d. 晦庵集 Hui-an Ji. https://ctext.org/wiki.pl?if=gb&res=137778&remap=gb.

Ziporyn, Brook. 2012. *Ironies of Oneness and Difference: Coherence in Early Chinese Thought; Prolegomena to the Study of Li*. Albany: State University of New York Press.

Ziporyn, Brook. 2015. "Harmony as Substance: Zhang Zai's Metaphysics of Polar Relations." In *Chinese Metaphysics and Its Problems*, edited by Chenyang Li and Franklin Perkins, 171–191. Cambridge, UK and New York: Cambridge University Press.

Zong Fubang 宗福邦, Chen Shinao 陳世鐃, Xiao Haibo 蕭海波. 2004. 故訓匯纂 *Collected Usages of Words in Classics*. Beijng: Shangwu Yinshuguan 商務印書館.

Zuo Commentary/Zuozhuan 左傳. 1980. In 十三經注疏 *Thirteen Classics with Commentaries*. Beijing: Zhonghua Shuju 中華書局.

Index

For the benefit of digital users, indexed terms that span two pages (e.g., 52–53) may, on occasion, appear on only one of those pages.

ai 愛 (care, love), 54, 62–64, 70, 78, 232–33

Ames, Rogers T, 15–16, 33, 57–58, 60–61, 83, 238, 251

Analects, 11–12, 33–34, 48–49, 54, 55–56, 58, 59–60, 63, 65–66, 68, 72, 74, 76–77, 78, 80, 84, 85, 86, 87–88, 89–90, 92, 97–98, 100, 101, 102–4, 108–9, 110, 111, 114–15, 137–38, 139–40, 143, 145–46, 151–52, 157, 158, 163, 169–70, 176, 177, 179, 182–83, 184, 191–92, 193, 194, 202–3, 207–8, 209–10, 215, 221, 222, 227–28, 229, 230, 241–43, 244–45, 249–50, 258, 259–60, 261–63, 264–65, 271–72, 273–74, 277

Angle, Stephen, 4–5, 46–47, 203

Aristotle, 6–7, 14–15, 42, 57, 137–38, 200, 201, 206, 219, 220–21, 263–64

autonomy, 20, 204, 210–12

Bai Tongdong, 251–52, 303n.31

Bell, Daniel A, 237, 251–52, 301n.7, 303n.27

Berlin, Isaiah, 204, 208–10, 212–14, 219, 245–46

bie 別 (differentiation), 2, 18–19, 117–18, 120, 121

blood-*qi* 血氣, 158–61, 163

Book of Changes (*Yijing* 易經), 2–3, 31, 33–34, 35, 38, 42, 119, 121, 122, 124, 128–29, 179, 262

Book of History (*Shangshu* 尚書), 2–3, 12–13, 50, 54–99, 100, 114, 146–47, 157, 225, 235, 249, 262

Book of Poetry (*Shijing* 詩經), 2–3, 54, 64, 99, 140–41, 262, 277

Book of Rites (*Liji* 禮記), 2–3, 35, 74–75, 76, 77–79, 85, 87–88, 99, 101, 103, 118–19, 121, 123, 125, 143, 181, 204, 205–6, 207, 216–17, 227–28, 230, 243–44, 259–60, 261–62, 264–65

Book of Rituals (*Yili* 儀禮), 74

care
care ethics, 53, 67, 68–69, 70, 72–73
care respect, 113–14
See also filial care

Chan, Joseph, 217, 237, 251–52, 289n.2, 300n.9

Chan, Wing-tsit, 36, 37, 46, 54, 56–57, 58, 70, 97–98, 118–19, 178, 182, 194, 202–3, 222, 227, 260

cheng 誠, 161, 275, 277

Cheng Yi 程頤, 181, 182–83, 186, 188–90

Christianity, 186, 213–14

Chuci 楚辭, 131–32

Chunqiu Fanlu 春秋繁露, 124, 163, 180–81

civility, 86, 90–92, 272–73

Classic of Filial Care (*Xiaojing* 孝經), 102, 103, 107, 108, 111–12, 114–15

competency, 20, 210, 211–12, 214, 216–17

conformity, 16–17, 27, 30, 31–32, 33–34, 35–36, 37, 47, 125–26

Confucianism
Neo-Confucianism, 2–3, 46–47, 181
progressive Confucianism, 1, 2–5, 10–11, 19–20, 21–22, 87–88, 137, 175–76, 192–93, 194, 268, 277, 278–79

cosmogony, 38, 40–41, 42

cosmology, 16–17, 27, 29, 119, 129, 158, 186–87

330 INDEX

Dao, 36–37, 42, 53, 106, 107, 108–9, 128–29, 133–34, 137–38, 144–45, 159, 163–64, 165, 178, 181, 190, 259–60
Daoism, 2–3, 157
Daxue 大學. See *Great Learning*
democracy
  Confucian democracy, 20–21, 238, 250–51, 252, 253–54
  democratic activism, 21–22, 240–41, 249, 250, 254
determinism, 202, 207
Dewey, John, 150, 238, 251, 300n.17
differentiation. See bie 別
Discourse on the States (Guoyu 國語), 28, 63, 147, 159
Dong Zhongshu 董仲舒, 36, 124, 163–68, 180–81, 228

education
  civic education, 21, 171–72, 257, 265–79
  moral education, 170, 171–72, 257, 270–71
  See also *jiao* 教
egalitarian, 13, 127, 227–28
equality
  economic equality, 219–20, 226–30
  gender equality, 2, 10–11, 18–19, 117–18, 126–36
  moral equality, 219–20, 230–33
  numerical equality, 20, 220–23, 232–33, 236–37, 238
  political equality, 3–4, 20, 219–20, 223, 233–39
  proportional equality, 20, 219, 220–21, 222, 223–27, 229–30, 232–33, 237, 238–39
equilibrium, 2, 18–19, 43, 50–51, 117–36, 158
Erya 爾雅, 98, 146–47
ethics
  Confucian ethics, 17–18, 30, 53, 54, 56–57, 61, 72, 97–98, 213–14, 257
  See also care ethics

family
  elder and younger siblings, 49–50, 97–98, 118–19, 144, 147, 151
  husband and wife, 49–50, 117–29, 130, 131–32, 133–34, 135–36, 137, 140–41, 222

  parents and children, 49–50, 97, 104, 108–9, 118–19, 137, 144
Fang Ying-hsien, 54, 55–56
Fan Ruiping, 288n.19, 290n.3
feminism
  feminist care ethics, 53, 73
  radical feminist, 131–32
filial care, filial piety, 2, 4–5, 18, 86, 97–116, 118–19, 146–47, 274–75, 277–78
freedom
  Confucian freedom, 20, 199, 203, 207, 208–9, 212, 213–14, 215, 216–17
  positive freedom, 212, 214–15
free will, 199–203, 217
friendship, 2, 10, 19, 105, 137–56
fu min 富民 (enriching the people), 227–28, 265

gender, 2, 10–11, 13, 18–19, 68, 72, 117–36, 191, 219–21, 274–75
Gilligan, Carol, 61, 71–72
God, gods, 74–75, 76, 78, 89–112, 171, 186–87, 188, 201–2, 203, 231–32, 271–72
gongfu 功夫, 5, 58–59
grammar
  cultural grammar, 2, 18, 74–93, 258
  formal grammar, 81
  functional grammar, 81
  social grammar, 83
Great Learning (*Daxue* 大學), 111, 118–19, 181, 215, 241, 275
Guoyu 國語. See Discourse on the States

Hall, David, 83, 238, 251, 301n.30
harmonious society, 45, 224, 225, 228, 229
harmonization, 16–17, 33–34, 38, 39, 43–44, 47, 162, 168
harmony
  cosmic harmony, 40
  deep harmony, 16–17, 40, 46–47
  dynamic harmony, 2, 4, 16–17, 27–52
  environmental harmony, 27, 44, 50–52
  family harmony, 117–21, 123, 125–27, 128, 133, 135–36, 277–78
  "Great Harmony," 35, 36, 42
  intra-personal harmony, 162–63

INDEX   331

social harmony, 47–48, 49–50, 51, 80, 229–30, 268, 277–78

he 和 (harmony), 2, 4, 15–17, 27, 30, 31, 54, 118–19, 142

he-tong 和同 (harmonious unity), 29

heart-mind (*xin* 心), 29, 30, 48–49, 160–61, 164–65, 166, 168, 183, 202–3, 206, 217, 259–60

Heaven (*tian* 天), 12–13, 35–36, 37, 40, 49, 51, 107, 119, 128–29, 144–45, 159, 163–64, 165, 166, 167, 177, 180–81, 183, 237, 268–69, 271–72

Huang Yong, 284–85n.35

Inner Canon of the Yellow Emperor (*Huangdi Neijing* 黃帝內經), 158–59

Ivanhoe, Philip J, 286–87n.1, 289n.3, 301–2n.8

Jia, Jinhua, 291–92n.24

Jiang Qing, 117, 136, 245, 251–52

jian-zheng 諫諍 (remonstrate and expostulate), 103, 107, 112–13

jiao 教 (teaching, education), 2, 4, 10–11, 21, 193, 258, 259, 261–62

jing 敬 (respect, reverence), 11–12, 18, 47–48, 77, 100, 102–3, 108–9, 112–13, 230

jun 均 (equal distribution), 227–28, 229–30. *See also* economic equality

junzi 君子, 29, 30, 33–34, 63–64, 137–38, 158, 176, 177, 178, 259, 260

justice, 20, 57, 71, 110–11, 126–27, 144–45, 210–11, 219, 225, 226, 235, 238–39, 252, 275–76

Kant, Immanuel, 14–15, 109–10, 210–11, 230, 231–32

Kim, Sungmoon, 252, 255, 302n.11, 306n.13

Kingliness (*wang dao* 王道), 20–22, 240–56

Kong Yingda 孔穎達, 121–22

Kongzi (孔子, Confucius), 2–3, 5, 7–8, 10–11, 14–15, 16, 18, 19–20, 29, 33–35, 48–49, 54, 56, 58–60, 62, 63, 64, 65–66, 67–68, 72, 73, 76–77, 78, 83, 84, 85, 86, 87–88, 89–90, 92, 97–98, 100–4, 105–6, 107–10, 111, 114–15, 137–38, 139–40, 143–44, 151–52, 157, 158, 159, 160–61, 162–63, 167, 168, 169–70, 175–78, 179–80, 181, 182–84, 185–86, 191–93, 194, 202–3, 205–6, 207–8, 209–10, 213–14, 215, 216–17, 221, 222, 223, 225–26, 227–28, 229–30, 241–45, 248–50, 258, 259–63, 264–65, 271–72, 273–74, 277

Kongzi Jiayu 孔子家語. See *Recorded Sayings of Kongzi's Family*

kun 坤 (Earth), 121–22, 124, 125, 129

Lai, Karyn, 59–60, 307n.5

learning (*xue* 學), 202–3, 257–58, 259–62, 264–65

li 禮 (rites, ritual propriety), 2, 4, 18, 33–35, 47–48, 49, 55, 64, 74–93, 100–1, 139–40, 142, 161, 162–63, 184, 221, 230, 242–43, 258, 262, 268–69, 273, 274

li 理 (principle, order), 46–47, 230

li 利 (benefit, profit), 227

liberty

positive liberty, 204, 212

negative liberty, 204, 209–10, 212

Liji 禮記. See *Book of Rites*

Li Zehou 李澤厚, 242–43

longevity (*shou* 壽), 2, 19, 157–72

loyalty, 109–10, 144–45, 179, 241–42, 244, 246–47, 275–76

Lu Xiangshan 陸象山, 184–85, 188–90, 191–92

Lü's Spring and Autumn Annuals (*Lüshi Chunqiu* 呂氏春秋), 107, 179

Mawangdui Silk Texts 馬子堆帛書, 38–39

mei 美 (beauty, beautiful), 54, 64

Mengzi (孟子 Mencius), 2–3, 5, 7–8, 12–13, 14–15, 18, 34, 49–50, 55–57, 63–65, 67–68, 69, 70, 71, 74, 86–87, 97, 101, 102, 104, 105–6, 107, 108, 110–11, 114–15, 120, 137–38, 140–41, 151–52, 159–60, 161, 162–63, 164, 169–70, 175–76, 178, 180, 190, 191, 192–93, 202–3, 204–6, 212, 221, 222, 226, 229, 234, 237, 247, 257, 259, 268, 273

332 INDEX

Mengzi, 7–8, 12–13, 33–34, 35, 45–46, 49–50, 55–57, 63–65, 67–68, 69, 70, 71, 74, 86–87, 101, 103, 104–5, 110, 111, 114–15, 120, 137–38, 140–41, 151–52, 159–60, 163, 169–70, 176, 178, 190, 191, 203, 204–5, 206, 209–10, 212, 216, 221, 222, 226, 229, 231–32, 234, 237, 247, 257, 259, 268, 273
meritocracy, 233, 234, 235–36, 251–52
Mill, John Stuart, 204–5, 212–13
ming 命 (fate, destiny), 102–3, 167–68, 183, 207
morality
  moral attainment, 54, 101, 142–43, 168, 169–70, 222, 232
  moral sensibilities, 12–13, 19–20, 55–56, 67–68, 97, 148–49, 175, 185, 190
  moral vigilance, 102–13, 114, 115–16, 274–75
Mou Zongsan 牟宗三, 14–15, 248–49, 303n.31

Ni, Peimin, 58–60, 299n.24
Noddings, Nel, 61, 67, 68–69, 70–71
Nussbaum, Martha, 48, 127–28

Okin, Susan Moller, 126–28, 132–33

Pettit, Philip, 63–64
Plato, 27, 40, 42, 48, 200, 263, 266–67
Puett, Michael, 288n.22, 288n.23, 288n.24

qi 氣 (physical energy), 29, 36–37, 38, 40, 46–47, 48–49, 149–50, 157–62, 163–64, 165, 166, 168, 171–72
qi 齊 (equal, equality), 2, 118–19, 225
qian 乾 (Heaven), 35, 42, 121–22, 124, 125, 129
Qian Mu 錢穆, 206–7
qijia 齊家 (harmonizing the family), 118–19, 241, 275

Rawls, John, 210–11, 219, 272
Recorded Sayings of Kongzi's Family (*Kongzi Jiayu* 孔子家語), 108, 243
relationship, 5, 10, 31–33, 42, 46, 48, 49–51, 70, 76, 97–98, 105, 108, 110, 115–16, 120, 121–22, 128, 137, 162–63, 170, 199, 210–11, 230, 232–33

ren 仁
  humaneness-benevolence, 53, 55–56, 60–61, 64–65, 69, 177, 178, 260
  humanity, 17–18, 53, 56–57, 60–61, 70
  ren ethics, 53, 72–73
  ren zhe 仁者 (person of *ren*), 56–57, 72, 157
ren zheng 仁政, 64, 69, 229, 240
ritual propriety. See *li* 禮
Rituals of Zhou 周禮, 74
ru 儒, 2–3, 5, 257

sage
  sagehood, 2, 4, 20–21, 144, 175–86, 240, 248–49
  sage-kings, 28, 29, 31, 50, 110–11, 140–41, 160, 162–63, 224, 240, 247–48, 254
  sagely politics, 240–41, 247–49, 255
Saint Augustine, 201
sameness, 28, 31–32, 33–34, 121–22
self-cultivation, 20–21, 118, 159, 161, 167, 184–85, 202–3, 212, 241
Sima Qian 司馬遷, 107, 180
Shangshu 尚書. See *Book of History*
sheng 聖 *See* sage
shi 士 (a scholar-official), 107, 264–65
Shi Bo 史伯, 28, 29–30, 31, 33–34, 44
Shijing 詩經. See *Book of Poetry*
Shun 舜, 110–11, 140–41, 175–76, 177, 181, 184–85
Shuowen 說文, 28, 56, 74–75, 98–99, 100, 123, 206
socialization, 56, 210–12, 221
social mobility, 225, 264–65
Socrates, 112, 200, 263
submissive, submissiveness, 102–3, 111, 130–31, 244

Tang Junyi 唐君毅, 14–15, 62
Taylor, Charles, 199, 214–15
Thirteen Classics 十三經, 29, 74, 107, 146–47, 157
tian zi 天子 (the Son of Heaven), 86, 107, 180, 227
tong 同. *See* sameness
Tuan Commentary 彖傳, 35
Tu Weiming 杜維明, 70, 83–84, 177–78

INDEX 333

virtue
cardinal virtues, 47–48, 64, 120
comprehensive virtue, 17–18, 53–54, 56–57, 60–66, 67–68, 71, 72, 73, 137–38
five virtues, 49, 56, 142
particular virtues, 62, 137–43

Walzer, Michael, 219, 238–39, 246, 275–76
wang dao 王道 (the "kingly Way"). *See* kingliness
Warren, Karen, 124–25
whole, wholeness, 38–39, 48–49, 130, 131–32
Wittgenstein, Ludwig, 81, 83–84
Wong, David B, 62, 88
Wuxing 五行, 48–49, 74, 140, 141–42

xiao 孝. *See* filial care
xian 賢 (the virtuous and talented), 21–22, 234
Xiaojing. *See Classic of Filial Care*
xin 心. *See* heart-mind
xin 信 (trustworthiness), 56, 72, 262–63, 277
xing 性 (human nature, characteristic tendencies), 7–8, 46, 221
xing 刑 (punishment, penal code), 78, 80
xiushen 修身 (self-cultivation), 160–61, 241, 275
xue 學. *See* learning
Xu Fuguan, 14–15, 303n.31
Xunzi, 2–3, 5, 12–13, 18, 34–35, 38, 40–41, 50–51, 65–66, 75, 88–89, 97, 98, 102–3, 105–7, 108–12, 114, 115–16, 137–38, 147, 151–52, 159–61, 162–63, 192–93, 206, 207–8, 212, 221, 224–28, 234, 235, 247, 258, 268–69, 274–75
Xunzi, 34–35, 40–41, 50–51, 65–66, 74, 75, 88–89, 103, 105–6, 108, 109, 137–38, 147, 151–52, 160, 162–63, 206, 207–8, 212, 213–14, 221, 224, 226, 227, 234–35, 243, 247, 258, 268–69

Yan Family Teachings, 119
yang 養 (fostering, raising), 28, 98–99, 100, 102, 112–13, 157, 160, 202–3
Yan Zhitui 顏之推, 119–20, 271
Yanzi 晏子, 29–30, 31–34, 118–19, 179
Yao 堯 (the sage king), 160, 175–76, 177, 184–85
Yao, Xinzhong, 210–11, 283n.18, 293n.5
yi 義 (rightness, appropriateness), 47–48, 49, 55, 64, 86–87, 88–89, 110–11, 139–40, 142, 144–45, 159–60, 221
Yijing 易經. *See Book of Changes*
Yili 儀禮. *See Book of Rituals*
yin and yang 陰陽, 18–19, 35, 36–37, 39, 40–41, 48, 53, 124, 128–36, 149–50, 158, 163–64, 165
yong 勇 (courage), 72, 144–45
you 友 (friend), 2, 10, 19, 54, 137–38, 146–47
See also friendship

ze 擇 (choosing), 20, 206, 207–8
zeshan 擇善 (choosing the good), 20, 104–5, 199, 208–14, 216–17
Zengzi 曾子, 72, 107, 108, 137–38
Zhang Zai 張載, 36–37, 38, 286n.16
Zheng Xuan 鄭玄, 118–19, 204–5
zheng 政 (governance, politics), 2, 250
zhi 智 (wisdom), 47–48, 49, 55, 64, 139–40, 142, 221
zhi 志 (determination, personal commitment), 114–15, 159–60, 202–3, 215
zhong 忠 (dedication), 262–63, 275–76
See also loyalty
Zhongyong 中庸, 33–36, 38, 48–49, 56–57, 97–98, 111, 168, 178, 212–13
Zhu Xi 朱熹, 46–47, 175–76, 181–83, 184–85, 186, 188–89, 228
Ziporyn, Brook, 45–46
ziyou 自由, 2, 204–6, 212
Zuo Commentary 左傳, 29, 79, 80, 85, 101, 118–19, 147, 149–50, 207
Zuo Qiuming 左丘明, 29